The Russian Idea

In Search of a New Identity

THE RUSSIAN IDEA

IN SEARCH OF A NEW IDENTITY

EDITED BY

WENDY HELLEMAN

BLOOMINGTON, INDIANA, 2004

First published in 2004.
Each article copyright © 2004. All rights reserved.

Library of Congress Cataloging-in-Publication Data

The Russian idea : in search of a new identity / edited by Wendy Helleman.
    p. cm.
  Includes bibliographical references and index.
  ISBN: 0-89357-314-0
 1. Christianity and culture--Russia (Federation) 2. Russkaia pravoslavnaia tserkov'--Influence. 3. Nationalism--Russia (Federation). 4. Nationalism--Religious aspects--Russkaia pravoslavnaia tserkov'. 5. National characteristics, Russian. 6. Russia (Federation)--Civilization--Philosophy. I. Helleman, Wendy E., 1945-. Title.

BR932 .R86 2004
197--dc22

2003022049

Slavica Publishers
Indiana University
2611 E. 10th St.
Bloomington, IN 47408-2603
USA

[Tel.] 1-812-856-4186
[Toll-free] 1-877-SLAVICA
[Fax] 1-812-856-4187
[Email] slavica@indiana.edu
[www] http://www.slavica.com/

Contents

Acknowledgments i

Wendy Helleman
　The Russian Idea: In Search of a New Identity 1

Part I.　The Russian Idea: Cultural, Historical, and Ideological Aspects

Vladimir K. Kantor
　Is the Russian Mentality Changing? 23

Mikhail V. Il'in
　Words and Meanings: On the Rule of Destiny. The Russian Idea 33

Vladimir S. Bibler
　The Russian National Idea: A Culturological Hypothesis 57

Leonid A. Sedov
　The Place of Russian Culture among World Cultures
　(An Invitation to Reflection) 73

Andrei P. Zabiako
　Antinomies of Russian Consciousness: Labor and Leisure 95

Evgenii B. Rashkovskii
　Civil Society: A Religious Assessment of the Problem 113

Part II.　The Russian Idea and Russian Religious Philosophy

Konstantin K. Ivanov
　The Orthodox Schism and Schismatic Communism 129

Aleksei V. Zhuravskii
　P. Chaadaev and V. Solov'ev: The Discovery of Islam 137

Leonid I. Vasilenko
　Cosmism and Evolutionism in the Russian Religious-
　Philosophical Tradition 151

Sergei S. Khoruzhii
    Neopatristic Synthesis and Russian Philosophy 165
Andrei V. Kuraev
    Pantheism and Monotheism 185
Glossary 213
Bibliography 253
About the Authors 263
Index 267

Acknowledgments

The present collection of articles on the Russian Idea represents the fruit of six and a half years spent in Russia as visiting professor in the Faculty of Philosophy at Moscow State University (1995–2002). But its preparation involved a truly collaborative effort of librarians, colleagues, and students who helped evaluate and translate them, and numerous other colleagues and friends, both in Moscow and North America, who helped check the translations. Together with my husband, Adrian, I taught philosophy in English for second- and third-year students in the Moscow State University Faculty of Philosophy. For this work we brought materials from North America, but we soon realized that our students should also be challenged in terms of the ferment of ideas in their more immediate context. So we asked librarians of Moscow State University to compile an initial list of articles representative of new directions in Russian philosophical thought since perestroika. The goal of our classes, getting students to discuss philosophical issues in English, was particularly well served by articles on the 'Russian Idea', as both the most provocative and popular of themes presented in recent philosophical literature. Our students were asked to read, evaluate, and discuss these articles, and then to translate them, in smaller or larger portions. Since these students were quite comfortable translating from English into Russian, our request - to help us produce an English translation - meant a considerable stretching of their abilities.

Special thanks must go first of all to our colleagues Tat'iana Grigor'evna Sokolova, Evgenii Mikhailovich Pertsev, Emma Grigor'evna Zvereva, Zara Gazisovna Muratova, Alexandra Borisovna Murza, and Asia Goloborodko. They have been ever supportive and encouraging as we stretched their students beyond their expectations in this exercise. Unless otherwise acknowledged, preliminary drafts of translations were prepared by second- and third-year students of English for Philosophy during the years 1996–2000, in our classes and the classes of our colleagues.

Deserving of special mention are students who worked on substantial portions or entire articles: Natal'ia Petrova who provided the preliminary translation for L. I. Vasilenko, "Cosmism and Evolutionism in the Tradition of Russian Religious Philosophy"; Masha Saikina and Lena Savchenko who prepared initial translations of K. Ivanov, "The Orthodox Schism and Schismatic Communism"; and Sof'ia Maltseva who provided preliminary translations of both E. B.

Helleman, Wendy, ed. *The Russian Idea: In Search of a New Identity*. Bloomington, IN: Slavica, 2004, i–iii.

Rashkovskii, "Civil Society: A Religious Assessment of the Problem" and A. Kuraev, "Pantheism and Monotheism."

The project has benefited from the help of a number of professional translators in Moscow, including Andrei Skvarskii, who translated V. S. Bibler, "The Russian National Idea: A Culturological Hypothesis." We are also very grateful for the careful work of Marina Utishinskaia in reading and checking many of the articles.

MGU colleague Emma Grigor'evna provided the preliminary translation of A. V. Zhuravskii, "P. Chaadaev and V. Solov'ev: The Discovery of Islam." Sergei S. Khoruzhii himself provided the translation of "Neopatristic Synthesis and Russian Philosophy" as he presented it at a North American conference on Georges Florovsky; unknown to us, this article had been published by *St. Vladimir's Theological Quarterly* (vol. 44, no. 3–4 [2000]: 309–28). While we acknowledge prior publication, the present translation was prepared independently. Aside from our immediate colleagues in the teaching of English for philosophy students, other colleagues of the Faculty of Philosophy, particularly Valerii Kuvakin, were enormously helpful in checking articles after they had been translated by students.

In North America I wish to acknowledge the help of Boris Jakim, Robert Bird, and Taras Zakydalsky in final work on these translations. I am also grateful for the help and encouragement given by James Billington, George Kline, Robert Scanlan, Larry Ort, Ol'ga Volkogonova, and Kathleen Parthé, who were ready to help on a variety of questions as these arose. Larry Ort of the Russian American Christian University (Moscow) gave us an unforgettable 'farewell to Russia' on 24 January 2002, our last day in Moscow, when he organized a conference (cosponsored by the People's Friendship University of Russia) on the 'Russian Idea', with presentations by Wendy Helleman, Igor Chubais, Vasilii Vanchugov, and Ol'ga Volkogonova.

Finally, I am most grateful for the substantial help of Elena Mitina on questions of Russian culture. Nonna Khaustova and Ekaterina Zaichenko of the Russian American Christian University in Moscow provided invaluable help, checking innumerable details. And finally a hearty thanks to Igor' Smerdov for his general helpfulness in so many aspects of getting the manuscript ready for publication, and especially his ready assistance in dealing with questions of copyright.

It is difficult to thank adequately all those who have participated in this project, from the early stages of analyzing potential articles, translating, checking, and editing them. I am especially grateful for the help and encouragement of my husband Adrian, who cooperated on the project from beginning to end. And finally we thank the International Institute for Christian Studies in Kansas City, and its Canadian branch, Christian Studies International in Toronto, who sponsored our work in Russia during these years. It is our prayer that this book may provide a service in reflecting both the struggle and hope for Russia as it emerges from a period of difficult transition.

Introduction

The Russian Idea: In Search of a New Identity

Wendy Helleman

> "The morning that will break over Russia after the nightmarish revolutionary night will be rather the foggy 'gray morning' that the dying Blok prophesied.... After the dream of world hegemony, of conquering planetary worlds, of physiological immortality, of earthly paradise, – back where we started, with poverty, backwardness, and slavery – and perhaps national humiliation as well. A gray morning."[1]

This was the prediction of Fedotov, as early as the 1940s, and it has proven to be remarkably accurate. The transition has been slow, laborious, and painful. Turning the Communist USSR into a modern Russian state was far more difficult than most could have imagined. As numerous former satellite states declared independence, Russia was reduced to a pale shadow of the imperial USSR, and its role on the world stage diminished accordingly. Communists, though they will not easily return to power, continue to cast a strong shadow over every attempt at revising collectivist structures; nor is it easy to change attitudes deeply embedded in the 20th-century Russian mind. In a context of continuing economic and political instability it is not surprising that issues of Russian identity and the "Russian Idea" occupy a central place in public discussion.[2]

---

[1] F. P. Fedotov, *Sud'ba i grekhi Rossii: Izbrannye stat'i po filosofii russkoi istorii i kul'tury* [The fate and sins of Russia: Selected articles on the philosophy of Russian history and culture] (St. Petersburg: Izdatel'stvo "Sofiia," 1991–92), 2: 198; cf. V. I. Mil'don, "The Russian Idea at the End of the Twentieth Century," *Russian Studies in Philosophy* 35: 4 (1997): 24–38, esp. 36.

[2] See M. A. Maslin, ed., *Russkaia ideia* [The Russian idea] (Moscow: Respublika, 1992); V. M. Piskunov, *Russkaia ideia* [The Russian idea] (Moscow: Iskusstvo, 1994); A. Gulyga, *Russkaia ideia i ee tvortsy* [The Russian idea and its creators] (Moscow: Soratnik, 1995); Robin Aizlewood, "The Return of the 'Russian Idea' in Publications, 1988–91," *Slavonic and East European Review* 71: 3 (1993): 490–99; and idem, "Revisiting Russian Identity in Russian Thought: From Chaadaev to the Early Twentieth Century," *Slavonic and East European Review* 78: 1 (January 2000): 20–43; Wendy Helleman, ed. *The Russian Idea: In Search of a New Identity*, Bloomington, IN: Slavica, 2004, 1–19.

Only a few short years ago names like Yeltsin, Zhirinovskii, and Ziuganov regularly captured the attention of journalists reporting on Russian affairs. Russia's problems were not only an internal matter. Yeltsin got international attention by jumping on the tank; he stopped a coup. His later antics are rather more forgettable. Zhirinovskii achieved center-stage by exploiting wounded pride for a nationalist backlash to Western-style economic reform. And Ziuganov found a more plodding revamp of the Communist Party rewarded by his near defeat of Yeltsin's 1996 re-election. Journalism gives instant news, but moves quickly from one "hot spot" to another. Once a country regains a degree of stability, however shaky, interest wanes. Political analysts have a little longer timespan in which to report, but philosophers rarely make it on the news. The materials of the present collection are an attempt to provide important background information on how Russians themselves perceived the events of those years in their own country; they also attempt to balance the focus on nationalism, and provide some necessary analysis from a philosophical and ideological perspective.

The Russian Idea

So, just what is the Russian Idea? What does the term mean? The words as such seem to be obvious enough, and need no further elaboration. Or do they? In Russian, first of all, there are two options for the adjective "Russian": *russkaia* or *rossiiskaia*, and only the former is of concern. Why is "*russkaia*" used here, and what is its significance? What is "Russia"? What does it mean to be "Russian"? What distinguishes Russia from the former Soviet Union, or the Russian empire of the 19th century, to say nothing about distinctions with respect to neighboring countries, to the east or south, and especially the west (Europe)? And what about the term "Idea"? In what sense are we to understand it, especially in combination with "Russian"? Are we talking about an Idea which has a Russian character, which happens to be Russian? Or about an Idea (conceptualization) of Russia, a Russian national principle? Where should such a principle come from? How should it arise? And who decides on the appropriateness of such a principle? Further, what does one exclude, or oppose, in affirming the Russian Idea? And finally, after we have come to grips with all these issues, we must still face the question: is it still relevant to discuss it?

Idea and Ideology

Ideas belong to human minds and human thought processes. They direct our thinking in two ways: to what is above and beyond us, or to what surrounds us

---

James P. Scanlan, "Interpretations and Uses of Slavophilism in Recent Russian Thought," in James P. Scanlan, ed., *Russian Thought after Communism: The Recovery of a Philosophical Heritage* (M. E. Sharpe: Armonk, NY, 1994), 31–61.

and forms our world of perception; they take us toward the divine, or to the world of our everyday experience. The ancient philosophers were not altogether wrong when they described the human soul as a bridge between two worlds.

Big and important ideas, like the Russian idea, take us back to Plato's Ideas: the timeless patterns or archetypes, objects of mental vision and perfect models for an imperfect world. Philo of Alexandria (1st cent. BC) posited these Platonic Ideas in the mind of God; they served as crucial blueprints for his creating the world. Philo's exegesis of Genesis deeply influenced the Christian Platonism of the Fathers in their analysis of creation.

In the West Descartes revived the ancient Stoic view of ideas as class-concepts of the human mind, to be analyzed logically. The emphasis of Berkeley and Hume on ideas representing sense-perception in turn influenced Kant's presentation of ideas as problematic extensions of reason in its judgment of sense-impressions. In affirming the limits of human reason, Kant also limited human knowledge of absolutes, like God, the soul and cosmos. The approaches of Kant and of Plato were much debated in late 19th-century Russia.[3] Idealism continued to accent the primacy of the soul, spirit, or mind, whereas nascent materialism accented experience and the data of sense-impression.

Ideology as a political term takes us back to the Enlightenment, to the French intellectual and writer Destutte de Tracy (1754–1836), who used the term "*ideologiste*" for someone tracing general ideas back to sense-impressions, thus rejecting metaphysical sources of knowledge. Although originally supported by Napoleon, it was later rejected as state policy and blamed for all the problems of the Revolution. Since that time for Europeans the term "ideology" has acquired negative connotations, especially in representing the 20th-century fascist dictatorial regimes of Germany and Italy. But in Russia, even today, "ideology" is free of such negative associations. Introduced with Bolshevism, it articulated a worldview differing radically from what preceded (tsarism and Orthodoxy); as an ideology it was based on philosophical assumptions, and provided the crucial legitimacy for exercise of power by the Communists, the basis of their authority. Its philosophically expressed worldview was oriented to implementation and action through political policies and programs. Once communist ideology was undermined, the regime fell.

Accustomed to an ideological underpinning for political action, Russians now feel lost without it. A pragmatic approach is unnerving, too arbitrary in an already unpredictable situation. And a deeply embedded distinction between an élite and the common people (with deep distrust of the latter), continues to pose

---

[3] A recent discussion of this debate may be found in F. Nethercott, *Russia's Plato: Plato and the Platonic Tradition in Russian Education, Science and Ideology (1840–1930)* (Aldershot, England: Ashgate Publishing, 2000), esp. 75–95, 106–21.

serious barriers to the egalitarian democratic thinking which equates *vox populi* with *vox Dei*. Russians, once thoroughly deceived by Communist promises, are also wary of new utopian proposals.

The *Russian Idea* as a patriotic nationalist attempt to fill the ideological vacuum continues to have significant appeal for national pride after the demise of imperial superpower status. Discussion of the Russian Idea from abroad has focused on the politically reactionary, if not dangerous, nationalist aspects of the Russian Idea.[4] While these aspects are not negligible, and demand some attention, they must be examined in historical context for a balanced appreciation.

A Unique Russian Worldview?

Nationalism thrives on an affirmation of the *unique character* of the nation, affirming characteristics which constitute its identity, and differentiate it from the "other." Scanlan has traced such a focus on "distinctive" characteristics to romantic concerns with ethnic identity, as the background to Chaadaev's critique of Russian culture.[5] While Russians have certainly been rediscovering 19th-century romantic and idealist thinkers, and have reacquainted themselves with a half-forgotten past,[6] Scanlan's critique of the Russian obsession with its unique character has focused on the dangers of retreat to isolationism and chauvinism. While not unjustifiable, such warning remarks sidestep the specific modern and contemporary factors which motivated renewed discussion of Russian identity in the post-perestroika context, when *Russia* once more gave its name to the bulk of

---

[4] Tim McDaniel, *The Agony of the Russian Idea* (Princeton: Princeton University Press, 1996); and J. P. Scanlan, "The Russian Idea from Dostoevskii to Ziuganov," in *Problems of Post-Communism* 43 (August 1996): 35–42.

[5] See J. P. Scanlan, "Is Russia Really in Need of Russian Philosophy?" published in Russian as "Nuzhna li Rossii russkaia filosofiia?" *Voprosy filosofii*, no. 1 (1994): 61–65. J. F. Herder's late 18th-century romanticizing description of the Slavs was well-known in Russia; Herder predicted that Slavs, because of their unspoilt rural and peace-loving character, would be the future leaders of Europe. Cf. Peter J. S. Duncan, *Russian Messianism: Third Rome, Revolution, Communism and After* (London and New York: Routledge, 2000), 10–11.

[6] Of special interest today is the early role of Moscow in throwing off the Mongol-Tatar yoke, and the role of Orthodoxy in so much of Russian history. Even if a revival of such themes in Russian history is regarded as part of a process of mythification, as is argued by O. Volkogonova ("Est' li budushchee u russkoi idei?" [Does the Russian idea have a future?], *Mir Rossii*, no. 2 [2000]: 28–52) and Michael Urban ("Remythologising the Russian State," *Europe-Asia Studies* 50: 6 [1998]: 969–92), the healthy element of reconnecting with the past is not to be ignored. It is clear that the Orthodox Church, for one, cannot look ahead to the future without once more exploring and coming to grips with the role it had in Russian society at the end of the 19th century. If the process of rethinking its current role demands a reassessment of history, at least today there is an openness which allows for such rethinking as a basis for new strategies for the future.

the geographical territory making up the former USSR.[7] If the outside world considered transition from the USSR back to "Russia" an almost automatic resumption of pre-1917 identity, for Russians themselves the move was not so obvious. In the late 1980s very few Russian citizens of the Soviet Union could actually remember the pre-revolutionary period; theirs was a Soviet identity. Nor had "Russia" ever assumed a role like that of other republics. Russian citizens had deliberately been scattered as a ruling élite throughout the republics; unlike other people-groups the identity of Russians, even if defined ethnically, was far more tied to that of the Union as a supra-national power.[8] If these factors of ethnicity were not crucial while a strong Communist Party controlled the highly centralized government, they took on "monumental consequences ... when combined with the decision to grant sovereignty and a right of secession to the republics," as Hough expresses it.[9]

While the USSR typically emphasized an internationalist vision together with its own multi-ethnic composition, after 1991 the focus of attention shifted to Russia as a singular nation-state, which must try to reincorporate the Russian

---

[7] "Russia," as such, played a somewhat ambiguous role within that Soviet "alliance." See J. F. Hough, *Democratization and Revolution in the USSR* (Washington, DC: Brookings Institution Press, 1997), 214ff., on the unique problems faced by Gorbachev in decentralizing power from Moscow to the provinces, republics, and regions, advocating a voluntary renegotiation of the terms of alliance. The biggest problem was posed by Russia itself as a truly "superfluous" administrative link between the central government and the regions; Hough argues that Yeltsin, understanding the dynamics of the problem, took advantage of the situation to demand that the Soviet Union itself become the superfluous level of government (214–16). As a result, a *Russian* Communist Party was first created as the central authority of the party was disappearing. Yeltsin manipulated the situation by reminding Russians also of their need for "independence," recalling the economic disadvantages which the Union posed to their own interests, while the the regions seemed to have all the benefits. Cf. ibid., 238–45.

[8] Ibid., 238. The Russian republic had been absorbed within the central government of the Soviet federation far more than had other republics. Moreover, the boundaries of national units within the Soviet Union had been determined on the basis of ethnicity and language, e.g. as Ukrainian, or Belorussian. Nationality eventually was recorded on internal passports, initiated during the 1930s, making it even more clear that a Ukrainian maintained that ethnic identity even when living outside of the Ukraine, in Moscow or elsewhere (ibid., 221–22). Communist thinking expected a withering away of the state, and fusion of its people groups (with economic integration). Of course, neither of these happened, and as early as 1917 Lenin made provision for a strongly centralized multi-ethnic state as an alliance (*soiuz*) in which the various nationalities had the right to secede (although the proletariat and its party would not exercise such a right); cf. Hough's analysis of Lenin's *State and Revolution*, ibid., 217–19.

[9] Ibid., 221. The reference is to Gorbachev's decision to actually allow the independence of the Union partners under *perestroika*. As long as the party was in control, the right of secession was nothing more than a formality.

population left stranded in the "near abroad."[10] Would it re-create an "imperial" Union identity, focusing on linguistic, cultural and religious factors making up its ethnic Slavic identity, or turn to a more purely civic (*rossiiskaia*) identity, since it too contained within itself many ethnic groups variously related to the central federal state?[11] Within this context the discussion of the *Russian Idea* was no luxury; it actively addressed questions of present and future contours of the nation.

Nationalism and Neo-Slavophiles

Nationalistic motivation has evidently united the Orthodox and Communists, the two major components of the "authoritarian" bloc formed in the early 1990s.[12] For nationalists, the nation embodies a supra-temporal principle, functioning like a "national idea"; appeal to such a principle justifies rulers in demanding extraordinary devotion from subjects, especially in times of crisis. Since ethnically based nationalism often supports hatred toward "other" groups (neighbors, rivals, or enemies), and leads to violence, if not to pogroms, reference to nationalist tendencies in terms of a "specter" are not altogether unwarranted.

Twentieth-century awareness of Russia as a nation separate from the USSR goes back to the "ideological explosion" of the 1960s and 1970s, although incipient nationalism was quickly discredited by repressive KGB action and splintered into factions.[13] The most well-known spokesman of resurgent Russian nationalism in modern times, Aleksandr Solzhenitsyn, has remained the outstanding

---

[10] Cf. Nicolai N. Petro, *The Rebirth of Russian Democracy: Interpretation of Political Culture* (Cambridge: Harvard University Press, 1995), esp. 88–90, on the rise of nationalism, and the need for distinguishing between Soviet and Russian identity.

[11] A perceptive discussion of these challenges, and the varied answers given at present, can be found in Vera Tolz, "Forging the Nation: National Identity and Nation Building in Post-Communist Russia," *Europe-Asia Studies* 50: 6 (1998): 993–1022, esp. 994–1006.

[12] Nationalism as a political phenomenon is usually thought to characterize historical movements of the 19th century, with the establishment of nation-states like Italy and Germany; the "nation" is defined as a community of people sharing a given territory and a single governing body, sharing ethnicity, culture, language, and/or history.

[13] A helpful discussion of the rise of Russian nationalism as a dissident movement of the last decades of the communist regime, particularly from the 1960s, can be found in the account of the well-known Russian journalist and social historian Alexander Yanov, in *The Russian Challenge and the Year 2000* (Oxford: Basil Blackwell, 1987); the first part is called "The Historical Drama of the Russian Idea and America's Soviet Debate" (17–88). This book pursues the theme of an earlier publication, *The New Russian Right*, warning against the rise of fascist elements together with nationalism taking advantage of a weakened communism during its final years.

representative of a neo-Slavophile approach in political thought from the time that he stood up to Soviet power in the 1970s.[14]

The political ideas of the Slavophiles can be traced back to the 1830s–50s, to the work of Khomiakov, Kireevskii, Aksakov, and Samarin, in their response to the official Uvarov trio (Orthodoxy, Autocracy, and Nationality);[15] attacking "official religion" as heresy, they appealed for secularization of power, and regarded official nationality as a perversion.[16] Especially their view of (Orthodox) *religion* as the true basis of freedom led them to oppose what they regarded as "Western" safeguards of human freedom in parliaments, laws, and constitutions.[17] Such typical Slavophile positions were repeated by Solzhenitsyn in his open letter to the Soviet leaders and the *samizdat* collection *From Under the Rubble* (166–73).[18] But over the years Solzhenitsyn's views have hardened into anti-democratic, anti-Western authoritarianism.[19]

---

[14] Aleksandr Solzhenitsyn, *Pis'mo vozhdiam Sovetskogo Soiuza* [Letter to the leaders of the Soviet Union] (Paris: YMCA-Press, 1974).

[15] Within the present collection the most extensive discussion of the Uvarov formula for Russian identity may be found in V. S. Bibler's "A National Russian Idea? A Culturological Hypothesis."

[16] Yanov faults the Slavophiles for underestimating the dangers of "totalitarianism" and being insufficiently critical of the despotic power of the state (i.e., the tsar as all-powerful and infallible). See *The Russian Challenge and the Year 2000*, 30.

[17] Yanov argues that their critique was unsuccessful in combating the skillful combination of religion with despotism, reaction with patriotism, and serfdom with nationality in Uvarov's formula (ibid., 20–21, 30–32). Slavophiles did have a limited appreciation of a democratic process in the *mir*, and worked hard to make the *zemstvo* a viable form of local democracy; cf. Petro, *The Rebirth of Russian Democracy*, 90 n. 10, where he mentions the pre-revolutionary attempts of D. Shchipov and B. Chicherin to foster a degree of democracy. Yanov recognizes the limitations of the Slavophile distinction between secular and spiritual *authority* within the nation, which they regarded as one big family, where love and goodness are operative, and no external guarantees are needed (*The Russian Challenge and the Year 2000*, 19–21; cf. 25–26); this he contrasts with the realism of American Calvinists who, assuming original sin, did not trust in human goodness and thus instituted balance and control to limit the *powers* of the various branches of government (23). Rather than advocating constitutional limitations on the power of the state, Slavophiles focused on separate secular and spiritual *functions*, not powers of state, and on *obligations*, rather than the rights of the people (25).

[18] Yanov (*The Russian Challenge and the Year 2000*, 20–22) gives a detailed comparison between the views of Ivan Aksakov, in *Teoriia gosudarstva u slavianofilov* [The theory of the state in Slavophilism] (St. Petersburg, 1898), 31–32ff., 180, and Solzhenitsyn's description of democracy in *Iz-pod glyb* (Paris: YMCA-Press 1974), translated by A. M. Brock as *From under the Rubble* (Boston: Little Brown, 1975), 21, 25. While not oblivious to the power of Russian despotism to destroy the soul, Solzhenitsyn attributes the origin of the problem (i.e., Marxist ideology) to the West, with its crisis of democracy and spiritual confusion; likewise, Aksakov speaks of the messianic significance of Russia, with Slavophilism saving the West from parliamentarism, anarchism, unbelief, and dynamite. For Slavophiles freedom is a spiritual phenomenon; a person must be free internally in order to become free politically. Yanov compares a quotation from V. Maksimov: "If we begin with poli-

Dissident groups helped prepare for the transition from an internationalist perspective.[20] A preoccupation with national identity does not inevitably degenerate to chauvinistic nationalism; a certain dose may even be healthy.[21] The issue peaked with the election gains of the ultra-nationalist Zhirinovskii in the 1993 elections, but has not disappeared. For this reason it is imperative to discern a discussion of the Russian Idea as a legitimate aspect of the period of transition, and distinguish this from less healthy nationalist forms which arose at the same time.

Statism

Writing in 1990, Dmitry Pospielovsky recognized the collapse of Marxist internationalism as an important correlate of contemporary Russian nationalism.[22] In

---

tical freedom, we shall unfailingly arrive at spiritual slavery. And that is what is taking place in the West at every step" (*The Russian Challenge and the Year 2000*, 21, quoting Maksimov, "Svoboda dukhovnaia dolzhna predshestvovat' svobode politicheskoi" [Spiritual freedom must precede political freedom], *Novoe russkoe slovo,* 18 June 1978). In the open letter Solzhenitsyn asked the Soviet leaders to keep for themselves "unshakable power, a single strong, closed power, the army, the police, industry, transportation, communications, natural resources, a monopoly on foreign trade, and control over the ruble – but give the people room to breathe, think, and develop!" (*Pis'mo vozhdiam*, 49). This Yanov compares with Konstantin Aksakov: "The people desires for itself one thing only: freedom of life, thought and word. Not interfering in the power of the state, it desires that the state not interfere in the autonomous life of its spirit" (Aksakov, *Teoriia gosudarstva* [1898], 41, qtd. in *The Russian Challenge and the Year 2000*, 168).

[19] Already in the answer to Sakharov, published in *Iz-pod glub,* Yanov detects a more rigid turning to an authoritarian political solution (*The Russian Challenge*, 171).

[20] Some scholars, in their analysis of Russian nationalism in the late 1980s, go so far as to claim that the break-up of the USSR took place under the slogan of establishing a Russian state. Cf. Petro, *The Rebirth of Russian Democracy*, 88–90, on the need to distinguish between Soviet and Russian identity (the latter less coercive). See also Petro on the price paid by Russia in service to the USSR (96–101). Russian recognition that being part, or even the leading partner in the USSR had not worked altogether in its favor, that it was accordingly necessary to re-establish itself as a nation, is discussed by other authors as well, including R. Paradowski, "The Eurasian Idea and Leo Gumilev's Scientific Ideology," *Canadian Slavonic Papers* 41: 1 (March 1999): 19–32, esp. 31.

[21] This was certainly the expectation of Dmitry Pospielovsky, "Russian Nationalism, An Update" *Report on the USSR* 2: 6 (9 February 1990): 8–17.

[22] Ibid., esp. 11. Among the groups active at that time, he focused his attention particularly on *pochvennichestvo*, the nativist movement idealizing the rural communal village life of Russia. It is of interest that Pospielovsky included among nativists not only Solzhenitsyn, but the Byzantologist Fr. Ioann Ekonomstev, the medieval scholar Dmitrii Likhachev (editor of *Nashe nasledie*), Igor' Shafarevich (co-author with Solzhenitsyn in *From under the Rubble*), Vladimir Soloukhin, and others connected with Pamiat', a movement with strong Orthodox and monarchist connections. These he wanted to distinguish from the less acceptable group Patriot, a nationalist movement sharing Pamiat''s clear opposition to the internationalist stance of the Communists, but in a more extreme, racist (anti-semitic) form, even combining neo-Stalinist or neo-Nazi aspects with statism.

1990, still within the context of the millennium celebrations of Russian Orthodoxy (1988), he regarded such nationalism as a healthy movement; like Solzhenitsyn, Pospielovsky looked to groups like Pamiat' and to the Orthodox church to restore Christian ethical values in society. But nationalist groups like the Patriots and other statists supported a far more extreme nationalist ideology aiming to re-establish superpower status, using a neo-messianic ideology.[23] If not constrained by state law-enforcement agents such groups certainly could pose a danger in exploiting problems of the transition period, like inflation, widespread unemployment and poverty, negligible wages, breakdown in the infrastructure of health care, social benefits, and communication.[24]

Messianism

Is messianic imperialism also a component element of Russian nationalism?[25] Messianism points to a conviction of being chosen for a particular task or role in history. Dostoevskii, Solov'ev, and Berdiaev all recognized the messianic aspect of the Russian Idea; Solov'ev was especially critical of chauvinist, imperialist messianic attitudes expressed by Danilevskii and Leont'ev in their discussion of Russia's wars with Turkey.[26]

---

[23] Cf. Igor' Torbakov, "The Statists and Ideology of Russian Imperial Nationalism," *RFE/RL Research Report* 1: 49 (1992): 10–16, on groups connected with the *samizdat Veche* of the 1970s, and more recently, those represented by publications like *Sovetskaia Rossiia*, *Den'*, *Molodaia Gvardiia*, or the All-Russian Socio-Christian Union for the Liberation of the People, known by its acronym, VSKhSON, a movement which arose in 1964, though it was all but crushed by the KGB in 1967; on this movement cf. Yanov, *The Russian Challenge and the Year 2000*, 178–79. Already in the early 1990s Torbakov observed various kinds of nationalism moving toward *statism*, the more extreme nationalist ideology aimed at re-establishing superpower status at a critical time of loss, using a neo-messianic Russian ideology to replace the vacuum left by the demise of communism (10–11).

[24] According to Torbakov, statism is fed by four concepts: an imperialism that does not recognize the liquidation of the USSR; an authoritarian, hierarchical neo-Eurasianism connected with L. Gumilev and S. Sankevich; anti-Westernism (like that of the neo-Slavophiles, or Limonov's *Manifesto*) affirming the sovereignty and priority of the state; and finally, promotion of a "third way" for Russia, with messianic expression of the Russian Idea, as in the work of film producer and writer N. Mikhalkov (12–15).

[25] On this issue, see also Yanov's discussion of Solzhenitsyn and his friends, *The Russian Challenge and the Year 2000*, 178–79.

[26] Indeed, the issue of a messianic vision, a sense of destiny and God-given mission, comes up repeatedly in articles included in this collection. Kantor speaks of the "nightmare" of messianism, which he connects with Russian isolationism (25). M. Il'in reflects extensively on imperialism and the "Third Rome" as part of the "rule of destiny," and a significant aspect of the Russian character (37, 41–49). He also discusses the messianic character of Marxism, with its rhetoric of a historic mission in service to mankind (51–52). For Bibler too the sense of a unique destiny, as a statement of a supra-national idea of sovereignty, can be traced back to "Moscow as the Third Rome" (64–

But messianic views were not confined to pre-revolutionary times. Marxists expressed their historic, messianic role in terms of being progressive, well advanced in science and space exploration to be properly equipped for their task of "civilizing" the world.[27] And we may well ask, with M. Il'in, whether Russia is now ready to leave its "imperial" civilizing destiny behind? The evidence points to reluctance in abandoning former spheres of influence, accepting newly defined borders, particularly when it comes to Belarus and the Ukraine.[28]

The issue of messianic vision demands consideration of the question of *religion in Russian culture*. Berdiaev's interpretation of the Schism as a tragedy of messianic thought is now well-known in Russia. Berdiaev's *Russian Idea* was preoccupied with a messianic mission for Russia, starting with the crucial role of "Moscow as Third Rome," to express a strong sense of a specifically Russian place and task in history. Among contemporary authors, K. Ivanov has focused quite explicitly on the problem of the nationalization of Orthodoxy, as it confuses the interests of church and state, and, in turn, opens the way for misguided utopian constructions.[29] Inasmuch as these are based on substitutes for religion they only lead to bitterness and disillusionment.

Ivanov's analysis of Russia's messianic calling is particularly significant for initiating a discussion of the respective spheres of authority of church and state, and distinguishing the conditions for being a faithful and responsible member of the church, from conditions for responsible citizenship. Issues of church and state, or religion and politics play a critical role in this context.

The Russian Idea and Russian Orthodoxy

Neo-Slavophiles like Solzhenitsyn, with their 19th-century predecessors, consider Orthodoxy to be the crucial factor for Russian identity. Orthodoxy, they argue, represents the key to holding Russia together. Indeed, Orthodoxy has been more closely tied to national identities throughout history than have most Protestant groups or Catholicism within their respective states. When religion and ethnicity

---

69), confirming Kantor's approach on messianic nationalism; he also typically connects the Russian Idea with empire-building, with imperialism, i.e., rejecting democracy (58, 62–63). In a similar vein Walicki has connected the temptation of messianism and totalitarianism with the "Russian Idea," though he recognizes that messianism typically characterizes a time of chaos and uncertainty. Cf. A. Walicki, "Po povodu 'russkoi idei' v russkoi filosofii" [On the russian idea in Russian philosophy], *Voprosy Filosofii*, no. 1 (1994): 68–72.

[27] Cf. Il'in, 51.

[28] The re-establishment of closer ties with Belarus has been an ongoing concern of discussions with its leader, Lukashenko, during the past years. Connections with the Ukraine were strengthened after Putin's March 2001 visit; negotiation of energy policies reflects Russia's desire to reassert its influence there.

[29] See his article "The Orthodox Schism and Schismatic Communism" in this collection, 129–36.

coincide they give a powerful sense of identity. However, this strength in expressing identity can also hide a significant weakness. Nationalized religion is problematic when political power structures dictate priorities, or interfere in the appointment of leaders. Moreover, what unites a core segment in a nation can also serve to divide those alienated by it. Can the Russian Federation afford to alienate its Islamic and other ethnic component groups?

So we come back to an important question at the heart of the discussion of the Russian Idea, identity, and ideology. *Is Orthodoxy able to fill the current ideological void?* Is it the legitimate socio-political structure to do so? As a religion its prime concern is the relationship between God and human beings. Still, as Kuraev affirms, it has its own tradition of philosophy, and does express a religious worldview.[30] It certainly supports a system of ideas opposing the materialist and communist ideology which, even though it is no longer imposed as state ideology, has left its legacy in deeply engrained public attitudes and laws on property, to give but one example. And it can perform the crucial role of legitimizing contemporary political action, as with the patriarch blessing Putin and offering public prayers on his taking office.

What is *missing is the link from theory to practice and implementation.* What is the contemporary relationship of the Russian Orthodox Church (ROC) and the Russian state? It is not well-defined, and this is not accidental. The ROC has privileges, a role in the army and education, and receives help in rebuilding churches, but has not resumed its former role as state church. It relies on indirect means of influence.

Orthodoxy as Ideology? The Philosophical Dimension

Ironically, in Russian history ideology was introduced as a replacement for Orthodoxy. But ideology also meant a rejection of the Christian Platonist approach, emphasizing rather a naturalist approach to knowledge. However, consideration of Orthodoxy as "ideology" clearly implies a broadening of that assumed base of knowledge to include transcendental resources, based on divine revelation.

Of course, the Platonist approach was not without its problems, especially on the issue of creation. *Platonic Ideas* were accepted in the Christian tradition, as we noted, to explain the divine plan for the creation. These Ideas have divine status, but the creation as such represents an inferior embodiment of those Ideas. The Platonizing explanation tended to conflate "creaturely" with "fallen" status. Christian philosophers following the Platonizing fathers would always need to clarify their understanding of our world and humanity as an originally good creation, yet fallen due to human sin and disobedience. It is therefore not surprising

---

[30] See Kuraev's article in this collection, "Pantheism nd Monotheism," 185–212.

that in the Platonizing sophiological thought of Solov'ev, Florenskii, and Bulgakov, the status of creation remained a contested issue – on which Florovsky's corrective must be heard.[31]

Ideas are after all not just divine absolutes, although they have a transcendental aspect; they are human constructs. They depend on input both from above and below. In terms of religion and politics "input from below" means a degree of democratic expression must be honored; in the political arena there must be room for a plurality of options. But the issue of authority must also be addressed. Russians are obviously looking for some way of reintroducing an ideology, as a transcendental perspective to give a framework for action and for useful judgments on events. Certainly the renewed publicly acknowledged role of Christianity can make a difference here, contributing its own perspective on the value of human labor (or its exploitation), giving prophetic statements on the corruption which pervades the government and military, or articulating a vision of a Christian society. If it is not the task of the institutional church as such to give direction on critical issues of Russian society and politics, certainly those scholars and intellectuals who are Christian can help provide the vital link between Christian principles and their practical application.[32] The unfortunate 20th-century experience of over-reliance on utopian thought is by itself an insufficient reason for altogether avoiding imaginative deliberation on more perfect forms of social organization, business-arrangements or government, as an anti-

---

[31] G. V. Florovsky's critical article on creation, "Tvar' i tvarnost' [Creature and creatureliness], was first published in *Pravoslavnaia mysl'* (Paris), no. 1 (1928), and reprinted in translation as "Creation and Creaturehood," in *The Collected Works of Georges Florovsky*, vol. 3, *Creation and Redemption* (Belmont, MA: Nordland Publishing Co., 1976), 43–78. It is discussed in Khoruzhii, "Neopatristicheskii sintez i russkaia filosofiia" [A neopatristic synthesis and Russian philosophy]. See pp. 181–83 in the present volume. Florovsky affirms creation as an act of God's will, to be distinguished from divine generation as an act of his nature. This implies the heterogeneity of creation, and also allows for the freedom of the creature. It allows for history with an open outcome; death and finitude are not the only options, but are overcome in history.

[32] In St. Petersburg, Fr. Veniamin Novik has explored the difficulties of Orthodox believers actively involving themselves with socio-political and economic issues in terms of a vision for creatively transforming life in its fullness, one that he is says is rather unpopular among the Orthodox; see his "Social Doctrine: Will the Russian Orthodox Church Take a Daring Step?" *Religion, State & Society* 26: 2 (1998): 197–203. He recognizes that while in the Catholic Church priests also take no direct part in politics, that church has worked out a vision for a Christian society (198). At issue is the Orthodox attitude to social structures. A Platonist inclination influences them toward regarding "reality" as less important than the "ideal" construct. Lacking a concept of civil society, the Orthodox also regard as unnecessary any social initiatives through groups that could mediate government administration and the subject; according to Fr. Novik, the Constantinian model of imperial state Orthodoxy is still alive in popular psychology, considering a strong state, e.g. a monarchy, to be the most appropriate, even though democratic structures have been shown not to be in contradiction with the Scriptures (201).

dote to problems experienced in these areas. This remains a challenge for Russians, once more to dream constructively, to combine bold plans for the future with a sensible approach for implementation.

The Present Discussion: Authors and Isssues

The articles included in this collection for the most part represent a reaction to the post-perestroika reaction. They are keenly aware of the nationalist backlash to the "democratic" reforms of the early 1990s, with the rise of Zhirinovskii, and the use of the Russian Idea by groups around him, and also by Ziuganov. They have observed the "red-brown" alliance of the early 1990s, and heard Yeltsin's request to formulate a new Russian Idea appropriate for the time. While no quick solution could be produced, numerous authors evidently were stirred into writing on the subject, expressing concern over the request for a new (single) ideology to guide political action.

In the first section authors from various points of view deal with specific aspects of the renewed discussion of the Russian Idea, in terms of a so-called unique Russian mind, or mentality, a sense of destiny, and crucial choices made in service to mankind. They approach the topic from a variety of angles: linguistic, sociological, cultural (or culturological), and political.

With his article "Is the Russian Mentality Changing?" Vladimir Kantor argues that Russian attitudes *are* changing after the fall of communism. Reviewing typical Russian beliefs like collectivism (opposed to "Western" individualism), the "besieged fortress" psychology, messianism, and futurism, and dismissing most of these as myths, Kantor finds that many traditional attitudes are disintegrating and being replaced by Western ones. Since the 1950s, Kantor notes, the "apology for the private life" has had an impact which continues, even though the state still wishes to control the economy. Russian culture, according to Kantor, is coming out of a period of adolescence and entering one of adulthood.

Mikhail Il'in's critical discussion, "Words and Meanings: On the Rule of Destiny. The Russian Idea," begins with Belinskii's 1841 (Westernizing) characterization of a "motivating principle in history," Kireevskii's (Slavophile) elaboration of the "fundamental Russian mind," and Dostoevskii's attempt to synthesize these in terms of external and internal aspects of a Russian national principle in history. For the historical roots of the idea expressing Russia's self-awareness of its "imperial-civilizing" destiny, Il'in takes us back to epic heroes and legends of the forests and steppe, tales of passage and difficult choices. For the Russian formulation of Byzantine theocratic ideals Il'in examines the work of the eleventh- and twelfth-century thinkers Metropolitan Hilarion, Nikon the Great, and Nestor. Here he detects three foundations for the Russian Idea: 1) Hilarion's "chrono-political" formula, connecting Russian history with the spread and protection of Christianity; 2) Nikon's geo-political formula, looking at Russia with its far-flung regions, its towns and villages as a system of "islands" separated by watershed ridges; and 3) the archetype of self-sacrifice presented in Nestor's tale of the brothers Boris and Gleb, also attributed to Peter the Great's activities by Belinskii.

A synthesis of these motifs can be found in the themes of enlightenment, holiness, and glory applied to Russia as the "Third Rome," a concept elaborated especially by the 15th-century monk Filofei (Philotheus) to express a special role for Russia as "God-chosen." The concept of sacrificial service to mankind was not missed by Marxist Messianism, and Il'in portrays Lenin as a modern-day version of the tenth-century prince Vladimir, once more making critical choices for Russia. Il'in resists the urge to create new myths for the architects of "perestroika," even though Russia does not appear ready to give up on its "gods, tsars, and heroes." He urges great caution for those desiring to create another single national ideology, given the diversity and plurality within contemporary culture.

In his article "The Russian National Idea, a Culturological Hypothesis" Vladimir Bibler challenges the political expression of the Russian Idea, suggesting instead that the national idea is a linguistic and cultural matter; it is discourse, thought expressed in speech. Interpreted politically, as in Kiva's contemporary reworking of the well-known formula of Count Uvarov, Bibler warns that it focuses on the state at the expense of other components, and is clearly opposed to democracy (sovereignty of the person), civil society (the right of contractual agreement), and the independent development of culture, literature, and the arts. Not only does the Russian national idea represent pure nationalism; it leads to totalitarianism or fascism.

Leonid Sedov, in "The Place of Russian Culture among World Cultures: An Invitation to Reflection," uses comparative cultural analysis to examine problems of contemporary Russian culture, looking for deep roots in Russian history. Sedov attempts to decipher a "modal personality" of Russian culture by comparing typical attitudes to death and mortality in major cultures like the Chinese, Indian, and Judeo-European. His conclusion, that Russians prefer the "here and now," or "this-worldliness," leads him to question the depth of Orthodox religiosity, and to re-interpret Dostoevskii's characterization of Russia as "God-bearing" in terms of a pagan nationalism. If insistence on correctness of teaching and nationalistic pride in the superiority of one's nation characterized Marxism, it characterized Orthodoxy no less.

This article ends with an interesting character sketch of the Russian "modal personality," that of the gambler, with a certain irresponsible fatalism allowing him to taking chances. Truth, in such a context, is not abstract but pragmatic. There is also a certain desperation which characterizes the gambler's situation, for he cannot leave the game until it is over, and the unpredictability of the situation makes it hard to plan. Sedov similarly interprets "brotherhood" in terms of the cohesiveness forced upon those bound by the roulette wheel. Finally, he notes that this personality is characterized by a type of adolescence, one which can distinguish death from other kinds of leave-taking, but still regards it as a strange departure, in which the benefits are all for those left behind.

Sedov's portrayal is balanced by Andrei Zabiako's "Antinomies of Russian Consciousness: Labor and Leisure," which presents a strong case against the traditional reproach of laziness as a basic Russian character trait. He calls attention to the rhythm of a capricious nature, its short intensive summers alternating with long winters; the expansive sweep of the Russian landscape is also noted as an influential factor for Russian views of labor, or form, and restraint, fate and chance (*avos'*). He examines the worldview expressed in traditional monastic literature and the scheduling of the day by bells, funeral rituals, and fairy-tales which are as quick to mock the fool hoping for the sweets for which he did not work, as to glorify the clever rogue. Zabiako concludes that for Russians idleness is a temporary condition; labor is the norm.

In the article "Civil Society: A Religious Assessment of the Problem" Evgenii Rashkovskii begins by establishing a methodology for dealing with the religious aspect of civil society as a vital issue, particularly difficult to solve in rational discourse since it touches on spiritual reality. His introductory survey of the three basic principles of civil society (equality before the law, protection of property, and irreducible freedom of the person) gives clear evidence of the weight of responsibility carried by the individual in the context of civil society. In a historical survey he shows how Catholicism allowed more freedom for civil society, but especially the Protestant Reformation allowed for a more privatized sense of the covenant between God and man. Clear distinction between "what belongs to God and to Caesar" meant a powerful restraint on the ambitions of rulers.

The given analysis is helpful particularly when Rashkovskii applies it to the difficult transition period now experienced in Russia, where a totalitarian regime has collapsed; only civil society, and non-violence in settling differences, can prevent civil war. The liberalization of law, an unstable market economy, and the slow formation of new coalitions have added to an atmosphere of lawlessness, mafia presence, to which he adds two current problems: the traditionally large size of the state, with corresponding atomization of society, and a negative attitude to law, inherited from the Romantic views of the Slavophiles and passed on to *narodniki* and Marxists. Nonetheless Rashkovskii finds a source of hope in the revival of religion, from its negative (critical) role in the 1970s, undermining the atheistic basis of the state, to a more positive contribution in the last decade, encouraging the establishment of civil society and freedom of the person.

In the *second section*, which discusses the Russian Idea in terms of its foundations in Russian religious philosophy, authors approach things differently, from a more explicitly religious and Orthodox perspective, dealing once more with some of the topics introduced in the first section, but now with greater depth. The communist state was marked by its antagonism to religion, and by the assumption that religion would wither away, just as the state was to wither away, and all peoples would be fused in a single stateless paradise. Of course, communists reckoned too little with actual human nature.

Authors in this section take different approaches to the issue of the renewed presence of Orthodoxy in the public sphere; they use a historiosophical approach (Ivanov), look at the potential for interfaith discussion (Zhuravskii), re-examine cosmism from a religious perspective (Vasilenko), discuss the patristic factor (Khoruzhii), and finally, investigate the rise of syncretism and the occult (Kuraev).

In his essay "The Orthodox Schism and Schismatic Communism" Konstantin Ivanov recognizes the work of emigré writers on religious problems of Russian history, particularly the tragic 17th-century schism, and examines Berdiaev's connection of that event with attitudes of the intelligentsia and Bolshevik ideology. Only by regarding the schism as a tragedy of the messianic vision of Moscow as the Third Rome can one explain the subsequent shaking of the theocracy which it supported. Analyzing the "disenchantment" of Russians at that time, Ivanov turns to "nationalization of Christianity" as the prior spiritual catastrophe, the basis of such false dreams and utopias as we could find also among communists. For Ivanov nationalization of faith takes us to the heart of the problem. The collapse of a utopia of power meant turning to its alternative, anarchic nihilism. False idealization of the nation as "God-bearing," and false association of power and religion misled Russians to revolt against God, questioning his control over evil and suffering. Atheism arose from a false sense of compassion.

Aleksei Zhuravskii's article on Islam, "P. Chaadaev and V. Solov'ev: The Discovery of Islam," written against the background of current religious tensions in Russia, demonstrates that both Chaadaev (early 19th century) and Solov'ev (late 19th century) anticipated current positions on Islam held by noteworthy Catholic scholars like Karl Rahner. Discussion of Islam typically placed it in the context of the "opposition of East and West," or the major monotheistic religions (Judaism, Christianity, and Islam). Chaadaev was ahead of his time when, in the Philosophical Letters, he recognized the positive historical role of Islam as one of the major forms of revealed religion.

Zhuravskii shows how Solov'ev built on Chaadaev's position to develop an increasingly positive evaluation of Islam's role in history. From a more traditional and typical position in the earlier works like *Three Powers* (1877), where he emphasized the restriction of personal individuality in Islam, already *The Great Dispute and Christian Politics* (1883) recognized Islam as the capstone of a number of heresies going back to the Arians. Even more positive is the evaluation of *The History and Future of Theocracy* (1885–87), where Solov'ev recognized Islam as a religion tracing itself to Abraham. Finally, his scholarly article "Mahomet" in the Brokgauz-Efron encyclopedia presents a culmination of his study of Islam, allowing it a providential significance, as a type of "preparation of the gospel," such as can also be found in the Catholic orientalist Massignon. According to Solov'ev, the difference between the three major monotheistic religions is not to be sought in morality but in metaphysics. Solov'ev thus called for a reconciliation which treats the opponent on "God's terms."

Russians are rightfully proud of their role in space exploration. Their cosmonaut Iurii Gagarin was the first man to travel in space. Leonid Vasilenko's article "Cosmism and Evolutionism in the Russian Religious Philosophical Tradition" introduces us to the central ideas of cosmism and surveys four significant thinkers who supported cosmist views: Florenskii, Solov'ev, Bulgakov, and Berdiaev. He begins by asking some critical questions about the self-sufficiency of the cosmos, the aim of its evolutionary process, and the human factor, or human freedom. Already in the opening definition of cosmism in terms of a "world which as a whole is harmonious and organized according to reason, with soul ennobling it and promoting spiritual growth for mankind," he positions himself in terms of the Platonist tradition characterizing the work of Solov'ev and Florenskii. The article points to the significance of Russian religious-philosophical cosmism as a response to Western thought which did not look beyond rational factors, and ignored spirituality. Insisting on the inner spiritual depth of soul, whether human or cosmic, and the cosmic mission of human beings in the world, these thinkers provide a basis for new ways of thinking on social and cultural issues

Florenskii's positions are of interest not only for using a traditional Platonic dualistic approach to the distinction of our human world and the cosmos but especially for pointing to the crucial role of the church in allowing for man to become godlike, and thus overcoming dualism. Where Florenskii's view of life in the cosmos is static, Solov'ev has accented historical process and organic development, focusing on the role of the Logos and Sophia, or the world-soul, in the universal process of total-unity. Significant in this process is the primordial fall of man and consequent alienation from God, promoting fragmentation. In his discussion of re-integration, or unification, with a personal as well as a cultural historical aspect, Solov'ev pays attention to the question of East and West, and points to a special role for Russia in mediating between the brutal tyranny of the East and lack of spirituality of the West.

Bulgakov approaches cosmic issues from the perspective of the predominant social and economic problems of his time, recognizing our world as a field of struggle where human labor must help open up the future for life. Man has a crucial role in redeeming nature and transforming the world. And finally, Berdiaev, recognizing the end of an era of organic development signaled by technology and industry, emphasizes an eschatological view of our world, and accordingly focuses on human freedom and creativity as the answer.

With his article "Neopatristic Synthesis and Russian Philosophy" Sergei Khoruzhii takes a central concept of the work of Fr. Georges Florovsky, "Neopatristic synthesis," and demonstrates how it can be used to integrate traditional Orthodox theological concepts in a new philosophical tradition. He begins by examining Russian philosophy from the Slavophiles through Solov'ev as a school (the metaphysics of All-Unity) within the Western classical tradition, accepting a Platonist essentialist ontology, and expressing authentic Russian themes like integrality (*tselnost'*) but ignoring the spiritual experience of the mystics and ascetics. The theme of "glorification of the name" (*imiaslavie*) which showed promise of correcting these omissions was not productive among Mocow-based successors of Solov'ev mainly due to disruptions after the Revolution.

Khoruzhii finds a better opportunity for applying the experience-related themes of hesychasm and Palamist thought within a new Eastern Orthodox philosophical tradition which is personal, dialogic, and true to the patristic discourse. He calls it a philosophy of "energetic ontology," and demonstrates its potential from the theme of "Creation and the creature" as a helpful account of human status and human freedom. Recognizing the significance of Florovsky's 1928 essay "Creature and Creatureliness," Khoruzhii is confident that this direction of thought allows for valuable philosophical contribution in the future.[33]

And finally, Andrei Kuraev's "Pantheism and Monotheism" addresses the problem of popular syncretism combining Orthodox Christian belief with occult theosophical beliefs (like those of Mme. Blavatsky, the Roerichs, and Pomerants); the latter are typically based on pantheism, where God is indistinguishably intertwined with the world, and likewise to be sought in the depth of our souls. Kuraev begins his argument by contrasting the personal quality of God, versus the impersonal abstract divine Absolute of the pantheists; he then works out this contrast in terms of themes of creation, divine love, the presence of God in creation, human freedom, and evil.

How can the impersonal infinite Absolute create the relative and finite, he asks. While love is the strong point among Christian affirmations of God, the pantheist has no room for attributing love to the divine, for that would involve the impersonal principle in a personal interest for what is subordinate. For

---

[33] On this important article of Florovsky see also above, n. 31.

Christians God's love climaxed in his Son, Immanuel, God in human form. Among other things the incarnation means that created reality, though dependent and relative, is not an illusion; human beings are real, not just a microcosm, and have their own freedom of action. Finally, he argues that evil is not to be identified with God, nor with nature, as in the theory that harmony in the cosmos depends on the contrast of good and evil. Pantheism denies true freedom, has no room for the varied complexity of life as created, and makes no clear distinction between the relative and absolute, the perfect and damaged cosmos. Syncretism reduces major world religions like Hinduism or Buddhism to some variants of Christianity; distorting these religions, it also supports positions clearly incompatible with Christianity.

Thus the articles of this collection variously reflect the discussion of the "Russian Idea" which received considerable attention in the press of the early and mid-1990s. Although initiated mainly by nationalists and stimulated by Yeltsin's 1996 request of intellectuals to give a more balanced proposal, this discussion especially reflects political, ideological, cultural, and social concerns over the demise of communist ideology; the vacuum left by the long-imposed single ideological vision has not easily been filled. Nor is the discussion finished. Patriotic nationalism rose for some very specific reasons; a number of immediate historical conditions contributing to the loss of a sense of identity, like the question of borders, and of ethnic Russians living in the "near abroad," are slowly getting resolved. But there are also long-term cultural, ideological, philosophical, and religious factors, which are not as topical, and warrant ongoing attention. In fact, many of the issues raised by the discussion of the Russian Idea have a perennial character. The articles of the present collection have been translated to give a degree of balance to the discussion as it has reached the public outside of Russia.

Part I
The Russian Idea: Cultural, Historical, and Ideological Aspects

Is the Russian Mentality Changing?[1]

Vladimir Karlovich Kantor

1. Today's Fears, or, The Vicious Circle of Theoretical Planning

Nowadays it takes courage to read Russian newspapers and listen to politicians' and journalists' speeches. They always repeat the same old story. Russia has lost its identity. An alien set of values is being imposed, and Russia is on the point of disaster, a real apocalypse. Evil forces are trying to Westernize Russia, while our people just want to live their own way.

We keep on asking the rhetorical questions. Who are we, and whom should we be, just to preserve our identity? At issue is our self-identity, our mentality; we want to rediscover the "intellectual and spiritual structure" of our people, to use an older and more exact expression. Certainly, this structure has changed during the centuries of Russia's official existence as a state, just as the political system has changed. But some fundamental characteristics remain unchanged, and play a positive or negative role, depending on the situation. According to Russian Romantics and Slavophiles these characteristics are collectivism (*obshchinnost'*), *sobornost'*, and a strong Orthodox faith.

In the 1830s, when Russian society was greatly influenced by European ideas, such a Romantic approach received the canonical status of an official motto: Orthodoxy (*pravoslavie*), Autocracy (*samoderzhavie*), and Nationality (*narodnost'*). On these three cornerstones Russia seems always to have been established, and on them it was expected to persist unshaken into the future. With these characteristics we tried to distinguish ourselves from the West. In the more recent period of the solid "Iron Curtain" the trio appears to have been converted into a duo of Party ideology and Nationality. Nonetheless, the essential principle of the collective state was maintained in its opposition to the "corrupt individualism of the West."

If we turn to those like Chaadaev who criticized the culture of their time, without denying its original and specific features, we find a more pessimistic description of Russian culture. They supported their view by pointing to concrete features of Russian culture, like the tendency of Russians to renounce their rights, or the total subjection of the personality to the state. In moments of pop-

---

[1] "Meniaetsia li rossiiskaia mental'nost'?" *Literaturnaia gazeta*, 15 April 1998, p. 5.
Helleman, Wendy, ed. *The Russian Idea: In Search of a New Identity*. Bloomington, IN: Slavica, 2004, 23–32.

ular uprising, a wild arbitrariness characterizes Russians, but it is soon overcome, in turn, by a more cruel, arbitrary rule of state, returning the people once more to slavery. From recent history we are reminded of Russia's October revolution and civil war, with their slogan "everything is allowed" (according to Pitirim Sorokin); Bolshevist tyranny soon took its place. No tyrants from all the rest of Russian history could match such tyranny.

Taken individually, such points of view may be rather lopsided; but on the whole they complement one another excellently. For example, our people now enjoy "freedom," but there are still many grievances about the division of what was held collectively, about the "war of all against all" which also characterized Europe in the initial stages of capitalism. The person is now separate from the state; in fact, Russians have discovered that they are not truly collective creatures, unless we restrict our focus to the collective character of mafia structures. The social order has collapsed. At the same time the protagonists of "neo-collectivism" (*neo-sobornost'*) can only shed tears and dream of a Stalin-type "strong power" to drive everyone quickly back into the collective, back to the "orthodox-communist collective" (*pravoslavno-kommunisticheskaia obshchina*), to use contemporary ideological terminology.

So what do we have, the Gordian knot (which no one can untangle)? Is it true that out of "utter affliction, liberty is born, and out of liberty, slavery," to quote Radishchev? "Going from unlimited freedom, I finish with unlimited despotism," is the far stronger statement of Shigalev, in Dostoevskii's *Devils*. Or is it really true, as Gogol' claimed, that the sixth of the globe occupied by our country is a "place bewitched" from which no one who has been there can get away, in spite of all attempts? And does nothing ever change?

It is useful to turn our attention to the historical and cultural factors which created such a situation. Most Russian historians and philosophers of culture and history, both Realists and Romantics, maintain that the organization of the state and patterns of socio-cultural relationships which continue to exist to the present were shaped, in one way or another, at the turn of the 16th century. At that time, with the help of the Tatars, Russia was "Muscovized" (G. Fedotov). When Tatar power weakened and was overthrown, a centralized state was founded, one which was contemporaneous with Western European states, yet utterly unlike them.

This state was shaken by the reforms of Peter the Great and subsequent Europeanization, but was reanimated by the Bolsheviks. It was called a "constitutional government" (*gosudarstvo pravdy*, M. Shakhmatov), a "totalitarian state" (N. Berdiaev), or "monarchy of the people" (I. Solonevich), but its essence is portrayed in the section that follows.

2. The Nightmare of Messianism

Only those at the highest levels of power had rights, while its subject citizens had only duties, and accepted these, driven on by two aspects of their socio-psychological makeup, which played a role in Russian history far larger than is generally thought.

First of all, a "siege mentality" dominated the Russian people. They were always surrounded by enemies (which, indeed, was true), but without any natural barriers. If they wanted to build a fortress, stones were scarce. Unlike much of Europe, Russia was a land of great forests. But, as the historian S. Solov'ev emphasized, this did not contribute greatly to its defense, since wood can easily be destroyed by fire. The fortress built consisted of the "bodies of its inhabitants," as F. Nesterov remarked. Accordingly, personal interests counted for little; the interests of the state determined all others. This archetypal factor of popular psychology was exploited by the Bolsheviks when they declared the country under siege from the bourgeoisie.

A second important issue for Russia is its isolationism, and the messianism associated with it. While one tsar followed the other, and social structures came and went, this sense of isolationism and accompanying messianism remained.

This may be traced back to the Byzantine heritage which confirmed Russia as the only politically independent country of Orthodox faith; the heritage came via the Balkans, Serbia, and Bulgaria, who were unsuccessful in claiming the role of the "Third Rome." Cut off from Europe by the Tatars, the ideologues of Russian Orthodoxy eagerly accepted the praise of the defeated and humiliated Greeks, Bulgars, and Serbs, who passed along to Muscovy the role of being the sole savior of true Christian devotion (*blagochestie*).

The news fell on ears which were especially receptive at a time of liberation from many centuries of the Tatar yoke; it flattered the national self-esteem. In subsequent years such messianism underwent every possible modification and metamorphosis, but the feeling of pride remained: "We are solitary, but powerful, because we carry the light of eternal truth; being solitary is the native character of prophets."

It was no accident that the Bolsheviks so easily overturned the Western European experiment of a proletarian movement, and finally, with apparently solid grounds, appealed to the West to come and learn from the country of "victorious socialism." This Messianic madness, beginning with Dostoevskii, gained followers from a wide circle of the Russian intelligentsia, including those who accepted neither Orthodoxy nor revolutionary thought, and yet believed that something prophetic was being fulfilled in Russia. For example:

> And you, fiery element,
> Raging, and raving, and burning me up,
> Russia, Russia, Russia,
> Messiah for days to come!

This comes from Andrey Belyi's poem "To the Motherland" ("Rodine"), written in August of 1917. And these factors influenced Russian utopianism and the inclination to futurism (*budetlianstvo*), from Chaadaev and Hertzen, to Fedorov, Khlebnikov, and Maiakovskii. What does it mean? It means not accepting life today, or even tomorrow, in favor of life "after tomorrow." That was one of its poles – that of exalted dreams and thirst for universal harmony. But this futuristic messianism had another pole. Its pathos for the future actually encouraged the idea of social sacrifice, of sacrificing oneself and one's children, not just in favor of one's grandchildren, but for one's great-grandchildren – all in the hope of the "resurrection of the fathers" after death (according to Fedorov). The life of "the present day" was so desperate that a normal "tomorrow" could hardly be expected to follow on such desperate reality. In the language of state bureaucracy (accepted by every Russian inhabitant) "tomorrow" simply meant "never." The famous French thinker Joseph, Comte de Maistre, who lived in St. Petersburg for more than ten years (1803–17), wrote, "Having done all that that I myself can do, I am bogged down in fruitless waiting. *Zavtra* (tomorrow) – that is the terrible motto of this country."[2] And yet, on the other hand, "the day after tomorrow" could be seen clearly, like stars shining from a dark and deep precipice, almost to the point of hallucination, passing "through the mountains of time" (Maiakovskii), and was received as a miraculous transfiguration.

3. Tomorrow, Tomorrow, not Today!

In the sixth issue of the magazine *Golosa iz Rossii* (*Voices from Russia*) Hertzen published a letter to the editor of the magazine *Kolokol* (*The Bell*); to this day the true author is unknown. I will only quote some words from this piece, for, with a tough severity like that of Chaadaev, they characterize our mentality very well:

> Concern about the future is not a feature of the Russian character. Our words express a readiness to take all humanity under our wing; we are ready to become socialists or democrats, and speak of the highest honor with bloodshot eyes. But these are only words. In reality, we are afraid of any kind of work, and of thinking about the future. We live only in the present. Our civil servant steals so he can provide banquets with abundant food, and the merchant cheats to get a promotion for his son; the

---

[2] Zhozef de Mestr [Joseph de Maistre], *Peterburgskie pis'ma, 1803–1817* [Letters from Petersburg, 1803–1817] (St. Petersburg: Inapress, 1995), 45.

peasant [*muzhik*] works just to get drunk. There is no substantive concern about the future. In fact, in Russia those who do concern themselves about the future are rejected, and become the object of resentment and mockery. In other words, there is an incredible gap between the dream and the reality, one that characterizes no other culture. "Dreaming about the future" is altogether different from "concern about the future."[3]

To fulfil a dream we are willing to suffer and fight, even to be just "a cog in a machine," consoling ourselves with the thought of a "common enterprise," and of experiencing hardship for "the greater good." Concern for the future requires independent activity, laboring like a beaver to build one's own house, and working for oneself, which presupposes the independence of the person in a culture. But such a personality was never developed in the broad spectrum of the Russian population; they always worked for "the stranger," for Tatars, for a state budget, for the tsars, for lords, or for the Communist Party. Inability to do what one is not accustomed to, namely organizing the day's affairs, leads to a desire for living by "the present moment," at least until the fruit of one's work is taken away. It also prevents thinking of the transition from the present into the future, the real future, as in the proverb: "A new master means new orders; but I (myself) am not my own master." And that gives rise to the utopian dream of jumping through time, even through centuries, in which the suffering and absurdity of life as we now experience it will be justified.

Such is Russian "non-Euclidean mathematics," taking over the world where "all contradictions coexist" (Dostoevskii). Hence also the idea of the "single moment" (so meticulously traced in Dostoevskii's characters) which offers maximum success not by the increments of hard work over many years, or even the developments of many centuries, but at one go, jumping through the centuries. Only with such a dream of universal future happiness, equally available to all, can slaves be consoled. All the more, because slaves know no conditions other than the collective process which reduces them all to equality under compulsion. This is why the dream seems to have been fulfilled, although in fact it has been turned into just another modification of slavery; as Shigalev said, "All are slaves and equal in their slavery." In the popular consciousness it remains alive as a mythic reality, as an imaginary spiritual *sobornost* of "genuine equality" and collectivism: "How well we lived under Stalin!"

---

[3] *Golosa iz Rossii* [Voices from Russia], no. 6 (1859): 122–23.

4. The Possibility of Change

Is it possible for us to live differently? Do contemporary processes signal a change in mentality, or just another variant of the same old story? Are we repeating the reforms of Alexander II, with disintegration, and then another explosion? Above all, can our mentality change? It is very difficult to answer this question with a direct "yes" or "no."

In the 15th century, for example, it would have been very hard even to imagine that such a humane, fully responsible, and totally-European genius as our poet Pushkin could appear in this country. But it happened! Thomas Mann called him the "Slavic Mozart." With Pushkin came the rise of a class which educated its children on his poetry, focused on culture, and was open to every kind of European influence.

Such a transition was probably far more important than most social reforms. For the reforms which have a conscious influence on life result from the appearance of a class of people used to reflective thought; certainly Russian enlighteners thought in this manner. Russian poetry became like a second church, even replacing the servile state Orthodox religion, with its formal faith. Just as Christianity deeply influenced mankind, transforming barbaric people into civilized ones, so also Russian literature, which grew up on Christianity, was important in humanizing the enlightenment of the Russian mentality.

The intelligentsia, however, attempted to outwit the regular development of history, and leap from its present Russian condition into a hypothetical European future. Such self-deception ended in catastrophe. Humane traits were effaced, while more ancient aggressive, isolationistic characteristics of our mentality were restored, and gained the upper hand. These traits found new expression in the historical developments of Stalin's regime.

What has happened in recent years? The tyranny of compulsory unified thinking has disappeared. But many people are still complaining. It has become easier to breathe, but more difficult to live. Spirituality and the creative principle are disappearing. Political pressure has been exchanged for a socio-economic one. People no longer think of higher matters; they have become pragmatic, living according to Western ways and "selling their spiritual birthright for a mess of European pottage."

Of course one can retort with all sorts of banalities, claiming that no one stands in the way of a desire to live the spiritual life; Diogenes' barrel, i.e., serving as a nightwatchman, is always an option. After all, freedom has a price, and no price is too high for freedom. A culture which cannot resist the money-sack (even though it once stood up to the state), is reason for sadness; such spirituality deserves no pity. In any case, Western intellectuals are a constant reminder that writers and artists can live independently.

However, we would rather do without such banalities, and consider some concrete, highly-principled and meaningful changes in our culture during the last 30 years.

5. An Apologia for the Private Life as a Step to Emancipation

After expending enormous amounts of energy from 1917 to the mid-1950s, Russians neither proposed nor accepted any further messianist teachings. From Krushchev's time the basic intent was to live no worse than in Europe or America: "Let's catch up, and surpass America in the production of meat, milk, and butter." Both fear and love for the state disappeared. Thus, in the 1970s among the progressive classes of the *intelligentsia* an apologia for the private life was developed, in opposition to the collectivized life of the state.

In Russia the *intelligentsia* gives direction to social, public, movements. The October revolution, it is commonly maintained, resulted from the efforts of the Russian *intelligentsia* and Russian literature. And many now say that the 1917 revolution was a great breakthrough into a bright future just because of this, even though the aspiration was never realized; nowadays, however, it is the petty bourgeois and speculator without any higher aspirations who triumphs. Nonetheless, it must be conceded that the present changes are connected with a half-century (or more) of efforts by the Russian *intelligentsia* (i.e., dissidents and all accompanying literature, secret *samizdat* and *tamizdat* writings) to return to the road of Europeanization, from which it helped to push Russia in 1917. This is happening now, and in a very dynamic form. It is also noteworthy that today's radicals, i.e., nationalists and neo-communists, are not looking to new victories, but are just trying to save something from the past. Their concern is not only for the loss of territory and possessions, but for the spiritual legacy which, according to them, has been completely disowned.

Can we agree with them? I certainly do not think so. "Pure" nationalism has never worked in Russia; it has always clothed itself with ideas of universality. Only thus could Russia consider itself a bearer of ultimate truth (whether that of the "Third Rome" idea, or proletarian internationalism), and hold a sense of superiority over inconsistent, hostile foreigners.

This fundamental, archetypal mechanism of culture by which the Russian mentality is defined, has remained constant. One could identify it as an inclination for borrowing, or a craving for universal humanity, which Dostoevskii understood as an ability to accept European culture in its entirety. But the universal ideas are different today, because the value-orientation and geopolitical structures of our world (e.g., the idea of an open society, or market economy) have changed. And even if these take on the wild forms in which they now appear in

Russia, they no longer lead to isolationism because they have undermined the bug-bear of a "hostile milieu."

But what has this new universal idea given us? While the state is in collapse, a civil society has not yet taken shape. And now one hears the songs of the bards, "Today they talk about money!" It is true, indeed. For the first time in our history they do not propagandize loyal service but the capacity to work for oneself. Forgetting about the "happy future," everyone wants to be secure, not for the day after tomorrow, but for tomorrow. But all the while they live as before, "for the present moment." The fear of unpredictable acts on the part of the state is too deeply rooted; the state may seem powerless, but it is still replacing civil society with itself. It is more accurate to say that the state is powerless to protect the person, and has lost its power and desire to force citizens to work, but is as powerful as ever to hinder the development of an independent economy.

State structures still want to control the economy in order to collect a harvest of strangling taxes and bribes. Lawlessness still rules due to the present uncertainties, and now it is not even regulated by any ideology. Released from communist and party obligations, and without the concealment of political jargon, the rudeness described in Russian fiction has now become explicit. The nation is confused, like a sick patient after a hypnotic sleep. No one forces anyone to work, but people still need to learn to work in a different manner. That is why their eyes have an agressive look, even one of madness; they long for the stick to compel them to do something. The individuality of the other person is still completely neglected. A typical example: drivers, having made sure that they are not watched by the GAI [road patrol], rush about, disregard stoplights, and run over pedestrians, like hunters of unfortunate hares. It appears that without the stick "everything is permitted." We are still a long way from the realism of Westerners.

Yet we note the rise of a new generation, unlike the previous two "unbeaten" generations, from the mid-1950s. This generation does not rely on the state to build its life; it relies on its own efforts, intellect, talent, skill, and adaptability. This generation longs for independence, but no one knows whether it will be able to stop living from profiteering, and start producing domestic goods. To learn how to work independently without state control and compulsion is a task of historical importance and unbelievable complexity. Will it be achieved? It is clear that the path which has opened up does not lead to life in paradise, nor even to a bright future, but to a very difficult life, one no less cruel than the former (though in a different way); but at least it is a path to a free world. Will the Russian mentality, so used to existing under martial law, the rule of the stick and compulsion, endure this freedom? Can we even make a prediction under the present circumstances?

6. Giving up Myths – on the Way to a Mature Culture

It is obvious that many features which have characterized our mentality in the past are now fading and being erased. Gradually the psychology of a "Troy surrounded by Greeks" is also disappearing; with it, the corresponding sense of isolation and "lawful pride," of messianism and chiliastic futurism is also passing away. National myths, and especially that of *sobornost'*, are now subjected to scrutiny. According to S. S. Khoruzhii, who devoted a thorough study to the concept of *sobornost'*, it took shape in the work of A. S. Khomiakov, but the latter never identified it with the community and similar social groups. For Khomiakov *sobornost'* is not a secular concept; it pertains to the sphere of grace, the divine-human sphere. Khoruzhii notes, however, that

> that distinction was forgotten with frightening thoughtlessness, and easily renounced later on. *Sobornost'* was constantly, vigorously, and openly utilized, deprived of its beneficent essence, and reduced to a simple social and organic principle. This well-known sense takes us to the heart of the ideological evolution of Slavophilism.... In this degenerative process the ways of *sobornost'* and of socialistic ideas overlapped.... The same is true, in the long run, for all the communoid variations on the theme of collectivism, Soviet patriotism, and national bolshevism.[4]

The same point can be made about the idea of a "special path"; when the "Iron Curtain" was removed it could be seen clearly enough that every nation has its own special path, and that all nations, in their own way, have emerged, and continue to emerge from the barbaric structures of impersonal collectivism. The point also applies to statism (*gosudarstvennost'*), which supposedly comes naturally to the Russian people. We can say the same for the collective (*obshchinost'*), since the experience of the last 100 years teaches us that it is nothing more than a fiscal-state means of keeping people in complete submission, with "one responsible for all, and all responsible for one"; it is impossible to get away from such a formula. And we could go on with discussion of the *kolkhoz*, the factory collective, or numerous party groups with their compulsory submission of the person to the so-called collective decision, which typically meant no more than the decision of the leader.

A contemporary Russian writer, the emigré Alexander Zinoviev, has noted somewhere that Russia is nowadays becoming as boring as Holland and Belgium. But that can hardly be noticed yet. It would be better to say that Russia has never in its history had that kind of a boring life; it is a very unusual experience for her.

---

[4] Sergei Khoruzhii, "Khomiakov i printsip sobornost'" [Khomiakov and the principle of *sobornost'*], in *Zdes' i teper'* [Here and now], no. 2 (1992): 68–85, here 80–81, reprinted in idem, *Posle pereryva: Puti russkoi filosofii* (St. Petersburg: Aleteiia, 1994), 17–31.

That's why the new way of life will not get boring for the next 100 years. Soberness and common sense are still something new and unusual for us. Indeed, it is high time to stop entertaining the world with our troubles and tragedies, even taking pride in them as a mark of distinction. In any case, dreams of "beautiful and noble" tragedies are the lot of satiated, cruel-hearted people, who prefer to admire a house on fire from outside, with a psychology like that of Nero setting Rome on fire. Russia will remain Russia, of course, and the Russian mentality will remain the Russian mentality. No magician can make our problems, our troubles, and our peculiarities disappear. But perhaps the prolonged period of childhood of our culture is finally coming to an end; infancy and even "adolescence" are disappearing. Now "maturity" and adulthood are on the scene. To be grown-up is not an easy matter, for it implies more responsibility. But at the same time it is a kind of guarantee against the cruel and suicidal acts which characterize youth.

Words and Meanings: On the Rule of Destiny. The Russian Idea[1]

Mikhail Vasil'evich Il'in

This essay on "the rule of destiny" presents native Russian sources to elaborate typical ways of conceptualizing the self-consciousness of civilizations, and the historical empires or post-empire formations which are their political bearers. Our attention, accordingly, will focus on the "Russian idea," a concept similar to that of imperial secrecy (*arcana imperii*). Other concepts clustered around that of the "rule of destiny" will be discussed as needed. We will examine the self-consciousness of Russian civilization in terms of themes like choice (or fate), chance (*avos'*), faith, predestination, national spirit, and mind.

As an expression the "Russian idea" is used so extensively that people have gotten used to it. But as soon as we focus on it and pronounce it aloud, we somehow sense that it does not sound Russian. The very words "Russian" and "idea" do not fit together well; their forced combination is strained and semantically absurd. This is not surprising. We may regard it as the result of an abnormal borrowing process. It seems to be a loan-expression, the original meaning of which has been lost and replaced by another. Special research is needed to discover the true source of this borrowed phrase.

The source may be German: "*Russlandsidee*" on the pattern of "*Kaiseridee*." Or it may be French: "*idée russe*" on the pattern of "*idée fixe*," "*idée generale*," etc. And it is quite possible that the German or French phrases arose not in Germany or Paris, but in the salons of Moscow and St. Petersburg.

In fact, an interpretation of Russian destiny, and belief in this destiny using the foreign word "idea" can be found already in Belinskii's writings. As early as 1841 he uses the word as a universal term expressing the conception of a "motivating principle of history." This critic was clearly charmed by Hegelianism and wrote in his article on Russian folklore, "We would have been lost in the multitude of elements of which European life consists, all of which came from one source, and are nothing but a single, endlessly developing, and eternally self-moving *idea*."[2]

---

[1] "Slova i smysly: Po ustavu sud'by. Russkaia ideia," *Polis*, no. 4 (1996): 81–95.
[2] V. G. Belinskii, *Polnoe sobranie sochinenii* [Complete collected works] (Moscow and Leningrad: Izdatel'stvo Akademii nauk SSSR, 1953–59), 5: 346.
Helleman, Wendy, ed. *The Russian Idea: In Search of a New Identity*. Bloomington, IN: Slavica, 2004, 33–55.

And even though he also states that "There is not even a shadow of this in ancient Russian life," this assessment does not refer to the existence of the idea as such, but to its increasingly complicated unfolding, which Belinskii does not detect "in ancient Russian life." But Belinskii has no doubt about the presence of this idea and its self-revelation in the Russia of his own time. The development of this idea is evident in the figure and deeds of the Europeanizing Tsar Peter, whose essential character, according to Belinskii, consists in "the divine renunciation of his own personality in the service of eternal truth, a lofty self-destruction in the idea of his own people and fatherland."[3]

Unlike the Hegelian Westernizers with their predilection for the word-concept "idea," the Slavophiles, their brothers, expressed the same thought differently. According to I. V. Kireevskii, "The teachings of the holy fathers of the Orthodox church entered Russia with the first ringing of Christian bells. Under their guidance the fundamental Russian mind was formed and educated."[4] Here the "Russian idea" appears as an equivalent of the "fundamental Russian mind," a primordial expression with obvious Greek associations: *Nous, Logos, Sophia.*

In spite of external differences, "the idea of one's own people and fatherland" and the "fundamental Russian mind" are similar concepts, although they are mirror images of one another with a reversal of some secondary aspects. The dispute between Westernizers and Slavophiles was essentially between two branches of a single family of the free-thinking nobility, mostly on the question of how to enlighten Russia. Were they to take Saint Vladimir as their ideal, and develop those Orthodox principles from Byzantinism which had taken root for a long time already, even if they were corrupted by stupid peasants? Or were they to orient themselves to Peter the Great, and develop those principles of European education (Latinism) which had not yet been engrafted, once more, because of peasant vulgarization? Both the Westernizers and Slavophiles presented ideal models of enlightenment and pure patterns of Orthodoxy which had been revealed only to them, the select few. The actual composition of the Russian Empire and the real intentions of its subjects were regarded as insignificant, while the critical relation to the country and its people was sublimated into an exalted enthusiasm for Russia and the People. In fact both the external pattern and inner "secret," together with their adherents, turned out to be "infinitely removed" from the actual people and its polity, but not from their super-valuable ideas. It is quite understandable that beyond the purely theoretical sphere such ideals (of the Westernizers, Slavophiles, and the later "intelligentsia") had to be imposed

---

[3] Ibid., 150.

[4] Cited in V. V. Poznanskii, *Ocherk formirovaniia russkoi natsional'noi kul'tury: Pervaia polovina XIX veka* [An essay on the formation of Russian national culture: First half of the 19th century] (Moscow: Mysl', 1975), 180.

heroically on uneducated peasants, and required a revolutionary change of the evil political system into an ideal one.

In the post-Crimean period F. M. Dostoevskii tried to accomplish a real synthesis of the "idea" and "the fundamental mind." He tried to replace Belinskii's basic contrast between Russia *before* and *after* Peter the Great (i.e., between the period of the idea in its potential, in itself, and of the idea in its realization, for itself), as well as the Slavophile mirror image of the "fundamental mind" of primordial Russian Orthodoxy and the imitative stupidity poisoned by "Western rottenness." Both of these Dostoevskii tried to replace with a more productive antithesis between an alien-external ("Russian idea") and a truly internal view of the meaning and dynamics of Russian history ("that in which we believe").

This contrast is already drawn in the "Subscription Announcement for the Journal *Vremia* [Time] for 1861," published in a number of newspapers in September 1860. The article, signed by the publisher of the journal, M. M. Dostoevskii, but almost certainly written by his brother Fedor, emphasized the need to overcome the old simplistic antithesis between the Westernizers and Slavophiles: "To reconcile the followers of Peter's reforms with the national principle has become a necessity.[5] We are not speaking now about the Slavophiles and the Westernizers. Our time is quite indifferent to their domestic quarrels.[6] We are speaking of the reconciliation of civilization [the culture adopted, or "hijacked" from Europe – M. I.] with its national principle."[7]

---

[5] For Dostoevskii it is not only the Russia of the Westernizers, but that of all educated people, and first of all non-peasant Russia. "We used to condemn ourselves for our incapacity for Europeanization. Now we have changed our mind. Today we understand that it is just impossible for our mentality to be European.... We've been convinced at last that we are also an individual nationality, original in the highest degree, and our task is to create a new form, our own form, one that is native, taken from our own soil, from the national spirit and the national principle." Cf. F. M. Dostoevskii, *Polnoe sobranie sochinenii* [Complete collected works] (Leningrad: "Nauka," 1971–75), 18: 36.

[6] Today we are experiencing a spiritual and intellectual regress which makes us feel depressed. Already in the middle of the last century Dostoevskii could see clearly enough the necessity and opportunity of exchanging the simplistic black-white poles of "the West-Russia" for a more complicated intellectual construction. Nowadays, nearly 150 years later, publishers and even some ideologists try once more to breathe life into primitive schemes which are devoid of heuristic value, and impose them on public opinion. The "Subscription Announcement" may be one of the first, or even the very first text in which "the Russian idea" as a phrase is not used unintentionally; here it represents an obvious terminological and conceptional formation, with a claim to permanence. It is accompanied by expressions such as "the ideas of the people, without leaders, left to its own devices," and "the Russian idea" – both from an external perspective, but also by "a common foundation, one spirit, an unshakable faith in ourselves, and unlimited power," where the analysis is from within. In the "Subscription Announcement" "the national principle" is a relatively neutral idea.

[7] Dostoevskii, *Polnoe sobranie sochinenii*, 18: 37.

This counterpoint was developed in the substantive essay with which Dostoevskii opened the critical section of the first volume of *Vremia* (1861). Here one finds an objection to the basic thesis of the "Subscription Announcement." The objection is first presented in a generalized, impersonal form, as if

> Europeans would ask us: "What are you, Russians? You certainly boast that we [Europeans – M. I.] don't understand you, but do you understand yourselves? You are going to turn to your national principle, announce it in the papers, and distribute it on posters, are you? So you admit that you still have no notion of your own national principle; and even if you had one, it would be false, and you have rejected it, because to this very day you still haven't turned to it."[8]

Here two misunderstandings of the secret of the Russian national principle are contrasted, and brought together. The "national principle" is mysterious and vague, both for Russians and Europeans. Later on in the article the impersonal figure becomes clearer. He is a Frenchman, "not real, only imaginary, disembodied, fantasized." "Furthermore," Dostoevskii continues, "you asked to include the following in your announcement: you hope that in the future the Russian idea will become a synthesis of all those ideas which Europe has worked out so long and so persistently in its own separate nationalities."[9]

This passage emphasizes the "non-Russian" character of the very expression "Russian idea," which is put in the mouth of the so-called Frenchman. Moreover, by using this foreign word the national principle of Russia is put on an equal footing with the principles or ideas of European nations. Nor does Dostoevskii's answer reject such an intellectual perspective. It is simply added on, and broadened by the addition. "So we answer, 'Do you, dear sir, want us to declare quite directly what it is we believe in?'" In Dostoevskii's first use of the phrase "Russian idea," it serves only as an (outward and impersonal) expression of the complex set of ideas of the "national principle"; the other, contrasting side of the phrase is an inner, secret expression of the same principle, not in the nominative form, as subject, but in the form of a question, "What do *we!* believe in?"

In this way Dostoevskii established a rather refined and flexible method that, depending on the context and development of the logic of the discourse, allows one to pass from impersonal to individualized aspects, and to emphasize either the unique or universal character of the Russian national principle.

I will not take time to discuss all the twists and turns in the development of the concept of the "imperial-civilizing destiny of Russia," with its varied use of expressions such as "faith," "project," "intent," and, of course, the "Russian

---

[8] Ibid., 51.
[9] Ibid.

idea." I will only remark that in one way or another the final expression was connected either with an external, and thus foreign view of the civilizing destiny of Russia, or with a rather strict and sharp criticism of that destiny. Except in cases which nowadays have become quite widespread, in which the Russian idea is reduced to a simplistic "scarecrow" device, it opened up the possibility for conceptualizing a very important twin notion, a kind of "anti-Russian idea." That contrasting supplementary notion provided a broadened horizon for understanding Russia's civilizing destiny. A splendid example is the famous maxim of Vladimir S. Solov'ev, "The idea of a nation is not what it thinks about itself in time, but what God thinks about it in eternity." Here a transcendent perspective disputes and supplements the secular perspective of Russia as an Earthly City.

This undoubtedly individual achievement of Solov'ev is strikingly connected with ancient, if not primordial, ideas of the light, holiness, and glory of the Russian (Slavic) world. The point is that while the word-combination "Russian idea" is a very recent creation, the concept behind it, in fact the super-concept or conception, is not only many-sided and rich, but also deeply ingrained. The Russian idea, as a relatively marginal aspect of a wider Russian awareness of its historical destiny, is as ancient as our civilization itself. It is manifest in the very diverse attempts to express and fix the self-consciousness of civilization, the basis of the full achievement of an open political system which gave rise to Rus'-Muscovy-Russia-USSR-RF. The source of Russian self-awareness, mythological at first, and then expressed and sharpened in model texts which fixed the archetypes of our civilized consciousness, certainly deserves attention in this context.

The Choice of the Lot; the Testing of Faiths

At the root of the Russian conceptualization of historical choice we find an objective geo-political reality: the forest-steppe worldview of the continental "islander,"[10] the inhabitant of river and lake valleys in the midst of the "wasteland" of forests and steppes. In this context choice is a rush from one valley to another through dangerous and threatening stretches of forest or steppe. The feats of the epic hero Il'ia Muromets illustrate this. After his miraculous recovery, at the end of a patient 30-year wait for the sign of his fate, the coming of some foreign travelers, Il'ia begins to make his way to the capital, Kiev; he builds a road and thus connects the "islands" of Muromsk and Kiev. But he has to pass through deep forests infested by evil Solovian robbers. With difficulty Il'ia manages to make his way, and at the same time to build bridges and a road for those coming after him. Upon his arrival in Kiev, Il'ia continues such feats of

---

[10] V. L. Tsymburskii, "Ostrov Rossiia: Perspektivy rossiiskoi geopolitiki" [The island Russia: Perspectives on Russian geopolitics], *Polis*, no. 5 (1993).

road-building. He establishes frontier posts, and therefore roads to the "wilderness."

The instability and fragility of developing continental habitation did not allow this dialogue with destiny to unfold. The Russian with his hope in chance (*avos'*) awaits the next sign in the never-ending monologue of destiny, which may turn out to be a wonderful unforeseen crop or a famine, a saving gift or unexpected grief.

The subsequent taming of forests and steppes, and the initial intermingling with Baltic and Finno-Ugric peoples, the Scythian and Turkish tribes who occupied the steppe, contributed to the development of world-perceptions characteristic of the forest ("Don't make a noise, green leafy grove!") and of the steppe ("More and more steppe surrounds me, and there is still such a long way to go").[11] These eventually displaced the idea of choice as a breakthrough and building of roads, with the idea of choice as a roaming about without a road, guided only by forest and steppe landmarks. An original tradition which is rather close to that of the Scandinavians developed in the Russian north, first of all on the sea-coast (Pomor'e). It is represented by a distinctive version of the heroic path in the epic tale about Vasilii Buslaev, who rebels against a predetermined destiny and boldly states that he believes in "neither dreams nor sneezes."[12] He meets the "physical" challenge of a huge stone in his way with a leap, an artistic gesture in the spirit of Homer and Snorri Sturluson. The reply is just as "physical," a fatal blow and death.

For all the differences among the types of Russian world perceptions, and the much greater variety of spiritual worlds of the non-Slavonic peoples of Russia-Eurasia, one can recognize some mythic schemes as common to Eurasians. First of all, there is the myth in the well-known fairy tale about Prince Ivan and the Grey Wolf. Here the crucial moment is the definition of the route: if you go straight ahead, you'll be hungry and cold; if you go to the right, you'll lose your horse; if you go to the left, you'll be a dead man. The Prince's choice (losing the horse) is the vaguest and most ambiguous one.

The logic of the mythic scheme repudiates unequivocal and final choices, although, like frightening alternatives, these can be realized unexpectedly, and the choices remain with the hero throughout the story. Here a special inter-

---

[11] The respective quotations "*Ne shumi, mati zelenaia dubravushka!*" and "*Step' da step' krugom*" belong to old folksongs with the same titles. "*Ne shumi*" is by far the older song of a young man who expects to be punished for robberies committed at night; "*Step' da step'*" reflects the 19th-century "*iamshchik*" (coachman) experience of driving carts and troikas long distances in regular postal or transport service. *Trans.*

[12] The implied reference is to one who rejects superstitions, one who, as the proverb has it, "believes in neither dreams nor sneezes" (*ne verit ni v son ni v chokh*). *Trans.*

ference of the path-road mingles the "island" gullies with forest wandering, and the spaciousness of the steppes. This gives rise to the idea of an omnipresent road lacking concrete features, a road that runs through every place, and leads to some vague, secret happiness, granted in return for patience and hope.

The myth of indefinite choice and of the omnipresent road is developed and translated into a civilized context in the story of the trial of faiths in *The Tale of Bygone Years* (*Povest' vremennykh let*). In spite of its adaptation for the chronicle, this tale is a finished piece of work with its special plot and definite structure. It describes and thus defines the fundamental orientation points of the historical choice of Rus'. Foregoing analysis of the plot and structure of the tale, I will limit myself to an "objective" meaning of the civilizational choice expressed in this tale. The choice is conditioned by a historical calling. Toporov connects this calling directly with the origin of the Russian idea:

> We are speaking about the answer, given in response to an atypical situation, which is full not only of unexpected consequences, but even dangers. From the point of view of the princes of Kiev this challenge–question was given by Byzantium. The tension of this "challenge–response" situation was due not only, and not so much to the demands of Byzantium (to which Rus' was accustomed) but to the determination to formulate a "Russian" answer, one that was fundamentally different from the position of its spiritual tutor and patroness – Byzantium.[13]

Toporov's observation is quite right, but it applies chiefly to the religious and cultural aspect. In terms of the political aspect it needs refinement with an eye to the situation as "the testing of faiths." The challenge certainly came not from outside, but from within. The military dictatorship of the Riurikides (*Riurikovichi*), which consolidated the community of tribal unions with *polis*-like "islands" by a pyramidal structure of ancestral domains, expanded greatly during the reign of Sviatoslav. It was inherited by Vladimir, along with the problem of Rus' turning into an empire, and having to define itself as a civilization. Its continuing indefiniteness presented several alternatives, interpreted as a "choice of a faith": 1) becoming a "second Khazaria" and accepting Judaism; 2) or being transformed into an Arab-like enemy of Byzantium (accepting Islam); 3) joining the Western-European *Res publica Christiana* (accepting Christian religion from the Pope); 4) submitting to the polity of Rome (acceptance of Christianity from

---

[13] V. N. Toporov, "Rabotniki odinnadtsatogo chasa: *Slovo o zakone i blagodati* i drevnekievskie realii" [Workers of the eleventh hour: The *Sermon on Law and Grace* and ancient Kievan realities], in Toporov, *Sviatost' i sviatye v russkoi dukhovnoi kul'ture* [Holiness and holy men in Russian spiritual culture], vol. 1, *Pervyi vek khristianstva na Rusi* [The first century of Christianity in Rus'] (Moscow: "Gnozis" and Shkola "Iazyki russkoi kul'tury," 1995), 257–412, esp. 264.

the Emperor); and finally 5) affirming its independence as a state equal to Byzantium, excelling the West, not to mention the pagans (independent Christianization).

The choice was far from simple and by no means predetermined. To choose one of the alternatives of geo-chrono-political development and orientation necessarily meant giving an ideological justification for the decision in terms of an imperial-civilizational destiny. Each of the first four choices was both attractive and defective. The epic hero Vladimir (not a real person) rejected them, and instead of the passive role of a "convert" took on the active role of a "tester of faiths." Even a clear preference for the Greek religion does not mean that the choice was predetermined. Vladimir was baptized only after his triumph over the Greek empire at Korsun. And so the fifth option was chosen, a special, most undefined and ambiguous one: Byzantium was chosen "against Byzantium." The rejected religions (i.e., geo-political alternatives), and especially its native paganism, remained as orientations of Russian civilization.

The scheme outlined in the myth of the hero at the cross-roads, and developed in the legend about the testing of faiths, became an archetype in its own right for a vaguely understood and, more often, spontaneous discourse (i.e., the semantic organization of political actions) for the great majority of our ancestors and contemporaries, and almost all national politicians. Surprisingly enough, the political entity which chronicled the memory of a thousand years of history, and maintained in the form of legends and even literary echoes (like that of the "old Trojans") the memory of a tradition about twice as long, constantly characterizes itself as young, and still facing its decisive choice. There are numerous examples of such conceptualizations from P. Chaadaev to our contemporaries. They are not lies or self-deceptions. In fact, because of its multiplicity of meaning, its undefined character and openness, the initial choice of the "testing of faiths" turns out to be prolonged and unfinished, and must be reproduced over and over again. The disproportionately high degree of openness and the predeterminateness of the choice, on the one hand, allows Rus'-Muscovy-Russia-USSR-RF to be continually free, or, to be more precise, unconstrained in its choice; on the other hand, it postpones again and again to the future the drama of self-determination following on the choice.

The constant availability of freedom and the vagueness of the archetypal choice makes it open to the omnipresent path, the roadless space. The "heroic" version of this omnipresent path became extremely widespread. Its classical formulation was given by N. G. Chernyshevskii in 1861:

> The historical combinations are constantly drawn through the entire civic life of every man, and in these combinations the citizen must reject a considerable portion of his desires in order to promote the realization

of other desires which are higher and more important for society. The historical path is not paved like the sidewalk of Nevskii Prospect; it runs generally through fields, dusty and dirty, through thickets, and through bogs. Anyone afraid of getting covered with dust and dirtying their boots should not take part in public affairs.[14]

The idea of a roadless path, when both movement and the goal have no real sense, and the main and only real value is the overcoming of obstacles – quagmires, bogs, obstructions, or gullies – became dominant not only in the mind of the revolutionaries, but even in mass consciousness. The tautological reflection on the myth of the road going nowhere, on the creating and overcoming of difficulties, has become a source of mythologization for Soviet and post-Soviet political discourse; it has also presented an appreciable impediment to the modernization of politics and polity in our country.

The Historical Mission (Russia's Focus on Universal Service)

At the root of the civilizing idea of Rus' we find a decisive turn of the yet unfinished proto-empire, toward an accelerated reshaping of itself according to the most advanced model of that time, the Byzantine theocracy. This striving favored an immediate powerful and bold formulation of the ideas of its civilizing destiny. Intellectual advance turned out to be even more clearly defined than political advance. The three pillars of our culture, Metropolitan Hilarion (mid-11th cent.), Nikon the Great (d.1088), and Nestor (from mid-11th to early 12th cent.) defined the bases of the Russian idea. The first was the founder of a chrono-political conception, the second outlined the basic principles of Russian geopolitics, and the third translated the common Christian idea of sacrifice as the imitation of Christ (*imitatio Christi*) into a specifically Russian archetype.

Toporov has given a very convincing characterization of these three sources and three component parts of the Russian idea, or more precisely, the Russian sense of their own predestination:

> On the whole one can say that the intellectual work of Russian self-consciousness in Kiev, from the 1040s to the beginning of the twelfth century, finally resulted in three closely interconnected conceptions. At the same time, these conceptions became the moral imperatives of Russian life at that time. In one way or another, they found a continuation in the later development of Russian self-consciousness and, in particular, in socio-religious thought. These three conceptions may be formulated as follows: a) unity in space and the sphere of power (compare: *Povest'*

---

[14] N. G. Chernyshevskii, *Polnoe sobranie sochinenii* [Complete collected works] (Moscow: Khudozhestvennaia literatura, 1939–53), 7: 922–23.

vremennykh let [*The Tale of Bygone Years*], and *Slovo o polku Igoreve* [*The Lay of the Host of Igor*] as the most representative expression of this idea); 2) unity in time and spirit, that is the idea of spiritual succession (*SZB*, or *Slovo o Zakone i Blagodati* [*Sermon on Law and Grace*] – M. I.); 3) sanctity as the highest moral ideal of behavior and life style or, more exactly, a particular kind of sanctity which is understood as self-sacrifice, as hopes for another world and values *not of this world* (compare the texts of the Boris and Gleb cycle).[15]

Priority in outlining the contours of the formula of our national chrono-politics, and also in defining the roots of the Russian idea, rightfully belongs to Hilarion of Kiev, the first Russian metropolitan (*predstoiatel'*) in Kiev (1051–54).[16] The essence of the conception Hilarion proposed for the historical destiny of Rus' connects two important correlated schemes for the unfolding of history. The first is universal, and its plan on the whole follows the biblical and common Christian canons in distinguishing two key factors: the giving of the Law by Moses and the appearance of Grace and Truth in Christ. The second plan is Russian. Its history is marked by direct transition from a pre-law state: "At first we were like beasts and cattle. We didn't know the right hand from the left, and lived only by what is of the earth,"[17] to the state of Grace and Truth in Christ: "While the lake of the Law has dried up, the spring of the Gospel has overflowed; covering the whole Earth, it has reached us also."[18]

It must be emphasized that this did not come about of itself, but was due to St. Vladimir's ability to perform special deeds.[19] His feat was the direct and speedy transfer of Rus' to Grace and Truth in Christ under the influence of fully original aspirations:

---

[15] Toporov, "Rabotniki odinnadtsatogo chasa," 265.

[16] Hilarion is a key figure in our history and culture. He was an outstanding thinker and speaker, and in the years between 1037 and 1050 composed the *Slovo o Zakone i Blagodati*. The *Molitva* (*Prayer*), produced in sections, is also his and thought to be earlier, in part, than the *Lay*; and he wrote an *Ispovedanie Very* (*Confession of Truth*). Hilarion may well be co-author with Iaroslav Mudryi (The Wise) in composing the *Ustav* (*Church Rule*) as well as the *Pravda Iaroslava* (*Law Code of Iaroslav*), a very important part of Russian law. We may also assume his participation in the writing of old Russian chronicles, although the identification of Hilarion and Nikon the Great is clouded with doubt.

[17] *Slovo o Zakone i Blagodati* or *SZB*, 421–23; note that here and in further quotations I use the *Sermon on Law and Grace* according to the poetic divisions made by V. Deriagin in the separate Moscow edition of 1994.

[18] Ibid., 363–65.

[19] Ibid., 517–803.

A wonderful miracle! Other tsars and rulers, when they saw all that was done by holy men, did not believe, but subjected them to trial and torture. But you, o blessed king, have come to Christ without all that, only through the power of reasoning with your blessed insight and sharp mind, to conclude that there is one God, the maker of what is seen and unseen, what is in heaven and on earth...[20]

As a result, and through its self-renewal and ability to accept and fulfil the idea of civilization (i.e., Christianity) in an outstandingly pure and perfect way, Rus' gained the position of civilizational leadership.

Hilarion's formulation is confirmed and paralleled in other texts which belong to him, or are ascribed to him. Moreover, it organically permeated Russian conciousness, infected by the paradoxical idea of simultaneously entering onto the stage of world history and overcoming it. This could be treated by Hilarion as the lot of the chosen, but it could also appear much later as the lot of the cursed, as the "'the deceived son's' bitter mockery of his squandering father."

Such a chrono-political formula can certainly turn into the idea of "universal service," and sacrificing oneself (to Orthodoxy, to Europe, to communism, or to the civilized world); or it can turn into the reverse side of sacrifice, into aggressive impulses of "entering history," full of self-rejection and work on behalf of an alien history. At the same time Hilarion's formula also conceals positive moments of overcoming "abandonment" and a simultaneous striving for a universal synthesis (compare subsequent ideas of all-unity [*vseedinstvo*] or *sobornost'*).

The geopolitical formula of Russian destiny was outlined first in *The Tale of Bygone Years*. Nikon the Great, the brilliant compiler of chronicles and composer of many articles, may be regarded as its author. The general contours of "the model of focusing (on service)" were already outlined in the preface to *The Tale*, and developed in annalistic articles. Rus' is revealed in motion, yet as it were, frozen in its circling. Its motion is all turned inward. Rus' is turned toward its regions, the outlying areas, the countries on its outer borders, in order to connect them, to unite and concentrate them into a common "island" which has been formed of concentric circles. The basis for these circles is the external ("great") and inner ("small") Rus'. The very flesh of Rus' consists of its towns and villages, which in turn are themselves images of the self-sufficient islands of Great and Little Rus', with their endless spaces.

Interestingly enough, at about the time when Dostoevskii introduced the expression "the Russian idea," A. P. Shchapov conceived of the insular formation of Rus'-Russia by using this very same word:

---

[20] Ibid., 681–89.

Regional communities naturally acquired a diverse ethnographic organization and composition as a result of their formation through Slavic-Russian colonization among Finnish and other foreign tribes, and also as a result of a century-old striving for independence and individual control of territory. The main *idea*[21] of the physiological [i.e., "geopolitical" – M. I.] history of the great Russian people is the *idea* of consecutive historical-ethnographic *regional* self-formation, of diverse local organization, of the gradual birth and growth of the great Russian nation by admitting different foreign elements into its structure in the different regions.[22]

The geopolitical formula of the Russian destiny (idea) is defined more precisely in *The Lay of the Host of Igor'*. A new structural element is introduced there, *shelomian*. The term refers to a watershed ridge which breaks up the one island of Rus' into a multiplicity of islands. Every one of these islands turns out to be a different Rus' and the genuine Rus' is always "beyond the *shelomian*."

In *The Lay of the Host of Igor'* as well as *The Tale of Bygone Years* two strategies are outlined for consolidating Rus'; these strategies may be connected with Vladimir Monomakh and Oleg Gorislavlich. The first put his trust in something which can be called "a local autocracy" (*mestnicheskoe derzhavnichestvo*), i.e., the differentiation of the lands for the sake of a firm integration of the whole. He was the distant precursor of the idea of "The Island of Rus'." His opponent Oleg counted on expansion to the south to make the steppe a beach-head for the forced centralization of "disintegrating" Rus'. Gorislavlich may be considered the precursor of the concept of "the rush to the south," and the predecessor of Peter the Great's project of the conquest of Russia from St. Petersburg, the new capital. Although Oleg's failure certainly does not indicate that the conception as such was defective, the logic of our succeeding discussion indicates that Oleg Gorislavlich's success could have been no less fatal for Rus' than the Tatar invasion. Oleg's provocative expansion, which was accomplished on a smaller scale by his grandson Igor', turned out to be "a forging of sedition," throne-claiming, and despotic rule, when "throughout the lands of Rus' no ploughman worked, but only ravens croaked and shared corpses among themselves."

The third foundation of the Russian idea is the archetype of self-sacrifice and humanity. It follows logically from the general Christian imperative of the imitation of Christ (*imitatio Christi*). But in Rus' this principle was particularly sharply defined and emphasized. Nestor created *The Tale of Boris and Gleb*

---

[21] Emphases here and further are mine – M. I.
[22] A. Shchapov, "Velikorusskie oblasti i smutnoe vremia" [The regions of Great Russia and the time of troubles], *Otechestvennye zapiski* [Notes of the Fatherland], no. 10 (1861): 598.

(*Skazanie o Borise i Glebe*) which became more than just a text or literary work. He successfully presented a spiritual pattern which was repeatedly used and enriched by later writers and thinkers.

The archetypal significance of the *Tale* was demonstrated very well by Toporov.[23] I will not recount his analysis of this ancient text, nor his conclusions about its signifcance for Russian culture. I will confine myself to one citation:

> The story of Boris and Gleb is not only the tragedy of power, but the tragedy of all people bearing a moral consciousness when they face evil in an immoral environment. It is not the person who grasps at power, but power which grasps the person, because power cannot imagine that anybody could be free in relation to it. In this respect the *Tale of Boris and Gleb* remains relevant even today.[24] In fact, its lessons are even more valuable in our time. But does that mean that those who need them most will also adopt these lessons?"[25]

While accepting fully the spirit and moral sense of such an approach, I shall risk disagreeing with Toporov's conclusions. It is possible and morally necessary to feel, think, and act in such a way as long as one experiences the history of civilization, i.e., living by the Russian faith ("that in which we believe"). But one can become free not only by rejecting pre-civilizational mythological imperatives of power, opposing them with voluntary self-sacrifice. It is possible to become free by fully submitting to rationalized power, by rising above archaic self-will and the supra-civilizational will to self-sacrifice, by obtaining *freedom beyond* more simple freedoms: *freedom from* the history-as-destiny, and *freedom for* history-as-destiny.

This is possible, however, in the process of modernization, when the imperial mission and civilizational idea cease simply to be experienced, and start to be comprehended and used in a different way, more impersonally and more rationally. But this is the theme of the conclusion of the article cited, where Toporov discusses the destruction of the Russian idea from the perspectives of its rational reinterpretation. Remaining in the power of non-contemporary elements, even those Russians who were attracted by an imitation of European modernity must

---

[23] Toporov, "Ideia sviatosti v Drevnei Rusi: Vol'naia zhertva kak podrazhanie Khristu. *Skazanie o Borise i Glebe*" [The idea of holiness in Ancient Rus': Voluntary sacrifice as an imitation of Christ. The *Tale of Boris and Gleb*], in Toporov, *Sviatost' i sviatye v russkoi dukhovnoi kul'ture*, vol. 1, *Pervyi vek khristianstva na Rusi*, 413–600.

[24] Boris and Gleb, the first Russian saints, were sons of Prince Vladimir I, killed by their brother Sviatopolk in 1015. *Trans.*

[25] Toporov, "Ideia sviatosti v Drevnei Rusi," 1: 506.

inevitably overcome the temptation of self-contained (and self-satisfied) power through free and self-sacrificing service.

Self-denial, sometimes turning into self-flagellation, has always been one of our Russian complexes. While vividly manifest, this complex often lacks clarity because of its irrational elevation or confusion of soul. With Pushkin the early 19th century demonstrated accomplishments altogether equivalent to those of the European Renaissance, and initiated the tradition that could be called civilizational self-criticism. There were initially two versions, that of the Westernizers and that of the Slavophiles.

Belinskii thought that the "readiness to accuse oneself in the face of truth, selflessness, and self-sacrifice" was the most important thing.[26] Is the unintended echo of Hilarion's Orthodox self-accusation before the Grace and Truth of Jesus Christ, in Belinskii's enlightened self-accusation before the absolute truth of Reason, a coincidence? I certainly think that this is not a coincidence. The only difference is that the Westernizing Belinskii found an example of self-criticism and self-sacrificing service in Peter's activity. And so Belinskii attributed to Peter the set of genuinely Orthodox features fully in accordance with ancient prototypes of the prince-martyrs, "the justice and fairness of the tsar, everyone's free access to him, a readiness to forgive personal enemies and villains, and, upon seeing their repentance, a readiness even to elevate them if besides repenting they had abilities...."[27] Such re-interpretations are associated with the metamorphoses of the Russian idea and the transformations of the Russian faith. But that is another subject.

The Sequence of Transformations (Historical Hypostases of the Russian Idea)

These three basic sources and component parts of the Russian sense of its own fate and the special destiny of its civilization can reinforce and synergistically strengthen one another by unifying the three basic principles or ideas. Such a synthesis is always problematic, but when accomplished with a degree of success, it gives rise to some unique historical hypostases of a civilized self-consciousness, or metamorphoses of the Russian idea.

Interchanging secular Russia, or the "Russian World," with Holy Russia has become the archetypal model for the synthesis of the three basic principles of Russian destiny. Light and sanctity change into one another in two senses.[28] Once again this confirms the role of multiple etymologies (whether or not correct) in enriching words and concepts. In one way or another the Christianizing of Rus' and acquiring sanctity also means the enlightenment of our Motherland:

---

[26] Belinskii, *Polnoe sobranie sochinenii*, 4: 75.

[27] Ibid., 5: 150.

[28] Cf. Toporov, "Ideia sviatosti v Drevnei Rusi," 1: 475–77.

"And so Volodimer (i.e., Vladimir) himself is enlightened (*prosveshchen*), and his sons, and his land."[29] The story of the testing of faiths ends with these words. In this phrase the unique heroic feat of Vladimir not only unites sanctity and enlightenment (or education), but also associates light (*svet*) and glory (*slava*), a pan-Slavic, even ethnocultural source of the future Russian idea.

The motif of glory (*slava*) (and of word [*slovo*] as well as light [*svet*]) has a key significance for the self-consciousness of Rus', and probably for the Slavic world as a whole. Toporov has noted its variations in the "Speech" of Moisei Vydubitskii, the *Lay of the Host of Igor'*, the *Lay of the Destruction of the Russian Land* [*Slovo o pogibeli russkoi zemli*] and "further right up to Gogol'," [30] although the development of this theme certainly did not end with Gogol''s "bird-troika" (*ptitsa-troika*). On the contrary, it continued in new directions. We need only recall the image of Russia-Slavia created by M. Voloshin in the poem "Europe." "Rus' – the Third Rome – a blind and dreadful fruit," conceived in the heart of Europe-Byzantium by the "spokesman of Asia," Mekhmet the Conqueror, can be revived in a new destiny due to the radiance of glory:

> Fate leads him[31] on an ambiguous road
> Even in his name there is a double head
> Sclavus may be slave, but Slavia is glory (SLAVA)
> The halo of victory[32] covers the slave's head.

There are evident traits of Christ ("His cross [i.e., Slavism – M. I.] is universal service") in the image of the slave who offers himself for sacrifice and triumphs:

> Russia does not exist; she has burnt herself up.
> But Slavia will return to light even from ashes.

This also resembles the following lines of Tiutchev:

> Despondent from the burden of the cross,
> Throughout your entire expanse, Mother Earth,

---

[29] *Povest' vremennykh let* [The tale of bygone years], in *Pamiatniki literatury Drevnei Rusi, Nachalo russkoi literatury: XI–nachalo XII veka* [Monuments of the literature of Ancient Rus': The beginning of Russian literature from the 11th to the beginning of the 12th century], ed. N. A. Tvorogov (Moscow: Khudozhestvennaia literatura, 1978), 136.

[30] Toporov, "Ideia sviatosti v Drevnei Rusi," 1: 363.

[31] Slavism is implied in the text, i.e., the cultural basis of Russia which is perishing, and of Slavia now arising.

[32] The radiance of glory – M. I.

With the appearance of a slave, the Tsar of heaven
Walked about, blessing."[33]

The idea of the unity of "glory-holiness-enlightenment" was often repeated and reinterpreted as the essence of Russia's historical mission and the (logic) rule of its destiny. The perception or conceptualization of Russia as the Third Rome was especially productive. This formula was created by Filofei (Philotheus), a leading monk (*starets*) at the Eliazarov monastery. Using the model of Russia as the Third Rome which was only vaguely outlined by Metropolitan Zosima in the Paschalia "for eight thousand years" (1492), full of eschatological presentiments, Filofei in the second and third decades of the 16th century created a clear conception of the evolution and continuation of the earthly Orthodox kingdom. With clear step-by-step logic he outlined how falling away from Orthodoxy by unfaithful members leads to the special purity of those who are left. This can be traced in "The Petition to the Grand Duke Vasilii" (circa 1514–20) which speaks of "all the Orthodox kingdoms which hold to the Christian faith as transformed into your united kingdom."

The three stages of the process of consolidation are connected with the three Romes. The first Orthodox Rome was created by Constantine the Great (306–37) and destroyed by Julian the Apostate (360–63). According to Filofei, the heresy of Apollinarius was widespread under his rule, and finally destroyed the Catholics when West Europeans, "influenced by the heresy of Apollinarius, were enticed by Tsar Charles and Pope Formos," i.e., in the 9th century.[34]

The second Rome was the Orthodox Empire fully reconstructed by Theodosius (379–95), which existed as a Roman autocracy until it was corrupted by the Florentine Union of 1439, and finally destroyed in 1453. The third Rome, of all the Christian realms, was concentrated under "the present Orthodox rule of our Tsar who governs us and is the single Christian Tsar on earth, and holder of God's sacred throne, the sacred universal Apostolic Church, taking the place of Rome and Constantinople, who alone shines more brightly than the

---

[33] The inner connection and synonymous character of "*slava*" (glory) and "*slovo*" (word) permit us to unite these in the "word" for "blessing" (*blagoslovlenie*) and in the "glory" of "glorifying" (*proslavlenie*). Christ's blessing (*blagoslovlenie*) of Russia is expressed in the "miracle" of the reception of the call to prayer/Gospel (*blagovest'/evangelie*) and is accomplished in grace/the eucharist (*blagodat'/evkharistiia*), which provides the theological and cultural key to understanding Russian Orthodoxy, as was stressed already by Hilarion.

[34] *Pamiatniki literatury Drevnei Rusi.: Konets XV–pervaia polovina XVI veka* [Monuments of the literature of Ancient Rus': From the end of the 15th through the first half of the 16th century] (Moscow: Khudozhestvennaia literatura, 1978), 448.

sun in the whole universe."[35] Here again we find celestial light and earthly light connected with holiness and glory.

Such an ecclesiastic reinterpretation of political history does not indicate a disregard for the earthly political order. On the contrary, in his address to Vasilii, Filofei insists, "Indeed, if you organize your realm well, you will be the son of light and a citizen [!] of the heavenly Jerusalem."[36]

The tradition established by Filofei later received two different interpretations. One of these (Westernizing) eliminated its eschatological associations and introduced a moderate secularization of the idea of an Orthodox empire, predicting its unlimited prosperity and expansion ("there would be no fourth"). This imperial, super-power treatment which distorts Filofei's logic, originated with followers of the Westernizers who turned to ultra-patriotism, and is typical of the relatively recent past. Today such an idea is popularized by "critics" of the Russian idea and the conception of the Third Rome. For imperialists such a position is suspect: to justify one's civilization as a barbarian heritage (regarding every other empire and civilization as barbarism by definition) is, to put it mildly, an equivocation.

The second interpretation is associated with Old Believers who put a strong emphasis on eschatology in opposing Peter's innovations; it is also attributed to clairvoyants who foretold the advent of the Antichrist and the end of times. This conception is closer in spirit to that of Filofei, who did not yet see the coming of the end of times, but had a foreboding. Concentration of Orthodox purity in Moscow was a preparation for the second advent of Christ, and for the Last Judgment. "Heroic opposition to aggression and worldwide Russophobia," "Soviet Russia surrounded by fronts on all sides," "a bulwark of peace and progress," "an encirclement of hostility" – in all of these we find the dim primitivized reflexes of Filofei's conceptual archetype.

Aside from its interpretations, Filofei's conception is clearly founded on an evident demonstration of chrono-political movement by an Orthodox concentration in Muscovy, its purification being the result of the falling away of the parts of the Christian world that could no longer endure the trial. In spite of an external similarity to the idea of succession, or so-called transfer of empire (*translatio imperii*), the logic is different here. What Filofei says is not so much about empire as about civilization, or Christian civilization, to be more precise. In fact, he develops the formula of Russia's Grace (the unity of Christ's blessing and enlightenment), and God's choice of Russia for universal Christian service.

Such self-consciousness was so deeply ingrained in the thinking of our 16th-century ancestors that it actually became a founding principle of the specific

---

[35] Ibid., 452.
[36] Ibid., 440.

Russian version of Orthodoxy, the *Stoglav*[37] code, consolidated in 1551. It is characteristic that even such political antagonists and furious polemicists as Ivan the Terrible and Andrei Kurbskii, while accusing each other of "opposing" Orthodox Grace, accepted the fate of God-chosen Russian civilization as an unconditional truth, whether in the form of "the autocratic empire of the true Russian Orthodoxy" (Ivan the Terrible) or in the form of "the holy Russian kingdom" (A. Kurbskii).[38]

The definitive reinterpretation of Russia's civilizational calling occurred after the "Time of Troubles" (*Smuta*) under the early Romanovs. A number of conceptions of Russia's destiny arose under the slogan of "correcting" Orthodoxy, or opposing its corruption. One extreme was represented by the horror of schism before the "coming of the Antichrist" and end of the Third Rome, namely "the end of history"; another was represented by different attempts to "get out of oneself" and discover a new history beyond the limits of ancient Rus'. "One looks to the East, another to the West," was the observation of deacon Ivan Timofeev.[39]

A new mythology of the civilizational mission was constructed during the reign of Peter I. The very title of "The Father of the Fatherland, The All-Russian Emperor, Peter the Great" presents him as the equivalent of a new Vladimir. By fulfilling the aspirations of the 17th century, the faith was turned into a matter of practice; emphasis on precision of church ceremonies and correctness "to the letter" drove out the true spirit of Orthodoxy. Instead of a "testing of faiths" we find a testing of practice, whether in boat building, or amusement games, trips abroad to Europe and assemblies. However, as with Vladimir, the choice remained unfinished and unclear. The chronopolitical formula records an amazing breakthrough from extreme backwardness to the summit of progress. This accomplishment was due to the wonderful sagacity of the mythological hero; however, instead of Christian Byzantine theocracy we find the enlightenment of education and a German type of police state. The geopolitical formula is clearly represented by St. Petersburg, the frontier city which is half-Russian and half-European. This city is simultaneously presented as a support for the inner conquest or despotization of Russia, and an advance post for the "abduction of

---

[37] Literally, "One Hundred Chapters"; as a church code it prescribed rules for everyday life as well as rules for ecclesiastical behavior and rites. *Trans.*

[38] Ia. S. Lur'e, "Perepiska Ivana Groznogo s Kurbskim v obshchestvennoi mysli drevnei Rusi" [The correspondence of Ivan the Terrible with Kurbskii in the social thought of ancient Rus'], in *Perepiska Ivana Groznogo c Andreem Kurbskim* [The correspondence of Ivan the Terrible with Andrei Kurbskii], ed. D. S. Likhachev (Moscow: Nauka, 1993).

[39] G. Florovskii, *Puti russkogo bogosloviia* [Ways of Russian theology] (Paris, 1937; reprint, Vilnius: Litovskaia Pravoslavnaia Eparkhiia, 1991), 77; trans. by R. L. Nichols as *Ways of Russian Theology*, in the *Collected Works of Georges Florovsky* (Belmont, MA: Nordland Publishing Co., 1979), 5: 108.

Europe." Finally the complex of self-sacrifice and service is turned into a service to the emperor and empire ("imperial service," both military and civil service) and/or voluntary dedication to the mission of civilization (by the "intelligentsia"). In this way Russia's power and enlightenment become the new integrative "glory" of the country.

The enlightenment complex promoted the gradual development of the idea of Russia's destiny in service to mankind. Associated problems were studied thoroughly in the arguments between the Slavophiles and Westernizers. After Chaadaev the discussion of Russia's destiny and the lesson which Russia was to give mankind became the preoccupation of the entire intellectual and artistic history of the last century. At times "the new people," or "the critically thinking individuals," at other times the "intelligentsia" or "liberals," and at still other times "the revolutionaries" in endless argument with one another expounded with startling unanimity one and the same mission scheme of creating a future free of the prejudices sanctioned by century-old traditions.

The synthesis of many proposals in these ideological arguments was both complicated and at the same time supported by Marxist messianism. The historic mission of the proletariat turned out to be the historic mission of Soviet Russia, and then of the USSR. To justify such a mission the basic mythological scheme was reproduced once again. At the center was the figure of the prophet of genius, Vladimir Il'ich Lenin, carrying out a new "testing of faiths" (i.e., different versions of native revolution and international Marxism), and revealing in a wonderful way to Russia-USSR the most advanced scientific teaching, and the remarkable possibility of approaching the very highest level of civilization (the power of the Soviets as the most progressive form of direct democracy, the electrification of the whole country, etc.).

The geopolitical self-determination of the USSR reproduces the island model, although it proposes that the island potentially represent the entire world. The complex of self-sacrifice is also present, but displays exaggerated and often tragic manifestations.

The Soviet communist forms of the re-creation of the Russian idea were harsh and even grotesque at first. In the course of several decades they became gradually more complex. Although new possibilities arose for enriching the topic of the history of civilization for artistic and ideological dramatic arts, these were certainly not actualized. This can be explained largely by the desire to be considered scientific, which led to a simulation of rational discourse instead of full-fledged development of an artistic discourse and its gradual rationalization. However, quite a lot was done. An attentive, balanced, and neutral (*wertfrei*, i.e., value free) study of the Soviet transformations of the Russian idea may be useful to help liberate our consciousness from an inclination to see things as black-and-white, for this prevents us from distinguishing what is truly good, and causes us to declare the good a "verbal husk," and the "verbal husk" a good.

"Perestroika" and the formation of the "Russian Federation-Russia" called for efforts to re-create the fundamental myth of "the testing of faiths" and of a miraculous rise to the summit of world development. Even if the figures of Gorbachev and Eltsin have no appearance of greatness in contemporary historical retrospective, attempts to create myths have been undertaken and still are. Does it mean that the new version of the Russian idea (i.e., belief in its civilizational destiny) is perfectly natural and indispensable? I do not think so. The figures striving to play the role of christener, educator, or inspirer have failed to convince the Russian mass consciousness, and we realize that the time of "gods, tsars, and heroes" is receding into the past for Russia. However we are still a long way from saying goodbye to it. It is still with us. This is the source of all these outbursts of concern for our fate, and elections without choice. Yet at the same time we can already consciously and rationally evaluate, analyze and – in perspective – recast (i.e., split apart, distinguish) the meaningful and topical elements of our civilizational destiny, or of the so-called Russian idea.

Deciphering Predestination (The Proto-Rationality of the Russian Idea)

Must we now evaluate the Russian idea on the model "good–bad" or "progressive–reactionary"? Can we even do so? The unconvincing nature of unconditional criticism and one-sided apologetics makes us doubt that a positive answer to these questions is possible. The chronopolitical method allows us to raise the question in another way: has the Russian idea (together with the Russian polity and its civilization) become mature enough to discuss its (and their) transformation? The answer which I am inclined to give is the following: from many perspectives it would seem that the Russian idea may be mature enough, and in some sense even overly mature. The work on its rationalization began at least as early P. Chaadaev. Such facts must certainly be taken into account. However, looking at the matter from other perspectives, the Russian idea is still immature and underdeveloped, and in need of direct experience. That is why both attacks on it and enthusiastic appreciation (as I have just evaluated them, with considerable skepticism from the critical position of a "neutral" rationalism) are both justified and necessary. If we are to get rid of the Russian idea, clearly, we should go through it, to experience it; in this way we can turn the drama of the fate of civilization into a national tradition, and its rational-instrumental embodiment into a national self-consciousness that will allow us to overcome our fate.

How and by what means can this national self-consciousness be expressed? If the attempt is made to give it full and relatively final expression, then a kind of doctrine arises. This process is very familiar to us; we know it as the single true Soviet socialist "scientific ideology." The doctrinal construct may stress scientific or ideological features; it may appeal to the experience of the past or to ideal images of the future; it can be based on noble feelings or on common sense. Whatever the case, we shall have a more or less rationalized and modernized equivalent for our sense of our own fate. We will not even succeed in creating a fully valid, fully contemporary ideology. The result may be only a quasi-ideology, only one which simply explains "what we believe."

I would argue that a real ideologization of social consciousness is accompanied not by the elaboration of only one comprehensive and monopolizing quasi-ideology, but the presentation of a constellation of multiple interconnected ideologies, mature in civilized self-consciousness, penetrated with national cultural syntheses or combinations, and finally put into shape as ideologies of individualized social groupings and political organizations. The supposition that only a single national ideology can exist follows from using the word "ideology" in two senses. The first one is collective, a generalized expression of the presence or manifestation of an ideological principle. The second sense is quite exact and concrete. It refers to one or another fully completed system of ideological constructions. Accordingly, the expression "German ideology" may stand for "the ideological side of German life" (which is the sense supported by the title of the famous book of Marx and Engels, which could have been entitled *German Ideologies* if it had considered the separate ideological systems more systematically and carefully), but it can also serve as a name, or self-designation of a separate ideological system.

The very phenomenon of a "collective" ideology in its qualitatively defined form arises only from conditions of the contemporary world. Nor is it by chance that the very word "ideology" appears only at the beginning of the 19th century in the title of the four-volume work of A. Destutte de Tracy (1754–1836), *The Elements of Ideology* (1801–15). Cultures which have not yet achieved the level of modernity know only "precursors" of ideology in the form of what we often refer to as "spirituality" (*dukhovnost'*), i.e., mythologies, religions, or "ideas" of civilizational predestinations. A fully modernized national culture (with an equally modernized society and polity) presupposes the naturalness and necessity of the rise over a wide layer of a "spirituality" which has been revised with respect to its quintessence into the form of a "collective" ideology. This indispensable side of national culture is as variegated and diverse as the culture itself. The essential sign of a real (collective) ideology is pluralism, and competition among concrete ideological systems or ideologies, belonging to classes, parties, or communities, etc..

In my view, there can in principle be no single, integral national ideology as a system in an ideal national culture; yet, without a doubt, there must be a common space for ideological mutual interaction and mutual understanding, just as there must be intelligent argument or disagreement on substantive issues. At the same time one cannot help but recognize that in real situations ideological competition will often lead to formulating an ideological or even cultural hegemony. This phenomenon was brilliantly exposed by A. Gramsci (1891–1937) in his *Prison Notebooks*. It can reduce ideological competition to a struggle without compromise, which can provoke either a totalitarian homogenization of the political entity, or a revolutionary disruption of the political system.

Under Russian conditions neither the culture, the society as a community of the people, nor the political organization is completely modernized. We still have not achieved a full ideologization of our culture. Spirituality still dominates it. The imitation of ideology in terms of a "scientific Marxist-Leninist theory" has given birth only to a quasi-ideology, a form which converted the imperial-civilizing "spirituality." With its pretense at ultra-modernization Soviet communism could no longer reveal itself only as "faith," although in essence it remained just that. But Soviet communism could neither create a "collective" ideology, nor distinguish itself as a finished ideological system alongside other systems. It approached the latter with difficulty only through its inclusion in the international context.

The contemporary demand for a national ideology is depressing because it may well nudge us to form yet another monopolistic quasi-ideology with claims to hegemony. At the same time the need for spiritual consolidation in Russia, which stands behind this demand and is vital for the preservation and development of our national state, can be fully appreciated. It appears to me that such spiritual consolidation must be far more complicated and many-sided than its doctrinal expression, not to mention the invention in a year or in some "short historical period" of various "national ideologies," "state ideologies," "regimes of civil society" and similar grotesque texts well-known from the communist period. We must admit above all that spiritual consolidation requires also efforts which by nature are not contemporary and may even seem to be obsolete. We must complete what has not been fully accomplished by theology, rhetoric, scholasticism (which was hardly noticeable among us, except for some comparatively recent attempts at compensation), and the art of ritual as well as the other sides of civility. In all of this an essential role must be assigned to decoding the innermost secret of "what we believe" and also to rationalizing its comparatively distant counter-secret, the "Russian idea."

At the same time as we experience what has not yet been sufficiently experienced (i.e., the practice of spiritual revival) we must also provide a stronger foundation for rationalizing what has been attained. European experience shows that these two processes can proceed together, the one parallel to the other. It is necessary to outline the contours of the Russian idea more clearly, to reveal its main sources (literary monuments, examples of the "experience of destiny"). The interpretation of such sources by philologists, ethnologists, art critics, historians, and, not in the least, by political scientists, can provide the main thing we need now: to fill in the blanks and gaps in the understanding of our historical drama, and to explain the most troubled artistic and spiritual reflections of our civilizational destiny. Such work can help our fellow-citizens and especially our politicians avoid a slavish and senseless repetition of what has already happened (the "curse of history"). It can also help us avoid the naive project of creating a Russian idea once again in the form of some kind of "national ideology." If we can avoid these temptations, we can remain, as before, what we are. We will keep our spiritual and intellectual heritage, and it will cease to be a heavy burden which is poorly understood and even more poorly used. The subjects and roles of the drama of our national history will not be forgotten. We will even know them better; but most importantly, we will be able to use them differently, with more understanding and greater freedom.

The Russian National Idea: A Culturological Hypothesis[1]

Vladimir Solomonovich Bibler

> "A nation's identity is not built on a set of
> postulates, but through its language."

These reflections on the Russian Idea will not attempt to give detailed substantiation of the points made. It is not the intention of the author to give a theory or conception, but rather a hypothesis in which elements of imagination and of logic are, as it were, in equilibrium.

The present text is divided into two principal sections. The first section deals with the tempting nature of the Russian national idea as a single ideology, its dangers, its meaning and fundamental structure. The second section discusses the national idea in the 19th and 20th centuries and the relationship between national culture and the national idea. In that section we begin to deal with speech.[2]

---

[1] V. S. Bibler, "Natsional'naia russkaia ideia? Russkaia rech! Opyt kul'turologicheskogo predpolozheniia" [A national Russian idea? Russian speech! A culturological hypothesis], *Oktiabr'*, no. 2 (1993): 155–62; the title has been modified for this publication, to fit the part of the article translated here.

[2] All footnotes for this article were added by the translator. The original article included a further three sections which are not translated here because, although relevant for the theme of our collection, they rely too closely on nuances of the Russian language to be useful as an argument in translated form. Bibler's own summary is as follows: "The third section identifies the national idea with audible and – what is particularly difficult – silent, inner forms of language – the Russian language, with all its principal characteristics. The fourth section offers a brief formal definition of the national language as a national idea. In the fifth section, the most important one for me, I go into what I see as principal manifestations of the Russian national idea, that is the Russian language of the 19th and 20th centuries, such as Pushkin, Khlebnikov, or Andrei Platonov, or – if we cast our net into the future – Joseph Brodsky. Principal linguistic changes are personalized here from a specific perspective. For Pushkin, Khlebnikov, Platonov, or Brodsky the Russian *language* (and poetry as a crucial aspect of language, important for understanding the future) was the focus of poetic attention and main source of poetic inspiration. Their interest was in the poetic part of poetry, or inner language."
Helleman, Wendy, ed. *The Russian Idea: In Search of a New Identity*. Bloomington, IN: Slavica, 2004, 57–71.

1. Freeing Ourselves of Imperial Incantations

If in this section I discuss matters which are less interesting, I do need to sweep away tedious and frightening imperial ideological claims to make room for subjects really well considered and important. Unfortunately, our world of ideas is so littered that it really does need to be cleaned up.

Let us begin with the position that the communist idea, which has suffered a fiasco, needs to be replaced with a single national idea, a Russian national idea which would make it possible to reunite the scattered nation and the scattered peoples that are part of the Russian empire. It is a fairly well known point, one, in fact, we even get fed up with because it can be found in every newspaper and on every television screen. According to this view, the ideas and portrayal of democratic thought are something extra-national or alien to national interest. Democracy, of course, does have to be tolerated in the 20th century, but it fails to appeal as a slogan for the future, or to reflect the essence of the nation's life.

It would appear that the most direct and clear formulation of the meaning of the national idea has been given by the political scientist A. Kiva, although there is a compromising aspect, in that his definition follows that of Count Uvarov. In various recent articles Kiva has summed up the Russian national idea as Sovereignty – Religion – Nationhood.[3] Of course, there may be other options, ones even more comprehensive, where "Russian" stands for universal humanity, and all other persons, nations, or ethnic groups can acquire characteristics of what is considered "human" only if they enter the sphere of influence of Russian messianism in its complete form. You will recognize this equation of "Russian" with what is "human" as the one Dostoevskii makes, especially in *The Diary of a Writer*.

From my perspective, one reason why the Kiva-Uvarov formula is brilliant is that it accurately reflects the anti-democratic spirit of the troika, and in a topsy-turvy way also reflects (or rejects) the essence of democratization very accurately. Their idea negates what is most typical of democracy, or democratism, as an idea or way of life. Kiva's definition is exceptionally accurate! And when, for instance, S. Stankevich argues that those of the political "center" should take up Uvarov's definitions because our "reds" and "browns" discredit the idea, we should, I think, first and foremost try to clarify the essence of Kiva's definition, since it owes much of its power and clarity to being posed against the background of democracy and liberalism.

Kiva says that democratic values, human rights, and the unification of peoples are wonderful things, and that he fully supports them, but that our people

---

[3] The Russian terms are *derzhavnost'* (sovereignty, the holding of supreme power), *religioznost'* (religiosity or piety), and *narodnost'* (nationhood or "nationality").

are poorly developed, backward, and want something entirely different. Thus, for the time being we should put all these wonderful values aside and, instead, proclaim values that would be able to unify the people now. What follows on this argument is something we have gotten used to in the last few years, namely a reading of the hearts of ordinary people, to tell us that they want the three given ideas to be supreme. Accordingly, it is now our duty to share these ideas, defend them, and assure their supremacy. And after that we will wait for the right time to return to those magnificent values so dear to the democratic heart, but for which it is now still the wrong time. How long we may have to wait is not clarified; could it be until the start of the next millennium?

I would propose that there is more to this troika than pointed ideological meaning. It also conceals a very accurate and subtly devised structure. It seems to me that the core of the idea, both in Uvarov's version (Autocracy – Orthodoxy – Nationhood)[4] and in Kiva's mitigated formula of Sovereignty (Autocracy is awaiting its turn) – Religion (instead of the strong and clearly emphasized "Orthodoxy") – Nationhood (complete coincidence here), the central part of this troika, this triangle, is the idea of Sovereignty or Statehood,[5] something that is above everything else, above personality, above the individual, and above any creative cultural achievements of this people and this culture.

Anything, ultimately, can be sacrificed to preserve statehood. The main thing is that the state should continue to exist, a state that exercises authority (*derzhavnost'*) over other peoples and turns practical authority into a lofty idea, that is overturning it, and directing its authority into the future. The rest will come of its own accord. The other two components of the troika, the idea of Religion and the idea of Nationhood, are, in effect, concomitants. Their job is to give the inner ideological meaning to the word Sovereignty and to the notion behind it. You may remember that Mikhail Gorbachev, probably in his last month in power, said that he understood it all, that he finally realized, among other things, how close the Soviet Union was to falling apart, but he was still asking, "Are people really not aware that statehood is something that is above everything else?"

Movement towards this truly central idea, that of Sovereignty, has become a kind of framework within which all other ideas can be placed. Indeed, Religion per se is a great and significant idea, but in the Sovereignty – Religion – Nationhood troika, Religion has the sole meaning of sanctifying Sovereignty and of bringing all the people of this nation together, not around any specific state institute but around a state ideology that is truly fundamental, lofty, and cannot be reduced to any temporary claims: if you support (Orthodox) religion, the lat-

---

[4] The Russian terms are *samoderzhavie – pravoslavie – narodnost'*.
[5] *Gosudarstvennost'*.

ter (or the sovereignty it conceals) surpasses any of your personal ambitions, any idea that has to do with the fact that you are an individual. Whereas an idea put forward by Pushkin, Chaadaev, or Chekhov reflects the personalities respectively of Pushkin, Chaadaev, or Chekhov, the idea of Sovereignty is only an idea if it is given the aura of Religion, and that of a specific form of Religion as well (but I will return to this below). This represents the spiritual aspect of the matter. In Religion the idea of the state transcends the boundaries of personality and private relations. It is now linked not to the earth but to the heavens.

The second of the two "side horses" of this troika, one also having its own meaning, is the notion of Nationhood (again, I don't have in mind any kind of Nationhood existing beyond our triangle). Whereas Religion imparts maximum spirituality to the lofty idea of Statehood or Sovereignty, Nationhood makes it possible to see all people, strata, classes, and minor groups that live in this society as a single, many-headed (although in effect single-headed) people. Only a people who represent a single indivisible entity can be crowned by statehood, which is the power of corporate action by a people, primarily imperial action, externally directed. The people are the basis for the unity of the state. Without a "Nationhood" which is above and more significant than individuals, and merges them together into a kind of natural and indivisible entity, the idea of Statehood cannot be an idea either. It immediately withers away into an instrument for edicts to pay taxes, observe the law, or elect parliament. Religion, on the other hand, can become the living spirit of Sovereignty, linking it to the heavens, while the Nation can become the living spirit of Sovereignty as linked to earth.

This is the first group of issues to which I would like to pay attention. Religion and Nationhood are aspects of Sovereignty, or Statehood as the basis of society, and quite synonymous with it. In our triangle, Society as a concept is completely reduced to the concept of State, which is propped up by the ideas of Nationhood and Religion. These aspects stand aloof from society, from the intense, changeable, and dynamic life of the people, the classes, their culture. They represent a set of grim and immovable pillars which keep their identity through all the vicissitudes of history. This identity is also preserved with respect to a kind of uncertain radiant future. If the past and present are always dubious and constantly need to be interpreted anew, the process of projecting Sovereignty and all the other definitions toward the future means that we acquire something that is impossible to doubt and difficult to criticize, something that is molded out of fantasies about a messianic, internationalist, communist, or Orthodox future. This abstraction from the times, from motion and dynamics, as it looks straight ahead, grimly and immovably, to a purified "tomorrow," represents an essential component of Uvarov and Kiva's version of the national idea, even though this "tomorrow" is ultimately nothing more than the past, an invented past linked to a future that is uncertain, cannot be criticized, and is still always elusive.

However, when Kiva speaks about Religion (instead of Uvarov's Orthodoxy) and Sovereignty (instead of Autocracy), and uses Nationhood in inverted commas, he is clearly being devious, not in terms of a devious psychology, but of devious theorizing. Any form of statehood and any national patriotic movement, German, French, or Turkish, can come under his weakened troika: Sovereignty – Religion – Nationhood. Obviously, the troika needs a more definite and pronounced content to represent the *Russian* national idea: the national idea will not be Russian until we are more specific about our religion (Orthodoxy). It will remain something indefinite and elusive, and can even be found in the arsenal of our permanent enemies. Our Sovereignty will have a louder echo immediately upon our having deciphered it. The idea of Nationhood is also meaningless without being identified as *Russian*.

To come to the point, each of the three given principles is like a Trojan horse: Kiva's formula cannot be understood without fully taking that of Uvarov into consideration. Without that more clear definition, the Sovereignty – Nationhood – Religion formula is quite vague and empty. This is why the "brown" and "red" patriots put this formula more honestly and accurately, conveying its true meaning. Once again: each part of this troika, Sovereignty – Religion – Nationhood, needs an adjective to precede it, and the adjective has to be "Russian." But then we have come around full circle. We need to explain what "Russian" means. The answer is: Autocracy, Orthodoxy, and Collectivity (*sobornost'*), as the essence of Nationhood, as a kind of supreme embodiment of what is "truly human." I shall not go into the details of this self-evolving and self-defining concept at this stage. But let me stress another difficult point before I go any further.

Of course, in isolation, each angle of the national triangle, or troika, has a different, and increasingly deeper meaning. For example, Orthodoxy can certainly not be reduced to what Uvarov means by it. It is a universal branch or root of Christianity, and by no means restricted to its Russian form. Nationhood too received a deeper Slavophile meaning in the works of Aksakov and Khomiakov; it is not something different from the ideological attitude of the "people" that we have just spoken about. And so, Sovereignty, or even Autocracy as the focal point of the "Third Rome" doctrine goes far beyond the limits of a rigid imperial scheme.

Why then did I base my definitions on the superficial, simplified forms of these three components of the Russian national idea, edited down to a rigid, isolated, and ideological postulate opposed to any kind of citizenship? Nevertheless, I would suggest that there can be no other interpretation of these angles of the national ideological triangle. The reason is that, in entering the gravitational field of the national idea, these initial definitions are inevitably transformed, simplified, and ideologized. Orthodoxy which gravitates towards angles of Sovereignty and (Russian) Nationhood immediately loses its universal character and becomes firmly tied down to one dominant national group; and thus it approaches Uvarov's interpretation. Sovereignty, linked to Russian Autocracy, is transformed into an oppressive form of Statehood, which only makes sense as an antipode and negation of civic principles, and as a negation of the sovereignty of civil society in relation to the sovereignty of ubiquitous and omnipotent authority. Nor does Nationhood make any sense outside a national ideological scheme, and outside the antithesis of "the individual versus the people," once it enters the gravitational field of the angles of Orthodoxy and Sovereignty. The very meaning of Nationhood shifts to the pinnacle of Sovereignty and becomes personified in an authoritarian or totalitarian leader.

A unified people demand ultimate unity (or uniqueness) and attain it in a single powerful underlying cause, a troika which has been resolved for this purpose, as in German Nazism: *ein Volk, ein Reich, ein Fuehrer*. Sovereignty acts as a hoop to bring the other two components of the national idea together into an entity that is isolated and based on contradictions. In these contradictions the meaning of the entire formula can be found.

At the very beginning of my exposition, I said that in addition to a certain mystical messianic meaning, Uvarov's triangle possesses a clear and specific meaning, presupposing some kind of fundamental enemy. The triad makes no sense if it does not specify that against which, and the person against whom it is directed. It incorporates, and is even determined by a definite, clearly delineated and emotionally loaded idea of confrontation.

But this national idea with its three components, in which Sovereignty is the dominant component, also incorporates a fundamental and endless opposition, i.e., an opposition to democracy and civil society. I think that, strictly speaking, a national – sovereign – imperialist idea has no real positive meaning. Its real meaning is purely negative. In speaking about the priority of Statehood (with its spiritual and earthly characteristics), only one thing is meant: denial of the sovereignty of the individual, or, more precisely, denial of the sovereignty of the person in civic and cultural aspects. The idyll of a monolithic national monster conceals something that is far from idyllic, namely the destruction (or at least essential restriction) of the right of the person to form groups on the basis of agreement (i.e., such that they could preserve their fundamental sovereignty), whether these collectives have an economic, political, ethnic, or governmental character.

Democracy actually has two dimensions: the sovereignty of rights of the person, and agreement as the basis of all public institutions. All such institutions are based on consent between individuals. Institutions can be changed or abolished at any time on the basis of the right of agreement, which is put into effect for a specified period of time. Even if such agreements are formal, they have a deeply dynamic essence.

So let me repeat: Sovereignty, Religion, and Nationhood are purely negative concepts. Their essence is a systematic negation of democracy. If a single form of statehood is established once and for all, and if "the society-means-the-state" formula becomes predominant, then the entire system of continuously changing economic, cultural and social relations loses its human dimension. Society "withers away" to an all-powerful state pyramid, and as a result the idea of democracy also loses any sense of an idea. What remains is some kind of flaccid tolerance and a series of secondary institutions that recede before the supreme idea, Sovereignty – or Autocracy, if one sharpens the pinnacle. The same goes for Nationhood. In Uvarov's triangle, Nationhood has no positive meaning at all. Its meaning there is primarily negative, one of negation: a united people, or people as a single entity, who are above the individual, above the person, and above any particular subject. More than that: the only true individual is the people as a corporate body, while individuals as such are its parts, fragments, or "cogs." The idea of democracy once again ceases to be an idea. It becomes something intermediary: "when in Rome, do as the Romans do"; "we live in the modern civilized world, and have to sacrifice our principles for a selfish individual, a Petrov or Sidorov." Only a people (primarily the Russian people) can possess an idea. Given this interpretation, "the people" is a notion that implies negation of the sovereignty of the individual.

The same applies to Orthodoxy, inasmuch as it is drawn into the realm of Sovereignty. A state religion is an idea par excellence, the spiritual aspect of the authoritarian idol. But then it is clear that other personal ideas cannot be tolerated, or are hardly tolerable, while Orthodoxy is called upon to suppress such arbitrary "private" ideas. Spirituality which manifests itself in a single idea (it does not matter whether this is religious, communist, or any other), ceases to be spirituality in the sense to which I have briefly referred, i.e., that the individual is not merely a vehicle of economic, social, or other relations. The individual who achieves his or her complete earthly fulfilment is the sovereign and ultimate meaning of democracy. An idea produced by Pushkin represents Pushkin, and an idea produced by Tolstoi represents Tolstoi.

It is a principle of democracy (democratism or democratic relations) that each human being is an absolutely boundless universe, different from any other equally boundless universe. My existence is impossible without the existence of another human being who is equal to me, equally boundless like myself, although he or she is an absolutely different individual. But it is his or her being different from me that is essential for me. As soon as the idea of such interacting universes disappears, democracy ceases to be an idea. And it is absent from Uvarov's triad.

For the moment, this is all that I need to say with regard to the first part of my reflections. So let me pass on to the second part.

2. Statehood and the National Idea in the 19th and 20th Centuries

The equation of a national idea with the idea of Statehood (or Sovereignty) had a specific and important historical meaning for Russia, as it did for France or Germany in the 17th century and later, particularly in the 19th century, the period when nation-states were taking shape and being strengthened. The formation of nation-states was aided by state institutions that were powerful enough to prevent the disintegration of nations and to rescue their cultural identity. Moreover, in modern history such national identity has manifested itself fully particularly in simplified governmental or political structures, and in the impersonal power of the state. Culture, in the proper sense, was regarded as nearly identical to extra-national scientific reason, while natural speech was universalized in scientific and theoretical "Esperanto." It would appear that the cultural spiral of a "dialogue between various epochs" was unravelled into a trajectory of anonymous "generally-human" progress. Only the state kept its national sense. That, at least, was the superficial appearance, leaving aside the strange phenomenon (or noumenon?) of art.

We must note another aspect of the equation of a national idea with a national ideology, and the equation of a national ideology with state mysticism. Natural language, and especially inner cultural speech, was regarded merely as a means for expressing ideas that existed outside language, to express "word and deed" for the state or for the spiritual realm. "Word and deed" was the unifying force and symbol of national integrity. In the depths of the life of a nation, language (in the broadest sense) as the inner aspect of national culture, imparted organic harmony and diversity to this culture and to the true life of the nation. But on the outside this "unity" received a topsy-turvy external expression, being used as part of state ideology.

But the national idea, as a plan for the future of the nation, and the idol of statehood merged particularly closely and irreversibly in Russia in the 17th, 18th, and 19th centuries. There are several aspects to this. Although this subject deserves long and careful study, at this point I will just name them to make my reasoning clear.

In Russia there has been no (or almost no) cultural layer between the state-imposed unity of the country and its original, communal (or conciliar [*sobornyi*], to use the Orthodox term) unity. The middle layer was empty. There was no priority of law; the middle stratum of society was helpless. The image of a "burgher," a citizen, or self-reliant entrepreneur, someone who keeps his word, who owns his house and knows what to do with his resources and opportunities, all this was absent, even in cultural ideals. The petty, unfortunate, negligible poor man was both the reality and the ideal. The average man, the wonderful example of the golden mean, was neither part of reality nor an ideal, certainly if one excludes owners of the "landed estate" (*chelovek usad'by*) who were not such a small exception and did play a serious cultural role (but that is a subject for another occasion). So the national idea could be perceived and developed either in terms of military and state (imperial) power, or of the immobile (praise God!) depths of the life of ordinary people. But the troubling absence of relations based on agreement was felt constantly, and manifested itself in an inferiority complex, which can easily be perceived as "megalomania."

The Russian individual is a mere nothing, someone who can either be pitied or neglected. Of course, in the middle there was the great Russian culture. From the time of Peter the Great this culture was, in a sense, the only contemporary embodiment of the Russian national idea, an embodiment endlessly versatile; in other words, culture represented the actual modern unity of the nation. Moreover, it was an idea owing its existence from outside the state, being imported from foreign soil (as if culture grows with its roots downwards). And this idea not only supported a confluence of people, but strengthened the individuality and uniqueness of each human being. A small, unfortunate, and humiliated human being? Yes. But a free one as well, because he or she was freely invented, or freely put into existence by the pen, brush, or violin bow.

Nonetheless, in Russian culture as an embodiment of the Russian national idea from the 17th–19th centuries, there have been two strange gaps which pose an obstacle to understanding the mystery of its language, and turn the idea into an ideology. Turning to the first gap, we note that in the absence of an intermediary layer, culture took over its characteristic functions, whether legal, civic, or political, and concealed its own cultural/aesthetic idea, with its ultimate essence as inner language,[6] beneath a variety of ideological – philosophical, moral, religious, and social – postulates. Culture lost its own significance and became an instrument. The mystery of language was driven into oblivion by the "mystery, miracle, and authority" of Teaching, like that of the Grand Inquisitor in *The Brothers Karamazov*.

Let me explain my point more precisely. Culture, in both its aesthetic and philosophical aspects, possesses a transforming power so great that it can impart an aesthetic or philosophical essence to any external idea, and deprive it of its outwardly ideological character. I can put it more bluntly: such ostensibly ideological postulates, when transformed through the artistic element, have with their own special power given depth and focus to aestheticism itself, even to the artistic and philosophical conversion of culture. Gogol', Tolstoi, and Dostoevskii are

---

[6] The author deals with this in detail in other sections of the essay not translated here.

cases in point in literature. Another case in point is Silver Age religious philosophy, a philosophy where the philosophical aspect was sometimes, but not always, more powerful than the religious one. However, all this was happening in the invisible depths of culture, and was not even noticed by its makers; it became obvious only decades later. And the "linguistic mystery" of national ideas was shut off for about a hundred years. The reality was that the "idea of culture" was completely ousted by "ideas preached through culture."

But in the cultural core which replaced the missing membrane at that time, there was another glaring gap. Playing some of the leading social and civic roles of its civilization, Russian culture was shifting, as it were, towards the edges of the Russian world and approaching boundaries of other European cultures – French, German, and English, and (to a lesser extent) Italian and Spanish. Contact with other European cultures explains the unique character and great fruitfulness of Russian culture at this time. The work of M. M. Bakhtin and my own logical reflections have dealt with this as a shifting of our culture into the sphere of modern critical issues, even questioning that very culture; in other words, this was the making of culture par excellence, culture in the most precise and profound sense. But this very shift also clouded the inner linguistic "mystery" of the national idea. At the borderline of languages and cultures, at the very edge of the boundary, the element of language was disappearing, becoming as it were "translatable." Works of art, literature, or philosophy, on the other hand, possessed a meaning (or did they?) that existed outside language, especially outside of the syntax and semantics of inner language, i.e., of national life as such.

Once again, this role of language has been "borrowed" by the idea of Statehood, an idea that was also particularly powerful at the border areas; however, these are borders decorated with imperial and military colors. I wish to add, however, that within the endlessly expanding boundaries of the empire the very essence of the national idea in its basic form has been distorted and transformed into a messianic supra-national idea of Sovereignty.

But let me go back to what is the main point in this discussion. In the 20th century national movements, ethnic development, movements for independence or self-determination are assuming a new, special character. This character is very controversial and very paradoxical. It is connected with the destruction of immense imperial giants which originally gave this idea its emotional charge, its aura of genuine loftiness and spirituality. In this connection it has meant defense against other peoples, a tough, intense, and adamant defense of borders which could only be violated in geopolitical arguments, as was characteristic of German Nazism. Neighboring peoples were to be conquered, to guarantee the security of those borders. But a border might still be violated; ultimately, the idea of endless expansion of borders (for their own security) became identical to the idea of the global character of this (my!) nation, the idea of the state, or ideology.

This imperialist geopolitical fantasy of fierce resistance is falling apart today. In the 20th century, individual nations are increasingly identified with their former cultural mentality, and trying to get to the roots of their cultural identity. Accordingly, the national idea becomes a factor in culture-formation, not so much in the sense of the external security of a particular culture, of maintaining and guarding it, but in the sense of some "intervals" in what is a single process, from the 20th century to the 13th, then on to the 15th, and back to the 20th. A nation identifies itself as a specific cultural entity. An imperial megalopolis is replaced by the idea of a cultural megalopolis in time, all-powerful in linking epochs together and causing their interaction. Such an idea underlies modern nationalist movements not only in Russia, but also in Spain, France, Italy, Austria, and Britain.

These trans-epochal movements, let me repeat, are becoming a means whereby a nation seeks to attain its cultural identity, and above all, to preserve its language as a culture-shaping force. My native language, after all, is not only my individual language; whether or not I like it, I speak a language I have imbibed with my mother's milk, learnt from books and songs, and picked up in the street. I remain able to speak "my own way" if this part of my identity is more clearly linked to the identity of my nation, to its specific and unique linguistic identity. On the other hand, there is a paradoxical character in that, while a culture is developing as an entity over time, its identity is easily replaced by something that is at hand, well-known and customary. More precisely, by the equation in which the national idea means Statehood or Sovereignty. Here once again the temptation of a geopolitical diversion raises its head. The national idea, once more removed from "culture," acquires the familiar ring of Uvarov's triad. For Uvarov's formula stands for something that is right at hand, before your eyes and at the tip of your tongue. In launching movements for cultural identity, ethnic groups which have been incorporated in multi-ethnic states, like the Tajiks, Uzbeks, or Basques, also rush for ideas that are close at hand but in fact are diametrically opposed, and aimed directly against this idea of cultural identity as connected with the emasculation of their society and culture, via the formulae of the triads of which I have spoken.

At this point I wish to discuss a slightly deeper and more difficult aspect of the subject. The modern spiral of a nation's cultural and primarily linguistic identity is rooted in the past, runs through many epochs, and comprises attempts to draw into itself some of the most remote epochs, as parties in a modern dialogue between cultures. As we study such a cultural "megalopolis of smaller peoples," two important points must be observed.

In the first place, past epochs that are drawn into present-day reality, and are clamoring for a voice, are often epochs of barbarism, chauvinism, and outward expansion, epochs which have played out their historical role a long time ago but return to life in obsolete elements of a nation's culture or language. Moreover, the distant past as it is revived in the present is far from a neutral and culturally sterile thing. It carries along its bottom shells and seaweed of historical discord, brought back to life and growing on the fertile soil of modern historical convulsions. These voices from the past become part of the worst kind of nationalism, one which cannot accept its historical death. The blessings of art and learning turn into the evils of modern barbarity. Of course, generally speaking, these are inevitable, if unpleasant, concomitants of culture as it moves towards the epicenter of modern life. All things fall into place eventually. But this is poor comfort for our contemporaries. Let me repeat that the transition from good to evil takes particularly powerful forms among smaller ethnic groups, whether Basques, Catalans, or peoples of our Transcaucasia. Their survival and incorporation in the linguistic and cultural dialogue on the eve of the 21st century is one of the most important and fruitful signs of our times; but as we have also noted, the threat of good turning into evil is never absent.

In the second place, and as a reversal of the first point, smaller ethnic groups and their revived languages become free in an epoch of disintegration of immense imperial megalopolises, or, to put it in more general terms, in an epoch when state forms of national development are replaced by cultural, commercial, tourist, and personal forms of exchange, right across the borders of the European Community. But for smaller ethnic groups this abrupt liberation and penetrability of borders, particularly in Europe, often means, at least psychologically, a destruction of the beneficent shell without which the roots of their national identity cannot survive and put out shoots; or it seems that they cannot. And yet, it is not just a matter of appearance. Indeed, the protection of the state, taxes, borders, and an inflated sense of national pride are all essential for the initial growth of linguistic and cultural self-awareness. The temporary border is needed for culture to develop a toughened protective outer shell.

Once more, the idea of Statehood lays claim to top priority among national ideas, despite the radically different culturological meaning of the national idea in the 20th century, of which I spoke earlier. That is, if we apply general criteria.

One more point. It has become particularly obvious in the 20th century that "territorially endemic" characteristics of a nation are insufficient. It has become clear that the essential psychological characteristics of a people are a "portable thing" which penetrate borders and clan boundaries. In a strange way, they even become more pronounced in the nostalgia of emigrants, becoming more distinctive and putting out deeper roots when their bearers are far from home, but only if such emigrants have kept their language. Ethnic psychological characteristics become ten times more pronounced when concentrated in the native language of an ethnic group. This is not a matter of a few decades; at least a century has to pass before this process is realized. We can look at the first wave of Russian emigration. What must be emphasized now is the fact that ethnic psychological characteristics manifest themselves in individuals, and that in the 20th century individuals very easily lead a "cross-border" life. Tourism is not a marginal phenomenon today. It is becoming a constant feature of life. But this discovery of the 20th century coexists, scandalously, and even interacts with some of the most barbarous forms of ecstasies of power.

At this point, let us go back to Russia, where such collusion is particularly alarming. I think that anywhere in the Commonwealth of Independent States, say, in the Ukraine or Belarus, nationalism finds it easier to get on with the idea of cultural integrity and of democratism than it does in our country; I shall not speak about Central Asia now because that is a different case. In Russia it is a particularly agonizing issue because here the national idea has always been aggressively equated with the idea of empire-building. In Russia, all good and lofty words about a corporate spirit (i.e., conciliarity, *sobornost*), communal ownership, and so forth, are buried under the bombast of an imperial corporate spirit (*sobornost*), and under the messianic role of a supreme people who lead other peoples behind them, by force or otherwise – which is another matter and ideological problem. It proves next to impossible to tear the Russian national idea from ideas of imperial power.

There is only one solution – to realize that to equate the Russian national idea with Orthodoxy and Nationhood means to regard it as an idea of imperial omnipotence, and to accept or reject this equation accordingly. This is not just rhetoric or abstract theorizing. It is still being put into practice today. For Russia, to part with imperialism means to drop the national idea as interpreted by Count Uvarov or political scientist Kiva. Otherwise, Russia must accept the equation and abandon democracy, abandoning it definitively and hopelessly, because the idea of imperial, autocratic power is totally incompatible with democratic ideas.

That is how complicated these problems have become in the 20th century. In our day it is dangerous to make forecasts, but I think a horrid ending is highly probable. There are means of getting rid of this historical experience of imperialism, which draws both the nation and its culture into itself; but such means are very weak. We are forever sacrificing the idea of culture for the idea of Russian autocracy, namely for imperial suppression, including the suppression of the unique character of Russian culture itself. It is incredibly difficult to break this link. But, fortunately, I am a culturologist and it is not my job to engage in such forecasts. My job is to state facts and cautiously hope for the better.

In conclusion I will have to explain, very briefly, just to avoid arguing about trifles, why I need the word "idea" and the notion behind it in this discussion about the Russian language as the essence of the Russian national idea. Until now I have been able to use the word "idea" as a mere piece of phraseology. Now I must use the notion with it full weight. Without going into differences between meanings given to the notion by Hegel, Bakhtin, or even ourselves, I shall outline the general element in various interpretations and in various aspects of each interpretation, from Plato's ideas to modern logical notions (*predstavleniia*). Unlike a concept (*poniatie*), an idea possesses a completely definite meaning.

An idea is an intellectual entity which comprises a whole cluster of concepts. Or, more precisely, it is an infinite system of concepts or categories that are typical of a specific historical period or cultural era. From this perspective, it appears that there can be two definitions of an idea. In an idea an infinite multitude of concepts merge into a kind of system. Inner speech with its syntax and semantics, where the past, present, and future are blended together, is a logical and psychological equivalent of this system. The other definition is as follows: in an idea, the single fundamental focus gives rise to a countless number of specific concepts, categories, relations, judgments and conclusions. An idea, on the one hand, represents the product or result of the focusing of concepts, but, on the other, is the source and basic principle of a countless multitude of new concepts, more specific ideas, interactions, and judgments. Hence an idea radically transforms and deepens its own roots.

All well-known explanations of an idea, from the definitions of Plato, the Catholic Church, Hegel, or Bakhtin, can be summed up in the following formula, that of a certain identity of a specially focused and unfolded concept. Ideas represent the divergence of clusters of concepts, especially those concepts that go beyond the limits of purely emotional tensions, and transform that which is emotional and subconscious into something intellectual. In their own right, these clusters balance along the edge of the "ultimate problems of being." One typical feature of an idea, given such an interpretation, is that it stands for a culture which has points of contact with another culture. Typically, a comprehensive idea always lands in a risky situation where it comes into contact with another comprehensive idea. The entire wealth of such a culture is concentrated in ultimate questions about the meaning of life, with meaning itself as a kind of "question-and-answer" relationship.

Such ultimate questions, which are addressed to the other culture, or to one's own culture perceived as "another culture," are therefore important for comprehending the idea. These points are directly linked to Bakhtin's interpretation of an idea. This is the meaning by which I understand the structure of the "idea" in the title of this article.

But to return briefly to the Uvarov-Kiva triad (Sovereignty – Religion – Nationhood), let me be more specific. The "creed" thus offered cannot lay claim to the status of an idea, if we look at the definition of the word. It is a typical ideological postulate, a component of an extra-cultural ideology, which can represent the interests of a specific social stratum or party. And content is not the only problem here, as I said above. Form is also a problem. The formula suggested to us can neither give birth to a multitude of concepts, nor can it focus individual ideas into a kind of integrating nucleus, such as inner language. This Sovereignty triangle is something that has been definitively reprimanded and is now reduced to chattering. It lacks essential silence.

The Place of Russian Culture among World Cultures (An Invitation to Reflection)[1]

Leonid Aleksandrovich Sedov

We have just witnessed another decade of fruitless attempts to transplant onto Russian soil institutions such as law, market, and parliamentary democracy; all these institutions arose and were formed in different historical situations and different cultural climates. Today it is becoming quite clear that if we are to believe the popular saying of Tiutchev about the "inability to understand Russia with the mind," and the necessity of a "special standard of measurement" (*arshin*) to measure its "peculiar condition" (*osobennaia stat'*), such belief must be based on the real existence of the "peculiar condition." And however little intellectual effort might be required to maintain this "condition" for oneself, considerable strength of mind is needed to comprehend it.

Russia is not unique in this respect. A special standard should also be applied to understand China and Japan, India and the Islamic world. But the obstinate delusion that Russian culture is something marginal to Europe, or just a hybrid of East and West, makes it difficult to understand Russia as a truly original phenomenon, with special national features as important as those of the Chinese, the Indian, and Judeo-European worlds.

Our methodological approach dictates that we recognize differences among cultures in orientation on fundamental, existential questions. Answers given to such questions influence the values and public institutions maintained and developed in a given cultural type; they also influence the formation of a certain "personality" of the given culture (called a "modal personality"). Understood this way, a culture may be compared to a genetic code, or genetic axis on which historical strata are strung, connected in succession. The problem is to detect this axis amidst the great variety of different historical epochs, a task far more difficult than revealing the biological structure of genes, or mechanism of expansion of genetic programs. For culture reveals itself as a symbolic code; we cannot create a microscope to observe the configurations of basic symbolic meanings by which all the wealth of inherited cultural information is given.

---

[1] L. A. Sedov, "Mesto russkoi kul'tury sredi mirovykh kul'tur (Priglashenie k razmyshleniiu)," *Polis*, no. 4 (1994): 97–110.
Helleman, Wendy, ed. *The Russian Idea: In Search of a New Identity*. Bloomington, IN: Slavica, 2004, 73–93.

It should be mentioned here that the present author understands culture not as a combination of the fruits of spiritual activity, or the peaks of the human spirit and the process of its creation. Following modern sociological usage, culture is understood as the most common mode of orientation inherent in typical (modal) representatives of a nation, or a community; culture represents a certain sense of the world coloring all of national life at all levels.[2]

A particular culture forms the type of person who belongs to it, and gives a certain modal structure of personality. Naturally, when constructing such an abstract "modal personality," one must not forget the great variety of real individuals. Every person is unique; every person represents a microcosm with its own peculiar destiny, unique psychological makeup, etc. But the history of such "microcosmic lives" are the concern of the arts and literature. The role of scientific scholarship is far more modest, for it examines the "microcosms" in their multiplicity and in their interactions in the common "area of attraction" which we call culture. The abstract "modal person" of Russian culture is neither Pushkin, nor Uncle Vasia of the eternal line-up for more vodka; yet without such an abstraction it seems impossible to understand the one or the other, and certainly one cannot understand Russian culture.

With an eye to solving urgent political problems it is also necessary to understand the history of Russia and its "plot" in terms of the peculiarities of psychological makeup of the Russian "modal person." The author regards the notion that Russian history has, as it were, started anew after the 1917 October Revolution as a serious delusion, comparable to that which appeared among Russian publicists after the 1861 reforms, a turn of events no less significant than 1917. We need to remember how Kliuchevskii at that time defended the idea of continuity in Russian history. Many were asking why they should understand their past, when they had only just left it behind to rebuild their lives on a completely new foundation? Kliuchevskii answered that in their delight and enthusiasm at the way the reforms changed the Russian tradition, they forgot how much that tradition had itself changed the reforms.

The author certainly does not want to join those who blame Marxist ideology for all the misfortunes of Russia and of the world as a whole in the 20th century. Berdiaev's attempt to trace the destiny of Marxism in Russia appears to be

---

[2] Sometimes, with less precision, we give the name "national characteristic" to this essence which is so hard to capture. But our understanding of the term "culture" seems preferable, first of all, because this is not so strictly connected with the idea of a biological (genetic) means of transmission of traits; secondly, because it is not closely connected with anthropomorphisms and allows us to discuss issues in terms which are stricter in comparison with character epithets (like "angry," "greedy," or "energetic"); thirdly, because from our point of view and according to contemporary standards the most fruitful typologies of cultures (like Parson's classification) have been realized with the language of cultural value-orientations.

much better founded. He indicated that this ideology functioned here not in its primary form, but transformed by the strong influence of Russian traditions.

Marxist features could never hide the age-old Russian characteristics of the Soviet empire. Note the words of G. P. Fedotov on this matter:

> The new Soviet man was not so much molded in the Marxist school, as that he crawled out of the Muscovite kingdom into God's light.... Let's look closely at the features of this Soviet person – looking, of course, at a man who is building his life, not the one who is crushed underfoot in agricultural communes and factories, or in concentration camps. He is very strong, physically and spiritually, well integrated and simple; he lives at somebody else's bidding; he does not like to think or to doubt; he values practical experience and knowledge. He is devoted to (State) power, which has raised him from the mud and made him into a responsible master of the life of his fellow-citizens. He is very ambitious and quite hard-hearted toward his neighbor's sufferings – the necessary condition of a Soviet career. But he is ready to overwork himself, and his highest ambition is to give his life for the collective, the party, or the motherland – it depends on the times. Cannot we recognize in all of that the civil servant of the 16th century? Other historical analogies suggest themselves: a civil servant of the times of Nicholas I, but without the humane characteristics of Christian and European breeding; an associate of Peter I, but without the fanatic Westernism, without the national renunciation. He is closer to the Muscovite in his proud national self-consciousness: his country is the only Orthodox, the only socialistic one – number one in the world – "the third Rome." Contemptuously he watches the rest of the world, i.e., the West – without knowing it, liking it, or fearing it.[3]

Amid the conditions of Russian culture it became apparent that the ideological content was not as important as the ideological character of Russian consciousness itself – the "blank" that can be filled with any ideology, no matter whether it be Marxist, Orthodox, or nationalistic. Of course, the ideological content is not indifferent with respect to its consequences. It could be quite important for social structures and for the nature of social relations whether people believe in God or in an impersonal historical Law; whether they have at least a vague sense of the possibility of the continuation of earthly existence in the other world, or they are altogether devoid of such a sense. However, on closer investigation, these substantial moments often turn out to be just the varied verbal expressions of altogether similar "sensations."

---

[3] G. P. Fedotov, *Novyi grad* [The new city] (New York: Izdatel'stvo im. Chekhova, 1952), 147–48.

In any case, soon after the reign of Peter the Great, wide circles of the population supported an Orthodox ideology, in the form of a "brief catechism" with a collection of unclear and contradictory notions, the main purpose of which was to substantiate our advantage over the West. Marxism did not introduce the idea of imperial greatness to Russia. Nor is the socialistic outlook responsible for introducing an age-old hostility to the "rich neighbor," disrespect for personal and private wealth, or the sullen grumbling of the great leveling process. Saltykov-Shchedrin has brilliantly discerned such "socialistic" features of the Russian way of life long before any socialistic ideas penetrated Russia. Socialists were not the first to persecute ideological (i.e., including religious) heterodoxy in Russia. Was this not the stance of the Orthodox state, even more, of the church itself, in its attitude to Old Believers?

But how are we to construct this "standard" (*arshin*) to help us explain the actual characteristics of Russian culture and the structure of the Russian "modal personality"? It would not be useful to start with an empirical study, to dig up an unsystematic collection of varied features and characteristics, impressionistic sketches, and sometimes clever, but superficial observations. Rather, one should take as one's starting-point some fundamental characteristic, like a basic instinct or attitude specific to a particular culture.

It is natural to suppose that cultures differ. First of all, they differ in their orientation on the basic, most important problems of existence, particularly the problem of mortality and death. Using Weber's approach in sociology, it can be said that a person's attitude to death is the most important constituent aspect of his/her relationship with the Absolute; this in turn decisively determines the ethics of interpersonal relations, and in fact through that, the entire structure of human life.

There are four principal possibilities for correlating this-worldly, earthly life, with life in another world; corresponding to these, the problem of exiting this life to enter eternity can also be described in a purely formal way by juxtaposing key factors. These are:

1) a harmonic, unproblematical connection, with fluent transition from earthly life to other spheres of being, that can be expressed in a formula (+/+);
2) an attitude to life as something we participate in temporarily, with preference given to the other world (−/+);
3) an attitude to earthly life as an extremely responsible affair, full of troubles and dangers, a departure from which does not promise absolute de-

liverance; this is a tragic attitude, expressed in the formula (-/-); and finally

4) a preference given to earthly life over that in another world, whether because of a lack of faith in life beyond this earthly one (atheism), or because of the expectations of suffering and punishment in the other world ("fear of God") (+/–).

Let us now try to find empirical referents which conform to these formulas. In order to simplify the task only the following four cultures will be considered: Chinese, Indian, European/Christian, and Russian.[4]

Chinese culture solves the problem of leaving in the calm, optimistic way, which is also inherent in other cultures based on ancestor worship. Properly speaking, there is no leaving at all. A person with such an outlook on the world lives in a universe inhabited by the "living dead" who are still connected to him, and help him to live in this world. It is more accurate to say that the whole world, including the world of the dead, is "this" world; the Chinese, like no one else, honor old age and smile at a funeral. As T. Grigor'eva writes, for the Chinese wise man there is no death in the absolute sense; everything appears out of non-being and goes back to non-being; death turns into life, and life turns into death. But that which, on the level of philosophic wisdom, looks like the Dao, Eternal Peace and Absolute Nothing, on the level of folk customs appears in the form of rituals and customs, like the cult of ancestor worship and belief in the existence of the dead men among the living, though with a different appearance.[5]

On the question of death, there is hardly another culture where one might take the coffin wherever the head of state goes, as in the case of the Chinese Emperor; where a coffin could be a natural part of the interior of the house; where the gift of a coffin as a present to a seriously ill man would be regarded as a symbol of attention and favor; where the purchase of a coffin for elderly parents would be interpreted as a demonstration of filial love. Chinese regard death without fear, even with satisfaction. A dying man regards death as a forthcoming

---

[4] In offering his own approach in this typology of cultures the author understands that the global nature of his approach could rightfully engender the reproach of schematism and inattention to many concrete facts and details, and that this could easily lead to contradictions in use of the formulas for a given culture. Anticipating such reproaches, the author only urges his readers to remember that every statement has a purely comparative sense, revealing its truth relative to this or that culture, in comparison with other cultures.

[5] T. Grigor'eva, "Makhaiana i kitaiskie ucheniia" [The Mahayana and Chinese teachings], in *Izuchenie kitaiskoi literatury v SSSR: Sbornik statei. K 60-letiiu chl.-kor. AN SSSR N. T. Fedorenko* [Studies of Chinese literature in the USSR: Collected articles. To honor the 60th birthday of corresponding member of the Academy of Sciences of the USSR N. T. Fedorenko] (Moscow: "Nauka," 1973), 36–52.

distant journey to people he has not seen for a long time; and those who stay behind in this world often sell everything to arrange a magnificent funeral for their relative. The Chinese worldview is expressed in the words of Confucius: "Render all to the dead man as if he were alive."

The peculiar characteristics pointed out above partly explain the mysterious lack of religiosity in Chinese culture and the absence of any idea of the Absolute as a supernatural reality, separating earthly life and life after death.

The person with an Indian outlook also does not die. An eternal chain of regenerations in various forms and bodily incarnations await him. But, unlike the Chinese, the Indian attitude to life and death is colored with pessimism in everything connected with life. The chain of regenerations turns out to be a heavy burden, tying him to time, from which he must be liberated. Life in any form is suffering; liberation from it, an absolute and final death, is a blessing; and if the person dies and is turned into "Nothing," this merging with the Great Void – Atman – that is the destiny of the saints, the enlightened ones, the Buddhas. The Indian attitude to sorrow and to the burdens of life is expressed sharply in the Puranas. Even the existence of the fetus in the mother's womb is pictured as an inconceivable torture. The popular attitude to death is expressed in an Indian proverb: "It is better to sit than to walk, better to sleep than to be awake, and death is best of all."

In accordance with this disposition, life has always been cheap in India; contempt for earthly goods, and inclination to a voluntary death have been restrained only by the impossibility of breaking the chain of regeneration without prior attainment of the appropriate level of holiness. The absolute death of the saints, those who could stop the wheel of *samsara* (incarnations), means that those left behind are deprived of their share. This is where the idea of *bodhisattva* (or sojourn of the saints) comes from – even to the extent of their getting the ability to leave for Eternal Bliss, to the Great Nothing, to Nirvana – staying, nonetheless, among the living to help them throw off from themselves the heavy burden of being. So we can conclude that in dealing with the question of leaving life behind, in their description of the Absolute, the Chinese and Indian worldviews show many similar traits. What differentiates them, however, is an opposing relationship to this worldly existence. While Chinese culture is optimistic, Indian culture is pessimistic.

Strictly speaking, Judeo-Christian culture is more closely related to Hebrew culture with its global pessimism, with its lack of belief in an other-wordly existence, with its extraordinarily sharp, critical, and troubled relationship to the present, to what is given. The "global pessimism" of Hebrew culture even makes the very existence of Hebrew society altogether problematic; the stressful, stormy history of this people provides ample evidence of this. In Christian culture global pessimism is mitigated by the idea of resurrection. A Christian has the hope of salvation, but this hope is not as unconditional and unproblematic as in the Chinese or Indian types of outlook.

When the European dies, he leaves for an unknown place. He does not know for sure what is awaiting him in the other world, how his life will be evaluated by the standard of ultimate judgment; even that final judgment is an undefined and future matter. If earthly life is a preparation for death and for existence after death, then this world itself becomes only a preparation for the kingdom of heaven, to arrive after the second coming. That is why the entire existence of a person of European culture is a tense expectation, sharply aware of a provisional perspective, with the future dependent on the present life. Yet while this life is perceived as a "vale of tears" and "realm of sin," death too is seen as a problem, not a deliverance. A person of European culture believes that a pious organization of this life is a pledge and basis for the future one. Death, therefore, is understood as a loss, a sad event. The arrangement of this world at the service of the future is a particularly European feature, with which all the "progressivism" of European culture is connected. The latter combines striking individualism with a less evident, but no less important factor in European culture – human solidarity among those who remain in this world, full of determination to achieve their liberation with their own hands (even though among those who borrow this slogan it is often filled with different nuances of meaning).

Having completed this brief (and inevitably schematic) survey of three world cultures, filling thereby three sub-squares of our typological field, let us now turn to commemorative rites for the dead here in Russia, where they have been transformed into occasions for merriment and drunkenness. What do these rites tell us about the deceased? "It is such a pity for him," and "How much he has lost by leaving in an untimely fashion!" (i.e., "We are in such good condition, but what about him?") He is, as it were, beyond those left behind, the relatives, for whom the death of this person is a blow and a loss.

What, in this most Christian nation, is the source of such an amazing feeling of preference of any life over any death? Has not Orthodoxy inspired the same representations of paradise and hell, of the Resurrection of Jesus Christ, and of the Last Judgment, as those we find in Western Christianity? Yes, it has, but what about the results? Courageously we dare to affirm that Russian culture is characterized by an absence of the feeling for the eternal, even in its most primitive form, as we find it in the cult of ancestors. For many centuries the Christian faith remained an outward covering for pagan beliefs in "dwellings" and "waters"; it was easily adopted but also easily discarded. The experience of the revolution has destroyed, almost without a trace, the illusion of Russia's idealistic intelligentsia about the Christian base of the Russian nation, as god-bearing. The idea of Christ could find no enduring place in the pagan consciousness which lacked a crucial fourth dimension of time; consequently the portrayal of the crucifixion was effortlessly replaced by other pictures appropriate for the ceremonies and processions of the new epoch.

So, from this first observation, we make the bold admission that the reality of Russian culture and the Russian world view is accurately enough captured in the formula "Seize the moment" (*Carpe diem*), which, in the formal paradigm we have adopted in our work, is represented by the formula (+/-). This affirmation immediately introduces us to long-standing disputes about the religiosity (*religioznost'*) or non-religiosity of the Russian people, and the characteristics of Russian Orthodoxy. These controversies, from the polemic between Gogol and Belinskii right up to the October Revolution, have provided definitive empirical confirmation of those who did not especially trust the religious adherence of Russians; these disputes flared up with a new intensity on the pages of *Vestnik russkogo studencheskogo khristiansko-demokraticheskogo dvizheniia* (*The Messenger of the Russian Students' Christian-Democratic Movement*) of the 1970s.

It is impossible to deal with all the questions connected with Russian religiosity fully in only one article. However, we think that our approach contains an important clue to resolving numerous problems contained in it. Our construction, undoubtedly, takes us back to Belinskii and Chaadaev, who affirmed the absence of religious feeling among the Russian people. We may not share all the conclusions drawn by the "furious Vissarion" from the national features he noted, (his historical optimism was refuted by the much more furious "Vissarionovich"), but we can't help agreeing with his words to Gogol: "You believe that Russians are the most religious people in the world. This is a lie! The background of their piety is poetry, reverence, or the fear of God. A Russian utters God's name while scratching his arse. As for the icon: it's not fit for praying, but fit for covering pots. Look closely, and you will see that they are by nature a profoundly atheistic people. They have a lot of superstitions, but there is not even a trace of piety." And further, "Mystical exaltation does not characterize this nation at all. It has too much common sense, clarity, and practicality of mind for that, and in this, possibly, is to be found the "greatness of its historical destiny in the future.""

It is clear that however long one immerses oneself in such eloquent dispute, an affirmative answer to the agonizing questions can only be achieved through detailed consideration of the fate of the Christian idea on Russian soil. The point of departure for such consideration ought to be a desire to look "beyond outward signs," i.e., not allowing oneself to be confused by external attributes and names. Certainly, for many it will seem to be false, or even blasphemous, to think that an atheistic European intellectual could have penetrated the framework of a religious Christian mentality further than the Orthodox Russian who remained a heathen. Indeed, it was Merezhkovskii who wrote: "The choice is between paganism, pretending to Christianity, as in Tolstoi's outlook, or Christianity pretending to paganism, as with Nietzsche."[6]

Our methodology, however, calls upon us not to be under the delusion of religious tenets, but to try to recognize the influence of more original, more fundamental orientations of a culture to the ideas and representations which have been born on other soil and in other cultural climates. The Christian idea of resurrection and redemption may well have arisen as a ray of salvation in the gloom of global Jewish pessimism, and grown up on the foundation of a worldview characteristic of the European psychological type, pessimistic towards the earth; but when united with the optimistic pagan consciousness of the Slavs with their strong sense of locality, "earthiness," and merriment (which also characterized the Hellenic-Byzantines, earlier), it ended up altogether turned inside out.

Orthodoxy appeared as the fruit of this union, and its Christ reminds one as little of the Jewish-European, as the joyous, fat Buddha of the Chinese with wrinkles on his belly resembles the Indian prototype. Did not Marxism also undergo this sort of transformation in Russia or China? Within a few decades Chinese Marxism will resemble Daoism or Confucianism more closely than the Marxism of its European origin. To understand how much Soviet Marxist bureaucrats and their present heirs from the camp of the "patriots" reproduce the stereotype of the mentality of their predecessors one need only read Saltykov-Shchedrin or the chief of police Baron Dubelt.[7]

The mentality of people of a pagan culture lacks religiosity in the sense of an absence of perspective on eternity and resurrection, but certainly not in the sense of denial of the existence of God or the gods. As long as life on this earth is perceived as the greatest good, transcendental life is either altogether denied or takes on the appearance of some arbitrary power, which is independent of people, manages destinies, and is the bearer of good; or, as in Islam, it poses as a more or less exact projection of earthly good to the heavens (this is the most optimistic variant of this cultural type, as it concerns the connection with the transcendental). Accordingly, Christ is transformed to fit the larger view which merges Him with this supreme manager, losing the features of his incarnation of the divine; thus an irresistible wall is set up between humanity and heaven.

Properly speaking, the continuous generation of heresies in Byzantium had one basis. Christ the Savior, the son and envoy of God, turned out to be a stranger in the world where any life "here" was better for a man, than any

---

[6] D. S. Merezhkovskii, *Sobranie sochinenii* [Collected works] (St. Petersburg: Izdatel'stvo tovarishchestva Sytina, 1914), 9: 152.

[7] *Apologiia L. V. Dubel'ta v zashchitu otechestvennykh ustoev* [Apologia of L. V. Dubel't in defense of patriotic foundations], *Golos minuvshego* [Voice of the past], March 1913.

"there," inaccessible for him. V. Solov'ev noted that all Byzantine heresies presented just diverse variations on one single theme: Jesus Christ is not the true son of God, the only begotten of the Father; he is not God incarnate; his nature and humanity are separated from the deity and not united with the divine being; and, therefore, the human state can rightfully keep its indisputable independence and leadership. A worldly optimism, given to the heathen in his sensation, compels him to deny such things as redemption, unity with God, the consecration of material and sensible things. The human being in the world of paganism is a finite form, without any freedom, while God represents infinite freedom without any form. God and humanity are fastened on two opposing poles of being, and there is no connection between them. As a result, in 9th-century Byzantium a situation arose in which emperors adopted Orthodoxy, once and for all, as an abstract dogma; and Orthodox hierarchs gave their blessing to the paganism of common life for many centuries. Orthodoxy in Byzantium was indeed driven into heresy.

Such a separation of the earthly and divine led to an exaggerated asceticism, at least of a part of pagan society. It is, so to speak, the reverse side of the conception that this world is the best of all worlds, and a reaction of some people of this world (religious ones) to the unrestrained turbulence of the flesh and uncontrollable earthly pleasures. Some with a religious sense begin to hate particularly acutely everything that is earthly, sinful, or corporeal, when people around them consider that which is earthly and corporeal as the most meaningful. Under such conditions, Christianity, with its softened attitude to human sinfulness (the human being after all is a fallen angel, but an angel nonetheless) gives rise to monophysitism with its "stony insensitivity" to the divinity of man. Monophysite asceticism sees in man only what is evil, dirty, and bestial, that which should be eliminated and tortured so that he can be turned into an angel. It considers the world a trap for man, from which he should escape with all his might. This is exactly what makes this world repulsive, and denial of its temptations provides the basis for pagan holiness – from *Stolpniki* and *Skoptsi* to L. N. Tolstoi, inclusive. This riot against the earthly "optimistic" passions of fellow-tribesmen is related somehow to the other riot, that of European atheists (of the Renaissance, or Nietzsche), which is pointed in the opposite direction, against the original pessimism and organic asceticism of their cultural environment.

But it is important to mention that however Christian "pagan holiness" may look outwardly, in reality it leads to enslavement by this world and service to all its masters, to submissive agreement to placing the world at the disposal of the prince of this world. The pagan environment treats saints and monks with a mixed sense of respect as intercessors before God – the bearers of good, and with regret – since monastery and prison easily combine functions, insofar as both monk and prisoner, in the eyes of pagans, are just losers who have left, or gotten out of the game.

One of the purest variations of a culture of the optimistic earthly kind is Islamic culture. Islam is a consistent and sincere Byzantinism, free of internal contradictions. It presents itself as open, and a complete reaction of the Eastern spirit against Christianity; in the Islamic system dogma is closely connected with laws of life and individual belief is in absolute agreement with the political and social order (V. Solov'ev).

In Islam we find the clearest embodiment of a sense of the gap between what is earthly and divine, of consideration for the earthly as what alone is given to human beings, and for God as a power which governs the given environment, and demands from human beings blind obedience. The Muslim regards the world as a firm stronghold, certainly not allowing for any progress, or moral perfection. The ideal is simplified in such a measure as to ensure immediate realization. Muslim society can have no other purpose except the broadening of its material powers and the delight of earthly blessings. The only task of the Muslim State was to extend Islam by means of weapons, and to govern those who have correct beliefs with unlimited power, according to the rules of elementary justice prescribed in the Koran.

Russia received Orthodoxy through its contact with Byzantium; this faith was then already constituted in its dead, dogmatic form. Preachers of Christianity, the first monks and priests, were naturally the representatives of the "pagan holiness" described above. Their arrival in the cheerful land of Kievan feasts and clowns, fist fights, and collective drinking could not take place without severe conflict. However, from the very beginning here one can find in embryo the entire further perspective on the Russian Church's degeneration into a semi-state institute in service to the prince of this world. The transformation of Christianity in the context of Slavic this-worldliness was prepared in its Byzantine history. This is also the starting point of the future schism of the nation into optimistic supporters of the patriotic idea of Russia as "the Third Rome," or Second Israel (or the liberator of the workers of the whole world), and the supporters of orthodox asceticism, who refused to see in the present revelry the best order of things. The notion that "in love we find a synthesis of unity and freedom" was already given, and also achieved in the existing Russian Church; and so it is not an ideal to be achieved through countless hurdles and hardships, while these have all but come to represent the main distinguishing feature of Russian Orthodoxy. The Orthodox Church became a state establishment in Russia, "a kingdom of this world."

"How is it possible?" the reader may insist, "Have not the best, the most subtle minds of Russia, like Dostoevskii, for example, confirmed that Russians are a chosen 'god-bearing' people?" Let us admit that we too have heard such affirmations, and felt embarrassed. However, a more careful reading of Dostoevskii has destroyed our doubts. Even more, it strengthened our affirmation that the Russian people is "god-bearing," but it is not Christian, that the main idea of Russian Orthodoxy is belief in its own national God, one who sanctifies Russian national characteristics and its isolation. This belief is a belief in the God who leads to victory, and who, for the Church, is an organizer and inspirer of these victories. "The Russian people are all in Orthodoxy," Dostoevskii wrote in the last diary notes before his death. "Orthodoxy is the Church; the Church is the crown of the building, and will be that forever."

This nebulous formula is clarified when we read the remarks of Shatov in *The Devils*. Shatov is the main character expressing Dostoevskii's ideas about the divine character of the people. "Any nation," he says, "is a nation only to the point when it has its own peculiar god, and rejects all other possible gods without reconciliation, and when it believes that through its own god it can win and drive the other gods out of the world." It is hard not to agree with this, meaning that in the sense of this optimistic, life-affirming sense of its own superiority the Russian people always has been a "god-bearing" people. But we must also agree with Merezhkovskii, who does not see anything Christian in this idea, and even suspects some hidden godlessness here. The reason is that here God does not create the human being, but the human being creates God (just like Nietzsche's "In God people respect their own virtues. They thank themselves for themselves – this is why people need God"). To generalize, as Merezhkovskii rightly emphasizes, it is not Orthodoxy that becomes the main feature of the Russian people, but belonging to Russia becomes a necessary and sufficient condition for Orthodoxy. "Russian" means that one belongs to Orthodoxy, i.e., that one is right. The contours of the unshakable crag of Russian pride come through the nebulous formula of Dostoevskii about the "god-bearing" people.

Thus we consider, on the one hand, the optimistic attitude to this world, and on the other hand, the pessimistic one as an indicator of the crucial difference between a Russian and European sense of the world. This fundamental difference, which is much more deeply rooted than any dogma and tenet of faith, decisively influences the destiny of original and borrowed symbols of faith, institutions of ideas and ideals, transforming them into something that goes well with the spirit of a borrowed culture. This influence can be traced in almost every phenomenon of the national spirit, but leads to a subject that is beyond the scope of our present article. Therefore let us limit ourselves to one example from church architecture, which colorfully illustrates our position concerning the fundamental difference between European and Russian culture:

> Entering beneath the mighty vault of Western cathedrals, the Christian realizes that he belongs to a sinful, fallen world, but at the same time he

hears the appeal to the tireless struggle for liberation; and he is given a view of paradise in the cut-glass windows with their wonderful coloured glass, which beckon one upwards. Russian Church architecture with its bright colors, with its golden and green domes crowned with triumphant crosses is inspired by the opposite theological idea. The Orthodox Christian does not strive to subdue nature, or force it to go beyond its own boundaries, but, on the contrary, with love appeals to the Holy Spirit to come into the flesh of the soil, our mother, to consecrate and transform it. There, where the eucharist is celebrated, where believers gather together as one family with children and infants, there the land blazes forth with colors of the heavenly kingdom; everything inside the church is full of light and joy, and heaven comes down to the earth.[8]

The typologizing of culture which has been given, and set in motion with a formal method, seems to allow us to determine a series of additional characteristics of the cultures described, and fundamental enough to give a decisive account of a number of phenomena and relationships derived from them.

Theorem 1. A pessimistic attitude to "worldliness" arouses interest for "what is otherworldy," "extraordinary," "unknown," "strange," and vice versa. This statement is based not only on common sense but also on much deeper philosophical generalizations that find a very close connection between a striving for truth and a pessimistic attitude to life. Socrates was the first to feel not just the tragic character of existence, but actual despair in the face of life. He was the father of the understanding of truth. At the beginning of the *Phaedo*, Plato portrayed Socrates asserting that the man searching for truth secretly desires death, and that truth is harmful for life.

But perhaps the most convincing revelation connecting the search for truth and rejection of life is that of Nietszche, who wrote about science as a submission of life to truth, as a terrifying act, as the fanaticism of some otherworldly person. He quite reasonably considered striving for truth a repudiation of the temporal in preference for the eternal, and a preference for what exists with respect to what does not, thus undermining the free enjoyment of life. According to Nietszche science erected the very same cult of the eternal, i.e., that same hatred for life, on the ruins of the religion which it destroyed. A hostility to abstractions also characterizes Russian writers of a conservative inclination, such as A. Grigor'ev, K. Leont'ev, Iu. Samarin, I. Aksakov, and M. Katkov. They all praised life, oppos-

---

[8] N. Zernov, "Anglikanstvo i pravoslavie" [Anglicanism and Orthodoxy], *Vestnik Russkogo studencheskogo khristianskogo dvizheniia* 106: 4 (1972): 57–68, esp. 58.

ing it to what, from their perspective, were dead scientific schemes. The hero of one of Grigor'ev's novels is named *Vitalii*, meaning "alive, vital." Leont'ev emphasized the importance of what is arbitrary, typical, and bright, rather than abstract theories.

The pagan-Islamic outlook on the world, immersed in what is earthly, and regarding what is otherworldy only in terms of abstract power which is applied to this world, naturally worships (even on earth) only the manifestations of an external power, the crude fact, which does not require any internal ideal justification. V. Solov'ev considered this as the source of the neutral stance to truth, and the respect for every successful and skillful lie which has always characterized the East. Religious systems of an Islamic type are based on such an outlook on the world, and Solov'ev demonstrated repeatedly that Russian Christianity and Islam are alike, although the place of God is often occupied by the tsar or state.

So, according to this theorem, cultures are divided into those which are open to what is unknown, strange, and also realize the value of truth (Indian, European); or those closed to such matters (Russian, Chinese).

Theorem 2. A pessimistic attitude to death causes a "this-worldly" kind of activity. One can hardly expect much concern about our world from people waiting for an unconditional transition into another, better world, and who consider their earthly existence as a more or less accidental episode before eternity. This is the source of activity of Russian and European cultures and of the passivity of Indian and Chinese cultures. The cross-combination of traits received gives greater precision in depicting the attitude of any culture to what is strange and unknown. For example, in the case of European culture, active interest is displayed as a "cognitive-scientific" orientation; while the passive interest of Indians can be described as a "contemplative" orientation; active absence of interest of Russians appears as "hostility" or active xenophobia; while in Chinese culture there is a passive absence of interest, or "arrogance."

Further investigation in our typological field allows us to note the diametrical or "diagonal" difference of opposing cultures. Such is the position which the Chinese culture takes in relation to European culture, and the Indian culture with respect to the Russian. A peculiarity which on the first glance seems purely formal, namely, the similarity or dissimilarity of the signs of the formulas which describe them, is worthy of attention, for it makes diametrically different cultures seem similar. We conventionally call these parameters the difference of potentials. Thus, we have two cultures with different potentials (the Russian culture $+/-$, and the Indian one $-/+$), and two cultures without such a difference (the European culture $-/-$, and the Chinese $+/+$). The attempt to attach some substantive meaning to this formal description led us to the conviction that this example of ours is in some complicated way connected with that which T.

Parsons calls "the achievement orientation" of the second pair, and "the ascriptive orientation" of the first.

Theorem 3. Cultures which have a difference of potentials are characterized by an ascriptive orientation. In those cultures where a difference of potentials is absent, the achievement orientation dominates. While this theorem represents the greatest difficulty in terms of its rational foundation, let us try to support it with a heuristic metaphor, and then with some empirical illustrations. It is metaphorically possible to imagine a culture where the "difference of potentials" is absent in terms of a field which is not charged, in which, accordingly, there is no unidirectional movement of particles. On the contrary, the culture which is characterized by a difference of potentials looks like a charged field in which particles move in a well-defined direction. If we endow particles with the property of being oriented one to another, then in the first case each of the particles, not knowing beforehand the vector of movement of neighboring particles, will begin by estimating them from the point of view of that toward which they move, namely, action or achievement. In the second case, as soon as the direction of movement is given, the place of the particle gains decisive significance for the orientation in the structure, relative to the situation of these particles in the hierarchy, the order of caste, or some other classification system.

The conception of the difference of potentials also leads to the conception of the possibility of applying measurable procedures, i.e., looking at our formulas not as only qualitative evaluations, but as formulas in which a plus and a minus can have different quantitative meaning. In accordance with these meanings the derivative characteristics will also change. For example, we can examine a culture of the Judaeo-European type. The meaning of the minus in the numerator of the fraction here oscillates in a diapason from the maximum in the case of Judaism to the minimum in the Catholic variant of Christianity (where a minus remains as such, since even the Catholic outlook on the world is characterized as a pessimistic one). If the denominator is thought to be constant (i.e., in the negative sense) the increase of the meaning of the numerator has to lead to the reduction in the difference of potentials, and an increase in activity.

Empirically this is confirmed by a comparison of Protestantism and Catholicism. The more pessimistic Protestant culture has shown itself more active, more achievement-oriented and less oriented to caste than Catholicism. Materialism, under the conditions of European culture, means further problematization, right up to a full rejection of salvation on this side of life, which leads to hyper-practicality and hyper-achievement of the European kind (with all the consequences associated with that); or it is partly compensated by a heightening of optimism in the lower part of the fraction (scientistic optimism, progressivism).

In Russian culture the decrease of difference between potentials is either a result of the increase of religiosity, in the sense of belief in life after death, or a result of the more pessimistic estimation of the present. In the first case activity is reduced with the increase of achievement (movement toward the Islamic sense of the world and then to the Chinese, although the Russian and Chinese cultures cannot on principle draw closer together, because the significance of a minus in the numerator of the Russian fraction does not change, turning into a plus, as in China). In the second case the increase of (the potentiality of) achievement is accompanied by a greater openness for what is strange and unknown. Both Russian Old Belief (*staroobriachestvo*) and sectarian groups can be examined in the light of these two possibilities. In any case, our analysis does not contradict Russian historical reality: members of the Russian Old Believers movement and many members of millenarist sects showed themselves to be the most sober, diligent, enterprising, and literate part of the peasantry; they were "representatives of a mind and civil consciousness among the ordinary people of Russian society."[9] On the other hand, materialism has sharpened and maximized the traits corresponding to the outstanding significance of all components of the formula: activity, xenophobia, and the practice of ascription.

The peculiar characteristics of Russian culture mentioned above give a formal base for systematic description, although it stands to reason that the exclusively ideal-typical sketch we use can never lay claim to the all-round scope of empirical reality in all its riches and contradictions. It gives us only a "visual angle," or method for constructing some "geometry of relations"; if it does not permit us to explain the history of the Russian nation and to foretell the future of Russian culture, it does allow us to understand something of the historical destiny of Russia and the peculiarities of its social organization. It is obvious that for a more detailed introduction to the problem, we need a more detailed elaboration of the deduced formulas, and a closer study of the mechanisms of influence of one culture upon another, right up to the point of measurement of cultures; Japan and Ancient Europe at the point of transition from paganism to Christianity seem to be the most interesting from this point of view. Also important are efforts of grasping the sources of initial optimism or pessimism of a culture in characteristics of early upbringing and relationships within the family, peculiar to that culture. All of this belongs to the direction of movement prompted by the methodology we have chosen. But for the present we will try to outline some further consequences resulting from the basic position regarding the Russian worldview suggested above.

---

[9] V. Andreev, *Raskol i ego znachenie v narodnoi russkoi istorii* [The schism and its meaning in Russian popular history] (St. Petersburg, 1870).

The first feature of the Russian national character, rooted in the "here and now" and "this-worldliness" of the Russian outlook, may be called "responsiveness." "Russian logic" means a high responsiveness, even a disproportionate reaction to the present, the given and visible. Like any other spiritual peculiarity, responsiveness is neither good nor evil, but turns into one or the other according to circumstances. It is displayed in blind rage and in increased aggressiveness as an answer to slight injury (in the form of misbehavior or boorishness) and in the famous "bread-and-salt spirit" of hospitality, the desire to please "here and now."

> The motley soul! First man presents himself as a pure dog, now he is sad, feels sorry, indulges in caresses, and mourns for himself..." (I. A. Bunin).

We have already mentioned characteristics of orthodox-Islamic society, like freedom from ideal justification for the factual state of affairs, or worship of a crude manifestation of external power (theorem 1). Taking into consideration this peculiarity of our national culture, we can assert that in some aspects Russian society is more liberal and humane than any other. Unprecedented freedom from obligation flourishes here – there is no other place in the world that allows for so wide an opportunity to neglect one's work, to steal public property, to substitute words for action, and to disregard words as action. Society makes no great demands on the person, nor does the person make great demands on him/herself (freedom from conscience). Everyone knows that people deceive one another, but no one feels indignant at this, for the truth, understood in the Russian manner, has nothing in common with abstract truth. This is the truth for "here and now," a pragmatic truth for this very moment. A person not infected with the prejudices of other cultures can certainly breathe freely in such an atmosphere, and the fashionable Russian will never exchange this special freedom for any freedom of speech (it is not valuable for him) or for any legal guarantee (he does not believe in it).

Another result of this "here and now" attitude of the Russian outlook is a cheerful carelessness, a wastefulness that is so attractive in direct lively communication, and is often contrasted with European dryness. But we soon discover that it also represents an inability to plan, to look ahead and think about tomorrow.

Then again, the formula that we are investigating results in recognizing another quality of the Russian character, namely the feeling of being caught in a desperate situation. "What is given is given," "There is no place to escape," "Live once," "It's better here and now, than there and hereafter." All such formulations in various ways capture the instinctive affirmation of Russians that "in the hereafter" there is nothing.

This desperation is akin to the desperate relationship which connects gamblers: either the circumstances of the game allow no one to leave the table before the game is over, or the psychology of the player will not allow him to leave the game, even if he has won fabulously, and all the more if he has lost and strives to win it back. In brief, any heated playing relationship among gamblers, however long-standing this may be, has a basic formula: "whoever leaves loses; whoever stays wins." This formula also provides the basis for non-religiosity, for the hopeless reality of relationships in Russian society, where no one allows himself to leave the game before it ends, and matters like departure, emigration, suicide, and divorce are more strictly censured than anywhere else. What is more, you yourself will not escape the fear that it can get still worse, but that you will not be allowed to return to the table. And what about death?! Death is not voluntary, it is a total loss for you; you are leaving when you have lost utterly and left everything to others.

Hope in fortune, chance, coincidence; ability to risk and inability to work – these are typical features of the reckless person repeatedly portrayed by Dostoevskii. Trust in fortune or luck has accustomed our countrymen to a staggering dependency, irresponsibility, to customary waiting that some one, whether God, or the authorities, or any one else, will take some interest in you, think for you, and give you orders. Millions of people crowded around the wheel of historical roulette, now winning and then once again losing everything that was won – this crowd is waiting for manna just to fall down from the Heavens, for the opportunity to ignore work, and simply open their mouths for food.

His majesty "Chance" or "Lady Luck" are often portrayed with the image of the all-powerful officer; all responsibility and all initiative is given to this figure for a time, but later he will have to answer the revolt which demands the paradise not yet come down to earth; he must answer for defeat, starvation, for lagging behind the "German." For the authority figure is itself flesh of the flesh of this mass, cannot foresee the future, and is also better at squandering resources than working and maintaining them. So it is difficult for him to provide everything which the dependents, in their confidence, hope for; and when he gets tired of taking care of such "orphaned" people, he begins to take advantage of opportunities, allowing his own stomach to become his prime concern, and leaving events to go the "way of history."

Is it not because of this total irresponsibility and lack of initiative that the Russian adapts so ideally to life in the army or the camp? Russian society was always divided into "fathers" who provided benefits and "sons" who benefited by them. Fathers embody popular ideas about sources of total happiness, and know the secret of attaining victory, grandeur, or abundance. Tsar, baron, general; leader, regional committee secretary (*obkom*) – these are the different forms of "plenipotentiary benefactors." They are allowed to do everything. They represent destiny. It is possible to murmur against destiny, but it is foolish to oppose it with your own will, to teach or prompt it. It is possible to rebel against destiny, finally, only to submit once again to it. But nothing sickens a Russian more than watching a close colleague actively "making" his life, and, what's more, with prospects for the future. At this the Russian spirit rebels, even Dostoevskii's genial spirit; here we find the initiative for persecuting the bourgeois, *kulak*, "Yid," or anyone else who shows circumspection, thrift, or individuality. And what is most often placed over against such things is "brotherhood," a factor not found as such in nature – but there is more than enough of it in our nature.

It is true, Russian thinkers never had a unanimous view on the question of brotherhood. V. Solov'ev, however, noted that "to do some good for our countrymen voluntarily can be compared to squaring the circle."[10] Moreover, what aspect of Russian social cohesion could have given birth to this ideal of brotherhood as deposited in the national character, "in spite of centuries of suffering, in spite of barbaric coarseness and rudeness implanted in the nation, in spite of centuries of slavery, and foreign invasions?" (Dostoevskii).

In the first place: the responsiveness and generosity of soul, of which we spoke earlier. These are also rooted in the Russian preference for this world, for the "here and now" which characterizes their outlook. Next, there is the fear of being left out of the game. Solitude is unbearable for the typical Russian. He seeks to live in a close group, gregariously, communally (*soborno*), able at any moment to glance over at his neighbors and compare his life with theirs ("what applies to them, also applies to me..."). Everyday conflicts arise among those who are at close quarters, whether on the bus, at the stove, or the counter. In critical periods of history, like those of Ivan the Terrible or Stalin, a crowd may even be inclined to kill those who are brothers, while at other times the prevailing atmosphere is one of "games with departures." The desperation described above assures resistance for a society which appears doomed to a speedy collapse; and this resistance is startling for every one who observes from within the small but exhausting "war of all against all," and awaits the end which – see there! – is approaching, to put an end to the community's existence. The centripetal drawing power of the roulette wheel is apparently not such a weak source of integration. Hang on, wait for chance, be patient, do not trust even your closest acquaintances, but, above all, do not think that in some other place things are better: whether on this side of life, or at the boundaries, it is still worse. Beware of those who say that "things are always fine there, where we are not (i.e., the grass is always greener on the other side of the fence)."

The secret of Russian fatalism is held in the desperation and optimistic estimation of a "this-worldly" situation, although on the face of it unbelief in life after death ought to give birth only to fear of death, and a tenacious clinging to life. Indifference and contempt for life, which played such an enormous role for

---

[10] Solov'ev, *Pis'ma* [Correspondence] (Moscow, 1923), 54.

the kind of courage displayed by Russians in wartime, were well described in I. Bunin's story "The Celestial Birds." The fatalistic Russian saying that, "Although you cannot die twice, you cannot avoid one (death)" is founded not on belief in God, or in paradise, but on a completely pagan and almost animal attachment to life ("Birds are such animals, my brother, that they do not think about paradise, and are not afraid of freezing").

All the traits and psychological characteristics mentioned above remind one of qualities more often used when speaking of adolescence; they involuntarily suggest the possibility of approaching an analysis of Russian culture from the perspective of genetic or growth psychology. This potential is supported in that the coincidence of the Russian psyche with the structural psyche of an adolescent, is not limited to the complex of traits enumerated in the above presentation, but also takes us straight to the very fundamental relationship from which these traits are derived. The formulation of the Russian relationship with death as we have proposed has a direct correspondence with the infantile relationship as S. Freud formulates it in his work *The Interpretation of Dreams*: for the child ... death is strange, and has the force of *leave-taking* (Freud's italics) – the person has left, and has stopped annoying the living. The child does not distinguish the manner of leave-taking, how the absence has come about – whether through distance, through a breaking off of a relationship, or death. Beyond this it is only necessary to mention that Freud's observations are applied to children from the age of 4 to 10 years. But the psychological structure of Russians can be compared to that of much later adolescence, when the distinction between death and other disruptions is already clearly understood. Nonetheless, a relationship to death as a strange departure from which the one remaining behind receives gain ("he has stopped annoying"), still manifests itself.

It is extraordinarily interesting to compare the place and role of the idea of Orthodoxy in 19th-century views of Russian society, with the idea of Marxism as it took root in 20th-century Russian society. However paradoxical it might seem, we discover that in terms of their functional role in this system, Orthodoxy and Marxism appear almost synonymous. The important similarity here is an assertion of correctness of teaching, the conviction that the Russian (Soviet) people as such are the only possessors of correct teaching. Moreover, when either the moral-religious or scientific content of such teaching is forgotten, it turns into a nominal foundation for the exclusive privileges favoring one nation at the expense of others, as Solov'ev mentions in his comments on the Slavophile idea. From the affirmation that a people is truly Christian we cannot draw the apparently necessary conclusion, that in all its external and internal affairs and relations it must live up to its Christianity, and must not give offense; rather, the opposite conclusion follows, that it is allowed to do everything to support and defend its own interests. Solov'ev denied Slavophiles the right to speak on behalf of national self-consciousness, proposing that the people actually think and feel differently. However, the bitter truth is that one can hardly find a better characterization of Russian self-consciousness than in the following words of Solov'ev himself, if we can free it from the subjunctive mood:

> If we believed the Slavophiles and accepted their statement about the Russian people as a statement about their self-consciousness, we would have to imagine these people like some Pharisees, righteous in their own eyes, exalting their virtues for the sake of humility, despising and condemning their own fellow creatures for the sake of brotherly love, and ready to wipe them from the face of the earth for the complete triumph of their own meek and peace-loving soul. If indeed, further, the essence of the Russian national spirit was truly expressed in Katkov's cult of popular power, then our Motherland would appear to us in the form of a stupid athlete, who instead of conversation can only show us muscles and shoulders."[11]

These words are very relevant today, now that so-called "patriots" of all kinds, from Marxists to Fascists, are trying to play on the timeless strings of national pride and arrogance, for what is perhaps the final accompaniment to the dance of death, a dance for which the world is waiting, just in case it should bring to power these apostles of a Russia which is "forever right."[12]

---

[11] Solov'ev, *Rossiia i vselenskaia tserkov'* (Moscow, 1911), 49. Cf. the Herbert Rees translation *Russia and the Universal Church* (London: G. Bles, 1948), 43–45, and 56–58. The correspondence is not exact since Rees translates an abbreviated version which Solov'ev wrote in French and published in Paris as *La Russie et l'Église universelle*; Solov'ev explains his inability to publish the complete version in Russia at the time, 32. *Trans.*

[12] As a final note, the author would like to warn the reader that he did not intend to convince him irrefutably of the culture types described in this article. Cultures and civilizations, with their thousand-year heritage, are open to gradual external influences and sudden mutations which follow disturbances in the environment and shocking experiences along the thorny path of history. However all these processes represent themes for special investigation, and need their own methods; this is why we have not dealt with them in the context of the present article.

Antinomies of Russian Consciousness: Labor and Leisure[1]

Andrei Pavlovich Zabiako

> "Truth represents a contradiction for the human mind, and this contradiction becomes evident once truth is verbally formulated.... Thesis and antithesis together give us an expression of truth. In other words, truth is an antinomy, and it cannot help being that."
> P. A. Florenskii, *The Pillar and Ground of Truth*

Discussion of the contradictions of Russian consciousness represents an old tradition in Russian literature, both fictional and philosophical. Meanwhile, the historical, ideological, and psychological context of this discussion is constantly changing, giving modern nuances to an old theme. Current research in the humanities allows for reduction in the bitterness of these contradictions, as they are experienced in a peculiarly Russian and tragic way. After M. Foucault, C. Levi-Strauss, or our M. M. Bakhtin, contrasting phenomena like conditions of madness and intellectual sobriety, or the comical and serious, are regarded as typical of any ethnocultural mentality, in active interaction as *pairs of opposites* or *binary oppositions*. Spiritual entities which make up parts of the pairs may be designated as *categories of spiritual experience* or, when speaking about intellectual entities, *categories of consciousness*.

Inasmuch as categories of spiritual experience are considered as stable conceptions and feelings, charged with high significance for a people, they acquire the character of *constants* in an ethnic culture. Such an approach to our theme brings discussion of contradictions in Russian consciousness into calmer, deeper channels. Judgments about the spontaneity or unregulated character of the Russian nature lose their impact. On the contrary, a new task now arises, namely to explain the complicated structure of categories of spiritual experience, for its composition gives Russian culture its wholeness (*tselostnost'*).

The present essay, which provides a continuation of ongoing work on this problem, will focus attention not on "cosmological" categories of consciousness

---

[1] A. Zabiako, "Antinomii russkogo soznaniia: Trud i prazdnost'," *Literaturnaia ucheba*, no. 4 (1998): 161–76.
Helleman, Wendy, ed. *The Russian Idea: In Search of a New Identity*. Bloomington, IN: Slavica, 2004, 95–112.

(those of top and bottom, left and right, order and chaos) but on "existential" ones: holy and sinful, divine and demonic, native and foreign, will and power, and other similar categories. These are the concepts by which Russians have traditionally oriented themselves in cultural matters, and defined themselves in vitally important circumstances.

Let us begin with labor, and the antinomies of labor and leisure as these form the basis of culture. As is well known, this theme has been hotly debated.

Realities of History and "Liberal Anecdotes"

The 11th-century monk Theodosius of Pechora, one of the first Russian authors, in his essay on patience, love, and the fast reproached his monastic brothers by saying,

> And now I, unworthy as I am, on the basis of my understanding of the precepts of the good Lord, tell you that it is fitting for us to feed the poor and strangers through our own work, and not to remain idle, scurrying about from cell to cell. Have you not heard Paul saying, "Nowhere have I eaten my bread free of charge, but I worked by night and preached by day," and again, "The work of my hands has served both myself and others," and once more, "May the idle not eat." But we do not do any of this.

This reproach against the laziness of his compatriots resounded at the dawn of our native literature, and has been repeated so often that in time it acquired the character of a cliché. Rarely is any new literary 'account' concerning the Russian people, ancient and contemporary, introduced without discussing the inclination of Russians for doing nothing.

In a recent work on the history of Russian culture in the 19th century, B. F. Egorov's discussion of the Russian character affirms without evasion or reserve that "the laziness and irresponsibility of a slave are easily combined with deception and theft" in our national life. In folklore this combination is even developed as typical, historically rooted, and spiritually justified. "The majority of Russian fairy tales build their themes around theft: heroes steal apples, the feather of a firebird, or a horse.... And these actions are treated as a feat, not a vice!" the author exclaims.[2] It is remarkable that more than a hundred years ago F. M. Dostoevskii also heard much about similar "links" between Russian "passivity" and views that "whoever among the people was an activist, was also a

---

[2] B. F. Egorov, "Ocherki po istorii russkoi kul'tury XIX v." [Studies in the history of 19th-century Russian culture], in *Iz istorii russkoi kul'tury* [From the history of Russian culture] (Moscow: Shkola "Iazyki russkoi kul'tury," 1996), 5: 59–60.

kulak and swindler." These the author of *Diary of a Writer* regarded as "liberal and wanton anecdotes."[3]

Meanwhile, history clearly shows us that already at the end of the 10th century, long before the appearance of these accusatory writers, Russia had become a great state. Can it have obtained its power by seizure and misappropriation of alien goods? In moving to new territories Eastern Slavs settled on what was practically uninhabited and infertile land. In the West things were different; Franks, Germans, Goths, and other new European nations robbed the ancient riches of the empire, and settled on fertile lands, a significant part of which had long been well tended, and was covered with Roman roads and towns. Could it be that, like Scandinavians, Slavic-Russians acquired glory and power from brigandage and banditry? For Ancient Russia the epoch of distant warrior raids into alien territory ended with the death of Sviatoslav in 972. His son Vladimir (Sviatoslavovich) did not inherit the spoils from his father; nevertheless he and his son Iaroslav the Wise were especially praised by contemporaries for the power of their state. How did it grow? Only through the labor of a nation which in two or three hundred years turned the wild plain into a "country of cities," and thus made a deep impression on European guests.

The conception of the laziness of Russian people, so widespread in our national literature, has been kept alive by a persistent critical depiction of the Russian people. But it is a typical cultural myth. From the earliest time the Russian people have worked, and worked stubbornly, without sparing energies; but this labor did have its own peculiar characteristics.

The Russian Attitude to Labor in the Circumstances of Russian History

In answer to those who accused Russians of laziness Dostoevskii wrote:

> It is only too clear and understandable that everything happens according to the well-known laws of nature and history, and that neither stupidity nor the humble abilities of Russian people, and certainly not shameful laziness, can be considered as the cause of our meager production in science and industry. One kind of tree grows in a certain number of years, and another takes twice as long. Everything depends on the position of a people in nature, on circumstances, and on what is most important for them. Here the causes are geographical, ethnographical, and political; there are thousands of causes, all of them clear and exact.[4]

---

[3] F. M. Dostoevskii, *Dnevnik pisatelia: Izbrannye stranitsy* [Diary of a writer: Selections] (Moscow: Sovremennik, 1989), 204–09.

[4] Ibid., 205.

Labor on the land provided the very foundations of great ancient and medieval civilizations. What was the position of the Russian native land worker with respect to nature? How did the Russian ploughman feel about the conditions of nature of Eastern Europe?

The climate of the Russian plain is diverse. Our greatest national historian, V. O. Kliuchevskii, remarked on nature mocking even the most careful calculations of its Russian (*velikoross*) inhabitants. The peculiarities of the climate and soil deceive even the most modest expectations. Having once gotten used to such deceit, the thrifty Russian, losing his head, tends to decide on the most hopeless and unreasonable plans, opposing the whims of his own courage to the capriciousness of nature. This inclination to tease fortune, to play with success is the essence of Russian *avos'* (chance).

There is one thing of which the Russian is certain, and that is appreciation of the clear summer working day; nature allows him very little time for work on the land, and he knows that the short Russian summer can be shortened even more by unexpected, unseasonably foul weather. This forces the Russian peasant to hurry, to work hard in order to do much in a short time, to gather in the crops from the field on time, and then to remain all fall and winter without any business. So the Russian has gotten used to working hurriedly, feverishly, and quickly, and then resting during the enforced leisure of autumn and winter. Not one European nation is as capable of such intense work for a short time as are the Russians, but it seems that nowhere else in Europe can we find a people so lacking in the habits of plain, temperate, moderate, and continuous labor as in Russia.

Thus, from ancient times nature forced the Russian to work hard with great zeal, but not in a rhythmic way and, even more significantly, without sure hope except in *avos'*: "stick to *avos'* as long as it is not spoiled." The element of fortune has only become stronger in the peasant attitude toward work. While it encouraged the bold youth in a worker, it also taught him to accept unfortunate circumstances without an outburst of despair, but patiently to start his work over again, once more without firm hope. *Avos'* became not merely a part of the Russian attitude towards labor, but a part of the Russian attitude towards life.

> The Russian particle *avos'* briefly sums up the topic that permeates all Russian language and Russian culture, i.e., the topic of fate, of inability to control events, of living in a world which cannot be understood and cannot be controlled by rational consciousness. If everything is alright for us, this is certainly not because we mastered some new knowledge or skill, and subordinated the surrounding world to our control, but simply because we have been fortunate. Life is unpredictable and uncontrol-

lable, and there is no need to rely too much on one's mental capacities, logic, or rational activity.⁵

The tendency to think in terms of *avos'* is certainly a constituent part of the Russian way of thinking and life, but that does not mean that it is highly valued; according to the Russian proverb, "those who rely on *avos'* will have much opportunity for fasting."⁶

According to the brilliant Russian philosopher and historian of culture F. A. Stepun,

> [T]he labor of creating the powerful Russian state was certainly immense, but it was never labor as hard-working Europeans understand it and as Russians now also understand the word; for it was not stubborn, slow, consistent work, with systematic conquest of the resistance of materials by means specifically invented for this.
>
> When reading any Russian history one gets the impression that the Russian people has not so much battled with the land, as fearlessly taken it captive. So this *land, taken captive*, has worked for the Russian people, and there was no need for Russians to really work on it. The constant outflow from Russia in colonization, and steady influx onto grain-growing plains which must be settled and sown with haste, deprived Russians of both the necessity and possibility of careful, thorough working of the soil. In one way or another the people developed virgin land; without a clear instinct of state construction they took from it only as much as was needed to give it meaning and justify further expansion. Thus the centuries revealed an uncultured, barbarous style of managing the land, and with it a careless attitude towards the beloved soil. The land beyond one's own borders was regarded as a source of food as much as that already under the plough."⁷

Peasants worked on expanses of virgin land not their own in service to wide-ranging state plans for appropriating new territories and resettling the population. This policy began early, with the reign of Andrei Bogoliubskii (ca. 1111–74), and his immediate successors, who strengthened the northeast of Russia. However, the peasant was not only a co-worker of the state but also its opponent, for peasants escaped from state oppression to free lands and developed these, until once again the state overtook them; and their grandchildren renewed

---

⁵ A. Vezhbutskaia, M. A. Krongauz, and E. V. Paducheva, *Iazyk. Kul'tura. Poznanie* [Language. Culture. Knowledge] (Moscow: Russkie slovari, 1996), 79.

⁶ "*Kto avos'nichaet, tot i postnichaet.*"

⁷ F. A. Stepun, "Mysli o Rossii" [Thoughts about Russia], *Novyi mir*, no. 6 (1991): 221–22.

the search for new virgin lands. Although this does not justify negative management habits, it does help explain them; we should not look to an inborn tendency to lazy ways, but an ancient craving of the Russian people to live in freedom on free land, and an aspiration of the state to acquire new territories.

Labor and the Russian View of the World

According to historical developments, the eastern Slavs spread themselves out especially on the East European plains. V. V. Veidle has remarked that

> [T]he first fact of Rusian history is that of the Russian plain, and its impetuous expanses. With its wide-flung waves of endless expanse, the boundless land was much more fully an embodiment of infinity than the sea, for the seas still have a shore, and there are other farther shores to which a Columbus or Sinbad have sailed. But the land was like an infinity: land, and yet more land without end, not attracting anyone to any specific goal, expressing only its own infinity. Russian expanses call on one to travel, to wander, and spread about in them, rather than search for any new countries and new affairs among strange peoples; hence no translation of the word *prostor* (scope, spaciousness) itself can be given; it is colored with a feeling which can hardly be understood by a foreigner, and which explains why the West European world, broken up and partitioned, may appear cramped to the Russian. This is why the Russian understanding of freedom is so different from the Western one, for it is not the right to construct what is yours and to affirm yourself, but the right to escape without any affirmation and without constructing anything.[8]

No matter how far Slavic peoples migrated to the north and east, no matter how much the Russian land was enlarged, it still seemed endless, without a furthest boundary in the world. This *feeling of the vastness of inhabited space* left a deep imprint on the Russian spiritual outlook.

> Such a height, a height up to the skies,
> Such a depth, the depth of the ocean,
> A wide expanse throughout all the land,
> Deep are the pools in the Dnepr river.

The ancient Russian transferred the breadth, expanse, and sweep which he perceived and valued in nature to both the deeds of human hands and to spiritual life.

---

[8] Cited in E. V. Barabanov, "Rossiia i Zapad, vzgliad izdaleka" [Russian and the West, a glance from afar], *Voprosy filosofii*, no. 10 (1991): 58.

Let us listen carefully to Russian folklore: what is it that the Russian soul longs for in our epic tales and fables? It is unrestricted freedom (*volia volnaia*). How does it amuse itself? With dashing boldness, sweeping and unrestrained. At times the Russian soul, throwing its weight around, knows no limits, and proceeds to the point of forgetfulness. And this characterizes every event, both at work and in the wild revelry of celebration.

Both positive and negative consequences of the sweeping character of Russian attitudes to labor were noted by Dostoevskii; he compared it with German attitudes. In Germany

> everyone, or at least the vast majority, accept their status just as it is, regarding it calmly, without envy or suspicion. Even so, labor that is established and constructed over the centuries is attractive for its well-founded methods. Everyone knows how to approach their work and master it fully, since it has been assigned almost from the day of one's birth. Here everyone knows their occupation, but they also know nothing except their occupation.[9]

The expanse of the Russian plain gives an opportunity (as Veidle observed correctly) "to escape without affirming or building anything." Even if it nourishes a dream about speedy escape, it has done little from time immemorial to assist the Russian spirit to consolidate a habit of bringing work which has been started to full completion. Instead of bringing to fulfilment results already acquired, Russians have long preferred satisfaction with what is already attained, and amusing the soul with thoughts of new ventures. Finding these, they leave behind previous tasks and fling themselves with zeal into a new undertaking. That is why from ancient times our Russian history is full of gaps, always striving to break away from its roots, with even an enthusiasm for such destruction. But afterwards Russians find it difficult to recover.

Among the peculiarities of the natural landscape Stepun particularly emphasized the feature of "formlessness." From ancient times it left a firm impression on Russian spirituality, and its traces can easily be found in contemporary Russian life. "Every denial of form," Stepun writes,

> every struggle against form conceals within itself two internally opposed but nevertheless often connected principles: 1) the principle of mystic confirmation of the Absolute that is beyond any existing form and cannot be fully represented in any shape; and 2) the principle of barbarous rejection of all forms of cultural creativity. It is characteristic for the basic theme of the Russian landscape, for the theme of the Central Russian

---

[9] Dostoevskii, *Dnevnik pisatelia*, 279.

plain pouring out into Asia, that both principles resound in it with equal power.

A sparse network of railways and mainroads, a rare scattering of towns and country estates built of stone, with endless cart-tracks, now swampy, now dusty, with trembling humpbacked bridges which one needs to drive around by fording or wading, with long-legged thatch-roofed *izbas*, with peeling paint, made of unshelled pole-fences; here everything is placed at random (*avos'*), rutted and beaten, everything is put together one way or another, just as it appears, stacked and maintained from material at hand. There is an amazing unity of style based on total submission of the form of the living structure to the formlessness of the settled land; but there is also barbarous lack of inclination to culture, and pure Russian obstinacy in its age-old squalor. Yes, squalor! It may be the most exact definition of Russian village life. But it is, no doubt, necessary to remember that the national conception of squalor and ugliness expresses a keenly felt dialectical link between expulsion from the world and salvation in eternity, between visible abandonment by God and mysterious concealment in Him, between a barbarous cynic negation of the forms and laws of normal life and a mystic negation of creativity as the highest form of a life of spiritual intensity.[10]

The category of labor finds spiritual depth and metaphysical foundation in a relationship with a worldview. Its peculiar characteristics are defined by interconnection with the spheres of spiritual experience as these rise above the practical side of life; we may refer to them as "expansiveness" (*razmashistost'*) and "struggle-against-form" (*formoborchestvo*).

Labor as a Value of Russian Culture

From earliest times Slavs excelled not only in endurance in labor but also in skilled work of high quality. From an early period the technologies of the treatment of clay and metal which they mastered were of a high quality for that period. The Slavs used tempered iron and knew the technique of welding, expressed in "the words *nado*, 'an appliqué, a construction, a strip of metal welded on the sharpened blade of an iron tool' (cf. Serbo-Croatian *nado* 'steel', Slovenian *nado* 'applied strip of steel'); also the verb *naditi* 'to weld, to rivet' … demonstrating

---

[10] Stepun, "Mysli o Rossii," 220–21.

the rather early acquaintance of Slavs with a technology which in the future would provide the high quality of Slavic cold-steel."[11]

But at the same time it is well known that in the natural sciences and technical innovation Russia has lagged behind Western Europe considerably in modern times. How can this be explained? Comparing "uninventive," "passive" Russians with "active" Europeans distinguishing themselves in science and industry, Dostoevskii wisely noted:

> But while science was being invented there, passive Russians showed themselves to be active in a way no less inventive: they were creating a kingdom, and *consciously* creating it as a unity. For all of a thousand years they beat off cruel enemies who otherwise would have invaded Europe. Russians colonized the farthest regions of the endless motherland. They defended and strengthened outlying districts under their control so well that we, a modern cultured people, only add to it by undermining their accomplishment.[12]

An industrious approach, not only in tilling the soil, but in any affair, was considered highly virtuous by all sectors of traditional Russian society. Vladimir Monomakh begins the story of his life saying, "And now I'll tell you, my children, about my labor, how hard I have worked in traveling and on hunting trips since I was thirteen years old." And he finishes his narration with a sense of fulfilment of duty, with the words, "There were eighty and three great marches in all, but the rest of the lesser ones I can't even remember.... Whatever I asked my boy to do I also did myself, in war and while hunting, by night and day, in heat and hard frost, not letting myself take even a moment of rest."

In his *Precept* Vladimir Monomakh is careful to give these reminders:

> Don't be idle in your house, but see to everything yourself; don't rely upon the "*tiun*" [servant, household manager—A. Z.] or boy, so that those who visit you will mock neither your house nor your dinner. When you are at war, don't be idle; don't rely on the commander of the army. Don't indulge yourself in drinking, eating, or sleeping. Set watchmen yourself, and at night when you have posted guards, lay down near your warriors, and get up early. Don't remove your weapons in haste, too lazy to look around, for you know how suddenly a man can be killed.

---

[11] A. F. Zhuravlev, "Material'naia kul'tura drevnikh slavian po dannym praslavianskoi leksiki" [Material culture of the early Slavs, based on early Slavic words], in *Ocherki istorii kul'tury slavian* [Studies in the history of Slavic culture] (Moscow: "Indrik," 1996), 138.

[12] Dostoevskii, *Dnevnik pisatelia*, 206.

The everyday life of a man in Ancient Russia (*Rus'*) was filled with labor. In his thorough investigation of the lifestyle of ancient Russia D. Prozorovskii notes that "the activity of the day began with the morning's divine service in the depths of the night. In his will Vladimir Monomakh advises that the sun should not find one still in bed."[13] The day began with matins well before the rising of the sun, although the time fixed differed in different centuries and parts of Russia. In the fourteenth century church bells for matins rang at two o'clock in the morning in summer, and in winter at three o'clock; this corresponds approximately to the time for beginning daily work. According to ancient Russian calculations of time the proper beginning of the "day" fell at approximately four or five hours after midnight (for Moscow it was at four o'clock, in Novgorod at five o'clock). After breakfast peasants left home to get to their daily affairs, artisans started work, employees in service hurried to their duties, and in Moscow boyars arrived at the courtyard of the ruler. Markets opened for business in the second hour of the "day," at six to seven o'clock by present-day reckoning.

From ten to eleven o'clock they had dinner, after which "midday" began, a time of rest after dinner until one or two o'clock in the afternoon. That time was usually spent in sleeping. Russian beliefs even had a notion of "*poludnitsa*," an evil female spirit putting to death anyone working at midday. "Sleeping at midday was instituted by God," Vladimir Monomakh declares in the *Precept*. After this, work lasted until the evening; at nightfall ancient Russians took supper and went to bed. Anyone who could attended afternoon vespers, the afternoon service which began at about the tenth or eleventh hour of the "day" (i.e., at about three–four o'clock) in the 13th century; in the 17th century it began much later. Thus, on the 30th of May, 1685, evening church bells sounded at the fourteenth hour of the "day."

Labor as a Category of Religious Consciousness

From pagan times labor was sanctified by the performance of religious rites, enacted according to a calendar and performed daily at home. Christianity maintained this ancient tradition; it is well known that traditional Russian culture required the Orthodox to pray at holy icons before beginning any important affair, to ask for help and goodwill from heavenly powers, cross themselves, and only after that get down to work. *In the traditional Russian worldview labor had its practical importance, and was also a constituent part of religious life.*

Convincing evidence of the great significance given to labor in ancient Russian culture is found in the reference to saints and heroes who accomplished

---

[13] D. Prozorovskii, "O starinnom russkom schislenii chasov" [On the ancient Russian counting of hours], in *Trudy II-ogo arkheologicheskogo s″ezda v Sankt-Peterburge* [Proceedings of the second archaeological conference in St. Petersburg] (St. Petersburg, 1881), 2: 172.

exploits of faith as "laborers" (*trudniki*); their spiritual life of holiness was called "toiling" or "labor" (*trudnichestvo, trud*). Kirill Turovskii describes the image of the monk in terms of a hard-working bee, astonishing everyone with its wisdom. With such strongly pronounced religious overtones the Russian conception of labor acquired the character of a category of religious consciousness.

The Orthodox Church, however, did not preach any religious motives for economic labor. Responding to worldly cares with reproach, they quoted Jesus' words: "Therefore I say to you, do not worry about your soul, what you will eat or drink, or about your body, what you will wear. Is not life more important than food, and the body more important than clothing? Look at the birds of the heavens, who neither sow nor reap, nor gather into barns, and yet your heavenly Father feeds them. Are you not of far more value than they?" (Matthew 6.25–26). Religious enthusiasts implemented these words literally in their mode of life; the phenomenon of "*iurodstvo*" (God's fool) became more widespread in Russia than anywhere else. Meanwhile very few laymen, monks, and not even a Father-Superior was free of economic concern. Although we learn from hagiographical tales that Sergei of Radonezh set his hopes on miraculous help from the heavenly Father, they also give us reason to claim that the aroma of pine shavings is clearly noticeable in the fragrance of his holiness.

Nevertheless, *during the Russian Middle Ages, and even much later, Orthodox theology remained silent on the high religious value of labor*. Church writers preferred to speak about the saving power of almsgiving, thus focusing on the distribution of welfare rather than its creation. Of course, Orthodox thought did not altogether avoid the theme of creative economic activity, as we see from the life of Joseph Volotskii (or Volokamskii) and his concern for the strength of practical life, with the monastery at its center; according to Volotskii the Church had a responsibility for its children. However, like much ancient Russian theology, this Father-Superior gave a more practical, rather than theoretical expression of his concern.

A serious beginning for an Orthodox theology of labor can be found in the Domostroi. Sil'vestr's treatment of early codes of practical wisdom did stress the religious meaning of everyday work as a means by which the pious Christian could "save his soul ... serve his lord, and please God." Although the intrinsic religious value of labor was not yet presented, and the precept is directed to the moral acquisition of wealth, it is important that the commandment of "righteous labor" in the *Domostroi* was equivalent in value to that of pleasing God with almsgiving.

There was no further consistent development of such an initiative of Sil'vestr, to express the intrinsic religious value of labor within Orthodoxy. In Russia we find no development of an ethics of labor such as Protestants had, nor a teaching like the Catholic "theology of labor."

As a result socialists were the first to work out the idea of the value of labor for Russian consciousness. In 1905 Sergei Bulgakov affirmed the socialist "apotheosis of labor as a basic moral principle, because it puts the sanctity of labor at the foundation of the economic system."[14] Christian socialism had no strong roots in pre-revolutionary Orthodox Russia; thinkers or enthusiasts ready to preach a Christian "sanctity of labor" were a rare exception in the church community.

At the beginning of the 20th century the common Orthodox people still handed socialists-agitators over to the police; among them the predominant conception of labor was no more Christian than at the time of St. Vladimir. There is considerable ethnographical evidence to support this. Among important religious motivations for labor we find reference to fortune telling, superstition, and pagan rite.

Ordinary Idleness and Mythological Idleness

Initiatives for individual labor, thus, did not come from strong Christian motivation for dynamic ecomomic labor; add to that the slavish dependence of the village population, and dictates of the state burdening all social levels with the weight of government service. These added a sense of compulsion and innocent suffering to the common Russian conception of labor. Yet all this does not meant that idleness became the secret dream of the culture, or that an ordinary loafer and cheat came to play the role of a romantic hero.

In his *One Day in the Life of Ivan Denisovich* A. Solzhenitsyn has shown convincingly how a thirst for work, even labor under the lash and without personal gain, left a deep imprint on the Russian soul. Who does not know provincial men of elderly or middle age who at the end of the work week one and all virtually "topple onto" their kitchen gardens; there is nothing that can break them away from it, even if the work has no profit? "They are resting."

People in towns and villages love to have a true rest from work, and in earlier times festivities were often celebrated for days and even weeks in rural areas. This topic should be examined separately. *But for Russian traditional culture celebration as idleness for the sake of idleness and indulgence of laziness, has always been categorized negatively.*

The lazy man was the object of contempt and scorn. The laziness of monks in tending to church services was censured with great indignation. Vladimir Monomakh admonished against idleness in practical work; Russian folklore and tra-

---

[14] S. N. Bulgakov, "Neotlozhnaia zadacha (O soiuze khristianskoi politiki)" [Urgent tasks (On Christian political union)], in *Khristianskii sotsializm: Spory o sud'bakh Rossii* [Christian socialism: Debates on the fate of Russia], ed. V. N. Akulinin (Novosibirsk: "Nauka," Sibirskoe otdelenie, 1991), 35.

ditional literature too is filled with reproach against ordinary laziness. Witness the sharp-witted speech of an old Russian sage:

> My beloved friends and brothers, do not become like the idle slave – do not sleep too long, do not lie around too long, get up early, go to bed late!... Lying around will do you no good, will not deliver you from grief, nor bring you salvation, for it does not move God as does entreaty, nor does it purify you from your sins; it does not gain you honor and glory, or give you beautiful clothes to wear, provide for honeyed drinks to consume, or sweet meals to eat! If you are a fool, a lazy one and sluggish, you will never have the reputation of a good man, and master in your own home, and you will never see yourself in a position of authority, nor will you ever be in the good graces of God, or of your lord and ruler. Moreover, misfortune hits the shins of the idle man, and debt pushes him at the neck, poverty has taken up residence in his house, and disease always lies on his shoulders, despondency on his head, and mockery in his beard; his desires are just words, but there is a bitter taste on his teeth, grief on his tongue, and sorrow in his throat, a dryness in his liver, hunger in his stomach, and indigence has built its nest in his purse.
>
> Such a man who is lazy and loves to lie about is not a master in his house, is not a husband for his wife, is not a father for his children, and good men do not associate with him. He is too lazy to live in a village, nor does he belong in the *posad*.[15] They do not let him live in the *selo* [large village], nor is there a place for him in town. He walks up and down the street, peeps in the windows like a hungry dog, and scratches himself on corners like a dirty pig. Idleness adheres to him and hangs like a backpack on his shoulders, and poverty has already built a nest in his bosom; sorrow hangs on his hips, and boredom has tied his legs.
>
> Oh, such misfortune! Laziness attached herself to him like a beloved wife to her husband. And often he sighs, but does not want to give her up. Cursed devils are his beloved friends, long sleep his beloved father, a nasty limp his mother; he loves obstinacy and wilfulness, and hangs onto them, afraid of losing them as if they were his brother and sister. Reproach, abuse, and dishonor which they heap on him he accepts, like snow falling down on his head. And, accursed, he becomes accustomed to living from someone else's labor, as if he were a worm eating away at a cabbage. Because of his great misery he sleeps too much, and during his sleep devils present him with dreams and visions. Waking up from

---

[15] Designates the area around the town where merchants and craftsmen live. *Trans.*

sleep, he gives in to dreams which bring him even greater loss; he inherits endless grief! May the Lord God save us from that by the prayers of His Virgin Mother and all the saints. Always, today, at the hour of our death, and through ages of ages. Amen.[16]

The anonymous sage gives an eloquent and exhaustively expressed repudiation of idleness. The language overflows with elements of popular humor, and bears the stamp of a national attitude towards idleness. It is hardly necessary to develop the theme "Laziness as the mother of evil" any further. Such literary wisdom says it all. And given such a concerted effort of repudiating idleness in the various levels of Russian society, it is doubtful that an "everyday" kind of loafer could become a typical figure, or laziness the norm for a traditional way of life.

What then about the saying, "We have no Russian tales at all about hard and creative work, but many tales about wonderful presents to a hero; just look at the tale of Emelia-the-Fool." How should we regard this lazy-bone folk hero who obviously "exists not by work, but only by a miracle"?[17]

E. N. Trubetskoi took these questions seriously. In his work *"Another Kingdom" and Its Seekers in the Russian Popular Tale* the writer comes close to agreeing that "in the Russian tale sympathy with laziness and theft borders on an apotheosis of the lazy-bone thief."[18] He is well aware of Emelia-the-Fool and his stealing a feather from the firebird; however, he refrains from direct interpretation of this magic tale with its motifs of laziness and theft as expressions of "Russian character." When he explains basic principles of the tale in terms of Russian spirituality, Trubetskoi especially emphasizes "the lower" level, and "vulgar feeling for life."

> Here is the source of the vulgar, earthly tale, for which the "other kingdom," which is sought, functions as an ideal fulfilment of satisfaction. Separating "vulgar earthly" tales into a special group, and distinguishing the "vulgar feeling of life" from Russian spirituality as a whole, the philosopher tells us clearly that "such an understanding of life characterizes only the lower, everyday ground-floor level of a tale, where magic as such does not yet start."[19]

---

[16] "Pouchenie k lenivym" [Address to the idle], in *Krasnorechie Drevnei Rusi (XI–XVII vv.)* [Early Russian Oratory (16th–17th centuries)], ed. T. V. Chertoritskaia (Moscow: Sovetskaia Rossiia, 1987), 303–04.

[17] Egorov, "*Ocherki po istorii russkoi kul'tury XIX veka*," 60.

[18] E. N. Trubetskoi, "Inoe tsarstvo i ego iskateli v russkoi narodnoi skazke" ["Another kingdom" and its seekers in the Russian popular tale], *Literaturnaia ucheba*, no. 2 (1990): 102.

[19] Trubetskoi, "Inoe tsarstvo," 101.

In spite of such a careful approach, Trubetskoi was not able to avoid sociological simplification of folklore, especially in writing of "the ideal of theft" embedded in the tale, and the "social utopia" of people of the lowest kind of spirituality. Trubetskoi's exaggeration of the tale's rapprochement with reality is understandable, for he wrote the work during the Civil War. That is why he was led to say things that were certainly true:

> With our own eyes we have seen how the Utopia of the idler and thief, and the dream kingdom of the fugitive soldier has been realized. "Three-story houses" and other people's purses have been seized; printing presses have already long brought to life thoughts of a bottomless wallet, fast-running jack-boots and flying carpets that give a fleeting glimpse all around. Thieves and fugitive soldiers are everywhere. The deserter successfully becomes "the highest minister" and rules the realm in place of the tsar.[20]

Modern research on folklore has advanced our comprehension of motifs of idleness and theft in Russian fable. In this connection we must mention the thorough work of the Tartu-Moscow semiotic school which published, in its serial editions, some of B. F. Egorov's reflections on the Russian character. This research rightly considers the magic fairy-tale with characters like the notorious Emelia-the Fool (Ivan-the-Fool, etc.), where the hero exists "not by work, but by a miracle," to be the godmother of the mythological tradition.

Moral categories of idleness and theft lose their normal force in the magic fairy-tale. Instead we find mythological motifs of miraculous action or non-action, miraculous acquisition of the firebird's feather, the Herculean horse, the enchantress-fiancée, or the miraculous gift of the pike-fish.[21] An unusual idleness, exaggerated by narrative embellishment, signals the hero's participation in an unreal world, and hints at his relationship with fantastic events and creatures. The real "fairy-tale" begins when, in ways pre-determined by myth, the hero acquires the capacity for magic (i.e., he "steals"); demonstrating an agility unusual

---

[20] Ibid., 105.

[21] The stories referred to here are all traditional Russian tales and typically involve the character Emelia. The stealing of the firebird's feather refers to Ershov's traditional, well-known fairytale "Konëk-gorbunok" ("The Horse with a Hump"). The enchantress-fiancée also represents a traditional theme characterizing fairytales about "Vasilisa Prekrasnaia" (Vasilisa the Beautiful) or "Tsarevna-liagushka" (the Queen-frog), in which the frog on the road is converted into a fiancée who can give the hero miraculous help, for instance, in winning a competition among three brothers; the stories typically end with troubles caused by monsters (like Koshchei or Zmei, the snake), and the hero must rescue the girl from the kingdom of the monster. In the story of the gift of the pike-fish, Emelia, a good but lazy chap, after catching the pike-fish, sympathizes with it when it asks him to let it go; once he does so the pike proceeds to make all his wishes come true. *Trans.*

for common people, he next resolves his destiny as best he can, to the disgrace of hardened pragmatics. Fairy tales maintain the ancient idea that magic exceeds what is ordinary; they appreciate mythical idleness as a prerequisite for magic activity.

It is useful to note that the nonactivity of the "utopia of riches" or the "robber's ideal" finds expression not only in magic fairy tales but in all of Russian folklore. Having once discovered "worldly vulgarity," Trubetskoi also quickly discerned national mockery at the lazy man's dream of those fairy-tales portraying "the possibility of not working at all, yet eating and drinking sweets, and wearing clean clothes." A good example is the tale of the man who saw a stove full of food when he walked up into the sky. "The fairy-tale foresees the tragicomic finale of the illusory rise, which inescapably leads to his fall," Trubetskoi notes. Not having found his way down to earth, the man began his descent from the sky by a rope of twisted cobweb, which soon came to an end; and so the man who loved to eat without paying for it, fell down from the heights and landed in a swamp. The Russian philosopher sums up the moral lesson of the fairy-tale as follows:

> This is the image of the man [*muzhik*] who was deceived by the sweet dream, and could not find a safe return from utopia to reality. His lot was to dangle between heaven and earth on the fantastic rope made of a fine cobweb; the inescapable end of his journey was the marshy dirty swamp.[22]

Leisure in a Traditional World-View

All use of time not devoted to labor is called leisure. But we must ask: should every kind of idleness be considered blameworthy by public opinion? Representatives of traditional Russian culture were familiar with different kinds of leisure. *Understood as laziness, it has been blamed resolutely by traditional culture. But leisure has also been treated quite differently as a condition of spending a special period of time, as a feast-day.*

The time of the feast-day is time without labor; but participants are not reproached, even though the simplest of everyday work is not done: the floor is not swept, and the oven not lit. Even today aspects of folk culture still forbid engaging in any type of work (like housekeeping) on specified holidays. Why is repudiation of regular activities not only encouraged, but even dictated on special holidays?

The basic reason for such repudiation of work is found in archaic views about the structure of the world, many of which are still maintained in traditional Russian cul-

---

[22] Ibid., 104–05.

ture. This archaic picture of the world consists of *two parts,* one of them occupied by the life of people on this earth. Inhabitants of the other are extraordinary non-human creatures, gods, spirits, and ancestors who have left the earthly life. This second part represents "*another*" world. Habitual existence for inhabitants of the respective "worlds" takes its course, but their ways differ absolutely. While life on earth consists of everyday work, that "other" world is not burdened by labor; gods and spirits from time immemorial have been characterized by the use of inherent power and might, and require no labor to accomplish what they wish. Ancestors who have finished the course of life honorably are also in a state of bliss in that region of wonderful abundance.

In an interesting literary fragment from the early 10th century Ibn-Fadlan gives a famous description of the funeral of a noble Russian; during the funeral ceremony the girl doomed to death looks down over the ritual gates into that "other" world, and tells participants of the rite that she sees her dead father and mother, her relatives, and her master sitting "in a garden which is beautiful and green."

Under normal conditions, communication between these "worlds" would not affect the basis of human existence. But at some specified periods of time, according to traditional views, the mutual presence of the two worlds is quite obvious, and their correspondence more intense. When in close contact with unusual non-human creatures ruling over the course of human affairs, the person must divert soul and body from routines of everyday concerns, free mind and heart from petty cares, and devote himself to the special business of communication with these creatures. Customarily, food was prepared for these creatures, making them a present in the form of a sacrifice; they must be placated with prayer, ritual song, or dance. Human beings themselves also became participants in the sacrificial meal, and thus the abundance of food and consumption of intoxicating drinks were important parts of the festival.

Leisure as Category of Religious Consciousness

The essential concept of ritual leisure was the idea of communicating with unusual non-human creatures. Since the archaic consciousness regarded these powerful non-human beings as sacred, the time of communication with them was also a *holy time.* Indeed, Eastern Slavs used notions such as "holy," "holy time," and "holy days" to signify the meaning of these holidays.

Anything that distracted from communication with these *holy beings,* whether earthly concerns or economic problems, could be judged in terms of contempt, causing wrath and trouble. For example, among the Slavs there was a belief that cripples are born to parents who pay no attention to the work that is forbidden on holidays: "the day is holy and our work is asleep."

This does not mean that people of a traditional culture experienced the holidays with only bright and joyful feelings. The concept of the "holiness" of holidays meant that these days would be filled with the particular power which could imbue earthly life with the power of grace; but such power could also turn out to have ruinous consequences. According to traditional views, during the time when the "other" world is opened to "this" world, non-human creatures who communicate with human beings may either be dangerous and hostile to human beings, or bring them good. The conviction that holidays "might be "holy, bright, pure, and good" on the one hand, but also "evil, foul, dangerous, unchristened, terrifying, burdensome, crooked, empty, and useless" on the other,"[23] arose from the intertwinement of Christianity with pagan religion in ancient Russian culture. In the East Slavic tradition, for example, there was a firmly rooted belief that on holy days, and especially the winter holiday, extending from Christmas Eve (6 January, New Style) till Epiphany (19 January), the souls of dead relatives would come to the house; a special meal was prepared for them. They were awaited cautiously, "met" with all due respect, and after being "fed," were "seen off" with all piety, in the hope that these souls would be satisfied with this reception and would not bring any harm.

Ethnographic research into traditional Russian culture of the 19th and early 20th century likewise reveals a noteworthy peculiarity. Those boys who were to go into the army were liberated from work several weeks before departure; village inhabitants allowed them to do what was usually strictly forbidden: to go about all day well-dressed, walk around in company from house to house, to drink without limit, and to fight in the streets. Why did the peasant community not block such endless revelry? It can be explained by the fact that recruits were considered as those who have temporarily fallen outside of their normal condition; they no longer belonged to the normal peasant world, nor had they yet joined the world of soldiers. In this "abnormal" transitional period, they were allowed to loaf about idly. *Idleness* for the traditional Russian culture is *an abnormal, temporary condition. The normal condition is one of labor.*

---

[23] S. M. Tolstaia, "Prazdniki" [Feasts], in *Slavianskaia mifologiia: Entsiklopedicheskii slovar'* [Slavic mythology: Encyclopedic dictionary], ed. V. Ia. Petrukhin (Moscow: Ellis Lak, 1995), 323.

Civil Society: A Religious Assessment of the Problem[1]

Evgenii Borisovich Rashkovskii

Although the scope of the present article does not allow for a separate historical examination of the religious aspect of civil society, international publications carry a wide range of historiographical documents in which this problem plays an important role.[2] And this is not without reason.

The religious "issue" is of a very special kind. It is connected with vital and urgent issues which actually exist in the destiny of every human being and every community, but can be considered through strict rational interpretation only with difficulty. The subjects of religious thought cannot be clearly opened or discussed in normal discourse because the "last things" (*to eschaton*) cannot be embraced by the theoretical and logical conventions of an "earthbound" mind.

The integral presence of these subjects in human thought and experience can easily be discovered in every area of the social and human sciences, but again can only be described and interpreted with difficulty, and conditionally. So the primary task of this article is an interpretation of the immutable and elusive presence of spiritual reality in what appears to be an especially earthbound problem, that of civil society.[3] But allow me, first of all, in connection with the chosen topic, to propose some general perspectives on this problem.

---

[1] E. B. Rashkovskii, "Grazhdanskoe obshchestvo: Religioznoe izmerenie problemy," *Put'*, no. 7 (1995): 130–53. In its present translation this article has been somewhat abbreviated.

[2] The most detailed historiographical work discussing the religious aspect in particular is that of A. Seligman, *The Idea of Civil Society* (New York: Free Press, 1992).

[3] The different approaches of contemporary scholars in the social humanitarian sciences dealing with the religious aspect of civil society are given in Rashkovskii, "Tretii mir – Rossiia – Izrael" [The Third World – Russia – Israel], *IE&IR* (journal of the Institute for Economics and International Relations [MEiMO: Institut mirovoi ekonomiki i mezhdunarodnykh otnoshenii], no. 3 (1993); as well as in his "Tserkov', gosudarstvo, grazhdanskoe obshchestvo" [Church, state, civil society], *IE&IR*, no. 4 (1994).

Helleman, Wendy, ed. *The Russian Idea: In Search of a New Identity*. Bloomington, IN: Slavica, 2004, 113–26.

1. Some Premises[4]

Difficulties in the discussion of civil society reflect not only the logical complexity of human thought, but also the complexity of real paths of history. And it is no coincidence that renewed discussion of civil society has been connected with attempts to comprehend a series of anti-communist revolutions in Eastern Europe.[5] In spite of socio-cultural immaturity, the societies of these countries outgrew ideologies of socialistic change and the atheistic pressure accompanying them. They made the transition even without deep comprehension of the principles of personal dignity, of law-regulated society, or social support; nor were they able to combine these concepts in practice, although in the final analysis they cannot to be ignored, and can be connected only with difficulty.

Today three religious sources of the modern idea of civil society – Catholic, Protestant, and the secular liberal-emancipatory tradition (including the social-democratic tradition which it has produced) – act and interact in our world, in the East, West, North, and South. Sometimes they act in different and even unpredictable combinations.[6]

But it is astonishing that all three sources of modern understanding of civil society reflect and also partly share three fundamental ideas; furthermore, these ideas, strictly speaking, cannot be demonstrated, and are accepted primarily by intuition, or on faith. They are:

---

[4] In an introductory survey, not translated here because it depends heavily on analysis of Seligman's *Idea of Civil Society*, Rashkovskii emphasizes the conditioned, historical character of civil society, and delineates three basic principles (equality before the law, protection of property, and irreducible freedom of the person), thus giving clear evidence of the weight of responsibility carried by the individual in the context of civil society; it differs from a traditional society in which power is connected with property, the corporate body is more important than the individual, and one's position in society is prescribed by birth and status. In his historical survey Rashkovskii shows that while Catholicism allows a degree of freedom for civil society, the Protestant Reformation, encouraging a more privatized sense of the covenant between God and man, gave a clear impetus for emancipatory movements in Anglo-Saxon countries (of the 17th and 18th centuries), for what he calls the "synthesis of ideas of sacral agreement within the human soul, and rational agreement in the sphere within which people interact." In Europe it was Kant who based his view of the irreducible moral sphere on freedom as it characterized civil society; from that perspective Hegel and Marx appear regressive. Continental European socialism did contribute values of the dignity of human life, individually and as a group, and of social justice. *Trans.*

[5] This too has been thoroughly documented by Seligman in his *Idea of Civil Society* (see n. 2 above).

[6] Cf. Rashkovskii, "Puti demokratii na iskhode XX stoletiia: Mirovoi kontekst" [The ways of democracy at the end of the 20th century: In world context], *IE&IR*, no. 10 (1993).

- the presence of an immanent mind in the world;
- the presence of an immanent solidarity in society;
- the presence of an immanent autonomy in man.

None of these ideas are empirically founded, or "scientific." Instead, they are the objects of a particular worldview and of faith, and seem to be connected with a deep, philogenetic inner human experience which can hardly be expressed. Scholarship attracted to an unconditioned "scientific" character finds it much easier to prove exactly the opposite, namely the connection of social reality with antagonism, intrigue, and enmity. Extreme concentration on something elementary and base in man often reveals a powerful factor for cultural degradation.[7] And one might argue for the desirability and social necessity of scientific forms at the foundation of society's inalienable need to share in rationality, mutual interdependence, and flexible, versatile interconnections. But rationality of one kind is just not enough for these three ideas. Because in the real acts and processes of historical and cultural creativity, these ideas arise not only as objects of empirical and theoretical understanding, but also as objects of belief. And we understand belief as Vladimir Solov'ev did, in the "good sense" of life.[8] Moreover, this life is seriously infected with sin, lack of communication, and alienation. Under such conditions we discover that in some respects the existence of the other person, the existence of connections between people, the existence of society, the world, and even my own existence, are objects of faith, especially when we look closely look from a psychological and epistemological angle. The reality of these objects is hard to prove, but can easily be guessed at, if we consider their opposites. Nonrecognition of these objects, or lack of belief in their existence often indicates a psychologically split personality, ranging from a comparatively light form of autism, to full clinical breakdown.

Not only in psychological, but also in socio-historical terms can these values of faith, once again, hardly be proven (in the sense of a strict and complete "scientific" demonstration), but only be guessed from consideration of the opposites. Lack of faith in that deep and inexpressible "good sense" of life may reveal itself as aggressive non-acceptance, or valiant appropriation by zealots of an ideology which regards only itself as being in the right; in either case it appears as

---

[7] The liberal mentality has often been accused, not without reason, of misunderstanding the value of the human subconscious layers of emotions; actually, the success of psychological analysis in the 20th century is connected with attempts to compensate for and correct the historical weakness of liberalism. Cf. P. Roazen, *Freud: Political and Social Thought* (London: Hogarth Press, 1969), 248.

[8] V. S. Solov'ev, *Sochineniia v dvukh tomakh* [Works, in two volumes], ed. A. F. Losev and A. V. Gulyga (Moscow: Izdatel'stvo "Mysl'," 1988), 89.

the presupposition of an extreme human atomization, and so also of a totalitarian hell, whether in its "black" or "red" versions.[9]

The world of values necessarily attracts scientific arguments, but it does not follow them to their conclusion.

This discussion takes us rather far from our chosen topic, into the sphere that Berdiaev called "apophatic sociology."[10] Within the present context of research we must satisfy ourselves with the thought that a moment of faith is inalienably present in the spiritual economy of civil society; when we underestimate it, we risk throwing the whole problem into confusion.

2. "What Belongs to God" and "to Caesar"

Study of its historiography may lead one to think that the concept of civil society is connected particularly with personal rights and freedoms. But that is certainly not the case; we may go even further and state that it is quite wrong. Without consideration of group rights it is impossible to resolve the problems of civil society. This applies not only to highly developed countries of Europe, America, and Japan, where the question of group connections is critical and well-articulated, but also for the majority of the human race, which is non-Western.

When we address the social bases and guarantees of freedom and human dignity, we cannot ignore the freedom and dignity of the group; indeed, the social status of a person is most often realized through identification within groups, social links, and connections. So the question of personal status naturally leads to the issue of the status of political parties, confessions, professional unions, and ethnic, or cultural communities. Nowadays in highly developed societies the question of individual and group rights receives full attention, and focuses not only on those who are organized, active, and enterprising, but also the socially weak, the ill, the aged, the poor, children, people with low social adaptibility, or residents of poor areas.

Let me stress once more the connection between group rights and rights of the person, or "anthropological" rights. The person is not only connected with primordial primary groups (on the basis of blood, neighborhood, or occupation of land), but also tries to express himself in the completely modern context through connections with others, through cooperation in different types of group or cultural events, through interest groups, or through longstanding, formal means of non-utilitarian communication. All this requires investigation and

---

[9] Rashkovskii, "Totalitarizm kak mirovoi fenomen XX veka i sud'by Rossii: Sotsiokul'turnoe izmerenie" [Totalitarianism as a world phenomenon of the 20th century and the fate of Russia: A socio-cultural assessment], *Vostok* [The East], no. 5 (1993).

[10] N. A. Berdiaev, *O rabstve i svobode cheloveka: Opyt personalisticheskoi metafiziki* [Of human slavery and freedom: An essay on personalistic metaphysics], 2nd ed. (Paris: YMCA-Press, 1972).

appropriation of vast moral, organizational, and material resources. And in this connection organized groups, whether or not they like it, have to establish and develop contacts with each other and with the state. The character of these connections depends not so much on the specifics of group and state interests, but on the internal characteristics of group and state institutions. It depends, for example, on the degree of the group's intentions for good (or ill),[11] on the degree of the state's intentions for good (or ill), and its application of law and order.

Development of society means absorption of the person in a multitude of inalienable or chosen socio-cultural connections. In the final analysis, the principle of socio-cultural estrangement, or alienation, is rejected in civil society. But it is not denied vigorously, nor as a matter of necessity. The person must find or create the juncture of group connections for himself or herself. This principle of personal freedom or self-determination, introduced right in the middle of social life, opposes civil society to traditional societies, to those of a half-traditional (authoritarian), and to those of a secondary traditional type (totalitarian).[12] For all three types try to impose a socio-cultural and spiritual status on the human person externally, while civil society takes seriously the human need for socio-cultural and spiritual self-determination.

At this point we must face the question of the religious meaning of civil society, in terms of an external guarantee for the positive freedom of the person's spiritual self-realization in communication with others. According to the American theologian Kent Greenawalt, the problem of the interconnection between civil society and the deeper needs of the believer can be described by means of two mutually opposing premises:

1) "What belongs to God" and "to Caesar," however they might be interconnected in real life, are mutually incompatible, and thus need some distance from each other.

---

[11] I use the terms "good intentions" and "ill intentions" not in the ironical sense common for modern Russian semantics, but in a direct etymological sense, i.e., in the sense of the intent of individuals, groups, or state institutions on deliberate enmity or violence.

[12] In this respect I would like to draw attention to the contemporary Russian philosopher A. A. Ignat'ev, who says that by imposing a strict, external regulation on the inner world of the person or group, thereby repressing the creative scholarly work which is so important for a post-traditional society, societies of a totalitarian-socialist type play a role functionally analogous to that of traditional societies. Cf. Ignat'ev, "Tsennosti nauki i traditsionnoe obshchestvo (sotsiokul'turnye predposylki radikal'nogo politicheskogo diskursa)" [The values of science and traditional society (socio-cultural premises of radical political discussion], *Voprosy filosofii* [Philosophical questions], no. 4 (1991): 26. There is no need at this point to elaborate on the role of strong religious motivation for modern scientific creativity, which also has complex connections with the structures and ethos of civil society.

2) But "what belongs to God" is variously and often deeply projected in different human groups, types, and realities.

It follows from the very specifics of human spirituality that the presence in the world of "what belongs to God" does not imply a complete uniformity of spiritual and practical orientation. Accordingly, the multiplicity of internal human structures and external self-realizations is rooted in the very depth of religious experience.[13]

In developing this position of the American theologian we can state that rejection of this internally defined multiplicity means reduction of the person, the rational, free, and responsible being to the lowly condition of a state slave, a helot, or prisoner (*zek*), or to the condition of "delta" and "epsilon" in Aldous Huxley's anti-utopian work. This also applies to both the very strict traditional societies, and to a secondary, vulgarized totalitarian neo-traditionalism.

Acceptance, on the other hand, means that through the spirituality of one's own nature, and links in the complexity of modern social relationships, the person is condemned, as it were, to the non-idyllic freedom of self-discovery and self-realization. That is the religious correlate of the problem of civil society. And here we can agree with Ralph Darendorf, who points out that through its insistence on the positive aspects of human freedom ("freedom for"), civil society appears to be a kind of "quintessence of freedom."[14]

I anticipate a substantive objection to the above theoretical construction; it can be accused of Christian-Centrism (or Western-Centrism), because the difference between "what belongs to God" and "to Caesar" is closely associated with Christianity and has been more seriously articulated in Western Christian areas. We could respond to this accusation by arguing that any developed religious tradition is based on a differentiation of the sacred and profane, and on the deeply rooted character of what is sacred in the inner experience of the person. And so we may conclude that there are restrictions, whether legal or moral, on powerful earthly ambitions.[15] And these restrictions, combined with the functional complexity of modern society, provide some of the very early and later premises of civil society.

---

[13] K. Greenawalt, "The Role of Religion in Liberal Democracy: Dilemmas and Possible Resolutions," *Journal of Church and State* (Waco, TX), 35: 3 (1993): 513–15.

[14] R. Darendorf, "Moral', instituty i grazhdanskoe obshchestvo" [Morality, institutions and civil society], *Put'*, no. 3 (1993): 191.

[15] Cf. S. N. Eisenstadt, "'Osevaia Epokha': Vozniknovenie transtsentdentnykh videnii i pod"em dukhovnykh soslovii" [The axial era: The emergence of transcendental visions and the rise of clerical classes], in *Orientatsiia – poisk: Vostok v teoriiakh i gipotezakh. Sbornik statei* [Orientation – Research: The East in theories and hypotheses. Collected articles], ed. V. I. Maksimenko and L. I. Reisner (Moscow: Nauka, 1992), 42–62.

One more important observation must be added. Civil society does not commit itself to protecting and developing the religious traditions of particular groups. It only creates the preconditions, so that these groups can maintain or develop their own traditions. It is like some kind of well-intentioned "Caesar" who reveres what belongs to "God" but does not dare invade his territory.

3. Beyond Western Borders

In one way or another, the modern world with its many varieties of civilization cannot ignore an investigation of civil society such as we have initiated with this essay. Let me once again remind the reader of its essence, the problem of a minimum of law and order, and freedom:

1) in the legal sphere as such,
2) in the sphere of economic relationships, and
3) in the sphere of individual spiritual self-determination of the person.

Although the endlessly different forms of civilization and culture in the modern world might suggest different forms of approach, different forms of correlating and subordinating these three problems, the investigation itself remains unchanged. The reader may have guessed already that we are talking about non-Western areas. Indeed, conditions of the modern world allow for universalization not only of the obvious elements of Western science and technology (in areas of knowledge, economy, and government); the investigation of civil society itself has also become universalized. The important question is not *whether* non-Western societies were influenced by this investigation, but *how* they were influenced.

During the course of more that 150 years, imitations or pseudo-constitutional models of civil society were known beyond Europe, North America, or Japan; they appeared somewhat later in Latin America, then at least partly in the Middle East and Liberia, and even in India, thanks to the British colonial administration. But these societies were quite traditional, authoritarian, and hierarchical, and did not have their own socio-cultural conditions for establishing civil society. This meant that they were historically condemned to an evolutional or violent transformation.

Strictly speaking, the process of creating objective conditions for civil society in non-Western countries is a matter of only the very recent past, when an egalitarian view of law and of legal order, linkages appropriate to a market economy, and an understanding of the universal character of human dignity somehow penetrated and got established in these societies.

Naturally, the process of establishing elements of civil society in Third World and post-communist areas cannot, and should not be judged according to the stricter conditions of the European-American tradition. In the Third World one finds a special "cultural ecology" by which modern democratic processes are realized through forms of semi-traditional leadership and self-organization of primary groups: clans, blood relationships, castes, or territorial connections.[16] The dynamics of mutual penetration of traditional-hierarchical and egalitarian-judicial forms of self-organization go so deep that some outstanding experts on the Orient and Africa have found these dynamics even among the most active, developed groups of modern tribal or ethnic societies.[17]

As for establishing the conditions of civil society in Third World countries (especially if we speak of societies of the Eastern hemisphere, with strong blocks having a traditional orientation and concept in their socio-cultural memory), here the process of social self-discovery and realization of the human personality is connected with the following two premises:

1) with the deepest, inalienable connections of the person within the group: the person holds within himself a very strong imprint of its un-mediated connections within the group, while going beyond to the "market" of social ideas, platforms, and communications;[18]
2) with the extremely important function of individual and unique inter-group mediation; such mediation is vital, considering contemporary conditions in the East, and includes mediation between competing primordial groups, between modernized interest groups, intergroup coalitions, state institutions and international structures.[19]

At this point it is appropriate to pose the question of how the development of truly egalitarian structures of civil society can coexist with an activation of primordial groups and atavistic psychologies in the contemporary East. The answer is simple: through group mobilization and group participation in the strug-

---

[16] Cf. A. B. Zubov, *Parlamentskaia demokratiia i politicheskaia traditsiia Vostoka* [Parliamentary democracy and the political tradition of the East] (Moscow: "Nauka," 1990).

[17] Cf. Chr. Fürer-Haimendorf, "The Problem," *Seminar* (New Delhi), no. 14 (1960); M. K. Moharatra, "The Tribal Politicians of Orissa: Socialization, Recruitment, Ascent and Role Behaviour," in *Asie du Sud: Traditions et changements* (Paris: Centre national de la recherche scientifique, 1979); and N. Chazan, "Africa's Democratic Challenge," *World Policy Journal* 9: 2 (Spring 1992): 279–307.

[18] Rashkovskii, "Indiia vos'midesiatykh: Sotsial'noe znanie, lichnost' i obshchestvo" [India of the eighties: Social knowledge, personality and society], *Aziia i Afrika segodnia* [Asia and Africa today], no. 6 (1985).

[19] Modern historians think that the history of the Indian intelligentsia began precisely with this process of individual inter-structural cooperation; also that the history of modern Indian society, of parties, professional unions, and scientific institutions began with their participation. The same can be said about the rise of the Indian state system. Cf. M. Torri, "Westernized Middle Class: Intellectuals and Society in Colonial India," *Economic and Political Weekly* (Bombay) 25: 4 (1990).

gle for "markets" of resources and goods, whether material, informational, or related to status. A society consists of various groups. The less these groups communicate with one another, the more disorganized and violent the intergroup struggle in critical conditions of society and history. This question is vital not only for Third World countries or the East, but also for the West and Russia. And now it is time to focus on our own problems.

4. Russia

We start the discussion of the Russian situation with the assessment of one of our contemporary specialists on Africa. The collapse of totalitarian (or communist) and semi-totalitarian regimes in the late 1980s and early 1990s provides eloquent proof of systems of liberal-democratic communities having the strongest social and historical resources in the contemporary world and present historical conditions. But for the overwhelming majority of non-Western countries this truth gives rise to more questions than answers. There is no universally valid kind of transition to a liberal-democratic society, even when the distant perspective of a liberal-democratic future appears attainable and well-founded. But at present the collapse of totalitarian social chains (or those of its authoritarian leader) appears as the condition for mass organization, and also for sociocultural marginalization of enormous classes of people.[20]

This scholarly analysis applies also to contemporary Russia and those post-communist countries where, for all their swollen nationalism, ideas of social and national solidarity against dictatorship did not contribute to strong integration during the post-communist period.[21] Ideas of civil society, while not alien to reformers in Russia, were nonetheless understood in a very specific way in the late-communist and post-communist period, unlike Western countries with strong chains of rationally and legally elaborated relationships, or Eastern countries with strong chains of traditional or non-traditional primary groups. The Russian context appears to be characterized by the extreme atomization of individuals over against an all-encompassing power which claims everything for itself.[22] When the super-government of the Party finally exhausted and destroyed itself, the costs of deep social transformation were revealed in speedy group-formation,

---

[20] Cf. Th. Mkandawire, "Africa and the Changes in Eastern Europe," *Newsletter of the European Association of Development Research and Training Institutes (EADI)* (Geneva), no. 2 (1993).

[21] If we look at the history of developed national anti-totalitarian movements in three "socialist" countries: Poland, the Czech Republic, and Hungary, we note that these movements were deeply influenced by modern universal humanitarian and legal values. This turned out to be a guarantee of their future stable development.

[22] Allow me to recall just one slogan from the official jargon of the last decades of the dictatorship, at one time generally accepted, but now reminiscent of the theater of the absurd: "the stable growth of the leading role of the Party."

criminalization dictated by the "logic" of competing gangs of the Mafia, belated clericalism, and ethnic competition influenced by the same "logic." Russian history is not known for fostering the security of group and legal connections, and the present situation features a confusion of dangerously explosive emancipation processes of individuals, groups, or corporate structures.

The view that principles of law and legal order are alien to Russia appears to me rather simplistic. It can readily be opposed by a study of liberal and liberal-conservative ideas in Russian history, by study of the gradual humanization of legal relationship after the reforms of the 1860s, and by study of the influence of Russian thought, from Vladimir Solov'ev, Boris Chicherin, and Andrei Sakharov, on contemporary standards of legal theory.[23] But even from the perspective of a less strict understanding of civil society, there are two things which cannot be ignored in a reflection on the slow, difficult transition of Russia from totalitarianism to standards of normal dignified modern life in community.

The first we have already discussed briefly; it pertains to the abnormally large size of the government and state. This question is deeply rooted in Russian history and connected with an Oriental tradition resisting division of power and property. It also contributes to the extreme atomization of Russian society, and of substantial parts of the greater Slavic region.[24] Modern historiography speaks of the tradition of "patrimonial" institutional structures of Russian society;[25] I would prefer to call it a tradition of *irresponsible sovereignty*.

Imperial Russia substantiated this tradition with categories of quasi-Christian divine power; the Soviet period used Leninist categories of "negative theocracy."[26] The ruling power, accordingly, regarded itself responsible to existent or imagined transcendent powers, but never to its subject people. A clear historical example of this tradition can be found in the 20 articles of Peter the Great's military regulations: "His Majesty is a self-ruling Monarch, who does not have to answer for his actions to anyone in this world; but as a Christian

---

[23] A. Walicki, "Nravstvennost' i pravo v teoriiakh russkogo liberalizma kontsa XIX–nachala XX veka" [Morality and law in the theories of Russian liberalism of the end of the 19th–beginning of the 20th century], *Voprosy filosofii*, no. 8 (1991).

[24] Atomization of the majority of Russian society, together with relatively strong clan structures in the ethnic periphery, is one of the most important sources of modern Russian interethnic conflict; cf. D. B. Malysheva, "Etnicheskie konflikty na Iuge SNG i natsional'naia bezopasnost' Rossii" [Ethnic conflicts in Southern Russia and Russian national security], *IE&IR,*, no. 3 (1994).

[25] Cf. R. Pipes, *Russia under the Old Regime* (London: Weidenfeld and Nicolson, 1974).

[26] Cf. Rashkovskii, "Opyt totalitarnoi modernizatsii Rossii (1917–91) v svete sotsiologii razvitiia" [The experience of totalitarian modernization of Russia in the context of sociological development], *IE&IR*, no. 7 (1993).

Monarch he has the power to rule his lands and State and govern them according to his own will and good intentions."[27]

This tradition of irresponsible sovereignty which resulted in part from eco-geographical and cultural difficulties of the entire period of state-formation of Russia, also left its deep and painful imprint on the process of nation-building in all its multiple aspects.[28]

There is a second unfortunate factor in the spiritual evolution of Russian society in the last two centuries; we must note the strong ideological influence of romantic right-wing (or better, anti-right-wing) nihilism. It became influential through the mutual interconnection of ideas of Slavophiles, *narodniki* and Marxists in the Russian context; these ideas impacted the development of formal law, and the view which restricted law as an expression of bourgeois-individualistic self-interest.[29]

Contemporary political publications, in both the foreign and Russian press, like to stress that the instability of market development, relative liberalization of legislation, and ideological pluralization of society as they characterize contemporary Russia, all have a price in Mafia violence; such violence in turn calls for reaction from both the state and an opposition inclined to authoritarianism. But that is only one well-recognized, negative side of the issue. The other is less visible, but more complicated. That is the slow, unpredictable process of the structuralization of society, its economic groups and coalitions, professional societies, parishes, political and sub-cultural unions. The entire complicated problematics of group and social self-assistance presents a serious challenge for the atomized, state-oriented human psychology of the recent past.

Referring to the severe atomization of modern Russian society, in light of the theme chosen for this essay we must also connect this issue with problematics of the study of religion.

For a long time already, writers, historians, philosophers, and psychologists have paid attention to a real complexity in the Russian religious-cultural tradition, the tradition rooted not only in Russian history, but in the spiritual traditions of the Western Mediterranean and Byzantium. I am referring to the collision between the depth and refinement of the inner space of the person, and the

---

[27] T. I. Shvorina, *Voinskie artikuly Petra I* [The military regulations of Peter the Great] (Moscow: Voenno-iuridicheskaia akademiia Krasnoi Armii, 1940), 25.

[28] Let us recall the poem of M. Voloshin:
"... Comissars – that's where you find imperial folly,
the explosions of revolution – among the tsars..."

[29] The correlation of these three ideological layers of Russian history was mentioned as early as 1909 in *Vekhi* (*Landmarks*) in B. A. Kistiakovskii's article "V zashitu prava" ("In Defence of Law"). See also the article of A. Walicki cited above, "Nravstvennost' i pravo."

relative constraint, if not repression, of forms of its external activity.[30] During periods of harsh foreign invasions or the rise of native despotism, this collision could serve individual or group self-preservation, even though at times it might result in an outburst of useless reaction or suffering, again for the group or individual. In some critical circumstances the enormous reserve of human patience and inner depth could turn around into "meaningless and pitiless rebellion." The history of communist dictatorship in Russia has shown that especially during periods of history with the most unfortunate circumstances, such self-immersion of the socially-alienated person who has adjusted to centuries without freedom can reveal itself as a powerful form of individual, group, or even national self-preservation. This also means that adjustment to freedom (or even to social conditions of semi-freedom) requires a structural transformation of the internal world of the person. The half-conscious reserve of internal dignity and freedom has to develop outwardly, find a way to express and recast itself, and slowly suppress the "lawlessness" of Mafia and officials. This will lead to genuine modernization for Russia. But to achieve it may take years and years.

The last three decades of Russian history, from the 1970s through the 1990s, were characterized by a powerful religious boom. In this respect Russia has become a different country. During the first two of these decades this boom played a rather negative role, seeking to separate atheist totalitarian power from its inner legitimization, protecting the human environment from its irresponsible sovereignty. Fortunately, the great experiment of creating a permanent and irreversible totalitarian-atheistic society in Russia failed.

It would have been self-deceptive to claim that the Russian anti-totalitarian revolution, of which the religious boom was an inalienable part, distinguished itself for being constructive and consistent. But the 1990s brought a positive connection between the religious boom and processes which established the first serious premises of civil society in Russia.

In the first place, the religious boom revealed the necessity of a more precise organization of values of the inner space of the individual, i.e., the necessity of that "sacral agreement" that gives form to human existence for active and conscious experience in this world.

Secondly, development of different religious and religious-cultural institutions makes a society more structured, more deeply penetrated with connections and intergroup relationships of the primary group. Civil freedom needs a minimum of those principles of the ethics of life, work, and moral self-discipline, which are conditioned on the "sacral agreement" (including vertical

---

[30] Berdiaev, "Problema Vostoka i Zapada v religioznom soznanii Vl. Solov'eva [The problem of East and West in the religious consciousness of V. Solov'ev], in *Sbornik pervyi: O Vladimire Solov'eve* [First collection: On Vladimir Solov'ev] (Moscow, 1911).

human/divine, as well as horizontal human/human relationships). Out of an amorphous nihilism which lacks such agreement one can expect, in the final analysis, only a tyranny of irresponsible power and "lumpen" innergroup support.

An examination of socio-cultural obstacles to establishing civil society in Russia will discern at least three interrelated obstacles that seem to be more obvious, and indicate results of atomization:

1) a self-centered approach of individuals or groups deeply rooted in our culture, a feeling of exclusiveness, misunderstanding of values characterizing different forms of human experience, and a pathetic syndrome reminiscent of an elementary narcissism which considers only ours to be "true" teachings;
2) lack of appreciation of the reality of mutual inter-confessional and inter-ethnic understanding as a necessary premise for the normal life and development of any human group;
3) the present general condition of "Russian ideology" which, without knowing Russian history or understanding much about the modern world, reveals itself as some fermentation of idealized illusions of communism and idealized specters of imperial-orthodox Russia. And it is hard to say what is most astonishing in this parade of phantoms, the degree of general moral exhaustion of the people, the passionate immersion of millions of people in previously quite unfamiliar commercial activity, or the self-defensive function of meaningful skepticism, unique in Russian history.

5. Inner Space

We arrive at some conclusions. In modern Russia the difficult path of civil society is still the only alternative to a destructive civil war, whether in an open or semi-open form; war has already become a reality for many post-communist areas. And for civil society the theory and practice of non-violence[31] in its different forms – legal, moral, or religious – provides the only dignified and functionally acceptable regulator.

---

[31] It is a pity that the relevant Russian term *nenasilie* has a lot of negative connotations. The more adequate term, Gandhi's *satiagraha* ("active non-violence"), is still not used in the Russian language (cf. Rashkovskii, "*Satiagraha*: Revoliutsiia nenasiliia" [*Satiagraha*: Revolution without violence), *Put'*, no. 4 (1993). Let me remind the reader, in this connection, that L. Tolstois's *Tsarstvo Bozhie vnutri vas* (*The Kingdom of God is Within You*) was one of the sources of "*satiagraha*" teaching. Cf. M. K. Gandhi, *An Autobiography, or the Story of My Experiments with Truth* (Ahmedabad: Navajevan Publishers, 1940), 99.

Moreover, in speaking about civil society the term "religious" has to be interpreted in a broad sense, in terms of the deep, inner familiar connection of the person with others, with the world around, and with the Divine Presence. And when we speak of a religious understanding of civil society, we must not forget that according to the Sermon on the Mount[32] forgiveness and making peace belongs to human kindness, and can be fulfilled on earth; it is not restricted to a divine perspective.

To conclude, let me stress once more that the sense in which we understand the term civil society does not give a photographic picture of reality, but points to a universal, typical principle growing out of reality, even if it has a special connection with the powerful influence of Anglo-Saxon legal traditions in the modern world. Nonetheless, this article has tried to show that the idea of civil society also absorbed much from the intellectual-spiritual achievements of continental Europe, the Slavic world, and India. Thus it is not hard to discern features of a general, universal human achievement.

This ideal typical principle necessarily absorbs within itself the conflict between the social-cultural trends of individualization and collectivism which are immanent in any developed society; it does not prescribe one universally valid solution. Yet this principle is necessarily based on the idea of agreement, as some kind of ideal which I would even dare to call "Kantian"; by that I mean that it is connected with "things in themselves," with things difficult to express and immutable, with human dignity as the core of community.

Because only nihilism and violence clearly or (in poetic language), "weightily, roughly, and visibly"[33] verify themselves in the spiritual sphere, the principle of civil society requires a certain schooling of soul. In part this education is provided by religious experience, the experience of faith, or, in the words of the apostle Paul, experience of the "assurance of what is not seen" (Heb. 11.1) which can also be translated in terms of "being convinced of what is not seen." Such experience is not given to everyone, but when it is mediated through a system of interhuman connections it can become a reality for everyone. For it creates that inner space of the human person, and through it, also the inner cultural space which gives birth to a self-consciousness capable of opposing the powers that manipulate and humiliate people. So, the path of establishing civil society leads us not only through clarification, institutionalization, and optimization of human interests and antagonisms, but also through a willing self-sacrifice in prayerful and daily work.

---

[32] I am reminded of the Beatitudes, given in the Sermon on the Mount (Matt. 5.3–12) which are heard with every celebration of the Orthodox liturgy.

[33] The Russian text "*vesomo, grubo, zrimo*" represents an ironically contextualized citation from the poetry of Vladimir Maiakovskii and refers to some kind of irresistible evidence. *Trans.*

Part II

The Russian Idea and Russian Religious Philosophy

The Orthodox Schism and Schismatic Communism[1]

Konstantin Konstantinovich Ivanov

1. "Holy Russia": Spiritual Roots of the 17th-Century Schism

This essay is devoted to religious issues surrounding the 17th-century schism in the Orthodox church. I wish to discuss 19th-century problems which led to the appearance of communism in Russia but are essentially connected with that schism. On this question we are indebted to Nikolai Berdiaev and, even without fully supporting his positions, must credit him for discernment on spiritual issues of Russian history.[2] In his *Origin and Meaning of Russian Communism* Berdiaev drew connections between the schism and the ideology of the Russian intelligentsia, and also connected Russian Bolshevism and the ideology of the intelligentsia. As a religious thinker, Berdiaev examined religious motives at the foundations of Russian history, and even viewed the entire history of Russia from the perspective of the schism as a religious problem.

We must remember that before the revolution Russian scholars were prevented by state-imposed censorship from speaking freely about the schism. After the revolution Soviet historians neglected religious problems. But Russian emigré thinkers did study the schism, and among them Berdiaev went so far as to claim that schismatic behavior was common, and even defined Russian history tragically. But he warned that "it would be a mistake to think that the religious

---

[1] K. K. Ivanov, "Raskol'nicheskii kharakter russkogo kommunizma," published as "Intelligentsiia i khristianskaia mysl' v Rossii" [The intelligentsia and Christian thought in Russia], in *Fenomen rossiiskoi intelligentsii: Istoriia i psikhologiia* [The phenomenon of the Russian intelligentsia: History and psychology] (St. Petersburg: Nestor, 2000), 207–22.

[2] N. Berdiaev, *Istoki i smysl russkogo kommunizma* [The origin and meaning of Russian communism (Moscow: Nauka, 1990); the work was translated by R. M. French as *The Origin of Russian Communism* (London, 1937/1948). In my discussion I will start with quotations from this work, and will also refer to Georges Florovsky's [Georgii Florovskii] *Puti russkogo bogosloviia* (Paris, 1937), trans. by R. L. Nichols as *Ways of Russian Theology*, vols. 5 and 6 of the *Collected Works of Georges Florovsky* (Belmont, MA: Nordland Publishing Co., 1979). I also use Vasilii V. Zenkovskii's *Istoriia russkoi filosofii* (Leningrad: Ego, 1991), trans. by George L. Kline as *A History of Russian Philosophy*, (New York: Columbia University Press, 1953). [Please note that translations of these works given in the text of the article here are original; page references to English translations of French, Nichols, and Kline respectively are given for the convenience of the reader. *Trans.*]

Helleman, Wendy, ed. *The Russian Idea: In Search of a New Identity*. Bloomington, IN: Slavica, 2004, 129–36.

schism arose exclusively from a superstitious adherence to ritual among the Russian people. At issue was the question of whether the Russian kingdom was truly Orthodox, and the Russian people really carried out their Messianic vocation. While the low cultural level of the clergy, ignorance, and superstition played a role, these are quite inadequate to explain an event of such magnitude, particularly judging by its consequence: the schism. Among the Russian people a suspicion arose that the Orthodox kingdom as "Third Rome" had been destroyed, and they were facing a betrayal of true faith."[3]

The well-known historian of Russian philosophy V. Zenkovskii also writes that the schism was certainly "a phenomenon of much greater significance than has usually been thought."[4] This schism was important, as other religious historians have noted, for the wave of apocalyptic feelings which took hold of the people, the shock at the terrible spiritual deception and betrayal of what was sacred. It seemed that the Antichrist had come, that the end times had begun. Florovsky agrees with Berdiaev on the source of apocalypticism: "It was certainly not a question of rite; the theme and mystery of the Russian schism was the Antichrist.... The entire sense and spirit of the first resistance to the schism consists not in "blind" commitment to specific rites or ordinary "trifles," but in this apocalyptic suspicion."[5] Suddenly it seemed as if the Third Rome had already become the kingdom of the Devil. Florovsky concludes that "the schism arose from disenchantment."[6] In other words, an initial spiritual "enchantment" had been lost; here we note one of the fundamental causes of the split in the church.

The Muscovite kingdom, which considered itself the Third Rome maintained a combination of conceptions, confusing an ideal of the kingdom of Christ, or kingdom of righteousness, with that of being a powerful state, ruling over the unrighteous. Berdiaev tells us that "the schism meant the discovery of a contradiction, resulting from that mixture."[7] According to Zenkovskii too, "it is important to note the idea of the special mission of the Russian people, of the Russian kingdom. It was precisely in the 16th century when this teaching about "Holy Russia" was first promoted."[8] Evidence for such a mood can be found in the (late 15th to early 16th century) position of Iosif Volokolamskii: "The tsar is like an ordinary man by nature, but in his position and authority he is like God."

---

[3] Berdiaev, *Istoki*, 10; cf. French, 11.

[4] Zenkovskii, *Istoriia russkoi filosofii*, 52; cf. Kline, 40.

[5] Florovskii, *Puti russkogo bogosloviia*, 69; cf. Nichols, 5: 98. Cf. Florovsky: "This frightened century ends with an apocalyptic convulsion, a terrible attack of apocalyptic fanaticism" (*Puti russkogo bogosloviia*, 58; Nichols, 5: 87).

[6] Florovskii, *Puti russkogo bogosloviia*, 67; Nichols, 5: 97–98.

[7] Berdiaev, *Istoki*, 11; cf. French, 12.

[8] Zenkovskii, *Istoriia*, 47; cf. Kline , 36.

Similarly, Metropolitan Makarii (contemporary of Ivan IV) is quoted as saying, "God has chosen you, o Sovereign, to rule this land in his place, and placed you on the throne, entrusting you with mercy and the life of all of great Orthodoxy."[9]

The schism was based on a popular perception of the Orthodox kingdom. Florovsky refers to the schism as a "socio-apocalyptic utopia."[10] This utopia was closely connected with the idea of "Moscow as the Third Rome," thought to have been introduced by the monk Philotheus in his correspondence with Tsar Ivan the Terrible: "Blessed tsar, you should observe and consider that all the Christian kingdoms have flowed together into one single state, yours, and that two Romes have fallen, while the third Rome is still standing and a fourth there will never be. Your Christian kingdom will never fall into the hands of others." Philotheus speaks of the "Christian kingdom" as the "kingdom of God." And in this sense "the theme of schism is not a question of the 'ancient rite' but 'a kingdom.'"[11] The utopia of Russia as a Holy Kingdom, for schismatics "turned out to be the kingdom of the Antichrist."[12] Zenkovskii notes that "Russian ecclesiastical consciousness paid a high price for the dream, for the utopian interpretation of the theocratic idea of Christianity," and continues that

> in the historiosophical poem about the Third Rome, ecclesiastical consciousness of the sacred authority of the tsar and of its own universal mission led to an identification of the two orders of existence. Since 'the natural historical process' could no longer be understood clearly as a 'holy kingdom' it was regarded as the kingdom of the Antichrist. An enormous sacrifice was brought by Old Believers on the altar of a sacred dream...[13]

Berdiaev notes that a "sharp nationalization" of the Russian church had already occurred by the time of the schism.

2. Nationalization of Christianity

We must be clear about the *catastrophe* of the nationalization of Christianity in Russia, and its catastrophic impact on the Christian church and its preaching. It was both an ecclesiastic and social catastrophe. But if we take a deeper look, we also find in it a punishment for the prior spiritual catastrophe of nationalization of Christianity in Russia. "The Orthodox faith is the Russian faith. If it is not the

---

[9] Zenkovskii, *Istoriia*, 48; cf. Kline, 36.
[10] Florovskii, *Puti russkogo bogosloviia*, 67; cf. Nichols, 5: 98.
[11] Ibid.
[12] Florovskii, *Puti russkogo bogosloviia*, 69; cf. Nichols, 5: 99.
[13] Zenkovskii, *Istoriia*, 54–55; cf. Kline, 41–43.

Russian faith, it is not Orthodox faith."[14] The consequences of this process are so far reaching that they are with us even today in explicit and crude forms of religious nationalism, simply identifying religious ideas with national ones. Many who call themselves "Orthodox believers" understand this as an expression of being Russian. Such "Orthodox" believers, when asked whether they believe in God, are puzzled: "What does that have to do with God?"

In Russian history nationalization of faith expressed itself in more dangerous ways, introducing proud dreams and irrational utopias. National and state interests, confused with religious ones, perverted them, and became perverted in turn. The roots of Russian communism can be traced to religious nationalism opening a wide path to substitutes for religion. The nationalist utopia modified itself into a Communist one (even though the latter long claimed an internationalist ideology). Russian ideology finally immersed everything in one irrational stream of distorted utopian religiosity, freely borrowing ideas from the West, including Marxism itself and ideas of Nietzsche, which once also seemed so attractive. Demagogic ideology can easily be manipulated. In contemporary history we find the same extravagant religious behavior, rushing from one extreme to another, ending with confusion.

3. The Schism and the Russian Intelligentsia

In the schism nationalized religious feelings were injured and expressed themselves most painfully. They began to focus on questions of power in political and secular life, and thus began to lose their religious content. The schismatic ideology finally gave birth to the godless revolutionary ideology of the Russian intelligentsia, one full of irritation and bitterness at human life, under the pretext of righteous indignation. If we look more deeply, we note that God himself was the object of their irritation. "The intelligentsia took on the schismatic character which is so characteristic of Russians. Themselves living in separation from the surrounding reality, which they regarded as evil, the intelligentsia worked out a fanatic schismatic morale."[15]

Berdiaev himself did not notice that the pain from such schismatic irritation had turned into rebellion against God, for he spoke of this revolt with sympathy. "The source of atheism was compassion with people, and the impossibility of being reconciled with God because of excessive evil and suffering in life.... It was an atheism arising from ethical pathos, from love of good and justice."[16] But what kind of compassion is this? Here we can easily recognize the approach of Nietzsche, who regarded compassion as the main obstacle for human develop-

---

[14] Berdiaev, *Istoki*, 10; cf. French, 11.

[15] Berdiaev, *Istoki*, 34; cf. French, 40.

[16] Ibid.

ment. And what kind of limitation does Berdiaev have in mind when he says that "the Russians became atheists out of pity, compassion, and the impossibility of enduring suffering"? Superficially the intelligentsia expressed their experience in terms of bitter criticism of the authorities. But above all, they expressed hereby an irresistible desire for personal self-affirmation. Criticism was experienced as a spiritual mission. A righteous self-consciousness characterized their ideology; later, in their collision with the government, the consciousness of the "martyr" also characterized them, if not overtly.

Even while criticizing the ideology of the intelligentsia, Berdiaev is completely on its side. In writing of the Russian intelligentsia naturalizing a perception of holiness and repentance, he says, "They did not understand the mystery of the Cross, but were nonetheless capable of sacrifice and self-denial. In this they distinguished themselves favorably from Christians of their time."[17] "Theirs was a structure of soul which gave birth to saints," Berdiaev writes of Dobroliubov and Chernyshevskii.[18] With reference to Dobroliubov he adds, "He had a strong feeling of being a sinner, and an inclination to constant repentance." And, "Chernyshevskii was a very humble man; he had a Christian soul and his character bore the marks of sanctity."[19]

Striving for utopian ideas, the intelligentsia wanted to escape the inner bankruptcy which, in the final analysis, had a spiritual origin, although Russian historians have typically reduced it to national and social causes, or considered it "groundless" (*bespochvennyi*). "Superfluous people" (*lishnie liudi*) first appeared among the bored aristocracy, and then among the pretentious "*raznochintsy*." In their very Russian concern with the question "to be, or not to be" for the state and society, they ended up asking in a simple-minded way, "What should be done?" (*chto delat'*) This credo of bored idleness seemed to be extraordinarily significant in the romantic culture of the time. Berdiaev lyrically sympathizes with the ideology of emptiness, explaining its romantic and pantheistic position on social problems in terms of its religious self-consciousness. He explains the appearance of "superfluous people" through social causes. "Discord with reality made Russian people inactive, and this produced a type of "superfluous people."[20]

Yet in its final substitution for religious feelings this ideology carried within itself a spiritual vacuum, more precisely identified as "nihilism." "Nihilism is a typical Russian phenomenon.... We are all nihilists, Dostoevskii says. The Russian intelligentsia denied God, the spirit, the soul, standards, and higher val-

---

[17] Berdiaev, *Istoki*, 39; cf. French, 47.
[18] Berdiaev, *Istoki*, 41; cf. French, 49.
[19] Berdiaev, *Istoki*, 41–42; cf. French, 49–50.
[20] Berdiaev, *Istoki*, 32; cf. French, 39.

ues."[21] A spiritual emptiness served as a "space" for the unfolding of utopian dreams. These dreams were mostly focused on the state: what kind of state ought it to be, or not to be, and what kind of state it really was. Berdiaev concludes that "the Russian intelligentsia was finally formed as a schismatic type. They always refer to themselves as 'we', and to the state and its authorities as 'they.'"[22] In this way they expressed the previously mentioned obsession of hatred towards the authorities. Yet theirs was a dreaming consciousness which regarded true reality as a strange "it," while the world of its dreams represented something much closer to itself, as "ours."

4. Russian Messianism: Church and State

Russians began to idealize their state and exalt their nationality. Russians themselves regarded their country as a bastion of Orthodoxy; the Russian people were likewise regarded as bearers of true Christianity, a "God-bearing" people (*bogonosets*) by nature and race. We need not look, with Berdiaev, for an analogy with Israelite self-consciousness, also considering itself as specially "chosen by God." Such a view was encouraged by 15th-century political and ecclesiastical-political events: the Union of Florence (1439) and fall of Constantinople (1453). According to Zenkovskii, "after the Union of Florence the Russian clergy completely lost confidence in the Greeks who welcomed this union. The Russian church began to consider itself the single guardian of Christian truth in its purity."[23] "After the fall of Byzantium they began to affirm strongly the idea of "a wandering kingdom"; the first two "Romes" (Rome itself and Constantinople) had fallen; where was the third, the new Rome? Russian thought adamantly and confidently considered Moscow as the Third Rome, for only in Russia, according to Russian understanding, was the Christian faith maintained in purity."[24] On the other hand, Russian tsars were constantly concerned about ruling a country such as Russia, which was notoriously difficult to govern. There was a strong temptation to acquire additional religious power over the minds and souls of the people. Berdiaev affirms "Ivan the Terrible ... [as the one] who taught that the tsar should not only rule the state but also save souls."[25]

Because the people connected their godliness with a cult of State, the spiritual shock of the schism was all the worse. This was caused by a disillusionment with both the State and Church. In popular consciousness State and Church were merged in such a way as to include even the sanctity of God. Here we note

---

[21] Berdiaev, *Istoki*, 37; cf. French, 45.
[22] Berdiaev, *Istoki*, 25; cf. French, 25.
[23] Zenkovskii, *Istoriia*, 46; cf. Kline, 34.
[24] Zenkovskii, *Istoriia*, 47; cf. Kline, 35.
[25] Berdiaev, *Istoki*, 10; cf. French, 11.

the introduction of an idolatry, for which, according to biblical teachings, nations are rigorously punished by God.

Russian scholars have long recognized false Christian ideas of authority among the causes of the Schism; yet analysis has commonly been restricted to external historical reasons. No doubt Russia inherited from Byzantium the state-church relationship of the Church submitting itself to the State in the person of the tsar. Most scholars who recognize such "reasons" for the merging of secular and Church authority imply unspokenly that whatever the reasons, they themselves need not take any responsibility for them. Although secular historiography may confine itself to such "reasons" our present discussion of the spiritual foundations of history looks for deeper reasons underlying the above-mentioned "reasons." Why have Russians appealed to the Byzantine tradition? Why have they adopted the diseases and distortions of this tradition in worshipping God? From which human roots have our national troubles arisen?

I am convinced that such roots exist, and that they determine our personal and national history. The roots of human responsibility lie in the depth of the soul, where an individual or a nation mysteriously defines its relationship with God. This is best expressed in the religious faith of a people or the distinct individual. It is not a matter of dispute, but the necessary background for the question being considered.

5. Residual Paganism in Russian Religion

The nationalization of Christianity represents a relapse of paganism in the Russian religious consciousness; it clearly testifies to an inadequate appropriation of Christianity in Russia. False religious ideas of authority, with their tragic consequences for Russian history, witness to this residual paganism. To define our paganism accurately we must also note failure in affirming essential Christian positions on repentance and the depth of human sin. Russian pantheism and paganism has essentially expressed itself in a failure of repentance, more than a tendency to rites or speculations.

The tragedy of Russian history focuses on problems of spiritual life and Christian faith in Russia. The problem of faith in Russia is often defined by "residual" pantheist and pagan elements in popular religious consciousness. Central to such an element is an "indulgent" attitude to sin, an overly "kind" attitude to sinners, and intolerance for punishment of sin, all rooted in an inadequate grasp of essential Christian teachings on repentance. On such a religious basis only two extreme reactions to authority are possible: a utopian idealization of power, or (after the first religious collision with the reality of authority, given in the Schism) its anarchic rejection.

In Russia the collapse of the utopia of power with the Schism generated an anarchic tendency: at first in the religious form of "schismatics" (*raskolniki*) and later, in the secular revolutionary intelligentsia. Both tendencies misunderstood a true Christian idea of authority. The utopian choice did so implicitly and essentially; the anarchic secular choice, formally and explicitly. Russian communism which arose from the combination of these tendencies, also took advantage of them after it had become established as state ideology. Without at this point analyzing all the political or social forces of that period of Russian history, I only want to clarify the spiritual channel of these events, and the peculiar spiritual problems determined by Russian history, namely the problems of sin and authority in correlation.

We conclude this discussion with a suggestion for solving these problems from a theological perspective. Although widely regarded as an affirmation of a strong central government, the assertion that "all authority comes from God" (Romans 13.1) must be understood in terms of a triangular relationship of God/authority/sin; we must reject its delegation of all authority to the state. A fuller Christian understanding of human sin and need for repentance can help solve Russia's problems with respect to the spiritual basis of political authority. It recognizes the righteousness of God that does not tolerate sin; the depth of salvation can only be understood by recognizing the depth of judgment on sin. Yet God did not give up on his people; he sent his own Son. God's love for mankind should not be confused with an all-forgiving humanistic tolerance and compassion blind to sin, which supports a political utopia demanding no repentance or sacrifice. God's love cost him his Son; it meant the cross.

True Christianity does not rebel against divine or human authority when experiencing the trials of life. Nor does it simply endorse any use of authority; repentance gives patience to accept earthly punishment, without excluding the right of opposing abuse of power. The example of Christ gives strength to endure unfair punishment. Repentance eliminates the split in the depth of our soul, first in its relation to God, and then in relation to earthly life and authority, both of which are given from God. Only repentance allows for a full eradication of the roots of religious schism, which has sent out its destructive shoots on Russian soil from the 17th-century schism to our communist and post-communist epoch.

P. Chaadaev and V. Solov'ev: The Discovery of Islam[1]

Aleksei Vasil'evich Zhuravskii

Introduction

Much profound scientific and theological research has already been devoted to the question of the relationship between Western European culture and the world of Islam, including the religious aspect of the question, which is especially important. The issue of such a relationship has once more become very real for Russian society.

One recent headline in *Nezavisimaia gazeta* claims: "Islam is also our fate."[2] It is difficult to argue with this. Numerically, Islam is the second largest religion in Russia, with 12 million adherents, according to official sources, but 20 million, according to Muslims themselves. Still, this issue has not yet received the necessary social, political, and religious scholarly attention. After more than 70 years of Soviet censorship we are only just beginning to examine how Islamic traditions were received and understood within the Russian religious-philosophical tradition.

As a historiosophical problem with immediate implications for the fortunes of Russia, the issue of Islam was raised in the 19th century by P. Chaadaev, and given detailed study in the works of V. Solov'ev. The present article will focus attention on these two writers, and will not examine the totally different understanding of the problem found in works of P. Danilevskii, K. Leont'ev, or N. Fedorov, all of whom took a more practical, political, and ideological approach.

Chaadaev

If Chaadaev was not the first to formulate the issue, he was certainly the first to give it detailed attention and to place it at the center of the historiosophical triad

---

[1] A. V. Zhuravskii, "P. Chaadaev i V. Solov'ev: Otkrytie islama," first published in *Poiski edinstva: Problemy religioznogo dialoga v proshlom i nastoiashchem* [The search for unity: Problems of religious dialog in the past and present] (Moscow: Bibleisko-bogoslovskii institut sv. apostola Andreia, 1997), republished slightly modified in *Khristiane i musul'mane: Problemy dialoga* [Christians and Muslims: Problems of dialogue] (Moscow: Bibleisko-bogoslovskii institut sv. apostola Andreia, 2000), 435–50.

[2] *Nezavisimaia gazeta* [Independent newspaper], Moscow, 30 March 1993.
Helleman, Wendy, ed. *The Russian Idea: In Search of a New Identity*. Bloomington, IN: Slavica, 2004, 137–49.

"the West-Russia-the East."³ In his *Philosophical Letters* the members of this triad were characterized not only geographically, but also through cultural and historical realities, each with its own distinct inner dynamic. The East represented all pagan and non-Christian civilizations based on the pre-eminence of material interests. In the East all intellectual work, no matter how outstanding, all that is lofty in its scholarship and habits, has served and still serves only the physical nature of the human being.⁴ The West, according to Chaadaev, represents an antipode to the East, as a Christian society that alone was "truly guided by interests of thought and soul." These interests are boundless in their nature and thus "Christian peoples must always go forward."⁵

However, it would be unforgivably simplistic to claim that in his historiosophical structures Chaadaev considered the East as some single entity subordinated to only one principle goal.

By the time of his *Philosophical Letters* he had already discovered the non-Christian monotheistic East of Judaism and Islam, which he opposed to the civilizations of India and China. He also discussed these with a deep respect quite unusual for Christian thought of his time.

In the sixth philosophical letter Chaadaev pursued a daring revision of firmly based historical reputations. This re-evaluation was done mainly by overturning pagan authorities and elevating biblical ones, and was undoubtedly polemical with respect to values of contemporary European and, more particularly, the Enlightenment tradition. He presented Moses, revealing the true God to his people, in opposition to Socrates, who left his people only faintheartedness and restless doubt. David, a perfect example of the most sacred heroism, was placed over against Marcus Aurelius, who revealed only a curious example of artificial magnificence, of splendid and boastful virtue. As time went by people began to consider Aristotle to be "the Angel of Darkness, who for several centuries bound all the forces of good among people," while at the same time they saw in Mohammed "a beneficial creature who contributed more than anyone to the realization of the plan of divine wisdom for the survival of the human race."⁶

---

³ The trend of defining Russian culture in terms of an opposition of East and West is found already in the works of A. S. Griboedov and his circle; cf. Iu. M. Lotman, "'Fatalist' i problema Vostoka i Zapada v tvorchestve Lermontova" ["The Fatalist" and the problem of East and West in Lermontov's works], in *V shkole poeticheskogo slova: Pushkin, Lermontov, Gogol'* [In the school of poetic words: Pushkin, Lermontov, Gogol'] (Moscow: Prosveshchenie, 1988), 228.

⁴ See the sixth letter from P. Ia. Chaadaev in *Polnoe sobranie sochinenii i izbrannye pis'ma* [Complete collected works and selected letters] (Moscow: Nauka, 1991), 1: 408; a translation can be found in Raymond T. McNally, *The Major Works of Peter Chaadaev* (Notre Dame, IN and London: University of Notre Dame Press, 1969), 151.

⁵ Chaadaev, *Polnoe sobranie sochinenii i izbrannye pis'ma*, 1: 409; cf. McNally, 151.

⁶ Cf. Chaadaev's sixth letter, 1: 396–97; cf. McNally, 134.

According to Chaadaev, the Islamic religion led to good results for people because it worked toward the elimination of polytheism and "spread the idea of a single God and a universal faith throughout the immense stretches of Earth, including regions that were regarded as impermeable to the influence of a common intellectual movement; thus, it prepared a great number of people for the final destiny of the human race."[7] Reflecting on the historical mission of Islam, Chaadaev ascribed to it not only a negative role, i.e., through its bringing union among Christians facing a common threat; nor did he ascribe to it a purely cultural contribution, i.e., the transmission of material and valuable knowledge to Europe. Islam is one of the expressions of revealed religion, and in an invisible, mysterious way is connected with Christianity. The enmity between Muslims and Christians is a socio-historical phenomenon, and is not of a religious nature.

> Islam presents one of the most noteworthy expressions of the common law; to judge it differently implies a lack of understanding of the universal influence of Christianity, from which it originated. The most essential property of our religion is its capacity to assume very different forms of religious thought, and the ability to co-ordinate its actions, even with error, if necessary, in order to obtain the final result. In the great historical development of revealed religion, the Islamic religion has to be considered as one of its branches."[8]

It has been shown that Chaadaev's first editor, I. S. Gagarin, corrected this passage with a very rigorous note: "In the last resort one can consider Islamic religion to be a Christian sect, as for example, Arianism, but it is impossible to go so far as to unite the truth with the lie."[9] Gagarin's judgement is not surprising, inasmuch as it belongs to the middle of the last century when such a point of view about Islam was widespread. But the judgements of another author, pronounced a century later, those of the historian N. I. Ulianov, who represents the second generation of the Russian emigration and was a pupil of S. F. Platonov, are more remarkable. In his article "The Basman Philosopher" (1957), where he gives a uniformly negative picture of Chaadaev ("There is no greater impostor in the history of Russian thought," etc.), the author pauses briefly to examine Chaadaev's views on Judaism and Islam: "He was impressed not by Islam itself but by its expansion over an enormous part of the globe." With its triumphant procession it has done more for the celebration of Divine Providence than "useless" Christian wise men, who are unable "to represent any of their fabrications with flesh and blood, or to inspire firm convictions in any human heart."

---

[7] Chaadaev, seventh letter, 1: 429; cf. McNally, 180–81.
[8] Chaadaev, seventh letter, 1: 429–30; cf. McNally, 181.
[9] Quoted in P. Ia. Chaadaev, *Sochineniia* [Collected works] (Moscow: Pravda, 1989), 589.

Our philosopher was fascinated by the striking sword of Islam. The Bible "with its show of unusual means" for maintaining the idea of a single God, instilled in him the same delight. He named any form of philosophy that recoiled in horror at massive slaughter "more stupid, than godless." Moses was a great figure not because he led the people out of Egypt and gave them the law, but because he did not hesitate to kill thousands of people for apostasy. That was the best means of introducing to human thought an immense idea which could not arise there independently." Chaadaev reproached "Christian wise men" for their failure to shed blood or be merciless.[10]

We will not comment on the rather free translation of quotations taken out of context, and truncated, without beginning or end. The things with which the author tries to charge Chaadaev between the lines are more representative. Chaadaev never expressed approval of Islamic expansion; in fact, he did not speak of it at all. His work focused on the expansion of the idea of a single God, monotheism. Nor did Chaadaev say a word about a striking sword of Islam, any more than he mentioned "useless Christian wise men" (an obvious case of juggling words). The discussion focused on ancient philosophers who could not develop a unifying idea of man and mankind – a theme that was rather trivial.

As for Chaadaev's conception of Islam, one aspect is striking. In discussing the ability of Christianity "to assume very different forms of religious thought," "the Basman philosopher" to some degree anticipated Karl Rahner's concept of "anonymous Christianity," which in our century has provided the basis for one of the directions of Catholic theology on non-Christian religions as an acute problem regarding the salvation of non-Christians. The concept distinguishes two histories of salvation, or to be more precise, two currents in the stream of a single economy of salvation. The first universal, "ordinary" one includes all known and unknown religions which have existed at any time and in any place from the moment of man's first appearance. God has always spoken to human beings, and his Word could take various forms: from the cosmic revelation of the covenant with Noah, to personalized prophecies and inspirations. The second current, that of the Bible and Christian revelation, is special, particular, and extraordinary. It is unique, but certainly not exclusive. The relationship between these two types of revelation is described as a convergence, an assimilation and agreement in eternity. Thus the full integration of these currents is possible only

---

[10] N. I. Ulianov, "Basmannyi filosof: Mysli o Chaadaeve" [The Basman philosopher: Reflections on Chaadaev], *Voprosy filosofii* [Philosophical questions], no. 8 (1990): 81–82.

at the end of time, while in historical time it is possible and necessary to search for ways of agreement between them.[11]

Solov'ev

Solov'ev's views on Islam and their relevance for us represent a theme which provokes bewilderment and doubt not only among professional specialists on Solov'ev's works, but even more so among Orientalists. For the former, these views give only an insignificant segment of his wide-ranging philosophical works, but for the latter they are nothing but the judgements of a dilettante. As a result, these views have received very little attention.

All his life Solov'ev worked at understanding Islam within the global framework of the cultural and historical opposition of East and West; this may be considered the dominant problem of Solov'ev's historiosophy. He found its solution in the combination of two one-sided truths within a higher fulness, in their mutual fulfilment:

> The great dispute of East and West has continued throughout the entire life of mankind. Even Herodotus ascribed its beginning to semi-historical times; he gives the first indications of that universal struggle between Europe and Asia in legendary events, in the Phoenician kidnapping of the women from Argos, and in the kidnapping of Helen of Sparta by the son of Trojan Priam. This dispute arose in ancient times, and even today creates divisions among mankind, interfering in its regular life. Having appeared before Christianity, and then been stopped for some period by this new religion, it was yet once more renewed by an anti-Christian policy in that very Christian world; such a fatal dispute can and must finally be solved by a true Christian politics.[12]

V. Solov'ev's general historiosophical concept is elaborated in more substance in his works *The History and Future of Theocracy* and *The Great Dispute and Christian Politics*, written in the second period of his scholarly work, which E. Trubetskoi called "utopian" and which is also designated as "theocratic."[13] The following gives a brief statement of its essence:

---

[11] Cf. Karl Rahner, "Christianity and the Non-Christian Religions," in *Theological Investigations* (Baltimore: Helicon, 1966), 5: 115–34. See also his later discussion of the issue, "Anonymous Christian," in *Theological Investigations* (Baltimore: Helicon, 1969), 6: 390–98.

[12] V. Solov'ev, "Velikii spor i khristianskaia politika" [The great dispute and Christian politics], in *Sobranie sochinenii* [Collected works] (St. Petersburg, 1914), 4: 3.

[13] E. Trubetskoi, *Mirosozertsanie Vl. Solov'eva* [Solov'ev's philosophical worldview] (Moscow, 1911). The three periods of Solov'ev's work he delineates are: preparatory – theoretical development of the main principles of a philosophical and religious world view (1873–82); utopian – research on methods for the actual realization of the Christian ideal for the whole of life (the utopia

There was a clearly marked opposition of two cultures, East and West, from the very beginning of human history. The basis of an Eastern culture is the total submission of the person to a superhuman force; the basis of a Western culture is the independent action of the person.[14]

In their own separate manifestations each culture includes extremely diverse and dissimilar elements, but all the distinctions of the individual forms cannot hide the main contrast, which was distinctly revealed already in ancient history. Proceeding from submission to a superhuman principle, the East has developed its own moral ideal, the main features of which are humility and submissiveness to the supreme powers in the social and political sphere, i.e., a patriarchal despotism that was the most consistently expressed in a theocracy, while it held an exclusively religious interest in intellectual activity; indeed all thinking and knowledge was connected with a theosophical idea.

The attachment of the East to legend and antiquity degenerated into exclusiveness and stagnation. From this point of view, for Solov'ev, an exclusive and immobile China represented the purest example of Eastern culture, but this was also the very reason why Chinese culture did not enter the common history of mankind, which presupposes movement.

The roles have changed in the West. Western culture was developed by the Greek republics and Rome, whose moral ideal was characterized by independence and energy, and whose public life was defined by self-determination. Here intellectual activity and artistic creativity was decisively freed from religion, unlike Eastern philosophy and theurgy; the Hellenic genius gave mankind pure philosophy and pure art. The vices of the Western spirit, accordingly, are personal pride, self-determination, and an inclination to discord.

Subordinated to "god," Eastern humanity sought the true God. This search determined the general course of Eastern Enlightenment. Originally a superhuman force was unveiled for man in the form of a revelation, and of an external power of nature.[15]

The West, trusting and worshipping the human principle, sought the perfect person; thereby it deified the person himself, and discovered in him a rabid animal. It became clear that the perfection of the person is not to be found in man himself. The East, however, did not recognize perfection in the person, but sought a perfect God, understanding him as perfect infinity (in India), as perfect light and goodness (in Iran), or as the perfect life (in Egypt). And this East has

---

of universal theocracy) (1882–94); positive – the positive values of Solov'ev's worldview are free of a temporal historical ballast (1894–1900).

[14] Solov'ev, *Velikii spor*, 4: 20.

[15] Ibid., 20–21.

developed a great thirst for seeing and feeling in reality the perfect Divinity which was revealed to it only in contemplation of mind and mythical incarnation. A more actual epiphany and continuous mediation between God and the person was required.[16] And both the false Man-God of the West, or Caesar, and the mythical God-Men of the East, called for a true God-Man. Christianity appeared as the revelation of the perfect God in the perfect person.

Undoubtedly the problem of the Christian East and Christian West was the main problem in Solov'ev's historiosophy. In their demarcation and division he recognized the greatest historical drama; in their mutual reconciliation he saw the greatest historical imperative. However, as he got further into this issue, Solov'ev turned to the experience of another East, the non-Christian East, which still in one way or another belonged to the world of biblical revelation, the East of Judaism and Islam; there he aspired to find the way to a spiritual reconciliation of the three religions that descended from Abraham.

Solov'ev's interest in that East was originally connected with his heightened attention to the Jewish question in Russia. His serious studies of Judaism, Hebrew, and the Hebrew Bible and Talmud were all connected with this issue.[17] In the article "The Sins of Russia" he affirmed that the most important of these were the system of forced Russification in outlying areas, the status of the Jews, and the absence of religious freedom.[18]

As for spiritual reconciliation, he followed the spirit of the time in assigning a special role to Russia. In his third speech in memory of Dostoevskii he wrote, "From the beginning Providence has put Russia between the non-Christian East and the western form of Christianity, between infidels and Latins."[19] The word "infidel" for Solov'ev is not a curse, but rather a conditional term, axiologically neutral, and a little ironical, to designate the monotheistic non-Christian East. Later in the same speech Solov'ev replaces "infidels" with "Judaism." The problem of Islam and, beyond that, of the non-Christian East in general, concerned him as a religious thinker and as a Christian whose conscience demanded, as he

---

[16] Ibid., 28–29.

[17] On Solov'ev's serious study of the ancient Hebrew language, the Bible, and Talmud in the original, see the testimony of F. Gets, *Ob otnoshenii Vl. S. Solov'eva k evreiskomu voprosu* [On Solov'ev's attitude to the Jewish question] (Moscow: Tipo-lit. T-va I. N. Kushnerev, 1902), 9–11.

[18] V. S. Solov'ev, "Nashi grekhi i nasha obiazannost'" [Our sins and our duty], in *Sochineniia v dvukh tomakh* [Works in two volumes] (Moscow: Pravda, 1989), 211; cf. Solov'ev, *Sobranie sochinenii*, 5: 443–46.

[19] Vl. Solov'ev, "Tri rechi v pamiat' Dostoevskogo" [Three speeches in memory of Dostoevskii], in *Sochineniia v dvukh tomakh* [Works in two volumes] (Moscow: Mysl', 1990), 1: 316.

noted in the third speech in memory of Dostoevskii, that he appeal to its very spiritual essence, and take it seriously.[20]

We must note that Solov'ev did not approach the problem of Islam as a specialist on the subject. He did not pretend to be one, but did emphasize that "the meaning of Mohammed and the religion founded by him was so important for the common destiny of mankind that any writer who is interested in religious philosophy, or the philosophy of history, does not need any special justification for forming his own judgement on the person and the mission of the Arab prophet, even without being an Orientalist."[21]

In the first place, V. Solov'ev raised the question of the place of Islam in the divine plan of history. Thus, in solving the problem of Islam he sought above all to find answers for two questions, the very same two questions which Christian thought had raised since it had first been confronted with the phenomenon of Islam, i.e. the time of John of Damascus. Those questions were essentially: why did Islam appear six centuries after the advent of the Savior (whose appearance is the culmination of the Christian understanding of history); who was Mohammed; what could be the religious status of a person who declared himself the "seal of the prophets"; and the question of Christ, who, though he was a prophet, outstanding among those chosen, was nevertheless only a creature of God. These are traditional questions for Christianity, but it is important that Solov'ev gave them essentially new answers. On this issue, as on a number of others, he anticipated much of what was to be discussed within 20th-century Roman Catholicism.

On this position I concur with authorities like Urs Von Balthasar or Monsignor Jan Rupp, who in dealing with the issue has written a remarkable essay about V. Solov'ev, "Le Message Ecclesiale de VI. Solowiew." Solov'ev's Christian treatment of Islam was amazingly close to that of the French expert on Islam, Luis Massignon, who represented the new position of the Church in its relationship to Islam, as determined by the Second Vatican Council.

We must also note briefly that the traditional Christian resolution of two ill-starred questions on Islam were as follows: that Islam was sent down by God upon the heads of Christians for sins with respect to the creeds, and was either one more Christian heresy or a new version of paganism; that Mohammed was a false prophet, an antichrist, or (as one more variant among many had it) that he was the cardinal Mahon who took offence because he had not been elected pope, ran away to Arabia, and at Satan's impulse created a new heresy.

---

[20] Ibid.

[21] V. S. Solov'ev, *Magomet, ego zhizn' i uchenie* [Mahomet: His life and teaching] (St. Petersburg, 1902), 4; cf. *Sobranie sochinenii*, 7: 203.

The evolution of Solov'ev's insights on Islam and his role in history reproduces, to some extent, the entire historical path of Christian conceptions about this religion. He first approached the problem in his small early work *Three Powers* (1877), where he examined Islam as the first historical force that excluded the individual person for the sake of the whole.

> In Islam everything is subordinated to the uniform principle of religion, and besides, this religion reveals itself with an extremely exclusive character, excluding any plurality of forms, any individual freedom. The deity in Islam is an absolute despot, arbitrarily creating the world and people, who are only blind instruments in his hands; the only law of existence for God is his arbitrariness, and for mankind, it is blind invincible fate.[22]

Thus at an early stage of his work, Solov'ev refused to admit that Islam had some independent historical value. We must note that his real knowledge of the Islamic religion at that time was poor and superficial, that it was determined by the stereotypes of Renan which were popular at the time: portraying Arabic philosophy as a barren flower; regarding Iranian poetry as the only valuable contribution of the Islamic world, though alien to Islam; referring to the best representatives of Islam, the dervishes, as "crazy fanatics"; portraying Muslim civilization as alien to progress; and so on.

In his work *The Great Dispute and Christian Politics*, written six years later (1883), Solov'ev already examines the problem of Islam in a rather different perspective, that of the long historical confrontation of East and West. The East is characterized by its tradition of affirming an insuperable precipice between the person and God; although this chasm was inverted and by Christ and directed towards a single God-manhood, Eastern Christian heresies like Arianism, Nestorianism, and Monophysitism restored, once more, its internal requirement of a division between the human and divine principle. In Islam, which arose not just as a heresy but as a different non-Christian religion, the East has found the most consistent, complete statement of its traditional basis.

Without attributing a Christian origin to Islam, Solov'ev sees in it the completion of the oriental rebellion against the God-man. All that was still held in an implicit form in Eastern Christian heresies was clearly expressed in Islam: the rejection of God's incarnation, fatalism, simplicity of cult, and the prohibition against making an image of the deity.

"The latent sin of the Christian East here becomes obvious, but this is also the historical justification of Islam."[23] So, the first step was from an unequiv-

---

[22] V. S. Solov'ev, "Tri sily" [Three powers], in *Sochineniia v dvukh tomakh*, 1: 20.

[23] Solov'ev, "Velikii spor," 1: 102.

ocally negative to a positively negative estimation of the role of Islam in history. The majority of Eastern Christians did not live according to the rule of their faith. (Cf. Solov'ev's well-known aphorism: "In Byzantium there were more theologians than Christians.") Islam thus concludes that the Christian law is untenable and provides another, more feasible law. "Thus, Muslims have an advantage over us, that their life is co-ordinated with their faith, that they live according to the law of their religion in such a way that, although their faith is not true, their life is not a lie."[24]

On a number of occasions in his further work Solov'ev comes back to this original justification of believers of other religions and unbelievers, in terms of faulting Christians themselves before them. Both in the work *Judaism and the Christian Question* (1884) and the essay "On the Decline of the Medieval World View" (1891) he affirmed that inasmuch as Jews and Muslims "persist" in their beliefs, and atheists in their unbelief, we should blame not them but Christians themselves, because they are not guided by Christian law in their own life.

In later works, Solov'ev gradually overcomes the excessive sketchiness of his views on Islam and its role in history. In the work *The History and Future of Theocracy* (1885–87) Solov'ev examines Islam in terms of its place in the general theocratic movements of human history. Aside from the main trunk of theocracy, beginning from Abraham through the Hebrew people, God also raised up numerous collateral branches. Islam, having received on behalf of Hagar and Ishmael the four-fold promise of the land, is one of such branches which arose from the very origin of the trunk. "By multiplying I will multiply your seed, and because of its multiplicity it will not be reckoned."[25] Thanks to Islam, the small Arab tribe has increased extraordinarily, has absorbed into its womb a multiplicity of peoples who submitted to them and converted, and has distributed the force of its name and its new religious idea to the whole southern half of the old historical world, from Morocco in the West to India and China in the East.[26]

Solov'ev's article "Mahomet: His Life and Teaching" (1896) is of special interest to us. The deformed name of the prophet, the one more customary for the Russian reader, is put only in the heading; in the text of the article Solov'ev already uses the correct form, Mohammed. We can regard this article as the culmination of Solov'ev's study of Islam. And it reveals use of source materials for Oriental studies which were very solid for that time. Solov'ev's biographer, V. Velichko, testifies that he studied works of the great experts on the East of that time: Caussin de Perceval, A. Sprenger, R. Smith, I. Wellhausen, A. Müller, and

---

[24] Ibid.

[25] Genesis 16.10.

[26] V. S. Solov'ev, "Istoriia i budushchnost' teokratii" [The history and future of theocracy], in *Sobranie sochinenii*, 4: 381.

J. Grimm; he also studied the Koran in European translations. During the course of his work on the article he constantly consulted the well known Russian Arabist, V. G. Rozen, and the *imam* of the metropolitan mosque, A. Baiazitov.[27]

Solov'ev's article represents not only a description of the life and doctrine of the prophet of Islam. It is an original, profound study of Islam, a sort of Christian apology of Islam. The positive historical and spiritual mission of Islam is proven first of all by its participation in the monotheistic tradition of the Middle East. This involvement was affirmed by Mohammed, who traced his faith through Ishmael to Abraham, whom both Jews and Christians respect. The mission of Mohammed had providential significance: "In Mecca was born a person through whom the ancient promises of God about Ishmael, his ancestor, were fulfilled."[28] Subsequently, this statement would become central for the Catholic Orientalist L. Massignon in his view of Islam.[29]

That is why it is not fair to raise the question as to whether Mohammed was a true or false prophet, nor can we rightly limit his mission to national and political problems. "Mohammed undoubtedly had a special religious genius."[30] All his actions were certainly guided by religious sanction. Mohammed's teaching about God and his properties, about his revelations, about God's commandments, about the destiny of the evil and the good – all of these positions were rather incomplete; still there was nothing false in it, and compared with the pagan religion of the Arabs it represented a great success of religious consciousness.

> The main limitation of Mohammed's worldview and of the religion established by him was the absence of an ideal of human perfection or of a perfect unity of Man with God – the ideal of true God-manhood. Islam demands from the believer not infinite perfection, but only the act of undoubted devotion to God.[31]

But Islam was able to attract many peoples to its history with its popular dogmas and simple commandments. For these peoples the religion of Mohammed became

> what the law had been for the Jews and philosophy for the Hellenes – a transitional step from pagan naturalism to a truly universal culture, and

---

[27] V. L. Velichko, *Vladimir Solov'ev, zhizn' i tvoreniia* [Vladimir Solov'ev, life and work] (St. Petersburg, 1902), 184.

[28] Solov'ev, *Magomet*, 12; cf. *Sobranie sochinenii,* 7: 210.

[29] Cf. Louis Massignon, "Les trois prières d'Abraham," in *Parole donnée* (Paris: Julliard, 1962), 287–89.

[30] Solov'ev, *Magomet*, 16–17; cf. *Sobranie sochinenii,* 7: 216.

[31] Solov'ev, *Magomet*, 79; cf. *Sobranie sochinenii,* 7: 280.

a school of spiritualism and theism in the initial pedagogical form acceptable to these peoples.³²

Certainly, one may say that Solov'ev here examines Islam as a sort of intermediate step to a higher religious stage, as a special form of preparation for the Gospel. But it is more important for us to consider other aspects. The comparative study of three monotheistic religions brought Solov'ev to a principled conclusion, one rather difficult for us to appreciate fully because it requires an understanding of the religious and national situation in Russia at his time; and this is also difficult since we are separated from Solov'ev's time by the Soviet period. He concluded that there is no fundamental difference between the religious laws of the Jews, those of Muslims, and the morality of the New Testament. The basic dispute lies not in the moral, but in the religious-metaphysical sphere. This recognition of ethical equality between the three religions provides an opportunity for mutual understanding, and for positive dialogue between their followers. It is not a question of concessions and compromises, as Solov'ev writes in the "Third Speech in Memory of Dostoevskii": "Our real task is not to *adopt*, but to *understand* the alien forms, to identify and to acquire the positive essence of the alien spirit, and morally to unite with it for the sake of a higher universal truth. Reconciliation *in essence* is necessary; the *essence* of reconciliation is God, and true reconciliation means treating the opponent not on human terms, but 'on God's terms.'"³³ At issue here is the relationship of Catholicism, Judaism, and Islam.

Concluding Remarks

Here we find the principled step to "the new religious consciousness" (a term used by Solov'ev), the essence of which may be expressed briefly in the formula: "It is not I who possess the Truth, but the Truth that possesses me." It goes without saying how relevant and important these ideas are for us today. However, in conclusion, I would like to reflect briefly on two observations which touch on contemporary problems of inter-religious and inter-confessional dialogue.

The first deals with the fact that for us the idea of dialogue far too often acquires a distorted, if not a false form. Take for example the understanding of dialogue as a union of two, in a struggle against a third; for example, Jews and Orthodox may be united in struggle against Protestants. Or statements like, "the dialogue with Islam is possible, but not with Jews, because the first respects the Virgin Mary, while the second does not." Another variant regards dialogue as an

---

³² Ibid.

³³ Solov'ev, "Tri rechi," 2: 316.

alliance of fundamentalists of varied expressions of faith. Here the enemy takes shape not only outside, but also within the religious group itself. This idea is extremely popular among members of contemporary Neo-Eurasian groups. One more variant is rapprochement between Orthodoxy and Islam on the basis of typological similarity. Two moments specially emphasized are: the priority of collectivistic values over individualistic ones, and the unity of spiritual and temporal powers.

The second observation is related to the coexistence of a plurality of religious groups within the state. Establishment of a democratic and law-abiding state, so much discussed these days, undoubtedly presents the necessary condition for the normal existence of the contemporary multi-confessional Russian society. But these confessions, religious groups, and communities also remain within society. The question is not only how the state would regulate relations among them, but also what resources they might find within their spiritual potential for coexistence, for mutual understanding and communication. V. Solov'ev's position presents us with an Orthodox answer to this question, and in my opinion this answer still remains to be claimed.

Cosmism and Evolutionism in the Russian Religious-Philosophical Tradition[1]

Leonid Ivanovich Vasilenko

As a scholarly perspective, cosmism regards the world as a whole in terms of balance, harmony, and beauty; it is full of light and organized according to reason. Cosmism looks for vivifying, creative sources in the world. Although we may be overwhelmed by depressing contemporary problems, cosmism regards the world and its history without a sense of tragedy; it is a fairly optimistic outlook. Cosmism considers the world from a variety of angles, distinguishing "visible nature," which is studied empirically and theoretically, from "invisible nature," which lies somewhere in the depth of visible nature. Only with the latter do we recognize the vivifying, creative powers of the universe, arranged in hierarchical order; these can be personified. They endow natural life and human culture with soul, and ennoble it. These powers can promote human spiritual growth, and this in turn becomes another factor of cosmic significance.

As a scholarly approach cosmism can easily be joined with evolutionism, since the latter also emphasizes the role of significant processes of ascent, complication, development, and world-formation, whether as a whole or in its separate parts. For cosmic-evolutionary thought "invisible nature" or the interior universe becomes a creative source and moving power of the process of world formation, determining its possible ways and aims.

Within the context of such an approach, evil is regarded in terms of disharmony, disorder, disfunctionality, or a state of chaos. The solution to these problems, accordingly, is to be found via incorporation within the framework of cosmic organization, and through the evolution of all that has somehow fallen outside of this framework. Nothing is unnecessary in the cosmos, nothing useless or malicious. Everything should have its own place to fulfil its own destiny, without pretension to anything beyond. With all its problems humanity is saved by returning to its lawful place.

These ideas are not complex, and are becoming more popular nowadays. Yet a number of theoretic problems hide beneath their outward simplicity. Let me point out three of them:

---

[1] L. I. Vasilenko, "Kosmizm i evoliutsionizm v russkoi religiozno-filosofskoi traditsii," in *Russkii kosmizm i sovremennost'*, ed. L. V. Fesenkova (Moscow: IFAN, 1990), 70–86.
Helleman, Wendy, ed. *The Russian Idea: In Search of a New Identity*. Bloomington, IN: Slavica, 2004, 151–63.

1) Is the cosmos self-sufficient? If we assume that the sum of what appears in our world is attracted in its relationship to unseen nature, and we use conceptions related to "invisible nature" to explain what is most valuable, most beautiful and most enduring in terms of evolution, would it then not be necessary to explain the "invisible nature" once more by a "more invisible nature"? And how far are we to go with such an explanation, to the very Source of life as such?
2) Evolutionary processes, generally speaking, go in different directions in our world. How do all these processes going in different directions contribute to the general process of world-formation? Is it directed towards one unified aim? And what is that aim?
3) Every person has a tendency to exceed the boundaries of their present condition, an aspiration to surpass their own nature, to go beyond their social and cultural conditions, even beyond cosmic being as a whole. Is this tendency evidence of disfunctionality, and thus to be suppressed; or, on the contrary, does it manifest freedom of human spirit, without which there could be no creative renewal of the world? Is this the human factor in evolution?

Russian religious philosophy at the end of the 19th and early 20th centuries regarded these as key questions. In answering them they investigated the problems of cosmism and evolutionism. Isolation from the results achieved by these scholars has greatly impoverished the work of Soviet authors writing on questions of the correlation between global evolution and problems of anthropology, ethics, and culture, as well as questions connected with the "noosphere."[2]

1. Some Comments on the Cosmism of Florenskii

P. Florenskii can rightly be linked with the tradition of "Russian cosmism." He wrote inspired works on the "ideal affinity" of the world with humanity, their interpenetration and interrelationship. He followed the pattern of ancient Greek philosophy in correlating the world and humanity in terms of a relationship of macrocosm (i.e., the Cosmos, the world on a grand scale, our surroundings) and microcosm (the world on a small scale, in terms of particulars or individuals). The latter he regarded as "the image and likeness of the Universe," bearing within itself everything existing in the macrocosmic world. Such a cosmic approach to the question of humanity, however, diminishes the fullness of personal being. To address this difficulty Florenskii claimed that both the world and hu-

---

[2] I. N. Moiseev, "Logika universal'nogo evoliutsionizma i kooperativnost'" [The logic of universal evolution and principle of cooperation], *Voprosy filosofii* [Philosophical questions], no. 8 (1989): 52–66.

man beings are equally complicated and inwardly eternal; this is why they can be regarded as parts one of another. Biologically we may consider the world to be the universal body of man; and from an economic point of view we regard the world as the sphere of human economics. "The world is the unfolding of man, a human projection."[3]

Florenskii examined such a "cosmic-anthropological union of two in one" within the context of traditional Platonic dualism, distinguishing the divine and the human in terms of "mountains and valleys" or the "higher and lower." That other world opposite our own is symbolically half-revealed within the realities of earthly being. According to Florenskii, this dualism can only be overcome in the Church, where reality is spiritualized, consecrated, and becomes godlike. *Theosis*, "becoming like God," is the final result of the salvation of the entire world through human salvation, accomplished in the Church by the power of Christ and his Spirit. Salvation overcomes the conflict of humanity versus the world. Here we note the "cosmic aspect of Christianity."[4]

Florenskii gave an ontological interpretation of salvation, using Christianized Platonic two-world dualism. Historical modes of Christianity influencing the world culturally or socially did not attract his attention very much. In his research on Florenskii S. S. Khoruzhii points out that this left him outside the

> main channel of Christian thought (of the time), which portrayed the existence of the world as a process of incarnation of God in humanity, through actual ontological growth and transformation of the world, proceeding to unity with God. This incarnational process was started and actualized by the creative activity of human beings, with the grace of God. Indeed, in freedom the human being, at the head of the council of all creatures, can lead this assembly to God-likeness, when acting by grace; but may also lead other creatures to death, through loss of grace.[5]

Unfortunately, Florenskii has a static picture of life, as did many Platonists. Dynamic processes like evolution or history have no ontological meaning. Any

---

[3] P. Florenskii, "Makrokosm i mikrokosm" [Macrocosm and microcosm], in *Chelovek i priroda* [Man and nature], no. 9 (1989): 71.

[4] P. Florenskii, *Stolp i utverzhdenie istiny* [The pillar and ground of truth] (Moscow: Put', 1914), 733 n. 478; cf. the French translation of Constantin Andronikof, *La colonne et le fondement de la verité* (Lausanne: L'Age d'Homme, 1975), 454. Florenskii's work has also recently been translated into English by Boris Jakim, *The Pillar and Ground of Truth* (Princeton: Princeton University Press, 1997).

[5] S. S. Khoruzhii, "Kosmos – Chelovek – Smertnost': Florenskii i orfiki" [Cosmos, man, mortality: Florenskii and the orphics], in *P. A. Florenskii: Filosofiia, nauka, tekhnika* [P. A. Florenskii: Philosophy, science, technology] (Leningrad: Akademiia nauk. Institut istorii estestvoznaniia i tekhniki, 1989), 14.

history of the world is evaluated negatively, as darkness, or "night, only one awful dream that lasts through the centuries."[6] Florenskii's philosophy reveals a cosmism without evolution; "transformation of the world" does not get beyond the walls of separate church centers, nor does it penetrate the density of the life in the universe, or human social activities.

2. World-Unity and World-Formation in the Work of Vladimir Solov'ev

Vladimir Solov'ev did examine the world in terms of historical process, with special emphasis on questions of the significance and aims of that process, the source of variety in the world, how it shows itself, and the inner co-ordination of various processes of formation and development. It is also important that, unlike Florenskii, Solov'ev did not stop at interpreting man as a microcosm, but turned to the idea of the supercosmic nature of personality. This idea was taken up also in the 20th century by Christian personalists, who did not reduce the person to any forms of its present being, whether natural, individual, or social. The Christian tradition settles this on its own terms, recognizing that man is created in "the image and likeness of God," and that God transcends the cosmos.

In the second place, Solov'ev supported organic thinking; he thought it necessary to consider any subject in its all-round integrity and inner connection with all other subjects. Evolutionism is a natural feature of such thought. Furthermore, he regarded the world in its entirety as an organic entity, a total unity (*vseedinstvo*) of great cosmic variety. He believed that any organic unity includes its own unified source, or has an acting principle causing that unity; when unity is accomplished, it becomes the image of that principle. In other words "an idea of total-unity must be its own definition of the unified central creature."[7] Here he alludes to a personification of cosmic total-unity, giving it a divine character with features of immanence and transcendence.

Thus Solov'ev provides the basis for inclusion of the Logos and World Soul – Sophia – in his conception, for these are the sources and foundation of universal total-unity. The Logos is the principle of being for formation of its structures. According to Solov'ev, Sophia also includes within herself ideal, perfect humanity. It is, as it were, the body of God in the world, an eternal soul of the world, and its dynamic principle. Real humanity and the world as it really exists belongs

---

[6] S. S. Khoruzhii, "Filosofskii simvolizm Florenskogo i ego zhiznennye istoki" [Florenskii's philosophical symbolism and its life sources], in *Istoriko-filosofskii ezhegodnik* [Historical-philosophical annual] 88 (Moscow: Nauka, 1988), 199.

[7] V. S. Solov'ev, *Sochineniia v dvukh tomakh* [Works in two volumes], vol. 2, *Chteniia o Bogochelovechestve: Filosofskaia publitsistika* [Lectures on God-manhood: Philosophical writings on current affairs] (Moscow: Izdatel'stvo "Pravda," 1989), 66. Cf. Vladimir Solovyev, *Lectures on Godmanhood* (London: Dennis Dobson, Ltd., 1948), 119.

to Sophianic total-unity only in part; for the greater part it is beyond Sophianic total-unity. And natural being is connected with the supreme total-unity through humanity, which bears responsibility for total-unity in our world.

At the dawn of history, however, humanity broke away from the original, ontologically indissoluble total-unity. This falling away provided the primary impulse for all world history. And this history reveals the consequences of the fall as the world from time to time is plunged into a deep state of crisis; but people also strive to get themselves free so they can establish a new existence. Solov'ev writes that "the world broke away from God through a free act of the world-soul that united it, and itself disintegrated into a great number of mutually hostile elements; all the multiplicity which arose must become reconciled with itself and with God, and must be revived in the form of the absolute organism by a long sequence of free acts."[8]

The world organism which fell apart nonetheless left something behind, preserving a certain ideal kernel for future total-unity in a hidden and potential form. Universal total-unity exists ontologically in eternity as the base of world integration, which must be accomplished in history. The gradual accomplishment of this process, first in the separate fragments of universal being, and then in the whole, provides the goal and meaning of the world process.

Solov'ev searched eagerly for manifestations of unifying powers in the human world, and also in various other parts of cosmic life. In his works we find references to the law of gravity in physics, to the chemical affinity of bodies, and to the structure and life of plants and animals. Here the world-soul opposes the process of chaos and disintegration. In humanity nature realizes and even outstrips itself as it attains to spheres of absolute being, for man is able to understand the inner connection and significance of all that exists, representing cosmic total-unity within himself: "humanity is the single mediator between God and material being, bearing the unifying divine principle into elemental multiplicity – as arranger and organizer of the universe."[9]

But humanity has broken away from God as the source of total-unity. This resulted in two variants of a cosmic worldview: *naturalistic cosmism*, as a consequence of the above-mentioned falling away as it enslaves man, and *spiritual cosmism*, as a deliverance from what is naturalistic, and entry into the transphysical structure of the cosmos as a whole, connected with Sophia and Logos. The second type of cosmism recovers the dignity of the human being, but as one already redeemed; it recognizes the human right to be spiritual focus of the universe, and gives humanity the power to embrace all nature in the soul and live one life with it, love and understand it.

---

[8] Solov'ev, *Chteniia o Bogochelovechestve*, 137; cf. *Lectures on Godmanhood*, 179.
[9] Solov'ev, *Chteniia o Bogochelovechestve*, 140; cf. *Lectures on Godmanhood*, 181.

These two kinds of cosmism also oppose one another in history: the first gives birth to every kind of idolatry and attracts demons that oppress the human soul. It takes revenge by means of magic, occult knowledge, and other forms of self-affirmation, for it can possess independent sides of natural life, at least in part. The second, on the other hand, longs especially for restoration of the inner unity of the human soul through restoration of its roots in the Sophianic foundations of the universe, and in the Logos. In this way a genuine spiritual direction of the deeper aspects of world life is possible; through labor and creativity it also allows for the real possibility of assisting the historical-evolutionary process of recreating and opening up cosmic total-unity.

This approach differs radically from the attitude to the world prevalent in the modern scientific-technological mentality, which cultivates a forced capturing of the world and an ego-centered structure of the human soul dominating its living environment. The tasks set by Solov'ev oppose the increasing powers of the ego, and the rational knowledge needed to expand and strengthen its domination. Solov'ev's "Sophianic" task serves the "supreme" project for the world and humanity, and requires a totally different structure of the human soul. Solov'ev remained faithful to the Christian tradition affirming humanity as bearer and co-worker of the power of grace spiritualizing the world only as it becomes renewed according to the image of Christ.

Solov'ev devoted special attention to the cultural-historical side of this process. He analyzed different world cultures and religions from the perspective of their affirmation of total-unity in the world. Solov'ev also made a thorough study of the history of philosophical thought from the same perspective, not excluding criticism of socialism, revolutionary movements, and their social projects.

A fundamental culturological opposition recurring in Solov'ev's work is that of "East-West." From Solov'ev's point of view, the battle between East and West helps explain the course of historical development, first within the Mediterranean cultural region, and then the whole world. In a small work, *Three Powers* (*Tri sily*), Solov'ev opposes the Western approach on questions of the organization of life (with priority given to self-affirmation and creative realization of personal abilities) to Eastern impersonal social organization and religion as it limits human freedom and creative powers. When taken to an extreme and realized consistently, both approaches bring human progress to a deadlock. "The first excludes the free plurality of separate forms and personal elements, free movement, and progress, while the second has just as negative an effect on unity and the general supreme principle of life; it breaks the solidarity of the whole."[10]

The struggle between these powers can be pursued for a long time with variable success, but without any substantial accomplishment. A "third force" is

---

[10] Solov'ev, *Sochineniia v dvukh tomakh*, 1: 19.

needed to create world total-unity; this force will not cease acting in the world but, according to Solov'ev, does need a special historical mediator for effective realization in history. The people called to that task should be able to "impart a living soul, to give life and integrity to a broken, dying humanity through its union with the eternal divine principle."[11] Acting not in its own interest or from of its own conviction, that people must rise above the oppressed creative and moral energy of the elements with their small, humble passions and interests, and must also avoid getting too greatly affected by Western or Eastern principles of life-organization.

Solov'ev says that the Slavonic and Russian people have a special historic mission as bearer of a collective power that creates a new path for human development in history; this path is to avoid the deadlock of brutal tyranny and spiritual stagnation of the East, as well as the absence of spirituality in Western civilization. Russia receives a special cosmic role in accomplishing total world unity. This has been a constant theme at the center of attention for Russian cosmism. In the 20th century the Rerikhs turned to it, interpreting it from their own point of view, as did Daniil Andreev in his main work, *Rose of the World,* which has now finally been published.

To sum up, we may conclude that Vladimir Solov'ev developed his own cosmist-evolutionist understanding of the world, with a strong emphasis on thorough integration of everything in the world, and struggle to overcome chaos and collapse. He did not pay much attention to the simple "struggle for existence" in the biosphere or social life; he was more interested in overcoming that kind of life, to raise it to its highest level of being. Questions of differentiation and selection were also secondary, although in Solov'ev's time scientific evolutionism attached fundamental significance to these phenomena.

This emphasis can be explained in terms of Solov'ev's organicist understanding of development; had he devoted more attention to different biological processes, he might have regarded world evolution as a differentiation of an organic whole along different, opposing poles, around which processes of integration would be organized in terms of growth. But he did not have such an organic view of the world; Solov'ev was so focused on overcoming the spiritual disruption of humanity that he would not seek another picture of future development. And he was not alone: this approach was shared by other early 20th-century philosophers, like S. Bulgakov.

---

[11] Ibid., 29.

3. Sergei Bulgakov's "Philosophy of Economy"

As a philosopher Sergei Bulgakov regarded all concrete questions from a cosmic perspective. Like Solov'ev, he interpreted cosmic being in its entirety as "an organism in potential,"[12] the universal human body. Just as Teilhard de Chardin made a re-thinking of modern natural-scientific evolutionism from a Christian point of view the aim of his life, so Bulgakov took as his goal a spiritual rethinking of contemporary economism, the aggregate of socio-economic concepts, all typically saturated with a spirit of economic utilitarianism, pragmatism, and materialism. Bulgakov posited the ontological value, spiritual importance and cosmic role of human labor, independent of social, state, or party interests. Labor is called upon to serve in establishing life on earth, to oppose the powers of disintegration and death, to ennoble life, and open up the riches of its creative potentialities in their highest form. But this calls for a discovery of ontological and cosmological aspects of Christianity that are still only weakly actualized, if at all.

"Justification of the world is a basic motif in Bulgakov's philosophical thought, expressed with an often emotional affirmation of the value of this-worldly being and the material cosmos."[13] Our world, moreover, represents itself as a struggle between powers of Life and Death. This struggle is necessary for world development and cosmic formation; it means the undaunted seizure and revival of huge masses of dead matter by the powers of Life. As a result, life penetrates where formerly there were no manifestations of it, reviving the power of life inherent, but oppressed by an enslaving death in matter. Death led to the collapse of the world as a whole, but Bulgakov affirms that the collapse could not prevent the revival of the world as a kind of organism and living whole: its true reality is maintained in potential form, hidden under the cosmos visible to us. Human labor and creative work must help to uncover this reality.

This view provides the impetus for Bulgakov's understanding of the cosmic human mission, which he shares with Solov'ev, namely to shift the balance of powers of life and death in that struggle towards fullness of life and a positive direction in the global evolutionary process. "Reaching self-consciousness and an ability to work on itself in man, nature enters a new stage of existence. Proprietary labor represents a new power of nature, a new cosmogonic factor in world-formation, fundamentally different from nature's other powers."[14]

---

[12] S. Bulgakov, "Mir kak khoziaistvo," pt. 1 of *Filosofiia khoziaistva* (Moscow, 1912), 80; trans. by C. Evtuhov as *Philosophy of Economy: The World as Household* (New Haven and London: Yale University Press, 2000), 132.

[13] S. S. Khoruzhii, "Sofiia – Kosmos – Materiia: Ustoi filosofskoi mysli otsa Sergiia Bulgakova" [Sophia, Cosmos, Matter: Foundations of the philosophical thought of Fr. Sergei Bulgakov], *Voprosy filosofii*, no. 12 (1989): 74.

[14] Ibid., 107.

Nature attains its salvation through human salvation, and that in turn is given through Christ. Both Florenskii and Solov'ev discussed such a cosmological meaning of Christianity. Bulgakov thus joins an older European tradition, regarding the human being as a "Messiah of nature" (Novalis) or "redeemer of nature" (Schelling). By "redeeming the sin of the original corruption of nature, through labor" humanity must cure the world "of cosmic disease," i.e., nature's isolation from the supernatural "soul of the world," and make the visible world transparent for the work of invisible creative powers.[15] Bulgakov assigns a special role to knowledge in transforming the world. For him knowledge is not primarily a means of capturing nature, but rather a support, defense and expansion of life and its partial resurrection. To return life to its genuine condition, scientific study of nature is not as important as an inner comprehension of its deeper aspects.

For Bulgakov Divine Sophia, the eternal Beauty and harmony of the divinely created cosmos, and ontological centre of universe, was also the source of inner comprehension of the world. She endows economic activity, religious and cultural creative work, philosophical and scientific knowledge, and even social progress in history with her Sophianic qualities.

> Whether we consider Sophia in terms of true insight, mythological inclination within Christianity, or mystified expression of urgent historical needs, a significant ethical power is hidden within Bulgakov's sophiology. In this power a sense of distance with respect to the transience of life is combined with a sense of protecting and preserving it. In loving the world he does not regard it as a source for the "satisfaction of needs," but as a priceless artistic creation; such love proposes asceticism, self-restraint, and rejection of the vampire syndrome of the present civilization. Such are the practical results of Bulgakov's sophiology, the essence of his "dogmatic basis of culture."[16]

4. Berdiaev: Cosmos, History, and Eschatology

With the rise of technical civilization the world somehow "moved" irreversibly along a dangerous path toward the breakdown of the organic and spiritual foundations of life. This is one of the main themes of Berdiaev's work. He did not believe that it was possible to restore old forms of social and religious life, and the corresponding relationships between man and the cosmos. Admitting that the past with its endless constraints was certainly no paradise, the human spirit

---

[15] Ibid., 123.

[16] I. Rodnianskaia, "Sergei Nikolaevich Bulgakov," *Literaturnaia gazeta* [Literary newspaper], 27 September 1989, p. 6.

must go forward, freely and fearlessly, rather than retracing old ways for salvation from contemporary troubles. This is why Berdiaev rejects Bulgakov's concept of history as a sacred necessity, Solov'ev's concept of world development as an organic process, and also Florenskii's attraction to the static cosmology of the Middle Ages and Antiquity; for him the end of the organic epoch has already come.

All of Berdiaev's philosophy is marked by his sense of the eschatological End; it is presented as a perfection of history, a summing up of all things, and Judgment. It also covers cosmic life. Judgment on humanity includes nature; the industrial-technological civilization, so pernicious for every living being, represents a realization of this judgment, at least in part.

> The machine has crucified the world's flesh; its fragrant flowers and singing birds have ascended onto that cross. This is the Golgotha of nature. In the inevitable process of the artificial mechanization of nature, there is a kind of redemption of the sin of inner constraint and enmity. The natural organism must die in order to be resurrected to new life. As the monstrous machines destroy natural organic integrity, they indirectly and tortuously set the spirit free from its natural connectedness.[17]

History as a tragedy of being must end in catastrophe, and has a transcendent path. Reliance on any historical determination is useless and deceptive; face to face with that End, it is necessary, rather, to enter the free spirit and creativity of the person.

> The Earthly spirit of humanity, proceeding along the path of the Snake, has hypnotized humanity with its tempting idea of progress toward an earthly paradise. Thoroughly seduced, human beings have not noticed the madness of such service to progress and submission to the fortunes of an approaching paradise. Progress flourishes in the cemetery, and the entire culture of such a perfected humanity is poisoned by a deadly venom. All the flowers of life belong to the burial ground.[18]

Humanity must obtain inner freedom to serve the cause of salvation and thereby liberate the world from sin. This is a key role for human beings as the cosmic center of being, the highest point of its compass. It is also in humanity that the power of God has created a special seed by which to implant the cause of salvation. "Incarnated as a human being and appearing on Earth, Christ is the

---

[17] N. A. Berdiaev, *Sud'ba Rossii: Opyty po psikhologii voiny i natsional'nosti* [The fate of Russia: Essays on war psychology and nationality] (Moscow, 1918), 236–37.

[18] N. A. Berdiaev, *Filosofiia svobody: Smysl tvorchestva* [Philosophy of freedom: The meaning of creativity] (Moscow: Pravda, 1989), 123.

absolute center of the cosmos. Through Christ humanity has gotten a cosmic significance; in him the soul of the world returns to God."[19] The human duty is to become free, and spiritual creative work is one of the important ways for becoming free.

Berdiaev anticipates the beginning of a new world epoch, a religious-cosmic epoch of creativity to be realized by a redeemed and spiritually free humanity. A new life is to be created, one that steps far beyond the frames of culture; in fact it implies a conversion of culture, revelation of the godlikeness of human nature, continuation of the creation of the world, as well as revelation of the cosmic character of humanity, its spiritual growth and ascent to truth, to goodness, beauty, and to the Origin. With its roots creativity extends to transphysical mysteries, the mystery of human freedom. Authentic freedom has a cosmic character, and is not chaotic. It has an inner connection with the hierarchical harmony of the Universe, and is almost unknown to modern humanity in its enslavement to natural and social necessity and loss of its original place in the hierarchy of universal being.

5. Conclusion

We have presented only a general sketch of fundamental directions in cosmist thought, but these open up a spectrum of ways to understand the problems of cosmism and evolutionism. They also pose the question of the future development of the ideological and spiritual foundations of cosmism. Problems of world development, for example, are not considered by Florenskii, whose cosmist views can be traced back to antiquity. The philosophical systems of Solov'ev and Bulgakov led them to more organically intertwined ideas of cosmism and evolutionism, each of them developing directions in cosmism according to the specific material foundations from which they preferred to work. And finally, we noted the mystical historicism of Berdiaev, in which the ideas of cosmism and evolutionism have lost independent significance, subjecting their energy to a powerful historical and eschatological mysticism.

These distinguished representatives of Russian philosophy arrived at conclusions which for them were not philosophical abstractions, far distant from real life, but ideological foundations giving direction for new paths in social and cultural development. They recognized an opposition between such a spiritualized and spiritually conditioned development and the basic direction of contemporary Western social thinking, which assigned little significance to spirituality. In the present epoch of global crisis, however, Western models have gotten exhausted, and lack positive ideas. At this point the long-forgotten Russian heritage can be revived, to initiate the search for future directions.

---

[19] Ibid., 141.

In response critics may point out that Russian religious-philosophical cosmism simply revitalizes an ancient mythology, reproducing an archaic worldview which is poverty-stricken and merits no serious attention. In fact, even though "mythological" forms of thought may be out of step with modern rationalist culture, they still have important advantages over the latter in addressing questions of critical aspects of man's being in the world. Even developed cultures maintain a tradition which builds on its more ancient spiritual content; this is also illustrated by the concepts explained above. Indeed, if we examine modern culture closely, we will find it presents a different kind of mythologizing, of a quality much lower than that found in Russian philosophy.

The fundamental problem is not one of the continuity of a tradition from the past, in spirit and form. It would actually be strange if this were not the case, for human beings remain the same in most aspects throughout history, no matter how great the changes in the natural, social, and cultural contexts of their activities. Problems arise from primitivization of the cultural-historical mythology and the spiritual content born of religion. Authentic interpretation is maintained by the fundamental spiritual traditions of the world. However, simplification of content inevitably occurs beyond the limits of these traditions, through socio-ideological use, for aims connected with such use.

We find an example of this process in the technocratic reduction by Soviet philosophical publicists of the term "noosphere," first suggested by Teilhard de Chardin and V. I. Vernadskii. Another clear example is the politicized socio-collectivistic propaganda of Slavophiles on ideas of *sobornost'* as an element of the Russian national consciousness. However, before the idea was politicized, A. S. Khomiakov and other authors discussed the fundamental significance of a communal (*sobornyi*) spiritual unity of the people, as a bearer of truth in its fullness. They affirmed the existence of such a mystical form of "collectivity" in the early Muscovite period of Russian history; so their attempt to create a "collectivized Russia" seemed to them a restoration of what had already existed in history. As a result, both history and the social project were mythologized. Fortunately they managed only to create a utopia needed not for scientific history, but to oppose the myth of Western civilization. Instead of a search for truth, ideological struggle arose and led to the degradation of Slavophilism to national arrogance and political utility.

Science has certainly rejected the Slavophile myth, but strictly speaking, it has a right only to reject the historical link. The content of the myth can be rejected only on the basis of nonscientific concepts, for myth appears and exists outside of a rationalist culture. Myth carries with itself a figurative-symbolical understanding of things, not rationally founded knowledge. It demands research from a hermeneutical perspective, in comparison and contrast with other myths of greater depth of spiritual meaning, and must be criticized on the basis of such comparison.

For Russian cosmism, things are different. It arose in reaction to the lack of spirituality of Western forms of civilization and scientific culture, and thus defended the idea of the universe, history, and the human soul having an inner depth which cannot be contained in any rational schemes. It also insisted that the realization of certain superhuman tasks in the world, like the cosmic mission, be entrusted to man. Of course, it was right in claiming that Western European culture had lost an understanding of such things.

Moreover, unlike the Slavophile myth, Russian cosmism defended the ideal of cultural universalism and spiritual openness, and this represents its value for us today, when trends of anti-cultural fanaticism and spiritual isolationism are very strong. If one wishes to argue with Russian cosmism it is first necessary to admit its truth and value, and in response propose a truth even deeper, more foundational. But it is much easier to reject cosmism in other ways, and it can certainly be rejected as something that is "not ours," "useless," or "irrational"; others may try to utilize it, and will hardly escape debasement. Those who witness such profanation will blame not those (or at least not only those) who effect it, but those profaned. The fruitlessness of it all is evident enough; even so, the creative development and intensification of Russian cosmism is possible, in service to the search for truth in different directions.

Neo-Patristic Synthesis and Russian Philosophy[1]

Sergei Sergeevich Khoruzhii

The two themes of Russian thought and Orthodox theology always remained at the center of Father Georges Florovsky's creative work. It has become a tradition to consider these two parts of his work in isolation, as if they have little to do with each other. Just recently a fundamental study of the work and life of Fr. Georges appeared in the United States;[2] although it is an excellent, thorough work, it takes this tendency of separating the two areas of interest to an extreme. The "Russian" and "theological" themes are treated in two parts of the book, written by different authors, and brought together almost incidentally under the same cover. Of course, there are reasons for such a separation. In developing his theological and ecclesiological ideas Fr. Georges did not usually consider their application to the concrete context of Russian religion and culture.

The chief and most general of his theological ideas, that of "Neo-Patristic Synthesis," seems at first sight to be an exception; in *Ways of Russian Theology* the author is persistent in applying this idea to the history of Russian thought. But it is easy to see that its application embraces only two aspects: Greek patristics and the "patristic style" are used as a standard for assessing various stages of Russian thought, and in the conclusion functions as a slogan and appeal, pointing to a fruitful way for future cultural work. Clearly, this is inadequate. Neo-patristic synthesis is not so much a slogan or standard of measurement, as a positive theological and historico-cultural viewpoint. And a serious approach to the ways and tasks of Russian thought from this point of view means, first of all, understanding what "restoration of the patristic style" means for the present spiritual situation, in both Russia and the world. This is what I plan to do in the present article. I shall try to outline briefly and in a preliminary fashion a method of resolving this task, especially as it applies to the development of Russian philosophy.

---

[1] S. S. Khoruzhii, "Neopatristicheskii sintez i russkaia filosofiia," *Voprosy filosofii* [Philosophical questions], no. 5 (1994): 75–88.

[2] Andrew Blane, ed., *Georges Florovsky, Russian Intellectual and Orthodox Churchman* (Crestwood, NY: St.Vladimir's Seminary Press, 1993).

Helleman, Wendy, ed. *The Russian Idea: In Search of a New Identity*. Bloomington, IN: Slavica, 2004, 165–83.

1. The School

The patristic and neo-patristic style of thought is characterized by Florovsky in constant comparison and contrast with the Western theological and philosophical tradition. Thus, I shall start by outlining a historico-philosophical scheme to demonstrate the correlation between this tradition and Russian philosophy in its various stages. For such a scheme it is convenient to use the concepts of "school" and "tradition" in the history of thought, making certain distinctions between them.

1.1. Slavophiles

As in all other main aspects, the period of the early Slavophiles is a prologue. Here for the first time the Russian consciousness was convinced of the "possibility and necessity" of creating its own philosophy, based on its own spiritual roots. However, that creation did not yet take place. It was quite clear that the tasks and goals of the desired philosophy would not be borrowed, but should come from Russian spiritual experience. But the exact nature of the relationship between this philosophy and Western philosophical thought was not yet determined, and remained unclear.

The task of creating a Russian philosophy was the responsibility of Ivan Kireevskii; what he contributed was not so much a distinct solution to the problem as some conflicting trends. On the one hand, his views on the contemporary state and development of philosophy were strongly influenced by Schelling, and remained within the frame of Schelling's concepts. This inevitably influenced his own view of Russian philosophy. According to a recent careful study, "Kireevskii strove to include the pure science of reason, which culminated in Schelling's "negative" system, into a "positive" philosophy, and consequently also into the future Russian philosophy."[3] On the other hand, Kireevskii claimed emphatically that the heritage of the Eastern fathers of the church should be the very cornerstone of this future philosophy; he stressed that patristic thought and its approach to issues of reason, human being, and spiritual life differed profoundly from paradigms of Western thinking. In this regard he is a direct and indisputable forerunner of neo-patristic synthesis. In the last period of his life there are indications of a different way of philosophizing, and we may agree that "his estrangement from Schelling appears quite considerable, and may even be taken as a matter of principle.... It looks as if he is proposing to give up altogether the world of late-Idealistic philosophy."[4] Khomiakov, on the other hand, was even

---

[3] E. Müller, "I. V. Kireevskii i nemetskaia filosofiia" [I. V. Kireevskii and German philosophy], *Voprosy filosofii*, no. 5 (1993): 128.

[4] Ibid.

less inclined to submit Russia's philosophical project to Western directions of thought, but like Kireevskii he had no constructive alternative to such directions. The project lacked substantive details. How should Russian philosophy relate to Western philosophy? The answer was not yet found, and the choice not yet made.

1.2. Solov'ev and the Metaphysics of All-Unity

It was Solov'ev who eventually made the choice. With him Russian religious philosophy ceased being an uncoordinated collection of preliminary efforts, and appeared as a fully valid philosophical system. Solov'ev's thought found many followers, and very soon developed into an entire philosophical direction known today as the metaphysics of All-Unity. Solov'ev's philosophy, as well as that of others who took this direction, had a very specific status in relating to Western thought. I shall describe it as follows: Russian religious philosophy defined itself as a *new school within the framework of the classical European philosophical tradition*. This crucial formula for positioning the newborn philosophy within the European context needs to be explained and substantiated in greater detail.

1.2.1. The Classical Western Tradition

First of all, let us specify the categories of "school" and "tradition" in the history of thought. It is natural to consider "tradition" as the broader category; within the framework of one tradition we find a variety of schools. What unites them? What constitutes the common basis of a tradition? Briefly, it is formed by the most general ideas of being, by ways of thinking, and by the organization of theological and (or) philosophical discourse. The former is the most essential for us now. It is important to note that besides a general position, which embraces the principle features of a theology and (or) philosophy, their nature, tasks, or system, the base of a tradition also includes a certain ontological foundation. We are not referring to the details of an ontology, which may vary greatly within a tradition, but the *type of ontology*, its skeletal structure and deep-rooted intuitions of being, which lie at the root of this framework. This constitutes a universal historico-philosophical category, and remains an "invariant" of a tradition, shared by all the schools taking part in it.

Next, we must specify what is meant by the "classical Western theological-philosophical tradition." We include with it the whole magisterial line of development of the European Christian era, from the patristics, via scholastics to the secularization of thought, and the formation of classical modern European philosophy with its landmarks: Descartes, Leibnitz, and German Idealism. What ontological foundation is associated with this tradition? It began with precursors of the patristics, but its roots were universally Christian, with the Fathers of the

4th century, common to both East and West. But already in the late 4th and early 5th centuries a special Western branch of patristics appeared, one that was to serve as the source of Western ontology. Its founder was St. Augustine. After his work the basic layer of ontological positions for Western Christianity was that of patristics à la St. Augustine, adopting his selection and editing of the Fathers (including, of course, his own considerable contribution on many issues). Among the distinctive features of this Augustinian "editing" one must emphasize the strong Neoplatonic elements which influenced all principal concepts, like the Augustinian doctrine of grace, predestination, freedom, evil, or sin.

Further contributions to this foundation were substantive, but at present it is sufficient to mention them briefly. What matters, first, is that the changes preserved the general type of ontology; one of its principal features is an ontological split, including two horizons of being, as well as the "essentialist" character of its foundational categories and relationships. It is also important that the two main stages introducing this tradition, Thomist scholastics and classical German Idealism, for all their radical differences, from our point of view (i.e., from the East) appear to proceed in the same direction, one that perceived and intensified the specific tendencies of "Augustinian editing." Here the principles of Reason and abstract thought were singled out, emphasized, and considered as a cornerstone, although in Augustine's own position this was moderated by strong existentialist motives and development of an intuition of the integral person. This philosophical tradition closed the gap with pre-Christian Greek thought, absorbing its concepts and positions unaltered, neglecting the work of transformation or translation within the context of Christian teaching, work which the fathers always considered indispensable.

One hardly needs to prove that Solov'ev's philosophy, and all Russian philosophy of the Silver Age, in its general type finds a place within the tradition outlined above. It adopted the tradition's methodological and epistemological postulates, defining philosophy, and determining how philosophical discourse should be constructed. It also adopted the system of categories of this tradition and, even more important, the skeleton of its ontology. It had the closest ties with the course of German philosophy, which influenced Russian philosophy in many different ways.[5] The influence of scholastics, on the other hand, was relatively insignificant. At the same time, Russian philosophy did not join any concrete direction of Western thought. From the very beginning it was an independent and rather separate phenomenon. The very reasons for its emergence had

---

[5] Cf. the radical opinion of L. P. Karsavin, "Everything really achieved by Russian philosophers should be included in the history of European and mainly German thought," in his article "Filosofiia i VKP" [Philosophy and the All-Union Communist Party], *Evraziia* (Paris) 20 (6 April 1929).

little to do with the appearance of professional philosophers, most of whom joined existing schools and trends. Its main driving motive was to express on a proper philosophical level the authentic Russian spiritual experience, that of the Russian soul and mentality, individual and national being, the religion and culture of Russia. So it had its own tasks and subjects for philosophizing, its own set of themes and ideas. These were the common elements embracing all systems and doctrines in Russian philosophy, yet at the same time separating the latter from the rest of the Western tradition. With their own respective value and character these elements, when compared with the aforementioned borrowings, were quite adequate to give Russian philosophy a status which can be expressed in the formula of a "separate school within the framework of a larger tradition."

Such a status raises a number of questions. *A priori* it may well be contradictory: if the tasks and aims of a new school are independent and not derived from the tradition, they could conceivably be incompatible with the tradition, and thus not be realized within its limits. Was it possible to express within the classical Western tradition the experience and spiritual principles which gave rise to Russian philosophy? This question was not given much theoretical consideration and the answer was provided not so much by reasoning as by life itself in the course of the historical existence of Russian thought. Today the answer is sufficiently clear. It is neither just positive or negative. The tasks of Russian thought could be realized within the framework of the Western tradition, but only to a certain extent or stage. These tasks did share some real common ground with the basis of the tradition. And since the decision to join the tradition, beginning with Solov'ev, had already been made, the optimal strategy for Russian thought was to explore this common ground and use all the given options fully.

1.2.2. The Metaphysics of All-Unity

This was precisely how Russian philosophy developed during the religious-philosophical renaissance. The intuitions and sources of the Orthodox outlook coincided with the ontological basis of the classical Western tradition in the philosophy of All-Unity. It is here, first and foremost, that the common ground turned out to be rather rich and extensive. In European philosophy the metaphysics of All-Unity existed from much earlier times in Ancient Greece. In his work A. F. Losev has demonstrated thoroughly that All-Unity served as a key idea and *Leitmotiv* for the entire ancient Greek worldview. It was introduced specifically as a philosophical category by Plotinus, and in Neoplatonism All-Unity obtained a deep philosophical elaboration; it was transformed by pseudo-Dionysius, along with many other Neoplatonic concepts, into a Christian theology, which already had some elements of this idea from St. Paul's teaching on the Church. After the patristic era, the theme of All-Unity accompanied all periods of the classical Western tradition; it was developed by Eriugena, Nicholas of Cusa, and Leibnitz, adopted within numerous mystical doctrines, and completed its development in Schelling and Hegel.

But this theme had just as great an affinity with Russian culture and Russian Orthodox spirituality. All-Unity was especially suitable for the philosophical expression of the values and ideals of this culture. An important *Leitmotiv* of the Russian mentality is a striving for wholeness, integrity, community, and unity, and aversion to any kind of fragmentation, division, separation, whether in the world, in society, or in the human soul. As Florenskii has reminded us, precisely this motif guided the deeds of St. Sergius of Radonezh, and found expression in the Trinity icon of Andrei Rublev. As principle of the perfect unity of multiple being, All-Unity ideally embodies this motif. Another motif closely connected with it which has both an ethical and aesthetical nature, is the theme of harmony, well-proportioned arrangement, and coherence of being. It appears to be the specifically Russian and Christian version of the ancient Greek ideal of *kalokagathia* (goodness and beauty). This ideal too is perfectly expressed in All-Unity. Finally we must consider the motif of *sobornost'* (catholicity), so ancient and so important for Russian identity, for both its social and religious content; it is also directly connected with All-Unity, and finds its philosophical basis in it.[6]

When Vladimir Solov'ev created the first philosophical system in Russian he chose to found it on the concept of All-Unity; this was a natural and organic development of the tradition. And it was quickly supported by others. At the beginning of the 20th century quite a number of major philosophical systems emerged within a short time: those of Bulgakov, Florenskii, E. Trubetskoi, Losskii, and Frank. Together they formed the first philosophical direction born in Russia, that of the Russian metaphysics of All-Unity. Together with the European philosophy of All-Unity, it belongs to the Platonic tradition, and represents panentheism according to its ontological type: the position which regards the world and all its phenomena as having its essence abiding in God.

Thus All-Unity provided the common meeting ground for the worlds of Western philosophy and Russian Orthodoxy. It was an important meeting, and to this day the fruits of the metaphysics of All-Unity provide the main content of Russian philosophy. Our present intention is not to dwell on these fruits, however, but to trace the path and understand where it led. The paradigm of All-Unity opened up considerable possibilities for the development of Russian philosophy. While the philosophical process (like other national processes) was characterized by unprecedented intensity and speed during the Silver Age, at the

---

[6] Cf. S. S. Khoruzhii, "Khomiakov i printsip sobornosti" [Khomiakov and the principle of sobornost'], in *Zdes' i teper'* [Here and now], no. 2 (1992): 68; cf. also his *Posle pereryva: Puti russkoi filosofii* [After the break: Ways of Russian philosophy] (St. Petersburg: Aleteiia, 1994).

time of the Revolution one could see that its possibilities were limited. The reasons for this limitation could not be fully understood because it coincided with the catastrophe of the revolution. Nonetheless, it was becoming clear that a considerable part of Russian Orthodox spirituality failed to find expression in the metaphysics of All-Unity, especially questions of Orthodox anthropology, concepts of man and his connection with God. There were also the important classical subjects of the Orthodox mystics and ascetics: the theme of the changeable character of human nature, of the dramatic struggle against the passions, the problem of the perfection and transformation of the soul, and deification of man by divine grace. These themes, all broad and rich in content, failed to find expression in the metaphysics of All-Unity, and escaped its constructions.

1.3. Russian Asceticism and Spirituality

On the other hand, Russia only experienced partial success in following along the course of European thought. Lack of full accord between the sources of Russian thought and the Western tradition was an explicit, recognized fact. Even as a school within this tradition, Russian philosophy never managed to become a school like others. There were always elements of strain, tension, and conflict. Criticism, and at times quite sharp criticism of the Western tradition, remained a feature of the work of Russian philosophers. It was directed at distinctive features of the tradition as a whole, its bias toward epistemology, abstract-speculative constructions, and one-sided systematization. Separate trends of the tradition were also criticized. Such trends might be fashionable for a short period, and even emerge as a stereotype, but this in turn would soon be subjected to devastating critique; it was called "overcoming" (*preodolenie*). In this way Marx, Kant, and Nietzsche were "overcome," and contributed to an attitude of permanent criticism.

Thus, while it was integrated into European thought, Russian philosophy was also becoming a critical corrective for it, taking on the role of self-criticism of European philosophy. Certainly this was not a useless role, but the positive tasks of Russian thought as such could not be realized in this way. As Florovsky has pointed out, "Orthodox theology ... is called to oppose other confessions not so much with rebuke as with the *testimony*, the *truth of Orthodoxy*."[7] The same could be said of philosophy. But here, in order to bear witness, one difficult condition had to be met: use of "new principles for philosophy," for which Kireevskii had already made an intense effort. It was becoming clearer that these had not yet been provided by Solov'ev.

---

[7] G. V. Florovsky, *Puti russkogo bogosloviia* [Ways of Russian theology] (Paris: YMCA-Press, 1983), 513 (italics Florovsky's).

1.3.1. *Imiaslavie*

Russian philosophy came closer in approaching these principles when it turned to the problem of the "glorification of the name" (*imiaslavie* or *onomatodoxy*); this refers to a special form of venerating the name of God, which arose at the beginning of the 20th century in a variety of independent monastic communities on Mount Athos and in the Caucasus. "Glorification of the name" represents a profound theoretical topic which arose directly from both religious practice and ancient roots of mystical traditions of Orthodoxy. It immediately caught the attention, interest and confidence of a great number of Russian philosophers; Bulgakov, Florenskii, Ern, and Losev became supporters of the movement and engaged in serious theological and philosophical analysis of its foundations. They were all agreed that the grounds for "glorification of the name" must be found in the doctrine of divine energies developed by Gregory Palamas in the 14th century.

This teaching synthesized all of Eastern patristics and is also a theological expression of the practice of hesychastic asceticism, but did not come within the orbit of the metaphysics of All-Unity; it had never been given philosophical consideration prior to this time. Its conceptions and positions were new for philosophy, and thus the problem expanded the previous base of Russian philosophy with new content. Under the Bolshevik regime this work was only partly completed, and its conclusions remained unknown for a long time. But rather unexpectedly this factor also played a positive role, for the new elements contained in hesychasm and Palamist thought could thus not be introduced into Russian philosophy as a simple complement to the foundations of the metaphysics of All-Unity (just as these also could not be used to justify "glorification of the name"). For further advance in Russian thought a rejection of that foundation was needed, not another complement. And the external force breaking up the established philosophical process may in its own way have facilitated departure from the previously well-trodden path.

2. "Kehre"

After the national catastrophe a withdrawal from the previous course of development in Russian thought took place in both branches of culture, and these would continue divided from that time. In Russia itself this meant departure into nonexistence. In the diaspora life continued; here it was not just a matter of departure, nor was the departure from the former path a sudden one. It took as much as a generation. Leading philosophers already established in their work continued to develop the metaphysics of All-Unity. It could hardly have been otherwise, but the time was ripe for change. Convincing proof of this may be found in the fact that however outstanding and brilliant, these philosophers left hardly any successors. Creative forces, far from being exhausted, began to find expression in other ways. One of the first philosophers to embark on a new path was Vladimir Losskii, son of the famous representative of the metaphysics of All-Unity and author of a system of intuitionism, Nikolai Onufrievich Losskii. His system focused precisely on all those themes which the metaphysics of All-Unity could only absorb Platonically (in all senses), namely the inner experience of Orthodoxy and a mystical-ascetic anthropology.

2.1. Palamist Asceticism

The turn toward these themes had many, far-reaching consequences. In contrast with the Moscow defense of "glorification of the name," where the turn was already noted, no preservation of foundations of the metaphysics of All-Unity were now implied. In fact, all links with that metaphysics were abandoned, nor were links sought with any philosophy whatsoever; it did not even claim to be a philosophical movement. For this turn, direct practical experience of the mystical, ascetic life of Orthodoxy was a priority, and theoretical concerns were of interest only inasmuch as its contents were relevant to this experience. In other words, attention was focused on hesychasm and Palamist thought, on spiritual practice and theology long since rooted especially in Orthodox monasticism connected with Mt. Athos. So it is certainly not surprising that the first important text in which this turn found expression was the (1936) work of a monk of Mt. Athos, Basil (Krivoshein), *The Ascetic and Theological Teaching of St. Gregory Palamas.*

What were the implications for the ways of Russian philosophy? Properly speaking, philosophical work was put aside for the time being. For normal development of theoretical thought the turn to ascetic and theological problems was a step backwards; yet it would be quite erroneous to consider the move only in this way. In fact, what was taking place was an essential deepening of the historical vision, and discovery of new links, roots, and sources of Russian thought. For all its value, our religious-philosophical renaissance could not claim to have depth of historical-philosophical reflection. At the time Russian philosophy could hardly trace its origins further back than Solov'ev, the Slavophiles, Chaadaev, and possibly Russian Freemasons and followers of Schelling. And its historico-cultural and historico-philosophical context consisted almost entirely of Western influence. But now the context was changing dramatically. Different phenomena and more ancient layers of Eastern Orthodox spirituality were recognized as having an importance for Russian thought, contributing to its genesis and tasks. So the turn, while appearing to be a turn backwards, proved to have a much deeper meaning: it meant discovery, return, and reflection on original sources.

2.2. Florovsky's Return to the Source

Not long ago such a turn-return of thought, bringing with it a new penetration into origins, was featured as a historico-philosophical notion: Heidegger's notion of *Kehre*. According to Heidegger, *Kehre* is a return which serves as a precondition of advance, and is necessary for reaching a new qualitative level. "Turn (*Kehre*) is the name for a spot where a serpentine mountain road turns almost completely backwards, in order to get closer to the pass."[8] And we can easily see that Florovsky's notion of Neopatristic synthesis is extremely close to it in meaning. It also affirms ways of advancement of thought in terms of return and penetration into origins; the only fruitful strategy for creative thought means retaining a living connection with the sources, correlating oneself with them as an everlasting pattern and standard. In both conceptions the ongoing role of the Source is built on the formula of St. Irenaeus often quoted by Fr. Georges, a *depositum juvenescens*: a self-rejuvenating and self-renewing inheritance; this is also in harmony with Heidegger's key reference to *arche*, from *archein* (Gr.): "The Beginning begins" (*Nachalo nachal'stvuet*).

However, Heidegger and Florovsky are not just speaking about return and connection with any Source. Both refer to a very definite Source. And at a certain point there is a crucial divergence between them, for the Sources are different, though both are rooted in Greek thought. For Heidegger the Source is pre-Christian and even pre-Socratic Greek thought, while for Florovsky it is Greek patristics or "Christian Hellenism," a "christened" "transfigured" Hellenism. One could explain and remove the divergence by saying that Heidegger deals with the source of philosophy, while Florovsky is concerned with the origin of theology. This is not completely unfounded as an explanation, but inadequate. Both thinkers approach their statement on the Source not as some limited methodological, but as a universal ontological position, referring not to the normal development of a discipline but to an everyday situation of life and intellect. According to Heidegger, *Kehre* is the "return to being," when thought achieves not just a position of comprehension, but achieves a special horizon of understanding, "the location of that dimension from which comprehension comes."[9]

---

[8] V. V. Bibikhin, "Delo Khaideggera" [The task of Heidegger], in M. Khaidegger [Heidegger], *Vremia i bytie: Stat'i i vystupleniia* [Time and life: Articles and speeches] (Moscow: Izdatel'stvo "Respublika," 1993), 5.

[9] M. Heidegger, "Briefe über den Humanismus," in Khaidegger, *Vremia i bytie*, 200. Cf. Martin Heidegger, *Platons Lehre von der Wahrheit: Mit einem Brief über den "Humanismus"* (Bern: Francke Verlag, 1954), 72; translated as "Letter on Humanism," in *Martin Heidegger: Basic Writings*, ed. D. Farrrell Krell (San Francisco: Harper, 1977), 213–65, esp. 231.

With this also "the light of the essence of being comes to light."[10] And thus thought achieves the "revelation of what was secret and hidden" which, according to Heidegger, is Truth itself, *Aletheia*. "*Aletheia* rules the origins of Greek philosophy."[11]

For Florovsky, however, the way of thought toward Truth is only through the witness to Truth; because the Truth is personal (for it is Christ, John 14.6) so also must the witness, provided by witnesses to him, be personal and living. And witnesses to the Truth – *testes Veritatis* – are none other than the Fathers of the Church. So the turn to the Origin is necessarily a turn to the Fathers: a neo-patristic synthesis, achievement of "the spirit of the Fathers," and inspiration from the "reason of the Fathers." "The teaching of the Fathers is a permanent category of Christian existence, a constant standard of measurement, and ultimate criterion."[12] For this reason "the renewal and the resumption of Christian Hellenism is always relevant ... as an orientation for all thinkers, not only for theologians."[13]

Thus Heidegger's position absolutizes the Hellenic Source, and that of Florovsky shows a similar absolutization of the transformed-Hellenic or patristic Source. Both appeal to Truth. It would be more just to regard the two Sources as mutually exclusive alternatives rather than compatible, for they relate to different spheres of experience and discourse. We may suppose that the two authors would have agreed with this. Even so there is much here that is not clear or simple. The question is an important one. It touches on many general themes, perhaps even the entire complex of themes embraced by the formula "Christianity and Philosophy," focused on the problem of whether the "phenomenon of Christ" and the "standard of Christ" involve something that (by removal, addition, or substitution) changes the very position and ground of philosophizing as such. When we reflect on this complex of themes, noting the distinctions between philosophy and theology, it may even be more important to recognize that both the (re)turn and Source, as well as all general events and dimensions of Christian existence, have a personal and dialogic nature, and belong to the element of "being-in-

---

[10] M. Heidegger, "Kehre," in Khaidegger, *Vremia i bytie*, 256; translated as "The Turning," in Martin Heidegger, *The Question Concerning Technology, and Other Essays*, trans. William Lovitt (New York: Harper and Row Colophon Books, 1977), 36–49, esp. 41.

[11] M. Heidegger, "Hegel und die Griechen," in Khaidegger, *Vremia i bytie*, 387; cf. M. Heidegger, "Hegel und die Griechen," in *Wegmarken* (Frankfurt am Main: Verlag Vittorio Klostermann, 1957), 267.

[12] G. V. Florovsky, "St. Gregory Palamas and the Tradition of the Fathers," in *Collected Works of Georges Florovsky* (Belmont, MA: Nordland Publishing Co., 1972), 1: 107.

[13] G. H. Williams, "The Neopatristic Synthesis of Georges Florovsky," in *Georges Florovsky, Russian Intellectual and Orthodox Churchman* (Crestwood, NY: St. Vladimir's Seminary Press, 1993), 292.

communication." "If there is any room for Christian metaphysics at all, it must be a metaphysics of personality."[14]

Let us come back, however, to the concrete turn that took place in Russian thought in the diaspora. It was certainly a turn like that discussed by Florovsky, namely a turn to patristic sources with attention focused on the latest Byzantine components, with a certain extension of these toward use of ascetic Fathers. Such an extension was in full accord with patristic principles, since a deep-rooted tie with the element of spiritual practice is the most important part of the criteria by which patristic discourse is structured and by which it checks itself (unlike the purely theoretical criteria of the classical Western tradition). The result of the turn, in its totality, can be described with the following formula: *discovery of Orthodox energetism*. It was a real discovery. By comparison, the Moscow prologue may be described as a false start. The turn to hesychasm and Palamist thought took place there with a preconceived aim (defense of "glorification of the name"), and with the burden of a definite philosophy (metaphysics of All-Unity). Now the extension of thought into mystical-ascetic Orthodoxy took place in a more fundamental and unbiased way. Discernment of this Orthodox element both in its essence and historical scope led to two important conclusions, one of them historical, the other philosophical.

In the history of Orthodoxy new important links and connections were clearly revealed for Russian thought, and taken together these amounted to a whole new lineage of succession on important issues. The reconstruction and study of this line was, to a considerable extent, the work of Fr. Georges, and was continued by Fr. John Meyendorff. To the classical patristics of the fourth century he not only added the Latin synthesis and new developments of the thought of St. Augustine; the Orthodox synthesis and new developments, firmly rooted in mystical-ascetic experience associated with Maximus the Confessor, were also added. Parallel with the Western development in theology associated with Thomas Aquinas, in Orthodoxy a new stage of theological clarification was achieved at the Hesychast Councils, and through teachings of Palamas, namely the 14th-century "Palamite synthesis," embracing the theme of God and man, once again basing itself on ascetic practice.

Later, this line of thought ceased to find intellectual expression and began its concealed "underground" existence, preserved in a few centers and in semi-esoteric schools of spiritual practice and guidance. But even during this period (called the period of "pseudomorphosis" by Florovsky) its influence was quite strong and profound, though only indirect and implicit. It found considerable reflection in the values and ideals of Russian culture, its literature, and the spiritual tasks which Russian philosophy tried to realize. This influence also

---

[14] Florovsky, "St. Gregory Palamas," 119.

stood behind the aforementioned tensions and divergencies between Russian thought and the Western tradition. Beginning with the work of St. Paissy (Velichkovskii) and the appearance of the Russian *Philokalia*, however, the patristic-hesychast line once more gradually rose to the surface of religious and cultural life. The "turn" symbolized its ultimate firm presence in the cultural consciousness.

2.3. Hesychastic Energetism

From a philosophical point of view, the "turn" brought about even more significant changes. It became increasingly clear that energetic, or else energetic-synergetic principles of hesychasm and Palamist thought thoroughly penetrate Orthodox ontology and anthropology. As was noted above, the philosophical-religious renaissance, having turned to these principles, did not draw such conclusions, seeking rather to combine energetic conceptions with the ontological basis of the metaphysics of All-Unity. Since this basis was essentially that of Christian Platonism, the "Moscow prologue" followed the way of Neoplatonism, which complemented classical Platonism with the Aristotelian notion of energy and a number of derivative concepts. Such a path may well be justified and natural for philosophical thought. But Palamist thought was not a product of philosophical evolution; it was born of a new mystical experience, both Christocentric and personal. It was also a synthesis, but a *synthesis of Christian experience*, and thus quite different from the Neoplatonic *synthesis of pagan philosophy*.

The dogmatic statement of the council of 1351 was as follows: human beings can be united with God not in essence, but only in energy. The first, negative part of this formula differed fundamentally from Platonic ontology. Moreover, analysis of the ontological foundations of Orthodox energetism inevitably leads to the conclusion that these foundations represent a special type of ontology, differing also from the whole ontological basis of the "classical Western tradition." In the Neoplatonizing line of St. Augustine, in the Thomist line supported by Aristotle, as well as that of German Idealism, in short, everywhere, the basis is *essentialist* in character, and alien to energetic conceptions, or at any rate does not give ontology a dominant role.

All of this allows us to proceed to more general conclusions. The "turn" of Russian thought was also a turn in the relationship to European philosophy and its historical-philosophical status.

The new content of Russian thought identified as organically consonant with long-standing tasks, turned out to be incompatible with its former status. The changes made it impossible to remain within the Western classical tradition as one of its philosophical schools. And a new status, adequate for the next stage after the "turn," was now also clarified. Its own historical lineage was based directly on patristic sources of Christian views; and it now had its own ontological basis. Both of these features testify definitively that the essence of Russian thought corresponds not to the status of a school, but to an independent and *different tradition*. To be more precise, it represents a stage or link in another tradition, one existing from ancient times.

3. Tradition

Thus we have seen that the "classical Western" or "First" tradition has as the following main representatives: fourth-century Fathers, St. Augustine, Thomas Aquinas, Descartes, and secularized Idealism. Alongside this we have noted a "Second" or "Eastern-Orthodox" tradition with its main representatives: fourth-century Fathers, Maximus the Confessor, Palamas, and 20th-century Orthodox energetism.

We recognized the essential "turn" in the repudiation of the choice for Solov'ev, and therewith a transition of Russian philosophy from the first tradition (where it belonged as one school) into the second tradition. One may assume that both its basic philosophical type and its principal positions will eventually agree completely with its initial intuitions and spiritual tasks, since for Russian thought the first tradition is "alien" while the second is its "own." The latter is indisputable, even while it raises many questions.

In contrast with the first tradition, the second was not a philosophical tradition at all until now. Earlier we compared the important role of Gregory Palamas of the second, with that of Thomas Aquinas in the first tradition. But if we approach the matter less formally, the comparison is really not quite justified. Palamas' thought, as is stressed by all authors of the "turn," is in organic continuity with the patristic discourse. Even more – *it is that very discourse*. It is organized according to the same structure and rules; the criteria to which it submits and by which it verifies itself include the same supra-rational component: fidelity to the mystical experience of communion with God, and to the communal (*sobornyi*) experience of the church. Here thought moves within the medium of "being-as-communication," in a personalist and dialogic medium.

What Aquinas did, for his part, was to change the discourse; scholastic thought decisively chose the Aristotelian paradigm in which thought is submitted to its own autonomous laws. In the East Palamas continued patristics; in the West Aquinas closed it. Scholastics, as the next stage, follows in the direction clearly given, to isolate the autonomous sphere of self-sufficient reason. It was not yet the final step in this direction, since Church dogmas were still kept. But if we look from within the sphere of isolated thought, to which scholastics was directing itself, dogma is already perceived as an external restriction, as a fetter on reason; the step which follows naturally and necessarily is the removal of these fetters, i.e., secularization. Such secularization brought on a free, unhindered reunification with ancient Greek origins of philosophical thought, and opened up ample opportunities for fruitful philosophizing, a process for which Descartes pointed the way. This was the way of Western philosophy, and to this day it has remained the royal way of philosophy as such.

Meanwhile the East chose the path of "endless patristics." This was in full accord with the main spiritual principle of Orthodoxy reflected in its very name: focus on the precise "correct" adherence to an orientation of being, the fundamental ontological vector from man to God. Preserving the patristic character of discourse, both personal and dialogic, and the patristic concept of man as "creature," given a beginning by God, and standing before him in integrity, one gives up the isolation of reason. Here dogma is no fetter on thought, but the basis which feeds and stimulates it; this dogma is a kind of idiom which brings to reason, in abbreviated form, the supra-rational (not anti-rational!) experience of integrity and personality, the experience of being-as-communication between God and man, which is altogether real, no less real than reason itself, and certainly no phantasm. But we must still answer the crucial question, how philosophy is to be developed in such a discourse? Up to this point philosophy has been absent here; is it possible at all to do philosophical work in such a context?

Of course, the final answer cannot be given here, for the question includes the very definition of philosophy and its relation to religion. But it is possible to point out some outstanding features. The second tradition, while not excluding philosophy, does change its character. In the first, the classical tradition beginning with Descartes, the world of thought is the classical Cartesian world. The thesis "*cogito ergo sum*" establishes the first law, i.e., the geometry of this world as a world of Cartesian rectilinear coordinates: indeed, since the pure *cogito* (I think) is a sufficient confirmation and verification of *sum* (I am) then for the world of thought the only thought that rules and determines its laws of motion (i.e., development of reasoning) is that which is equivalent to being, that is, self-sufficient thought. Extrinsic influences are removed, and thought moves along a straight line. In both the phenomenal and noumenal worlds, Descartes made the same discovery; he introduced the Cartesian coordinates of classical rectilinear geometry.

But in the second tradition the world of thought is not the world of isolated reflection. Here logical reasoning is influenced by dogma; the character of categories is influenced by the personal nature of ontology and anthropology, in which permanent "couplings and uncouplings" (to use the expression of Palamas) of reason and its extra-rational content are implicit. As a result we find not the Cartesian world of thought, but that of Einstein, for it is a world of curved geometry where we do not find only pure thought; here thought moves in accordance with modified and more complicated laws. We have already indicated that the second tradition cannot have a Platonic ontology. Now we see that it also cannot have a classical Cartesian method, and categorial construction. Rather, its distinctive feature is a non-classical, non-Platonic, non-Cartesian type of ontology. The creation of the latter requires a change of paradigm which is partly similar to the paradigm change experienced in the natural sciences in the 20th century.

3.1. Creation and Beginning

Philosophy begins from the Beginning (*Nachalo*), i.e., with the theme of the Beginning, beginning as such, the beginning of being, and beginning (of the process of) philosophical thought and speech. On this theme, as on most others, the classical philosophical tradition rejected patristic sources, regarding theological discussion about the Beginning in terms of Creation and creature as an archaic myth. Giving another beginning to the theme about Beginning, it comes closer to ancient Greek thought from the Eleatics. However, in this case, the second tradition puts forward a different approach with its own interpretation, providing us with a good example for discerning philosophical distinctions and possibilities for the "discourse of endless patristics."

These distinctions can be seen very easily. The central notion, that of "creature," is interpreted distinctively in Eastern patristics, not as an element of "metaphysics" (to use Heidegger's opposition) but of the "analytics" of phenomenological observation. The creature is a kind of being which has an inner predicate of being created, in the sense of being provided with a beginning (*nachalo*), of "having a beginning" (*nachal'nost'*) or of "being given a beginning" (*onachalennost'*). The creature is a *being to which a beginning has been given*, and accordingly "being created" (*tvarnost'*) is a principle of the inner form of that being which has been given a beginning.

In the classical tradition the status of the creature is simply resolved in terms of essentialism, with the ontological distinction between Divine Being and empirical being which is limited by *a priori* forms. Here there is no depth of reflection on the act of creation itself; it simply remains in the realm of myth. This is one reason why philosophy turned away from the patristic approach to the theme of Beginning. However, if we analyze just one feature of the act of Creation, its unforced character and lack of necessity, we conclude with the second tradition that Creation is characterized by an act of will; it has the character not of an essentialist but an energetic act.

Already at this stage we enter the sphere of anti-Platonic energetic ontology; when we look further it is clear that the elements of energetism are multiplied and intensified. Classical thinking gives up the holistic concept of creature, dissecting it into Mind and World, *res cogitans* and *res extensa*. Here the qualities of dynamism, activity, and self-mobility are almost exclusively connected with the former, Mind, which was isolated, removed from anthropology and also from the theme of Creation, as we have already emphasized a number of times; it is often interpreted as something infinite, without beginning, and confused with divine being. And Creation is interpreted in the sense of the creation of the World, Cosmos, or "nature"; thus reduced to a problem of "natural philosophy," it is marginalized among philosophical subjects. The second tradition, in contrast, develops the analytics of the integral creature as a being which has been "given a beginning"; this is not only of ontological significance but constitutes the main contents of ontology.

3.2. Florovsky's "Creature and Creatureliness"

The being "given a beginning" is *eo ipso* a historical being; thus the first problem of the analytics of the creature is that of being finite, the connection between its beginning and end. The patristic solution to the problem is profound and original, so much so that it was not properly understood until very recently with Florovsky's brilliant 1928 essay "Creature and Creatureliness," which Florovsky himself thought (justifiably) to be one of his best works. Its first thesis is that there is no necessary connection between the factor of "having a beginning" and "being finite"; the former does not entail the latter. According to a patristic maxim, "God did not create death" (Wisdom 1.13). Hence the empirically finite character (or mortality) of man is not a consequence of ontological creaturely status, and in contrast to Heidegger's teaching, finitude is not to be accepted as the definition of our being in this world. It represents only one of two possible outcomes, each of which is compatible with the human status; thus it is quite possible to reject it, recognizing it as a non-effective definition, one that can be overcome. As a result, the being which has been "given a beginning" turns out to have a very subtle and truly non-classical status, one that is dual and varying. Such creaturely status admits of being both finite and non-finite, or to be more precise, having a beginning without being finite, i.e., being "semi-finite" or "like a ray." As Florovsky put it, "The creature can be compared to a geometric sheaf of rays which spread out from the origin or some radiant to infinity."[15]

But we must remember that this image refers to the "creature before the fall." The image is not complete, and does not include the second ontological variant, that of "having a beginning" and "having an end," the totally finite creature. But history is unique, and allows for the realization of only one variant.

---

[15] G. V. Florovsky, "Tvar' i tvarnost'" [Creature and creatureliness], in *Pravoslavnaia mysl'* [Orthodox thought] (Paris), no. 1 (1928): 178; translated as "Creation and Creaturehood," in *The Collected Works of Georges Florovsky*, vol. 3, *Creation and Redemption* (Belmont, MA: Nordland Publishing Co., 1976), 43–78.

This means that from the beginning the situation of the creature and its ontological status includes a choice to be made, an act of self-determination of being, and also a predicate of freedom.

Thus the patristic definition of being in this world (*Dasein*), as "being created" or "being having a definite beginning" implies that this kind of being is fundamentally open, with two possible outcomes, and is provided with ontological freedom. Here ontologically the creature is an active and dynamic agent, and ontology becomes historical and eventful. The Creation cannot remain the only ontological event, isolated and self-sufficient. It necessarily entails a continuation, and starts a history. And, what is most important, this creature, alive, with a will and capacity for motion, makes its own independent and fully valid contribution to such a continuation. Ontology is not only eventful but also dialogic. In the classical Western tradition, on the contrary, the Creation, understood in cosmological and natural-philosophical terms, does not include the creature as an ontologically free agent, and does not, generally speaking, require any continuation. For the first tradition the Creation is an isolated event, a natural one *ex machina*; but for the second tradition, the theme of Creation is not so much an independent one, as the grand theme of the status of the created being in which the moment of creation is integrated. In this case the moment of creation is both the start and an integral part of the whole ontologically eventful and dialogically unfolding history or drama.

The drama of being involves a genuine and sharp dramatic development, for its subject is victory over death. Of the two outcomes of being open to the creature, one presupposes death while the other overcomes it. In this overcoming (*preodolenie*, surpassing, or ontologically transcending) the creature acquires qualities of the divine being, so that the outcome of overcoming finitude means unification with God (*obozhenie*), deification or *theosis*. According to Palamas this unification can only be energetic, i.e., a union of energies of the creature with divine energy (by the grace of the Holy Spirit). Thus the theme of Beginning, i.e., the theme of Creation and of the creature, is organically included in energistic ontology and finds in it a new non-classical solution.

This example is typical, and enables us to understand, even partly, how philosophical themes can be considered in the second tradition. The specific character of basic categories and concepts should, as a rule, lead to a new approach to problems, while the solutions will always depend somehow on the central principle, the pivot of the entire discourse, the principle of synergy, of energetic connection in an ontologically split reality.[16]

---

[16] An attempt at a philosophical presentation of this principle can be found in my *Diptikh bezmolviia: Asketicheskoe uchenie o cheloveke v bogoslovskom i filosofskom osveshchenii* [Diptych of

But it is certainly not necessary that all these solutions be radically new. Self-determination of Russian philosophy as a "different tradition" presupposes not autarchy, but dialogue with the Western tradition; this dialogue allows for proximity in concrete issues, and is only facilitated by the final acquisition of its own status and identity. Defining itself in terms of the first tradition, as non-Platonic and non-Cartesian thought, the second tradition thereby presupposes a single cultural space and field of problematics. Moreover, Western thought today is not only characterized by the "classical Western tradition." It includes strong, noticeably critical tendencies, and departure from what has typically been recognized as its main course. Derrida's slogan of the "struggle against logocentrism" rejects the basic principle of the whole tradition, the dominant role of the principle of self-sufficient reason. The philosophical situation demonstrates an active search and testing of non-classical paradigms, an influx of anthropological and psychological problematics, and intensification of the drive toward a holistic and dialogic view. The enormous influence of the work of Bakhtin is also important, for this work can function like a bridge, mediating between Russian and Western thought, and bringing them to closer unity.

So it is not self-evident that the "turn" of Russian thought should increase its distance from Western thought. Its essential significance is first of all an internal matter. The "turn" means an achievement of maturity, and ultimately of self-determination, i.e., that Russian philosophy raises its tasks not toward elevated obscurities such as the peculiarities of the Russian soul, the spirit of Russian culture, or the legacy of Orthodox spirituality. Rather, it deals with the clear, concrete phenomena which belong indisputably to its ancestry and history, like patristics, hesychasm, and Orthodox energetism. And besides that it means that these phenomena denote an independent theological-philosophical tradition, the philosophical dimension of which is yet to be developed. It is a difficult but possible task, and may provide a valuable contribution to the current search for new principles and ways of thought.

These are some of the important philosophical aspects of the conception of Neopatristic synthesis, and they show once more, and in a new way that this idea of Fr. Georges Florovsky has been a profound and fruitful one.

---

silence: Ascetic studies on man from a theological and philosophical viewpoint] (Moscow: Tsentr psikhologii i psikhoterapii, 1991).

Pantheism and Monotheism[1]

Andrei Viacheslavovich Kuraev

Religious syncretism is one of the most popular contemporary intellectual fads. Its followers think religions differ only in ritual. Esoteric philosophy with its respect for any symbolic rite, accordingly, can be combined with all religions. This position falsely equates cult and religion. Christianity, or Orthodoxy, is not just a rite; it has its own philosophy. Christian philosophical and theological thought is sufficiently independent and well-developed to defend an integral and consistent understanding of the world, humanity, and God.

In their efforts to suppress a *rational* understanding of theological problems, syncretists argue that Orthodoxy has inadequate resources to substantiate the faith, claiming (after one more presentation of the usual caricatures of Orthodoxy) that the Church only represents ritual, and that no one would dream of consulting church literature or its theologians to ask whether the Orthodox understanding of God, the world, and the Bible is really as primitive as they have been told.

That was the tactic of Marxist agitators; it has been adopted by advocates of the occult and sectarian missionaries who themselves present their beliefs philosophically. As a result they claim that "the Russian Orthodox Church has degenerated into a belief in ritual, something that Lev Tolstoi pointedly rejected."[2] In fact, Lev Tolstoi believed just that. He was deeply convinced that the Orthodox Church was degenerating into a belief in ritual. But Christians believe not in rituals but in the grace contained in the rites.[3] The disagreement between Lev

---

[1] A. V. Kuraev, "Panteizm i monoteizm," *Voprosy filosofii*, no. 6 (1996): 35–53 (slightly abbreviated).

[2] B. Sushkov, "Kogda my reabilitiruem L'va Tolstogo?" [When will we rehabilitate Lev Tolstoi?], in *Evangelie Tolstogo: Izbrannye religiozno-filosofskie proizvedeniia L. N. Tolstogo* [Tolstoy's Gospel: Selected religious-philosophical works of L. N. Tolstoi] (Moscow: Novosti, 1992), 4.

[3] Only journalists believe in such a ritualistic faith and find the Russian Church infected with this disease. Cf. the words of Bishop Mikhail Semenov (Old Believers): "So-called ritualistic faith, a slavish literal following of rite, is a myth. Our ancestors held vigorously to rituals because they sensed their enormous value. So the question arose whether they should 'double or triple the alleluia.' They went to the East to learn the answer. Is this a belief in ritual? For our ancestors ritual meant a clear writing down of dogmatic truth. We may fear that with the destruction of rite the truth of the faith can also be destroyed." *Tserkov'* [Church], no. 2 (1992): 22.

Helleman, Wendy, ed. *The Russian Idea: In Search of a New Identity*. Bloomington, IN: Slavica, 2004, 185–212.

Tolstoi and Vladimir Solov'ev was not about rite, but about philosophy. In his last book Solov'ev even portrayed Tolstoi as a servant of the Antichrist! Kozhevnikov, when he returned to the Church, rejected Tolstoi not because of a preference for rituals to tea parties, but because of the superficiality of Tolstoi's philosophy compared to the profundity of Christian thought. Bulgakov, Berdiaev, Frank, and Struve left materialism to come to Christianity not because of a need for "rite" but to find a philosophy that could explain human nature better than Marxism. They found such a philosophy in the Gospel and in the Christian tradition.

Indeed, Orthodoxy is not only rite or "belief" but also thought. "I know in whom I believe" (2 Tim. 1.12). Christian philosophy is capable of discerning views of God and humanity incompatible with the Gospel. If someone were to expound a pagan philosophy in a room full of Orthodox icons, we should not think of this as "reconciliation of religions." Neither Orthodoxy or paganism can be reduced to rites.

The Pagan Portrayal of God

What is paganism? I do not need to come up with a new definition. The Apostle Paul said clearly enough of pagans that "they serve the creature rather than the Creator" (Rom. 1.25). A pagan expresses his trust in the World with religious enthusiasm. Paganism worships everything that is not God: conscience, the nation, art, health, wealth, science, progress, "values common to all mankind," space, or the self. According to St. Ephraim of Syria, when the whole world was darkened and people were groping about, they worshipped as God everything that blocked their way. Self-worship is both the most dangerous and the most effective temptation. Indeed, every person is like God because we are "His image." But we are not God. In praying to his Lord St. Augustine says, "You are not some corporeal image, some emotional state that we experience when we are glad, upset, desirous, afraid, remembering, or forgetting something. You are not our soul, because You are the God of our souls" (*Confessions* X.25).

The human soul is beautiful and grand. "So also are the eyes beautiful and useful parts of the body; but when they wish to see in the darkness, their beauty and strength does them no good, and may even bring harm. The soul will only stumble over itself in trying to see without the Spirit."[4] The soul is godlike; but this is dangerous, for it is not God. In his Spiritual Homilies St. Macarius of

---

[4] St. John Chrysostom, "7th Homily on 1 Cor. 4," in *Tvoreniia: Besedy na 1 Kor. 4* [Works: Homilies on 1 Cor. 4] (St. Petersburg, 1886), 117; trans. in *Chrysostom: Homilies on the Epistles of Paul to the Corinthians. Nicene, and Post-Nicene Fathers*, ed. P. Schaff (Peabody, MA: Hendrickson, 1994 [repr. 19th-century ed.]), 12: 65.

Egypt reminds us that the soul comes from neither the divine nature nor the crafty power of Darkness; the soul is not God.

Here we note the great difference between Christianity and paganism. No Christian would ever think of himself as a part of the divine. God is not the highest peak of the human soul. Theosophists claim that a man must find "himself, the hidden God inside himself."[5] Even early Christian philosophers like Origen's teacher, St. Clement of Alexandria, wrote that "we cannot be compared to God, whether in substance, origin, or any particular human characteristic. We are a creation of his will" (*Stromata* II, 16). "We should not think that the Divine Spirit dwells in us like some part of God" (*Stromata* V, 13).[6]

These clear judgments of the ancient theologian have not prevented professional syncretists from claiming that their "synthesis" eliminates nothing substantive from original Christianity. Neither conscience nor knowledge prevented E. Roerich from saying that "in Christianity I follow the traditions of the first Fathers of Christianity."[7] E. P. Blavatsky claimed that she expressed an ancient Christian understanding of the world, yet spoke of the human being becoming "a receptacle of the World Soul, as Emerson expressed it so well: 'I, in spite of my imperfection – worship my own perfection.'"[8] But this is exactly what Clement and other Church Fathers warned against as a dangerous mistake. The fathers of the *Philokalia* openly declared their faith that "the Son of God came as a man in obedience and humility, and that by the cross and death he saved mankind."[9] E. Roerich is lying when she says that "authors of the *Philokalia* interpreted 'Christ' as the highest divine principle in us."[10] According to her, "the

---

[5] This expression comes from Kamenskii, president of the Russian Theosophical Society, cited in M. V. Lobyzhenskii, *Misticheskaia trilogiia, t.e. Temnaia sila* [Mystic trilogy, i.e. dark power] (Prague, 1914), 183.

[6] Cf.: "Only impious dreamers would suppose that the characteristics of the Almighty and the human being could be one and the same. For God says, 'You are impious, you who thought that I was altogether like you' (Ps. 50.21)" (*Stromata* VI, 14) or "In spite of the complete alienation of our nature from Him, He takes care of us" (*Stromata* II, 16). Cf. Clement of Alexandria in *The Ante-Nicene Fathers*, ed. A. Roberts and J. Donaldson (Buffalo: The Christian Literature Publication Co., 1885), 2: 163–629. For *Stromata* II, 16, see p. 364; for *Stromata* V, 13, p.465; for *Stromata* VI, 14, p. 470.

[7] *Pis'ma Eleny Rerikh, 1929–1938* [Letters of Elena Roerich, 1929–1938], ed. N. F. Bezrukova (Minsk: Belorusskii fond Rerikhov: PRAMEB, 1992), 2: 9 and 1: 281.

[8] E. P. Blavatskaia, *Teosofiia i prakticheskii okkul'tizm* [Theosophy and practical occultism] (Moscow: Izdatel'stvo "Sfera," 1993), 9.

[9] St. Theodore the Studite, *Nastavleniia monakham* [Exhortations for a monk], no. 123, from the *Dobrotoliubie* [Philokalia] (Jordanville, NY: Holy Trinity Russian Orthodox Monastery, 1963–66), 4: 184.

[10] *Pis'ma Eleny Rerikh, 1929–1938*, 1: 366. Cf. "Pray that God, who is within, help you preserve your purity" (2: 425) or "Every recovery is possible when the sick person takes heart or believes in

words of the prayer 'Do not lead us into temptation' mean the turning of the sick spirit to its Instructor, or to its highest Ego, either of which can guard him against his sin."[11]

Should I then require of *myself* the strength to resist temptations, forgiveness of sins, and healing? In the 1970s psychology students at Moscow State University diagnosed schizophrenia with the words of a popular song: "I quietly talk to myself…" Religious life is transformed into an endless novel of "talking-to-oneself."

Pantheism and Its Impersonal God

Pantheism is a vital existential need for occultists. Such neopaganism is based on the simple syllogism "God is everything; everything is God. I am a part of everything; so it follows that I am God." This self-divinization leads to acceptance of some rather dubious conceptions of the Universe.

Theosophists have come up with three pieces of "good news" for Europeans: there is no personality, no God, and no freedom. According to E. Roerich, "Mahatma rejects and contradicts the blasphemous human understanding of a Personal God. Mahatma rejects the God of Christian teaching."[12] Indeed, for the East, the idea of personality is connected with narrow-mindedness. According to the Mahatmas, "Personality is synonymous with what is limited." They reject the application of this word for the "Divine."[13]

But European philosophy has a different approach. Here the term "personality" has a long philosophical history. Even in pre-Christian philosophical thought theologians identified God with Personality. The word "*hypostasis*" (which in Christian theological language refers to a "mystery of personality") initially meant "a concrete existence (*sushchestvovanie*) that differs from any other." Aristotelian terminology, which was later accepted in Byzantine thought, interpreted *hypostasis* as a "second nature" (*priroda*), i.e., the concrete existence of a concrete object. Nature as such is abstract, pure understanding. There is no idea (nature) of a meadow where one could graze the idea (nature) of a horse. But God is real, concrete; he is not identical to our idea of him. So we can say that God is *hypostasis* (according to Aristotle's formula that "there is no nature without a hypostasis").

---

his healer, that is, when he raises the vibrations of the energy of *his own* heart so high, that it is able to accept the magnetic flow radiating from the healer" (*Pis'ma Eleny Rerikh, 1932–55* [Novosibirsk: "Viko," Algim, 1993], 409).

[11] *Pis'ma Eleny Rerikh, 1932–1955*, 36.

[12] *Pis'ma Eleny Rerikh, 1929–1938*, 1: 270, 272.

[13] *Pis'ma Makhatm* [Letters of the Mahatmas] (Samara: "Agni," 1993), 513.

Moreover, there is another term that can be applied to God: "*prosopon,*" the Greek word also translated into European languages as "personality" (*lichnost'*). *Prosopon* in its philosophical meaning is something recognizable, the specific attributes by which we can recognize a person. Is God "recognizable"? Can a person distinguish his experience of meeting a cat and of meeting God? Clearly, yes. So, God somehow differs from the world. E. Roerich's saying that she doesn't "understand how Christians can distinguish between God and ordinary realities"[14] shows her knowing of only a "cosmic" grace, not the genuine one. In the end, any serious philosophy and theology must conclude that God differs from the world, and not just qualitatively. Apophatic Christian theology aspires to establish the distinction between God and the world, not to dissolve him into it.

It is astonishing that theosophists cannot accept even the idea of a divine hypostasis. Perhaps Blavatsky's declaration "I believe in an invisible, universal God, in the abstract Divine spirit, but not in the anthropomorphic God"[15] is due to her usual careless manner of using terms. What does "abstract Divine spirit" mean? Does it mean one that "exists only in our mind"? Does "Abstract" mean "unreal"? Or "non-concrete"? Unrecognizable, or not to be understood? Can Blavatsky differentiate the Divine spirit from a mewing cat? Does she consider it possible to know God concretely? Indeed, God "cannot be understood" by our own mind in the sense of the grandeur of his Being. But Cyril of Jerusalem asked whether he could not at least take just what is useful, if he could not drink the entire river; and if he could not drink the entire sea, that does not imply that he was unable to distinguish fresh water from that of the ocean.

When Greek and pre-Christian authors of the early centuries spoke about God as *hypostasis* they considered God a real being, not an abstract image or symbol. Attempts of the Greeks to think of personality were limited; pre-Christian thought maintained a well-grounded prohibition against a personified representation of the Absolute. This prohibition was abolished by Christian thought after a radical re-interpretation of the term "personality" (*hypostasis*). Pre-Christian philosophers considered the divine incompatible with personality, because individuality meant differentiation between objects. And if the Absolute must include everything existing, it cannot be individual. Christian theology, on the other hand, realized the necessity of distinguishing nature, individuality, and personality.

Nature (*priroda*), or *being* (*sushchnost'*), first of all, consists of some specific attributes that a given object possesses. For example, human nature in the narrow

---

[14] According to Roerich, "Among these dogmas the most astonishing is that differentiating God from the Universe. All Eastern Pantheism is especially hostile to such an ecclesiastical position." *Pis'ma Eleny Rerikh, 1929–38,* 2: 266.

[15] E. P. Blavatskaia, *Pis'ma* [Letters] (Moscow: MCF, "Diana," 1994), 205.

sense differentiates a human being from animals, and from the angels. In the broader sense "human nature" is everything that characterizes man, independent of the fact that those features may be common to other creatures higher or lower, whether or not these differentiate the human from others. Attempts to understand "nature" mean searching for an answer to the question "What is man?"

Individuality consists of specific attributes that differentiate creatures of one and the same nature. There are differences between people. We can say that each of us has only a part of human nature, each in our own way. Recognition of individual features means understanding how, and to what extent, any given man realizes his humanity.

Finally, *personality* is the individual himself, having all the natural, individual features. As such, the personality is not qualified. Any characteristic relates to its nature. As for the personality, it describes the person who possesses these qualities, virtues, and energies, and realizes them. "Nature" answers the question "what," while "individuality" answers the question "how," and "personality" – "who."

Theosophy faces the same problem. The leader of the pre-revolutionary Russian theosophical movement, E. Pisareva, wrote that "Ancient Eastern psychology clearly distinguishes the immortal individuality of a man from his mortal personality. Everything personal dies with a man, but the entire result of his personal experience is saved in his immortal individuality, and forms its eternal content."[16] First of all, these words should be noted by those who think that "the law of karma" will provide them a better future. It will do nothing of the sort. Your personality will be destroyed. Your "who" will disappear, and only those different qualities which make up your individuality, only those small pieces of energy – or "*dharma*" – that are temporarily united in your life, will continue their way through the universe.[17]

But more important, we see here the great difference between Christian and pantheistic thought. Christianity assumes that as a concrete combination of my accidental features and actions, my individuality can be transformed, destroyed or even fulfilled to complete possession of human nature. But my personality, my Ego, remains and finds fullness of life in God. If a man's soul comes to God's final judgment with a burden that can not be taken into Eternity, it will be burned up with Eternal fire. But those things that a person cherished in his soul during life on earth that are worthy of Christ will be transformed by the love of

---

[16] E. Pisareva, "Karma, ili zakon prichin i sledstvii" [Karma, or the law of causes and effects], in *Korrektsiia karmy (chistaia karma)* [Correction of karma (pure karma)], ed. S. N. Lazarev and N. F. Lazareva, bk. 2 (St.Petersburg: Akademiia parapsikhologii, 1995), 2: 77.

[17] Pisareva here follows Blavatsky, who has written even more directly, "I believe in the immortal divine Spirit in every person, but not in the immortality of every person." Blavatskaia, *Pis'ma*, 205.

Christ. Even if a person comes with empty hands and an empty soul, only his individuality, not his personality will be burned. "Every deed will be revealed, and by the fire it will be judged. And those whose deeds will survive will be rewarded. But if a person's work is burned up, he will lose it, yet he himself will be saved, but only as one escaping through fire" (1 Cor. 3.13–15). Here is the difference from theosophy, which claims that "he will die" but "his deeds will live," while Christianity says the opposite, that "everything that is 'mine' can be abandoned" but I myself cannot disappear into nonbeing. The problem is not one of terminology but of meaning. What will survive – "I" or "mine"? Christianity does not proclaim "our deeds or karma to be immortal." It expects the "resurrection of the dead."

Christianity has revealed the personality in the human being, and has brought this revelation to the gates of Eternity. However, in history it was a bit different. Mankind realized itself to be God's image only after God revealed himself in the man Christ. In philosophy we always start with what is simpler, more obvious, i.e., with ourselves. Christian anthropology clarifies the teaching of the Trinity.

So personality is not the same as individuality, but is something special, and "other." Although personality is different, it is not qualitatively excluded nor in contradiction with the being that is "one-in-essence." Since personalities cannot be understood or characterized through qualitative differentiation, the "otherness" of personality is found beyond qualitative, concrete content. That is why one can think of a multiplicity of personalities, without destroying the unity of being. Philosophical monism does not contradict the concept of a Personal God, i.e., a God that has one being but three "faces," or is three with respect to personality, when each of those personalities possesses the entire fullness of the Absolute equally, and none of them differ one from the other. To be more precise, a God who is one in being, and three with respect to personalities.

So, Christian thought in distinguishing between individuality and personality accepts God as a "personality"; but such individualization does not limit his Divine Being. St. John of Damascus defined personality (*hypostasis*) as "something that exists by itself,"[18] i.e., an ability to exist and act independently, which is how "freedom" is also usually defined. John's definition means that human personality is freedom. And with a surprising intuition Pushkin expressed the very same idea of a human secret:

---

[18] St. John of Damascus, "Filosofskie glavy," in *Chelovek* [Man] (Moscow: RIC, "Kul't-informpress," 1991), 149; trans. by F. H. Chase, Jr. as "Philosophical Chapters," in *St. John of Damascuss: Writings* (New York: Fathers of the Church, 1958), 37: 68.

Based on Eternity
By the will of God
Independence of person –
Is his grandeur's lot.

"Independence of the person" is the "*hypostasis.*" It is neither some "second nature," nor something concrete, but the reality that acts consciously and freely. If the same meaning of the word "*hypostasis*" is applied to God, it refers to primacy of being in relationship to any quality. "Who" is prior to "What." "Who exists" (the hypostasis of the Father) does not derive from "What exists" (from the divine nature without personality), but "What exists" derives from "Who exists," according to St. Gregory the Theologian.

The hypostasis of the Father separates his being from the hypostases of the Son and of the Holy Spirit, which have their existence not "from the Father's nature" but "from the Father's hypostasis" in eternity, outside of time.[19] "Separating" does not mean that the Father's hypostasis "divides" from the other two, but "participates" and "coexists" with them. "All things have been committed to me by my Father" (Matt. 11.27). We do not recognize the difference between the "begetting" of the Son and the "procession" of the Spirit. Even more, we do not know how the "begotten" Son differs from the "unbegotten" Father. Actually, the most accurate answer may well be: none. St. Gregory of Nyssa shows clearly that these are apophatical terms. They indicate that there is some difference, without telling us what that difference is. We are not speaking about the difference of two things, but of two Persons. Ultimately, the entire teaching about the Trinity leads us to the mystery of Personality: there are three Personalities of the Eternal God that have no apparent differences when we analyze them from the perspective of "qualitative-nature," but differ existentially; "The Son is not the Father, yet He is all that the Father is," according to St. Gregory the Theologian. They have everything in common, and nonetheless are distinct. That is why we do not speak of "tritheism" or "three Gods." We do not think about them except as a unity, but in their existence they are each in turn a "hypostasis."

Pantheism and the Creation of the Cosmos

This intuition of Christian thought regarding personality has very important consequences for a Christian understanding of the world. The fact that God is Personal helps to explain the reality of the created, material world which exists

---

[19] St. John of Damascus explains, "The Son and the Spirit are led back to a single Initiator" and certainly not to an impersonal 'cause' but to 'the One who Causes,' to the personal Father"; cf. St. John of Damascus, *Tochnoe izlozhenie pravoslavnoi very* 1.8; trans. by F. H. Chase, Jr. as "An Exact Exposition of the Orthodox Faith," in *St. John of Damascus: Writings*, 176–88.

separately from God. Philosophy in the Middle Ages posed the problem of how the Infinite can give birth to creatures which are limited. If God is infinite, can the world created by him, or even any part of it, be finite? Using the language of contemporary physics we might ask, "How can infinite energy be realized in finite portions (the *quanta*)? On the condition that all energy is in an actualized condition (because God is an actual infinity), and that there are no external obstacles (because philosophical thought cannot accept anything that prevents the Absolute from being actualized, for he would not then be Absolute), we have to conclude that Creative Infinity must unfold itself into an infinite world, exhaust itself in this act of emanation, and further, identify itself with it. Accordingly, in the world thus conceived there can be nothing that differs in any respect from the Absolute. This does not just mean that "everything has a part of God," but even more radically that God is found in its very smallest particle and its every action. Actually, this is the language of theosophical thought when it "refuses to attribute 'creativity' and especially formation (i.e., something finished) to the Infinite Principle, saying that IT cannot create."[20]

From that we conclude that if "Parabraman, as Absolute Cause, is passive,"[21] he could not cause anything to exist. The Cause is without any result. And if it appears to us that something is not "IT," that simply means that our vision is defective. It thinks that something exists which is simply not there, and cannot even be there. Such a theory has a certain hypnotic power to make people think that there is nothing around them, and they should include themselves in that. Pantheism is nihilistic in character. It denies everything except "Parabraman."

Still, from a philosophical point of view such reasoning does not solve the problem. Philosophy has to comprehend the real world, not just depict internal logical fantasies. Even pantheism distinguishes relative from absolute being, although it has no resources to explain this difference. If the Absolute cannot cause what is relative, then where did the latter come from?

We may admit that divine creativity is somehow limited, "portioned." But who can limit the actions of the Absolute, or how? It can only do this itself. Infinite energy radiates particles from itself only if the source has some mechanism by which to control the outflow. So we must also allow a certain complexity in God to distinguish at least the source of divine creative energy from some "control mechanism." And this distinction we should make only within the context of theological monism, i.e., without affirming "two Gods" or a "Hierarchy of Absolutes." But any complexity in God nullifies the very idea of God as Absolute Unity and, thus, simple Being. So how can we affirm a complexity of God without also affirming a compound structure?

---

[20] E. P. Blavatskaia, *Tainaia doktrina* [Secret teaching] (Riga: Dziznavu ieva," 1937), 1: 41.
[21] Ibid.

This can be achieved only through a distinction between nature and hypostasis. The nature of Divinity is absolutely simple and united, without any nuancing or difference, without addition or complexity of structure. The "whatness" or quality of the divine nature is unchangeable, simple, and self-identical. But God's being goes beyond the divine nature. This is the Personality which goes beyond nature, which has no characteristic qualities of its own, yet is not something different than its nature. Personality refers to "Who," the subject that owns that nature and absorbs it. The Divine Nature is a source of his energy. It is one, absolutely simple, united, eternal, inviolable, and unlimited in itself. But God's nature and his Personality are not the same. The divine nature reveals itself in one way or another through concrete and definite "action," i.e., energy, in accordance with a personal, conscious, and free decision of God's Personality. And this is Divine Personality, which through its own free love wishes to create a multiform and complex world, and so diminishes the manifestation of its own infinite divinity that our world is not completely reduced to ashes by the abyss of the Divine light.

In Christianity this model of divine love is defined by the term "*kenosis*" – the self-diminishing, or self-exhaustion, of the Divine. This is the humility of God before the creature. Such concern of God for the world ends ultimately at Golgotha. "Without protest he abandoned the omnipotence and miraculous power which was his with the Father, as if they were just things, and became mortal like us" (B. Pasternak). In this *kenosis* the Creator allows one of his creatures to exist quite independently. God is related to the world not as an essence to its phenomenon, but as the Creator to his creation. God has his own essence, but it is not the world. This essence has its own manifestations in the world, but these should be called not the "energies of the cosmos" but "the uncreated energies of the Creator."

Models of an Impersonal Deity

To demonstrate that personality does not limit the Divine absolute, we will propose a philosophical experiment. Let us imagine an impersonal Absolute; this absolute substance does not know or control itself, nor does it possess self-consciousness or will. Blavatsky speaks about it as follows: "We refer to Absolute Consciousness as 'lacking consciousness,' because we assume that it must inevitably be like that ... Eternal Breath that does not realize itself."[22] Let us also imagine a personal Absolute; however, it is an infinite and completely perfect substance which knows itself, controls all its actions and manifestations, and has self-consciousness. So which one of these models of Being is more perfect and worthy of God?

---

[22] Blavatskaia, *Tainaia doktrina*, 102.

This experiment directs us to ontological analysis: we should think of the Absolute as some combination of all kinds of perfection in their highest (or better, unbounded) degree. Can we call self-consciousness and self-control a perfection? Yes. So, in thinking of the Absolute, we should admit that it knows itself. Can we call freedom a kind of perfection? It is obvious that a being can only be called perfect when it can act freely, independently and deliberately. So our self-representation of the Absolute is also more worthy when we consider it acting according to its own free will, not because of unconscious necessity.[23]

Understanding the Unity as a free and reasoning Personality is more appropriate than affirming some faceless Being. But let us continue our experiment on the theme of how to think in a manner worthy of God. Even someone non-religious and unbelieving can understand that the purest, loftiest, and well-developed theological conception is that which declares "God is love." And the model of Divine Personality that presents God's manifestation not just through his will, power, or intelligence, but through his love has greater depth, and is also more attractive.

Divine Love

So, let us try to compare this great theological thesis about God's love with ideas about God found in other monotheistic religions. We can first approach Allah, and ask if he is love; Islamic theologians will answer us that "Allah is first of all *will*, but of course he also has love for people." When we ask what this love is, and how it is shown, they answer, "He created the world. He sent his prophets to the people, and gave them his law." "So, was that difficult for him?" They answer, "No, the world is insignificantly small compared to the Creator's power." We get the same answers from Jews concerning Yahweh of the Old Testament. We are told that "Yahweh loves people. Despite his transcendence, he finds it impossible to be at peace without the love of human beings. He not only gives the Law; he begs people not to forget him."[24]

---

[23] We should also hear arguments for the other side, affirming that the "transition from a personal God to one that is impersonal is a long process of the maturation of spirit which has already gone on for several centuries, and that not only within Christianity," citing Sushkov, *Kogda my reabilitiruem L'va Tolstogo?*, 6. It is certainly possible to express such a conviction, but finding philosophical arguments to support it is much less likely to be successful.

[24] "In the final analysis, for the biblical God there is only a single concern, just as he is one: to seek the man who listens and gives himself to him; for complete power in possession of the entire world is not enough to please the will of Yahweh. That can only be satisfied through the free recognition from another will, the human. Yahweh can only be 'glorified' by human beings.... And God speaks to us thus as if he, who maintains the beginning and the crown of all, should need something from us." S. S. Averintsev, "Drevneevreiskaia literatura" [Ancient Hebrew literature], in *Istoriia vsemirnoi*

We ask next of Krishna (who is considered a Personal, Individual God and Creator) and learn that he did not simply create the world and give his revelation. He brought it to people personally, without an intermediary. He became a man, and not a king but a lowly servant. But did he become a man fully, and for all time? No, he only appeared for the time of the task assigned. Nor did he assume human flesh or a human soul for all Eternity. He blessed Arjuna for killing. He himself never experienced human pain or human death. He gave people the commandment to love him. But whether he loves people in return is not clear.

When we ask the God of the Gospels, "How do you love people?" the answer is, "to the point of my own death." His love not only created the world, but gave us freedom; it gave us the law, but also brought us prophets and wisdom. His love did not just take on human appearance; there was no appearance, for he became man. "All people of the Earth are blessed by the King who has come down out of Heaven, in the appearance of a slave." And we received the fulness of his love which he gave in denying himself to the point of self-sacrifice and death. "As if a man came, took up and opened his treasure, and gave away everything."

This is God, and such is his Love. He does not just love, but he is Love; he not only possesses this love, and reveals himself in love. He himself is this Love. The very essence of the Gospel is expressed in the words, "God loved the world so much that he gave his only-begotten Son." From the perspective of philosophy, this is an anti-pantheist manifesto. The gospel declares a separation between God and the world, and it is so large that it can only be bridged by the Incarnation and the Cross. In the realm of theosophy, where there is no personal individuality, where everything is dissolved, there is also no place for such a personal feeling as love.

The ancient critic of Christianity, Celsus, who did not discover that "God is love" in the Gospel, and ignored that same idea in the work of Plato, reasonably critiqued the religion of the Old Testament, saying that

> Christians and Jews are like frogs sitting around the pond, or like worms in the rain in a corner of the swamp.... They say that God reveals everything to them, and cares only about them; that while he pays no attention to the rest of the world, neglecting the movement of the heavens and forgetting his concern for the earth, he sends his prophets only to them, and does not stop sending them and showing his concern, that they may always be close to him. (Origen, *Against Celsus* IV, 23)

---

literatury [A history of world literature], ed. G. P. Berdnikov and Iu. P. Vipper (Moscow: "Nauka," 1983), 1: 276.

Celsus is right. A man is nothing more than a growth of mold at the edge of the universal swamp – if God is not Love, and is not capable of personal, loving Being.

So we are faced with a choice, to accept the Gospel with its idea of the One through whom "everything has its being, and without whom nothing would have come to be," who came down to Earth and became a man (John 1.3). The alternative is to regard humanity and its planet as nothing more than a dump for karmic garbage, and the cosmos living for itself, not even realizing that somewhere in its orbit mankind suffers and hopes. The world is neither richer when humans appear, nor poorer when they go. Two galaxies plus two more will always add up to four; it makes no difference to this multiplication table whether or not we earthlings know of it. The beauty of the world was created not for man, nor does it concern itself about him; it is essentially inhuman.

Those who wish to sense the difference between the wisdom of the East and Christianity are reminded of the words of A. F. Losev, "Does the Sun care about the Earth? Of that we have no evidence; it simply 'exercises an attraction in direct proportion to its mass, and in inverse proportion to the square of the distance.'"[25] Elena Blavatsky, on the other hand, writes that "Divine Thought has as little personal interest in them (i.e., the Highest Planetary Creative-Spirits) or in their deeds as the Sun concerns itself about a sunflower or its seeds."[26]

Theosophists misunderstood the Christian mystery of Divine love. When one of E. Roerich's followers timidly suggested that God is love, and that only a subject (not an impersonal law) can love, the tutor's harsh reaction was "Silence!" "The East *prohibited* any discussion about the Unspoken; only concentration on the great manifestations of the Mystery was allowed."[27] In another passage Roerich explained "divine love" as no more than the power of gravity in the cosmos: "Divine Love is the principle of attraction, or *Fokhat*, in its quality of divine love, of the electric power of their affinity and sympathy."[28] But Christians feel nothing less than a living love in the symphony of the world, a loving Personality. Not just a Law, Mind, or "gravitation," but a Personal and loving Will. That is why they so keenly experience the unity of God and the world, far more keenly than the pantheist. The Christian not only experiences the communion of the world with its Highest Principle (as do pantheists) but even knows the Name of this principle, the One to thank for that very evening and

---

[25] A. F. Losev, *Filosofiia, mifologiia, kul'tura* [Philosophy, mythology, culture] (Moscow: Politizdat, 1991), 130.

[26] Blavatskaia, *Tainaia doktrina*, 2: 201.

[27] *Pis'ma Eleny Rerikh, 1929–38*, 1: 439.

[28] *Pis'ma Eleny Rerikh, 1929–38*, 2: 12.

for the sunrise to come. Pantheists have lost this right, i.e., to say "Glory be to *Thee*, who has shown us the light!"

Christian revelation has taught us something about the First Principle that was unknown to unfeeling pagan metaphysics. Simeon the New Theologian once called Christ "our God who is not proud."[29] For this is how he acts with the people:

> When you [Israel] were born nobody cut your navel cord, washed you or swaddled you. Nobody took pity on you, and you were thrown out in the field because your life was scorned on the day you were born. But I passed by and saw you thrown out, lying in your blood, and ordered you – "Live!" So you grew up and became beautiful, and again I passed by and saw you. And behold, your time had come, the time for love. I extended the corner of my garment over you and covered your nakedness. And you became mine. I washed you with water, and washed off the blood, and anointed you with oil. You were dressed in expensive clothing, and adorned with gold and silver, and you were very beautiful. But you put your trust in your own beauty and used your fame, prostituting yourself, squandering your sexual favours as you shared them with every passer-by. You disgraced your beauty with such prostitution. How your heart must have suffered when you were doing that, like an unbridled prostitute. Usually men give prostitutes presents, but you were the one that was giving gifts to all your lovers and bribing them. So listen, you prostitute, to the word of your Lord! I will gather all your lovers and hand you over to them, and they will put an end to your prostitution and cut you with their swords. I will do to you the same as you have done to me when you broke your oath and destroyed our union. Yet I will remember my union with you, and restore an everlasting union with you, and you will remember and be ashamed of your sins. I will forgive everything that you did because I do not desire the death of those who are dying; so change your ways, and live!" (Ezek. 16.1–18.32)

Can any theosophical fastidiousness be found here? Is there anything unworthy of him, of whom we say "God is love" (1 John 4.8)? Like ecclesiastical mysticism, Christian theology has enough depth to experience and declare the inscrutability of God. Our "anthropomorphism" is secondary. It is not some relapse of paganism through misunderstanding, but recognition of the closeness between God and man that becomes understandable only after the experience of a theology of apophatical rejection.

---

[29] Cited in Archbishop Vasilii (Krivoshein), *St.. Simeon The New Theologian* (Brussels: Editions de Chevetogne, 1980), 221.

Divine Presence in the Cosmos

We must distinguish between anthropomorphism that has not risen to the level of apophatic thinking, and that achieved with its help. Pagan anthropomorphism arose from too hurried an appropriation of the "Incomprehensible." Christian "anthropomorphism" arose when the Absolute himself spoke in human language. The Incomprehensible wanted to be comprehended. He gave us the right, and even ordered us to talk about him, to announce the good news of our closeness to him. The word "Emmanuel" (God with us) is especially full of joy because we understand the endless distance between God and humanity. The one whom we cannot comprehend or express in words, has come to us. The Word became the Flesh. He sanctified the human words spoken to him and about him.

A central question of the history of Christian philosophy asks, "Why did the word become incarnate so late?" The New Testament tells us that people first had to understand monotheism as the only correct conception of God. Only after comprehending that God is Spirit could they realize the miraculous nature of his incarnation. Only after they learned that God is One and united, could they sense the mystery of the Trinity, the divinely united God. In a world full of paganism, belief in God's Son would have been too primitive without reminders of the Unity and Personality of God. Among pagans the incarnation of God in humanity is a regular, if miraculous event. But for Christians it is a miracle which cannot be understood, an unbelievable, unique event. That is because Christian thought fully understands the difference between Absolute and human being. God became a man. The Invisible made himself visible. What can be seen, can also be depicted. This is how the Orthodox icon was born.

The Christian Church has great mystics like Dionysius the Areopagite affirming that God is unknowable; there is also a certain Fr. Ivan from Nizhnii Vasiuk who affirms that for some days he saw something unusual, and accordingly painted a small icon. We could say that within the Christian church there is a strange, contradictory combination of mystical philosophy and pagan anthropomorphical practice. But in fact the Areopagite himself created a philosophy of the image. The church fathers themselves identify God as a Personality. Basil the Great gave us the genuine manifesto of Christian anthropomorphism when he advised that we take our understanding of the difference between human being and personality (*hypostasis*), and apply this to divine teachings.

Yes, Christians depict God as man. But not like the ignorant pagans mocked by Xenophanes.[30] God became human in Christ. Without ceasing to be what he

---

[30] Cf. Clement of Alexandria's quotation in his *Stromata* V, 14, of Xenophanes' famous description of human anthropomorphic depiction of the gods; cited in *Ante-Nicene Fathers*, 2: 470.

was, he became what he was not. In love and freedom God came to us. After the declaration that "no one has ever seen God," another follows: "The only begotten Son, who is at the Father's side, he has made him known" (John 1.18). The greatness of the Source of every being is not destroyed or lessened by the personalist understanding of God, or by portraying him as man.[31]

Pantheism has its own truth: any individual being can only *be* by participation in *Being* (with a capital letter). A stone, chain, or man exists only when its essence is connected by participation in that which embraces the entire Universe. Being is the utmost category of philosophical thought, and includes everything that exists. But such thoughts can be found in any serious Christian book on philosophy. The question is, whether it is possible for Being to be completely absorbed in all the individual particles of existence. The fact that God maintains the world within himself does not imply that God has no existence, or that he thinks of himself only within the context of the physical world. Nor is it necessary for consistency of thought to deprive that Being of the ability to think independently, to act freely and consciously, to love and create.

Pantheism claims that the search for an ideal basis of the world leads to pantheism. The world of ideas, forms, and numbers shapes its own matter, but is not of itself matter. From this it follows that our world is permeated by intelligence. Christianity too is familiar with the eidos-like, invisible, intelligent aspect of the world, but unlike pantheism does not altogether reduce that Intelligence to its life in the world's particles. We need not identify God himself as the world-embracing intelligent principle (or the intelligent-ideal aspect of the universe); God can create a world of ideal and numerical forms beyond himself, and these in turn envelop matter. Cognition of world harmony does not entail cognition of the Creator Himself, but the Divine Wisdom of the Creator. Accordingly, the ideal "Reality" known to the philosopher-pantheist is also accepted by the Christian, but Christianity finally places a Personal God beyond it.[32] Christians agree with pantheism on what it affirms, but they do not agree with pantheism on what it rejects, i.e., its denying the existence of the Divine Being beyond this world.

Pantheistic Appreciation of Our World

Pantheism thinks unworthily about God and the world when it regards the world visible to us only as an illusion and accidental manifestation of the in-

---

[31] Orthodox theology and canon law clearly forbid depicting God the Father in the image of man, because the Father was never incarnate. Cf. definitions of the Seventh Ecumenical Council.

[32] This is the kind of argumentation used by S. L. Frank in his last book, *Real'nost' i chelovek*, in his attempt to overcome the pantheistic tendency of the philosophy of All-Unity; trans. as *Reality and Man, an Essay in the Metaphysics of Human Nature* (London: Faber and Faber, 1965).

visible, faceless Absolute; such a view results naturally in world-denying nihilism. The Roerichs admitted that "we cannot say that our Earth and the Visible world are in opposition to the Absolute, or we would have to accept something existing beyond the Absolute, which is ridiculous."[33]

But this conclusion is doubtful. We can see that this world is certainly not the Absolute, is far from perfect, and also varied and complex. Besides, even within a context of "pure" philosophy this is not a necessary conclusion. The relationship between the Absolute and the relative is not necessarily a spatial one. God is "outside of the world" in the same sense that he is *beyond* the categories "outside" and "inside." He is not "extended" spatially. Moreover, the problem of the "limits of the Absolute" also arises for pantheist thought. Suppose the world to be "a sort of other existence" of the Absolute; suppose the world, matter, and human beings as emanations from the One. But how could that "other existence" relate to the Absolute? What could make the Absolute depart from its own limits, to enter the condition of "another" existence? Relative being still has existence. Why should the Divine imprison himself in imperfect forms? Who considers God more worthily, pantheism with its belief in a Divinity unconsciously and necessarily flowing out into a relative world, or Christianity as it proposes that God consciously and freely created the world of nature?

According to pantheism, it is a sin (more precisely, a mistake, or illusion) to notice anything but the Absolute in the world. Monotheism, however, allows for admiring and cherishing the world. Christianity says that the world of being is multiform even though everything arises from One Absolute Source. Christianity maintains ontological pluralism. It recognizes the Infinity of the Creator beyond what can be known, a real variety of the world, and its real existence outside of divinity. God in his love wanted the world to be complex and varied; in the fourth of his *Spiritual Homilies* St. Macarius of Egypt reminds us that when God brought the visible creation from non-being into being, he did so with great variety and diversity. Accordingly, the complexity and independence of the world is not a threat or fraud, but has religious value. Christianity knows the world to be thoroughly penetrated by Divinity. This sense of God's presence is based on the Christian teaching of the world's creation out of nothing.

Creation "Out of Nothing"

The Christian teaching about creation of the world "out of nothing" does not imply that "nothing" is some kind of "space" or realm surrounding the Absolute from without. The dogma of creation just explains that time and space, the world and humanity have no other cause for existing aside from God. In creating, God as it were empties out from himself some part of his being (which

---

[33] *Pis'ma Eleny Rerikh, 1929–38*, 1: 358.

becomes non-being), and in that non-being he creates new life that is not his, but ours.

Secondly, God fills the world because he is transcendent, and if he is transcendent, the world has no cause for being, or power of its own to maintain itself; rather, all that exists does so by participating in First Being, namely, the Transcendent Creator who fills the Universe (which is not identical to him) to support its being. God is not the world, and the world is not God, yet God is in the world and the world is in God. Under no condition is God to be comprehended as "a part" of reality which exists somewhere "near" the finite world. God is One in multiplicity, infinite in the finite, and transcendent in the immanent. Here we can only use the language of paradox, "the coincidence of opposites." God's presence is a mystery in our world. Still God is beyond the world; the world does not comprehend him, but God sustains its existence.

Pantheism and Anthropology

Aside from an unworthy portrayal of divinity and a primitive model of the universe, pantheism offers a distorted conception of the human being. Pantheism radically denies the existence of the human being. If pantheists are right, the person does not exist; it is only a location for the Absolute spirit to manifest itself. This does not ennoble the person, but unavoidably leads to the conclusion that "if I am a particle of the Absolute, then That exists, but I do not." Pantheism results in the annihilation of the self. E. Roerich says that "evil was born with the first appearance of consciousness."[34] This view of the source of evil supports a striving for complete extinction of consciousness.

How then can one escape such a trap, which appears so philosophical? The philosophical situation presented by pantheism is somewhat unusual. European non-Christian philosophy ordinarily asks for proof that God is not just a figment of our imagination. Pantheists, on the other hand, doubt the existence of this world; for them we need to prove that we are not a figment of the consciousness of Brahman.

Christianity opposed the muddle of absolute monism through the formula of St. Augustine and Descartes: "I think and therefore I exist." With sufficient logical basis I can always think that the entire world is just my dream; but I cannot think that I myself am just someone else's dream. I myself think, doubt, and search; and with every possibility of making mistakes as I search, I cannot doubt that, even to make mistakes, the person who is making the mistakes must exist, namely, I myself. V. Nesmelov said that "by ourselves we do not have the thinking capacity to resolve the existence of a consciousness alien to us."[35] The

---

[34] *Pis'ma Eleny Rerikh, 1929–38*, 2: 267.

[35] V. V. Nesmelov, *Nauka o cheloveke* [The science of man] (Kazan: "Chelovek," 1906), 2: 180.

philosophical facts are that "I" am capable of thinking about the Absolute, that "I" have an idea of Him in my consciousness. What of the Absolute thinking about me, and of my own thinking as something secondary, relative to the Absolute? This is just a philosophical model, not philosophical fact. Any hypothesis must be supported with fact, not kept aloof from them.

I exist, and this means that there is something else in the world besides the Absolute. That means that there are at least two of us. A man with a biblical upbringing who has learned to say "you" to God in prayer, cannot stop sensing himself as a reality. In his argument with Buddhism in *I and Thou*, Martin Buber claimed that a man has a sense of himself which cannot include the world.[36] Pantheistic monism requires the denial of my unmediated experience of my own being; it also requires acceptance of my being all alone in the Universe. There are no others. Buddhist monism leads to a denial of the capacity of saying "you" to God. His love, meaning that "everything that has appeared is indivisibly contained in his heart – does not know the simple opposition of one creature to another."[37]

Pantheism and Human Freedom

Absorbing human beings in "primary unity," pantheism cannot provide human freedom. If I am no more than a manifestation of universal substance, I cannot be free from what I manifest. It follows logically that "nothing exists but karma. All being is an endless chain of cause and effect."[38] Kant, on the contrary, affirmed the existence of God following necessarily from the phenomena of human freedom.

Kant starts from the widely accepted idea that nothing happens without a cause. The principle of determinism is also the most common law of the universe. And human beings are subjected to it. But there are exceptions, occasions when human beings act freely, without any pressure, nor automatically. If we say that every human deed has its causes, then only such causes should be praised. Without freedom there is no responsibility, nor can there be right, or morality. According to Kant, denying people freedom means denying morality. On the other hand, as I regard the causes that make other people act as they do in any given situation, I must admit that for the most part I myself act freely, to the extent that I can observe myself closely. I know that whenever the surrounding circumstances, my past, special features of my character and heredity do not influence me, there is always a split second in the moment of choice when I can decide what to do, and stand above myself. During this second, as Kant expresses

---

[36] Martin Buber, *I and Thou*, trans. R. Gregor Smith (New York: Scribner's Sons, 1958), 94.
[37] Ibid., 93.
[38] *Pis'ma Eleny Rerikh, 1929–38*, 1: 414.

it, the history of the entire Universe starts with me, as it were: neither in my past, nor in my surroundings is there anything that I can use to justify the baseness of what I am about to do.

So, we have the two facts: 1) Everything in the world lives in accordance with the law of cause, and 2) there are times in the rare moments of his freedom when a man does not follow this rule.

There is another principle. Within any given state there are people who do not follow its rules, diplomats who do not belong to the State and have "extraterritorial" right. If we do not follow the fundamental rule of the Universe, it may mean that we do not belong to it. Rather, having "extraterritorial" status in this world, we are envoys, followers of a different, nonmaterial world, where the principle of Love and Freedom is in effect, rather than the principle of determinism. So, if we are free, it means that God exists. The Russian contemporary of Kant, Gavriil Derzhavin expressed this idea in his ode "God": "I exist, and so do You."

The sense of human freedom is so much a characteristic of Christianity that even Metropolitan Antonii (Khrapovitskii) in his theological system (though it is not precisely Orthodox, for it leans towards pantheism) declared boldly that "while remaining subject to all material phenomena, God offered independent existence to the subject of moral phenomena."[39] To the extent that Christians think of human beings as rightfully higher than the cosmos, they can appropriate this statement. But occultists who consider human beings to be no more than a "microcosm" cannot use this argument, for they deny the freedom and independence of the world in general, admitting such features only for the fractions of the "macrocosm."

From this perspective pantheism cannot answer the question which Vladimir Solov'ev posed to Blavatsky: "If human consciousness is capable of decomposing divine light and breaking up absolute unity, what is its origin?"[40] In order to resist Unity, human consciousness or spirit must be other than Unity. How can it be different when it has never yet posed resistance? We must confess that it was a fraud, and the struggle between good and evil was no more than an intergalactic production of the struggle of Unity with itself. Or we must agree with the biblical claim that God actually created the world and humanity so that they differ from himself.

---

[39] Archbishop Antonii (Khrapovitskii), *Sochineniia* [Works] (Kazan, 1909), 3: 111.

[40] V. S. Solov'ev, review of H. P. Blavatsky, *Kliuch k teosofii* (The key to theosophy), in Solov'ev, *Sobranie sochinenii* [Collected works], 2nd ed. (Brussels: Zhizn' s Bogom, 1966–70), 6: 290.

Pantheism and the Question of Evil

Besides questions posed for "pure reason," ethical "practical reason" tries to break through the hypothetical charms of "all-unity." It refuses to idolize crimes or cannibalism. Identifying God with the world, or spirit with nature can disorient a man morally. Nature does not know the difference between evil and good. Things in the world just exist without burdening themselves with the sense of their own existence. If a person does search for the meaning of life he seeks something beyond this life, which does not mean "in death," but a search for something higher than his life, something which can consecrate and justify his concrete existence through its lofty character. We live for the sake of something else.

Searching means that something "beyond-this-world" already exists, for this search for meaning (or sense of lack of meaning) does not occur in the ordinary flow of events.

> For the most part it seems troublesome to us that, from the point of view of the objective empirical world, these insignificant, miserable double-legged animals called human beings find it impossible to arrange their life on Earth quietly, and are troubled by an internal dissatisfaction which is not understood; and all this is because of a glance from deep within, as evidence of our belonging to a deeper, different, fully reasoning existence. Even if we are powerless prisoners of this world, and our rebellion is senseless because of powerlessness, yet we, its captives, not its citizens, have a vague recollection of another genuine motherland, and do not envy those who have forgotten it.[41]

The ideas just elaborated are based on Vladimir Solov'ev (*The Justification of the Good*), Evgenii Trubetskoi (*The Meaning of Life*), and Semen Frank (*The Meaning of Life*). They agree in rejecting the simplicity of our world, arguing from the possibility of human moral judgment; we must distinguish between higher, spiritual, ideal being and a lower order of existence. The higher principle acts and attracts the lower to itself, but they are not identical. Human beings cannot be equated with the world (because they strive to depart from it while searching for God); nor is God to be equated with the world (because while living in this world human beings are drawn to him). And human beings are not to be equated with God, because they search for him, thus revealing a sense of distance from him.

According to E. Roerich, "The revealed Universe in its visible or invisible phases shows only innumerable aspects of shining matter, from the very Highest

---

[41] S. L. Frank, *Smysl zhizni* [The meaning of life] (Paris, 1925), 90.

to the very Lowest."[42] Russian Christian philosophers have argued that alongside "innumerable aspects of matter," human thought and passion for meaning brings humanity to God, far beyond the material world. The history of the world is not a history of the Absolute. What happens in the world and the human soul is not an act of the Divinity as such. God allows free action by independent sources of action; he has reserved for himself the capacity of not identifying with himself the wrong choices which we make. The possibility for judgment of sins opens up for the religious consciousness. Events in the world which result from human decision, without God's will, can be rejected from a religious perspective. The world is not God; sin can be called "sin" without being identified as "another existence of the Absolute."

If everything is God, the difference between good and evil must be predetermined in the thought of the Absolute. Whatever one might consider wrong, it is not necessarily unworthy of the divine; that is only an illusion. For the enlarged mind the "Absolute includes within itself all the manifestations of the universe."[43] "Everything" means evil too is included. Like other contemporary occultists Blavatsky was fond of the cabbalist saying, "As it is above, so also below."[44] The opposite is true as well, for Blavatsky quotes the cabbalist treatise, "Zohar says that everything existing in the lower world also exists in the higher one. The higher and the lower act upon and interact with each other."[45] But in "the lower world," among mankind, there is much dirt, ignorance, hatred, and, even worse, a conscious inclination to hatred, to destruction and evil. Combining this with the occult axiom "As above, so also below" leads to the conclusion that in "the united Divinity" of theosophy there is something that persistently desires evil for man.

This conclusion does not distort theosophical positions. "Living ethics" agrees with it, believing that there is a fully lawful place for evil in the Universe.

> There is no evil as such in the Absolute, but in the World all oppositions appear: light and darkness, spirit and matter, good and evil. I advise you to learn all the basic ideas of Eastern philosophy, the existence of the United Absolute Transcendental Reality, and the double Aspect in the Universe caused by it, as well as the illusory character or relativity of every manifestation. The action of opposites brings harmony. If one part were to stop acting, the action of the other would immediately become destructive. So the manifest world exists in a balance of opposing

---

[42] *Pis'ma Eleny Rerikh, 1929–38*, 1: 327.
[43] *Pis'ma Eleny Rerikh, 1932–1955*, 433.
[44] Blavatskaia, *Tainaia doktrina*, 2: 630.
[45] Ibid., 153.

powers. Good in the lower world can appear as evil in the higher, and vice versa. That is why all ideas in the manifest world are relative.[46]

If evil were to discontinue its actions in this world, universal harmony would be destroyed. Good cannot exist without evil, and the Absolute cannot stop displaying itself through evil. Moreover, evil is not just a condition of the Good, or knowledge of the Good. Evil is itself a basis of Being. "The ancients understood this so well that their philosophers, whose contemporary followers are cabbalists, regarded Evil as an "underlying foundation" of God, or Good."[47] Here we have an honest acknowledgment that the God of the theosophists has an evil basis. Good cannot even appear and act without evil helping it. Blavatsky's text is even more interesting if we remember that for Christian theologians the word "underlying foundation" (*podosnova*) is the same as "hypostasis." The hypostasis of evil is Satan. It follows that God is second in importance to Satan. Behind Good there is Evil, on which it is based. Good is an epiphenomenon, an accidental manifestation; Evil is essential being. As Blavatsky writes "The Cabbalists always portray Evil as a Power necessary for Good, providing the power of life and existence, which it could not have any other way."[48]

Christ says that his life came from the Father and from himself, not from the Serpent, or Evil. Trying to "reconcile" Christianity with other religions, theosophy "corrects" the Gospel: Good has its roots in Evil. "A shadow is not evil, but a necessary, indispensible relationship, an addition to Light and Good! The shadow is the creator (of Good) on Earth."[49] So, if Christ came to show the will of the Heavenly Father on earth and if "the creator of Good on Earth" is Evil, then whose will did Christ come to reveal? An occultist who resolves to be consistent will have to admit that the Heavenly Father, to whom Christ prays is … Satan.

Actually, theosophy does not refuse this step in saying that "when the Church curses Satan, it curses the cosmic reflection of God; it curses God himself as manifest in Matter or objectivity."[50] The world of occult pantheism has a lawful place for evil and Satan. So lawful that it does not distinguish Evil from God. Everything proceeding in the world is so intimately connected with the pantheistic Absolute that occultists do not wish to exclude even Satan from divine worship.

---

[46] *Pis'ma Eleny Rerikh, 1929–38*, 2: 341–42.

[47] Blavatskaia, *Tainaia doktrina*, 1: 510.

[48] Ibid., 1: 511.

[49] Ibid., 2: 269.

[50] Ibid., 2: 294.

Preaching total-unity of the world and a restricted distinction between God and the world leads inevitably to a sacralization of the world as given, including evil at work in it. Everything in the world is divine. Everything is God. Everything is good. There is no evil. The path from pantheism to immorality is logical: "One cannot affirm God as a synthesis of the whole Universe, Omnipresent, All-Knowing, and Eternal, and then divide Him from Evil."[51] The pantheistic Divine is basically inseparable from Evil.

As a result theosophical, not Christian ideas of "the One" turn out to be too "anthropomorphic." Christian views of the Divine place no human categories within the Divine Mystery. Divine transcendence and unknowability do not allow just any human categories to be subsumed under "the All-One"; apophatic thought limits the terms used for "Primary Being." Theosophists claim that the Absolute has a place for everything, and speak of God as being both good and evil, existence and nonexistence, male and female, light and darkness. Christian dialectical thought is different; he is beyond distinctions of being and nonbeing. It may even be said that through the creation of nonexistence, God can separate himself from created being.[52] That does not project nonexistence within God himself, for he is beyond human differentiation of good and evil. If God is not good that does not mean he is evil.

From its pantheistic premises theosophical thought logically deduces the relativity of all moral categories. Even F. Schlegel realized that pantheism, while verbally denying it, in fact did cancel the difference between good and evil. The followers of Schelling, and Schelling himself (after coming down with pantheism, as it were with an illness) declared that they desperately wanted to stop Germany's "inhuman pantheistic madness."[53] Indeed, if good and evil are equal in Universal Energy, the only thing left is to open the soul to unhindered acceptance of "the inspirations of life," entrusting oneself to the will of "cosmic storms" in which the Unified Spirit alone can breathe.

Actually, pantheism declares that nothing happens in the world. The Absolute does not let go of anything, and carries everything with itself, so all phenomena are equal to him, and all parts of being are equally perfect. No occupation could tear a person from this Perfection, just as no occupation could draw him nearer to That which is everywhere equally present. A person may seem to exist

---

[51] Ibid., 1: 510.

[52] "God is himself the initiator, and 'nothing'; for everything, being as well as nonbeing, flows out of him, resulting from him as its cause; for even 'nothing' is bounded, for it has being thanks to its being the nothing of that which does not exist." St. Maxim the Confessor, based on S. N. Bulgakov, *Svet nevechernii* [The unfading light] (Moscow: Respublika, 1994), 163.

[53] Cited in E. N. Trubetskoi, *Mirosozertsanie Vl. S. Solov'eva* [Worldview of Vl. S. Solov'ev] (1913; reprint, Moscow: MFF, "Medium," 1995), 1: 295.

and act, and through some deeds appear to change his status in the world; but this is only illusion, and must be abolished by purification of mind. The opposite is also true. Preaching of radical immoralism was used in esoterical cults as pantheistic training for adepts. In some Gnostic texts a female deity calls herself both prostitute and saint, both bride and groom, shameless and modest, war and peace.[54] In another Gnostic hymn, the one whom they call Jesus orders followers to dance around and answer "Amen" to all his mutually contradictory remarks.[55] In tantric Buddhism the limit between good and evil is crossed when a person betrays himself "consciously" in action, but even then in a group orgy they remain "pure," thinking of themselves as an undivided part of United Energy.[56]

It does not matter whether one achieves this "enlarging of mind" through deeds (as in tantrism) or meditation (as in gnosticism); the result is always the same. It involves crossing the boundary which human moral intuition senses between good and evil, because a realization of the radical unity of the world and one's own identity with it, is blocked by this "enlarging." As V. K. Shokhin expressed it, "that is how to tease the adept,"[57] bringing them to a "renewed" condition of openness to the pantheistic truth of the All-One revealing itself in the real contradictions of the world, in any display of good and evil. Once the moral boundary has been crossed, even in thought, it interferes with the clarity of all other differences.

Pantheism denies human freedom, dissolves and neutralizes all the colors of life, transforms all the categories of the relative world into the Absolute, and dissolves the Perfect Being in a damaged cosmos. Russian philosophers took the sense of good and evil as proof of human beings not truly belonging to this world. Vladimir Solov'ev proved the existence of God through the human feeling of shame. From this perspective it is quite impossible to consider the Roerichs as belonging to the *Russian* philosophical tradition.

---

[54] Cf. A. F. Okulov et al., eds., *Apokrify drevnikh khristian* [Apocrypha of the early Christians] (Moscow: "Mysl'," 1989), 308–15.

[55] "Gnosticheskaia khorovodnaia pesn'" [Gnostic choral song], in *Ot beregov Bosfora do beregov Efrata* [From the shores of the Bosporus to the shores of Ephrata], trans. S. S. Averintsev (Moscow: "Nauka," 1987), 143–45.

[56] Cf. Anand Nayak, *Tantra, ou l'éveil de l'energie* (Paris: Cerf, 1988), 107.

[57] V. K. Shokin, *Brakhmanistskaia filosofiia: Nachal'nyi i ranneklassicheskii periody* [The philosophy of Brahman: Beginning and early classical periods] (Moscow: "Vostochnaia literatura" RAN, 1994), 315.

Pantheism and the Poetry of the Cosmos

Nevertheless, there is an irrational, poetic argument for pantheism. The sense of the sacred harmonious character of nature can really take us past philosophy, to a pantheistic sense of the world as divine. Pantheism has its own poetry, perhaps even in contradiction with pantheist philosophical talk of an accidental conglomeration of dead particles. A pantheistic understanding of the world with its elements thoroughly penetrated by Supreme Life can warm one's heart. But such a poetry of pantheism is also part of a Christian understanding of nature. Orthodoxy expresses a sense of the liturgical harmony of the Universe. The world is not evil. Neither is it God, but we can feel Divine breath in it because (as a paradox of Christianity) Christ sent the Spirit to be "present everywhere and filling everything." One need only stand near the open doors of a country church in summer at the time of service, to feel how the prayers of the church harmonize with Russian nature, and notice a great positive "world-loving" attitude in Orthodoxy. Any Christian can repeat Tiutchev's reproach to the positivists:

> Nature is not what you think –
> It is not blind, not a soulless thing.
> It has its soul, it has its freedom.
> It has its love, it has its language..
> They cannot see and cannot hear,
> They live in this world as in darkness,
> For them the Sun does not breathe
> Nor is there life in the waves of the sea.
> The sun's rays have never touched their souls,
> And spring never bloomed in their hearts,
> For them the woods were ever silent,
> And for all its stars the night was dumb!

The world is certainly beautiful. It can be a source of religious experience, but not the subject of religious worship. Admiring the splendor of the world we risk losing sight of God in it.

That is why the Christian may experience the poetry of pantheism, but not accept its metaphysics. The beauty of the world tells the Christian that "there is even more Joy and more Beauty beyond me!" Nature does not consist of God: it points to him. Saint Augustine, in searching for Christ, learned about God:

> "What is God?" I asked the Earth, and it told me that it was not Him; everything living on it made the same confession. I asked the sea and the multitudes living in it, and they answered, "We are not your God; search higher." I asked the blowing winds and all the heavens with their creatures and they replied, "Anaximenes is wrong: I am not God." I

asked the sky, the Sun, the Moon and the stars, and they all said that they were not the God for whom I was looking. And I said to everything around me, "Tell me about my God – if you are not God – tell me something about Him." And they all cried, "He is our creator." My contemplation was my question, and their beauty was their answer. (*Confessions* X, 6)

Christianity has never been pantheistic, whether at its source or during its further philosophical development. A syncretistic identification of Christianity with Eastern Pantheism means a utopian violence upon reality. Grigorii Pomerants once offered an interesting criterion to identify a fundamental ideology: "an aggressive reductionism ... an aggressively violent simplification of life, developed in a mythic framework. What kind of myth? That is secondary."[58] According to this criterion contemporary popular religious syncretism can be identified as a fundamentalist movement. Everyone must think and believe identically. Christianity is reduced to fit the contours of Hinduism or "esoteric Buddhism." Religious practices and texts of all religions are reinterpreted according to theosophical conceptions, despite resistance. This is an experiment of aggression against history, a posthumous transformation of all great religious teachers of the past in favor of a fashionable contemporary faith. If contemporary intellectuals are inclined to Buddhism, Christ will be refurbished as a complete Buddhist. If Pantheism is popular, how else to think of the great Teacher but as a Pantheist![59]

G. Pomerants wanted to reinterpret all the sacred Scriptures of mankind to "agree with each other,"[60] not really trying to understand what *was* in these texts, but reading into them what he *wanted* to see there. Such historico-philosophical ventures should be avoided. It is far better to accept the right of Christianity to

---

[58] G. Pomerants, *Vykhod iz transa* [Exit from a trance] (Moscow: Iurist, 1995), 389.

[59] Pomerants himself could not resist the temptation. He interpreted Christ's cry on Calvary, "My God, My God, why have you forsaken me?" as an "ecstatic *feeling of unity with the world*, which can be broken, but only with extreme difficulty and lengthy suffering" (*Vykhod iz transa*, 504), although Christ never said that he was united with the world, but rather, that the world hated him. He was united with his Father, through the Spirit who is unknown and unacceptable to the world (John 14.17 and 15.26). Pomerants's last book has all religions accepting an ideal of "merging with the world"; here he openly turns Christ into a pantheist. According to Zinaida Mirkina and Pomerants, in religion the person does not look for God, but simply falls into "the depth of his own soul" (Mirkina and Pomerants, *Velikie religii mira* [Great religions of the world] [Moscow: RIPOL, 1995], 5), The apostles understood Christ "too literally" (ibid., 148). For centuries the truth remained silent, until Pomerants clarified the meaning of the Gospel; cf. ibid., 116: "The poetic meaning of the Gospel is the new image of the splendid human being. We attempt to uncover it in the same way that the meaning of Greek and biblical myths are uncovered."

[60] Pomerants, *Vykhod iz transa*, 559.

its independent specific positions, and not reduce the Christian to a Buddhist, or the apostle Paul to an "Initiate" in the occult.

Glossary

Aksakov, Konstantin Sergeevich (1817–60)

Slavophile writer on public issues, historian, linguist, and poet. He worked for abolition of serfdom, but without removal of the tsar.

Aletheia

Greek term for truth.

All-unity (total-unity, *vseedinstvo*), metaphysics of

Basic theme of Vladimir Solov'ev's philosophy; everything in this universe has a common source and common goal. Multiplicity and egoism represents a falling away from original unity. History tends toward reintegration, and in that process a crucial role is assigned to Jesus Christ, the Godman who reconciles God with humanity and the creation.

Anaximenes

6th-century B.C. Greek philosopher of the Milesian school who, with Thales and Anaximander, looked for a divine cosmic element to explain the variety of things in nature. He identified this principle as *air*, because of its infinite character.

Andreev, Daniil Leonidovich (1906–1959)

Russian poet and mystic, imprisoned from 1947 to 1957. His early poetry is characterized by expectations of doom and catastrophe. Important works are *Russkie bogi* (*Russian Gods*), published in 1989, and *Roza mira* (*Rose of the World*), elaborating a plan for world salvation through the combined efforts of the world's religions, published in 1991.

Antonii (Khrapovitskii), Metropolitan (1863–1936)

Russian theologian and pantheist living abroad after 1919. He was elected Chairman of the Holy Synod of the Russian Church in Exile, located in Sremski-Karlovatsky in Yugoslavia, and was responsible for its condemnation of the modernism of the Russian Theological Seminary in Paris, and more particularly, the sophiological position of Sergei Bulgakov as heretical (1925–27).

Helleman, Wendy, ed. *The Russian Idea: In Search of a New Identity*. Bloomington, IN: Slavica, 2004, 213–51.

Apollinaris (the Younger) (ca. 310–90)

Bishop of Laodicea (ca. 361), chosen in spite of excommunication for a heretical position on the nature of Christ (Apollinarianism); he denied the existence of a rational human soul in Christ, in an attempt to combat Arianism. Apollinaris was a teacher of rhetoric, and with his father, Apollinaris the Elder, translated the Old Testament as Homeric poetry, and the New Testament as Platonic dialogues when the emperor Julian forbade Christians to teach classical literature.

Apophatic theology

Eastern Christian understanding of God considers his essence as totally transcendent and unknowable; strictly speaking, God can only be designated by negative attributes. Thus we can affirm what God is *not*, but cannot express divine attributes describing adequately what he is.

Aquinas, Thomas (1225–74)

Dominican teacher and writer who became the outstanding representative of medieval Christian theology, often referred to as *scholasticism*; he studied in Paris with Albert the Great, and is well known for his defense of Aristotle, battle with Averroism (1269–72), and desire to harmonize reason with revelation. Important works are the *Summa Contra Gentiles* (1260) and *Summa Theologica* (1265–72).

Areopagite, Dionysius the – see Dionysius

Athos, Mt.

Higly secluded monastic establishment of Northern Greece, significant from earliest centuries of Christianity. From the 14th century it became associated with the ascetic discipline and teaching of Hesychasm.

Atman

The self, soul, or ego of Indian philosophy. It is variously regarded as the hypothetical carrier of karma, as identical with the divine, or dissolved at death and reunited with the world ground.

St. Augustine, S. Aurelius (354–430)

North African bishop of Hippo (from 395) who began as a teacher of rhetoric, and was converted by the preaching of Ambrose in Milan, after being attracted to Manicheanism and Neoplatonism. His outstanding works are the *Confessions*, *On the Trinity*, and *The City of God*.

Avos'

Almost untranslatable Russian word representing chance, fortune, fate, what is uncontrollable, the unpredictability of life.

Bakhtin, Mikhail Mikhailovich (1895–1975)

Famous Russian specialist in literary theory and aesthetics, whose ideas made a deep impact on Western thought in these areas. Upon graduating from the University of St. Petersburg in 1918, Bakhtin began his career in Vitebsk, Belarus, but quickly ran into problems with censors; he was arrested in 1929, and exiled to the Kazakh Autonomous Soviet Socialist Republic. He is well known for his work on F. Dostoevskii, *Problemy poetiki Dostoevskogo* (*Problems of Dostoevsky's Poetics*, 1929; reissued 1963); here he developed his view of the interaction of author, work, and readers to establish meaning within a socio-political context. Also important is his *Voprosy literatury i estetiki* (*Issues of Literature and Aesthetics*, translated as *The Dialogic Imagination*, 1975), where he developed a linguistic theory of polyphony, or "dialogics."

St. Basil the Great (of Caesarea) (ca. 330–79)

With his brother Gregory of Nyssa and friend Gregory of Nazianzus, one of the three Cappadocian Fathers who defended the Christian faith against Arian heresy and developed the Orthodox understanding of the Trinity. As bishop of Caesarea he wrote several works on monasticism, theological questions, and canon law.

Basman

Term based on the Turkish "basmach" referring to Islam.

Beatitudes

Series of "blessings" ("Blessed are the poor ... Blessed are the meek ... Matt. 5.3–12) given by Jesus as part of the Sermon on the Mount (Matt. 5–7), the teachings updating the law of Moses for a New Testament people.

Belinskii, Vissarion Grigor'evich (1811–48)

Russian literary critic, well known for his work on Pushkin (1843–46). He was notorious for his polemic with Gogol, asserting the non-religious character of the Russian. As a democrat and philosopher he wrote on public issues for journals like *Teleskop* (*The Telescope*, 1833–36), *Otechestvennie zapiski* (*Notes of the Fatherland*, 1839–46), and *Sovremennik* (*The Contemporary*, 1847–48).

Belyi, Andrei (actual name: Bugaev, Boris Nikolaevich) (1880–1934)

Symbolist poet and writer. Three of his novels are well known: *Serebriannyi golub'* (*The Silver Dove*, 1909), *Peterburg* (*Petersburg*, 1914), and *Moskva*

(*Moscow*, 1926–32). Also important are his books devoted to artistic theory, like *Simvolizm* (*Symbolism*).

Berdiaev, Nikolai Aleksandrovich (1874–1948)

Russian philosopher and writer on public issues who renounced Marxist materialism to return to Christianity, and was exiled in 1922. Important publications include his *Filosofiia svobody* (*Philosophy of Freedom*, 1911), *Smysl tvorchestva* (*The Meaning of the Creative Act*, 1916), *Filosofiia svobody dukha* (*The Philosophy of the Free Spirit*, 1927–28), *O naznachenii cheloveka* (*The Destiny of Man*, 1931), *Smysl istorii* (*The Meaning of History*, 1923; London, 1936), *Dukh i real'nost'* (*Spirit and Reality*, London, 1937), *Istoki i smysl russkogo kommunizma* (*The Origin of Russian Communism*, London, 1937), and *Russkaia ideia* (*The Russian Idea*, 1946). Berdiaev's thought is characterized by its concern for the person and the issue of freedom. He had high hopes for Russia fulfilling its historic task of mediating between East and West once the Soviet era ended.

Blavatsky (Blavatskaia), Elena Petrovna (1831–91)

Religious mystic who immigrated to the United States in 1873 and helped establish the Theosophical Society in New York City (1875). With the American lawyer and journalist Henry Steele Olcott, she established international headquarters for the Society near Madras, India, in 1878. Important aims of the Society were to foster universal brotherhood without distinction of race, creed, sex, caste, or color; the study of comparative religion, philosophy, and science, and study of the latent powers in nature and human beings. Her publications include *Razoblachennaia Izida* (*Isis Unveiled*, 1877) and *Tainaia doktrina* (*The Secret Doctrine*, 1888).

Bodhisattva

A state of wisdom attained by a Buddhist wise and holy man.

Bogoliubskii, Andrei (ca. 1111–74)

Early Russian tsar who wished to expand Russian territory, and in 1157 moved his capital from Kiev to Vladimir, on the Kliazma River, a city founded in 1108 by Vladimir II Monomakh, grand prince of Kiev. The community was important for trade along the Kliazma River until 1328, when Russia's political center was transferred to Moscow.

Bogonosets

Russian term meaning "godbearing," used by Dostoevskii to describe the Russian nation.

Buber, Martin (1878–1965)

Jewish religious philosopher and writer who emigrated from Germany to Switzerland in 1933, and then to Palestine. He is well known for his publication *Ich und Du* (*I and Thou*, 1922).

Bulgakov, Sergei Nikolaevich (1871–1944)

Religious philosopher, theologian, economist, and one of the ideological leaders of the Russian Student Christian Movement (RSCM); he left Russia in 1923. Like Berdiaev, Frank, and others he rejected Marxist materialism for Christianity, thereby stimulating the Russian Spiritual Renaissance of the early 20th century. Among his important publications are *Filosofiia khoziaistva: Mir kak khoziaistvo* (*Philosophy of Economy: The World as Household*, 1912), *Agnets Bozhii* (*The Lamb of God*, 1933), *O Sofii – Premudrosti Bozhiei* (*Sophia, The Wisdom of God*, 1935), and *Filosofiia imeni* (*The Philosophy of the Name*, 1953).

Bunin, Ivan Alekseevich (1870–1953)

Well-known story writer and first Russian to win the Nobel prize for literature (1933). His stories include "The Village" (1910) and "The Life of Arsen'ev" (1930). He followed classical traditions in his work, and emigrated in 1920.

Buslaev, Vasilii (Basil)

Epic hero, reveler and mischief-maker of 14–15th-century poetry connected with Novgorod.

Cabala (cabbala, kabala)

An occult religious philosophy developed by Jewish rabbis, using mystical interpretation of the Scriptures.

Caesar, "what belongs to Caesar"

The reference is to Jesus' New Testament statement on the paying of taxes, advising his disciples to give to God what belongs to God, and "to Caesar the things that are Caesar's" (Matt. 22.21).

Celsus

2nd-century Greek philosopher and fierce opponent of Christianity; his *Alethes Logos* (*True Doctrine*) dismisses the Christian faith as an uncultured attack on traditional Greco-Roman religion, the arts, and literature. This work survived primarily through Origen's thorough response, *Contra Celsum* (ca. 248), which claims a place for a Christian perspective in religion and philosophy.

Chaadaev, Petr Iakovlevich (1794–1856)

Russian thinker and writer, best known for his Philosophical Letters (1828–31). The sharp critique of Russian culture and religion in his first letter, published in *Teleskop* (*The Telescope*, 1836), while it cost him his freedom (he was declared mad), gave an important stimulus for discussions of Slavophiles and Westernizers on the role of Russia in the context of European civilization. He was the first Russian philosopher to synthesize religion, philosophy and sociology; many of his ideas were developed further by Vladimir Solov'ev.

Chardin, Teilhard de (1881–1955)

French philosopher, scientist, paleontologist, anthropologist, and Catholic theologian; he represents scientific evolutionism within the context of a Christian outlook.

Chekhov, Anton Pavlovich (1860–1904)

Famous Russian writer, well known for stories like "Palata #6" ("Ward #6," 1898) and the plays *Chaika* (*The Sea Gull*, 1896), *Diadia Vania* (*Uncle Vania*, 1897), and *Vishnevyi sad* (*The Cherry Orchard*, 1904). Combining humor with lyricism, his works explore themes characteristic of the intelligentsia of his time, their search for ideals, dissatisfaction with their "Philistine" existence, or resignation to the vulgarity of life.

Chernyshevskii, Nikolai Gavrilovich (1828–89)

Russian revolutionary writer and literary critic; a democrat, he was one of the founders of *narodnichestvo*. He was arrested in 1862 and sent to Siberia, but released in 1883.

St. Clement of Alexandria (ca. 150–215)

Christian Apologist, writer, and missionary theologian to the Hellenistic Greek cultural world, and also teacher of an important catechetical school in Alexandria. His most important surviving work is a trilogy including the *Protreptikos* (*Exhortation to the Greeks*), the *Paidagogos* (*The Instructor*), and *Stromateis* (*Miscellanies*). He prepared the way for the acceptance of Greek philosophy as an aid to Christian theological reflection.

St. Cyril of Jerusalem (ca. 310–87)

Church Father and bishop of Jerusalem from about 350. He finally accepted the Nicene position on Christ as God's Son, of the same substance as the Father, and participated in the 381 Council of Constantinople, where Arian positions were firmly repudiated.

Danilevskii, Nikolai Iakovlevich (1822–85)

Russian naturalist, sociologist, historical philosopher, and author of *Rossiia i Evropa* (*Russia and Europe*, 1869). His work provided a biological foundation for Russian nationalism, and anticipated Oswald Spengler's philosophy of history as a series of distinct civilizations. He supported absolutism as Russia's political heritage and influenced Konstantin Leont'ev among Russian political theorists.

Derrida, Jacques (b. 1930)

French philosopher and language theorist, famous for his rejection of metaphysics and "logocentrism" at the foundation of the Western philosophical tradition based on reason as a self-sufficient principle. His *Grammatology* emphasizes the primacy of the written over the spoken word (*logos*).

Derzhavin, Gavriil Romanovich (1743–1816)

Russian poet, contemporary of Kant, and representative of Russian classicism.

Descartes, René (Renatus Cartesius) (1596–1650)

French philosopher and founder of modern rational epistemology; he turned to mathematics for a new philosophical methodology, accepting only clear and distinct ideas as self-evident. His *"cogito ergo sum"* (I think, therefore I am) is often regarded as the epitome of the modern rationalist Western philosophical position. Important works are the *Discourse on Method* and *Meditations*.

Diogenes Synopeus (ca. 400–325 B.C.)

Greek moralist and founder of Greek Cynics. His guiding principle was simplicity of life, rejecting convention and accepting poverty, exemplified by living in a barrel. His aim was self-sufficiency as the basis for virtue and happiness. Opponents referred to his life as that of *dog* (Gr. *kuon*); accordingly, his followers were named Cynics.

Dionysius the Areopagite (pseudo-Dionysius) (ca. 500)

Syrian monk, known only by the pseudonym assumed from the 1st-century A.D. convert of St. Paul at Athens (Acts 17.34). He wrote a series of works in Greek combining positions of the 5th-century Neoplatonist, Proclus, with Christian theology and mystical experience; important are "On the Divine Names," "On Mystical Theology," "On the Celestial Hierarchy," and "On the Ecclesiastical Hierarchy," together with a set of letters written in a 1st-century Christian style. They influenced Western Latin medieval Christianity through translations by the 9th-century John Scotus Erigena, and commentaries by the 12th- and 13th-century Scholastics Hugh of Saint-Victor (Paris), Albertus Magnus, and Thomas Aquinas. In the East this work was influential on the

7th-century Maximus the Confessor, and the 14th-century mystic Gregory Palamas.

Dobroliubov, Nikolai Aleksandrovich (1836–61)

Russian literary critic, writer on public issues, and revolutionary democrat.

Domostroi (16th century)

"Household Book," a 16th-century codification of rules for daily life, family relationships, and care of children and property, attributed to Sil'vestr. It reflects the influence of monastic patterns of living on everyday Russian life.

Dostoevskii, Fedor Mikhailovich (1821–81)

Famous Russian novelist, thinker, and writer on public issues. Important works include *The Devils*, *The Brothers Karamazov*, and *The Diary of a Writer*.

Eleatics

School of philosophy founded by Xenophanes in Elea about 540 B.C., with important members like Parmenides and Zeno. It was monistic in ontology; Parmenides regarded the universe as one undifferentiated sphere, denying change and plurality of being, and accepting the evidence of reason at the expense of sense-perception.

Energetism

An Eastern 14th-century theological and philosophic principle affirming that mystic communion with God means union in energy, not in terms of divine essence. This position was developed by Palamas to refute accusations that Hesychast practice and experience of divine light assumed belief in two gods, of which one was transcendent, the other immanent. It was approved by the council of 1351.

St. Ephraim the Syrian (306–73)

Famous Christian theologian, poet and hymn writer, deacon of Edessa, also called "Harp of the Holy Spirit" and recognized as an authoritative representative of 4th-century Syriac Christianity. He composed theological-biblical commentaries and polemical works which have exerted a deep influence on both the Greek and Latin Christian tradition.

Erigena (Eriugena), John Scotus (810–77)

Irish theological philosopher, translator and commentator on works integrating Greek Neoplatonist philosophy with Christian belief, like those of (pseudo-)Dionysius, St. Maximus the Confessor, St. Gregory of Nyssa, and St. Epiphanius. He was well known from involvement in theological disputes on the Eucharist and predestination; both his *De predestinatione* (*On Predestina-*

tion, 851) and *De divisione naturae* (*On the Division of Nature*, 862–66) were condemned by church authorities, the latter for its inclination to pantheism.

Ern, Vladimir Frantsevich (1882–1917)

Russian religious philosopher and historian of philosophy. Two important publications are his *Sotsializm i obshchee mirovozzrenie* (*Socialism and the Social Attitude*, 1907) and *Priroda nauchnoi mysli* (*The Nature of Scientific Thought*, 1914).

Essentialism

Essentialism considers the nature of things independently of their actual existence, as an intelligible entity; it thus considers things which do not, or cannot exist in our world, hypothetical (unicorns) or spiritual (angels). "Essence" is based on the Latin verb "to be," *esse*, but the Latin did not distinguish greatly between *essentia* and *substantia*. Both terms for "essence" and "substance" go back to the Greek *ousia*, or "being," although medieval scholastic philosophy sharply distinguished them.

Eurasianism

An intellectual movement among Russian émigrés of the early post-revolution years. Eurasians regarded Russia as more Asian and continental, less a European and Western nation, and accented the Tatar-Mongolian period of Russian history. In the 1920s the movement was represented by N. Trubetskoi, P. Savitskii, G. Florovsky, L. Karsavin, and others; the important contemporary representative is Lev Gumilev.

Fedotov, Georgii Petrovich (1886–1951)

Russian historian and philosopher who emigrated in 1925. From 1926 to 1949 he taught at the Orthodox Theological University, Paris, and from 1943 to 1951 at St. Vladimir Orthodox Seminary in New York. Important works are his *Stikhi dukhovnye: Russkaia narodnaia vera po dukhovnym stikham* (*Spiritual Poetry: Russian Folk Belief in Spiritual Poetry*, 1935), *The Russian Religious Mind* (1946), and *A Treasury of Russian Spirituality* (1948).

Feodosii (Theodosius) of Pechora (d. 1074)

Old Russian writer of precepts and letters, monk and father superior of the Kievan-Pechorsky monastery, responsible for reform in its regulations.

Filofei (Philotheus)

16th-century church leader, father superior of the Trekhsviatitel'skii Monastery in Pskov, and author of epistles to Ivan Groznyi (Ivan the Terrible) as well as polemical works against astrology. The beginnings of the view of Moscow as the "Third Rome" are attributed to Filofei. Most significant is his epistle to

Vasilii III (between 1514 and 1521), stating that after the fall of Constantinople in 1453 (as second Rome), Moscow became the third (and last) Rome. Thus, as the only remaining true Christian state, Russia was justified in its imperial ambitions.

Florenskii, Pavel Aleksandrovich (1882–1943)

Russian religious philosopher and scientist, whose most important work is the *Stolp i utverzhdenie istiny* (*Pillar and Ground of Truth*, 1914). Unlike most other followers of Vladimir Solov'ev, Florenskii did not leave Russia as an exile in the early 1920s; for a number of years he tried to continue with scientific research under limiting conditions, but finally died in the *gulag*.

Frank, Semen Ludvigovich (1877–1950)

Russian philosopher and psychologist, exiled in 1922. From 1902 he co-edited the journal *Problems of Idealism*, and in 1909 was co-editor of *Vekhi* (*Landmarks*). Some of his important works are: *Filosofiia i zhizn'* (*Philosophy and Life*, 1910), *Dusha cheloveka* (*The Human Soul*, 1917), *Zhivoe znanie* (*Living Knowledge*, 1923), *Smysl zhizni* (*The Meaning of Life*, 1925) and *Real'nost' i chelovek* (*Reality and Man*, 1956).

Futurism (*budetlianstvo*)

An early 20th-century Russian revolutionary artistic school influencing both poets like Velimir Khlebnikov, who took great liberties in breaking up words, and painters like Mikhail Vrubel', one of whose best known pieces is "The Demon Seated" (1890).

Fedorov, Nikolai Fedorovich (1828–1903)

Russian religious philosopher, utopian futurist, and outstanding representative of Russian cosmism. His most famous publication is *Filosofiia obshchego dela* (*The Philosophy of the Common Task*, c. 1870).

Gogol', Nikolai Vasil'evich (1809–52)

Russian writer who influenced the development of satyrical writing and critical realism.

Goncharov, Ivan Aleksandrovich (1812–91)

Russian writer whose novels reflect important features of Russian society of his time. Of special interest is his *Oblomov* (1859).

Gramsci, Antonio (1891–1937)

Leader of the Italian Communist Party from 1923–26.

"Great October"

The so-called "Great October Socialist Revolution," of October 1917, resulted in the establishment of the Soviet Socialist State.

St. Gregory of Nazianzus (the Theologian) (ca. 330–89)

Famous 4th-century Church Father, theologian, and poet. He took a strong role in defense of the Trinity (God as Father, Son, and Holy Spirit), championing the full deity of Christ (as well as his complete humanity) against Arianism at the Council of Constantinople (381). With Basil he worked on the *Philokalia* (excerpts from Origen's work) and *Moralia* (monastic rules). He was an eloquent preacher; the *Orations* are among the most important of his writings.

St. Gregory of Nyssa (ca. 335–ca. 394)

Famous Church writer, orator, and brother of St. Basil the Great. He became bishop of Nyssa in 372, but his position was embattled by Arians. At the Council of Constantinople (381) he was a staunch defender of the Orthodox position, and greatly appreciated for his wise counsel. He wrote many theological, mystical, and monastic works; noteworthy are his *Against Eunomius* (refuting Arianism), *Catechetical Oration*, and *Life of Moses*.

Grigor'ev, S. T. (Real name, Grigor'ev-Patrashkin) (1875–1953)

Russian and Soviet writer, novelist. His works were first published in 1899; among his important works are *Aleksandr Suvorov* (1939) and *Pobeda Moria* (*Victory of the Sea*, 1945).

Heidegger, Martin (1889–1976)

German philosopher and important representative of 20th-century Existentialism. He was an original critic of technological society, alienation and inauthenticity. As a leading ontological thinker his fascination with "being" influenced many students of the time. His work showed a special interest in Pre-Socratic philosophy, Plato, Aristotle, and the Gnostics. He was also influenced by Søren Kierkegaard, Friedrich Nietzsche, Wilhelm Dilthey, and Edmund Husserl, the founder of *Phenomenology*, who especially influenced his doctoral dissertation (1914). His most important and difficult work, *Sein und Zeit* (*Being and Time*, 1927), asks the fundamental question about the meaning of "Being." It strongly influenced Jean-Paul Sartre in France and other Existentialists. Also significant is *Was ist Metaphysik?* (*What Is Metaphysics?* 1929), his inaugural lecture in Freiburg, discussing "*das Nichts*" (the nothing).

Helot

Ancient Spartan slave of state.

Hertzen (Gertsen), Aleksandr Ivanovich (1812–70)

Russian writer, thinker, and activist. In 1847 he left Russia, never to return, though he did not lose contact with activists within Russia. He edited a number of journals, like *Poliarnaia zvezda* (*The Polar Star*, 1855) and *Kolokol* (*The Bell*, 1857–67), and recognized the significance of changing public consciousness for social and political change. He appreciated Chaadaev's point about Russia's backwardness working to its advantage; under such circumstances Russia could avoid some negative aspects of European achievements.

Hesychasm

A form of asceticism which focuses on inner peace and illumination; the Greek *hesuchia* means silence, rest. Simeon the New Theologian (940–1022) encouraged a monastic discipline of prayer, using spiritual exercises with a specific posture, breathing patterns, and the Jesus prayer, to seek mystical union with God in Christ through vision of uncreated light. By the 14th century this movement came to be associated with the Mt. Athos monastic community, and was supported by Gregory Palamas (1296–1359), who argued for a distinction between God's transcendent unknowable essence and divine light as an operation of his energy. Hesychasm was revived in 19th-century Russia.

Hilarion of Kiev (mid-11th century)

Russia's first Metropolitan (*predstoiatel'*) in Kiev (1051–54), and author of *Slovo o Zakone i Blagodati* (*The Word about Law and Grace*), *Pokhvala kaganu nashemu Vladimiru* (*In Praise of Vladimir*), and *Ispovedanie very* (*The Confession of Faith*).

Historiosophy

A special term to designate the study of history from a religious perspective, taking into account the larger metaphysical context of events and the cosmos in which they occur. Historiosophy searches for supra-natural meaning and purpose in events, beyond the immediate, material and temporal context.

Homer (?8th century B.C.)

Epic poet reflecting the Mycenean period of Greece, and author of *The Iliad* and the *Odyssey*.

Huxley, Aldous Leonard (1894–1963)

English novelist and gifted critic whose work was noted for elegance, wit, and pessimistic satire. Early novels include *Crome Yellow* (1921), *Antic Hay* (1923), *Those Barren Leaves* (1925), and *Point Counter Point* (1928). His critique of 20th-century political and technological developments is most memorably expressed in *Brave New World* (1932), with its frightening projection of a psychologically conditioned society, showing the danger of utopianism for the human right to make free choices. Later works like *The Perennial Philosophy* (1946) reflect his growing interest in Hindu thought.

Ibn Fadlan (10th century)

Arabian traveler who described his journey through Bukhara and Khoresm to the Volga Bulgars.

Idealism

Philosophical tradition which emphasizes ideas, or what is ideal, and connected with mind, soul, or spirit as source and explanation of everyday reality as we experience it. It is usually traced back from the Greek philosopher, Plato, through Neoplatonism to Hegel, Kant, and their followers.

Il'ia Muromets (Il' a of Murom)

An important character in Russian epics of the 12–16th centuries, personifying the folk hero and warrior. At the age of 33 he miraculously recovered from paralysis and was sent to fight with dark evil powers.

Il'in, Ivan Aleksandrovich (1882–1954)

Russian religious philosopher making an important contribution to Russian idealism with his innovative interpretation of Hegel, *Filosofiia Gegelia kak uchenie o konkretnosti Boga i cheloveka* (*Hegels's Philosophy as a Doctrine about the Concreteness of God and Man*, 1918). Also important is his *Religioznyi smysl filosofii* (*The Religious Meaning of Philosophy*, 1925). He was greatly influenced by Husserl and associated philosophy closely with experience and religion.

Imam

Arabic term for a Moslem leader conducting services in a mosque, and also for an Islamic leader with political and spiritual authority.

Imiaslavie

Russian term for the Greek *onomatodoxy, or* "glorification of the name." It refers to a special form of worshiping the name of God which arose at the beginning of the 20th century in a variety of independent monastic communities on Mount Athos and in the Caucasus.

St. Irenaeus (ca. 130–200)

Early Greek church father, apologist. His most important work is connected with refutation of the Gnostics, *Against Heresies*.

Iurodivyi, Iurodstvo

Russian term referring respectively to the person who is crazy and the state of madness, it has been used for someone divinely inspired as "God's fool," and the fact of "behaving like God's fool," or a "fool for Christ's sake." The phenomenon was adopted from Byzantium, and became part of Russian life from the early 14th century. "God's fools" lived in towns or cities, but disregarded worldly riches, often leading a life of poverty, prayer, and fasting. While they were not really fools at all, they acted the part, and it was considered blasphemous to harm them. The phenomenon of "*iurodstvo*" was more widespread in Russia than elsewhere in Christendom.

Ivan IV Vasil'evich Groznyi (the Terrible) (1530–84)

First Russian tsar, from 1547.

Izba

Simple Russian home typically made of wood, often with decorative wooden window frames.

St. John of Damascus (673–777)

Author of dogmatic, polemical, historical, philosophical, and poetical works. His *Dialectics,* containing extracts from Aristotle and other philosophers, was translated into Slavonic as early as the 10th century.

Kalokagathia

Greek term literally meaning "beauty and goodness"; it represents an aesthetic and moral ideal of the aristocratic Greek classes, and is regarded as the equivalent of the Russian desire for harmony, coherence, all-unity.

Kant, Immanuel (1724–1804)

German philosopher, outstanding representative of the Enlightenment; his systematic work in the theory of knowledge, ethics, and aesthetics greatly influenced all subsequent philosophy.

Karma

A term of Indian philosophy referring to an action, deed, or movement. As a cosmic law, it is similar to the law of causality, of physical causation or retribution, the relation of cause and effect, also as it affects thought and the soul. It explains events in terms of what is inevitable and what is to be expiated.

Katkov, Mikhail Nikiforovoch (1818–87)

Russian publicist supporting Russian chauvinist Pan-Slavism (Slavic union) as an alternative to the revolutionary cause, with his writing in *Moskovskie novosti* (*The Moscow News*) in the 1860s.

Kehre

Literally, "turn." It was used philosophically by Heidegger to designate a turn which seems to take one backwards, but is the only way to proceed, to go forward. *Kehre* is a return which serves as a precondition of advance and reaching a new qualitative level, as on a mountain road where the hairpin bend takes one backwards, but provides the only means of approaching the pass.

Kenosis

A Greek theological term referring to the self-diminishing, or self-exhaustion, of the Divine, the humility of God before the creature, particularly in Christ's incarnation and suffering. The epitome of this attitude is expressed in Philippians 2.5–11.

Khazaria

East European state of the Khazar Turks, existing from the mid-7th to the end of the 10th century. Early in the 8th century its territory included the North Caucasus, lands near the Sea of Azov, much of the Crimea, and steppe land to the Dnepr River. It recognized Judaism, Islam, and Christianity as religions. It was destroyed by Sviatoslav Igor'evich in 964–65.

Khlebnikov, Velimir (Viktor) Vladimirovich (1885–1922)

Russian utopian poet; one of the leading activists for futurism in Russia, signing all their manifestoes. He was responsible for the Russian name for "futurism" – *budetlianstvo*. His combination of sound with semantic elements of verse influenced the poetry of Maiakovskii.

Khomiakov, Aleksei Stepanovich (1804–60)

Russian philosopher, poet, and publicist influenced by German philosophers Schelling and Hegel; he contributed greatly to Slavophilism, developing the theological and cultural basis of its positions. Khomiakov supported the abolition of serfdom in Russia and religious toleration. He in turn influenced the Russian spiritual tradition from Hertzen to Berdiaev; his ideas stimulated the creation of a distinctive Russian Orthodox theology.

Khrapovitskii, Metropolitan Antonii – see Antonii

Khrushchev, Nikita Sergeevich (1894–1971)

Soviet Premier from 1958 to 1964, remembered especially for his role in the 1962 Cuban missile crisis.

Kireevskii, Ivan Vasil'evich (1806–56)

Russian philosopher, literary critic, and publicist; together with Khomiakov responsible for founding Slavophilism. He was deeply influenced by German romanticism and also in close touch with the revival of Russian monasticism at Optina Pustyn'. His two significant essays are "On the Nature of European Culture and its Relation to the Culture of Russia" and "Concerning the Necessity and Possibility of New Beginnings for Philosophy" (1856).

Kiva, Aleksei Vasil'evich

A political scientist with a doctorate in history who has written numerous articles in recent years in *Nezavisimaia gazeta* (*The Independent Newspaper*), *Russkii zhurnal* (*The Russian Journal*), *Parlamentarnaia gazeta* (*The Parliamentary Newspaper*), *Novyi mir* (*The New World*), and *Literaturnaia gazeta* (*The Literary Newspaper*). He is a leading research fellow at the Institute of Oriental Studies of the Russian Academy of Sciences.

Kliuchevskii, Vasilii Osipovich (1841–1911)

Russian academic historian, considered the outstanding representative of Russian historiography of the late imperial period. Important works include *Kurs russkoi istorii* (*A History of Russia*, in 5 vols.; trans. 1911–31), *Petr Velikii* (*Peter the Great*, trans. 1958), and *The Rise of the Romanovs* (*Pod"em Romanovykh*, trans. 1970).

Kolkhoz

Russian abbreviation of *kollektivnoe khozhiaistvo* (collective management), the Soviet agricultural collective.

Krishna

A Hindu god, one of the incarnations of *Vishnu;* mythology presents two images of Krishna: a wise warrior king and divine shepherd.

Kulak

Russian word literally meaning "fist," but used figuratively for the rich and thrifty peasant who exploited his farm laborers. Kulaks were a major financial, social, and political factor in Russian village life before the 1917 Revolution. The early process of collectivization favored poor peasants at the expense of the kulaks; but the 1921 New Economic Policy favored their position. The 1929 drive for all peasants to join large cooperative agricultural establishments ended with "dekulakization"; as landowners, kulaks were considered capitalists and enemies of the people, with predictable results. Many were arrested, had their land confiscated, were deported or executed.

Kurbskii, Andrei Mikhailovich, Prince (1528–83)

Russian author of numerous works, including 3 epistles to Ivan IV; he is said to have originated the idea of "Holy Russia" as an extension of the imperial "Third Rome" concept.

The Lay of the Host of Igor (Slovo o Polku Igoreve)

Old Russian (12th-century) literary monument whose author is unknown. It was written after the campaign of Prince Igor' Sviatoslavovich (1185). The work calls for unity among Russian princes before the impending Mongolian invasion.

Leibnitz, Gottfried Wilhelm (1646–1716)

Germany's greatest 17th-century cosmopolitan philosopher, jurist, mathematician, diplomat, historian, and theologian. Author of the *Monadology* (1714), he developed a system of symbols for symbolic logic.

Lenin (real name Ulianov), Vladimir Il'ich (1870–1924)

Political theorist, supporter of Narodnaia volia (the People's Will), and leader of the 1917 Revolution, responsible for the ideological form of Marxism implemented in Soviet Russia.

Leont'ev, Konstantin Nikolaevich (1831–91)

Russian essayist, publicist, thinker, and literary critic. He questioned the Westernization of Russian industry, commerce, and politics (democratic egalitarian thought), supporting the Russian empire as an alternative for civilizing the East. His essays have been collected in *Vostok, Rossiia i Slavianstvo* (*The East, Russia and Slavism*, 1885–86). He also wrote novels, short stories, and his autobiography, *Moia literaturnaia sud'ba* (*My Literary Destiny*, 1875).

Logos

Greek for "word" and for "rational principle." It became a highly significant term for Christian thought because the gospel of John applies it to Christ, as the *Word* of God, while early Christian philosophers like Justin Martyr exploited philosophical overtones, using the term to assert that Christ was the foundational "word" through which creation came to be.

Losev, Aleksei Fedorovich (1893–1988)

Russian philosophical and religious thinker, with broad scholarly interests in the history of philosophy, typology of culture, philosophy, aesthetics, mathematics and philosophy of music. He did not leave Russia, but published the so-called Losev cycle of 8 books in the 1920s, of which the most famous are: *Antichnyi kosmos i sovremennaia nauka* (*The Ancient Cosmos and Modern Science*), *Filosofiia imeni* (*Philosophy of the Name*), *Dialektika khudozhestvennoi formy* (*Dialectics of Artistic Form*), *Dialektika mifa* (*Dialectics of Myth*), and *Muzyka kak predmet logiki* (*Music as the Subject of Logic*). In 1930 Losev was arrested, and the arrest of his wife followed soon after; in 1933 both were released. His work followed in the footsteps of Solov'ev, but he was conversant with contemporary German philosophical developments and supported *imiaslavie*. In 1953 he was allowed to resume publication, and the more important later works are: *Antichnaia mifologiia v ego istoricheskom razvitii* (*Ancient Mythology in Its Historical Development*, 1957), *Antichnaia muzykal'naia estetika* (*Ancient Musical Aesthetics*, 1961), *Problema simvola i realisticheskoe iskusstvo* (*Problem of Symbol and Modern Art*, 1976), *Antichnaia filosofiia istorii* (*Ancient Philosophy of History*, 1977), *Estetika Vozrozhdeniia* (*Aesthetics of the Renaissance*, 1978), and *Znak. Simvol. Mif* (*Sign. Symbol. Myth*, 1982).

Losskii, Nikolai Onufrievich (1870–1965)

Russian philosopher and representative of personalism and intuitivism, exiled in 1922. Important publications include: *Obosnovanie intuitivizma* (*Intuitive Basis of Knowledge*, 1919), *Osnovnye voprosy gnoseologii* (*Fundamental Problems of Epistemology*, 1919), *Svoboda voli* (*Freedom of Will*, 1927; trans. 1932), *Chuvstvennaia, intellektual'naia i misticheskaia intuitsiia* (*Sensory, Intellectual and Mystical Intuition*, 1930), *Usloviia absoliutnogo dobra (osnovy etiki)* (*The Conditions of Absolute Good: Foundations of Ethics*, 1931; trans. 1948), and *Personalistischer Idealismus* (*Personalistic Idealism*, vol. 5.4 of "Kant-Studien," 1959–60).

Losskii, Vladimir Nikolaevich (1903–58)

Theologian and son of Nikolai Onufrievich Losskii (1870–1965). Born in Russia, he emigrated in 1922 and lived first in Prague, later in Paris. During the German invasion he was active in the Resistance Movement. In his *Spor o Sofii* (*Dispute about Sophia*) he differed sharply with Sergei Bulgakov on sophiology. Important works are: *Misticheskoe bogoslovie Vostochnoi Tserkvi* (The Mystical Theology of the Eastern Church, 1944), *Smysl ikon* (*The Meaning of Icons*, 1952), and *Po obrazu i podobiiu Boga* (*In the Image and Likeness of God*, 1967).

Lumpen

Term applied to disenfranchised, uprooted individuals or groups, especially those who have lost status. Contemporary use is based on Marxist theory, which applied it to the lowest level of the proletariat, unskilled workers, vagrants, or criminals lacking distinct class identification and solidarity.

Macarius the Egyptian (300–90)

One of the Desert Fathers, also called Macarius the Great. He promoted the ideal of monasticism in Egypt and influenced its development throughout Christendom. A work of mystical theology attributed to him is considered a classic of its kind.

Mahatma

Indian term of respect, literally for a "great soul," and in philosophy applied to the super-individual, transcendental self, or Absolute.

Maistre, Jean-Marie (Joseph), Comte de (1753–1821)

French count, publicist, political activist, and Catholic philosopher. From 1802–17 he served on a ministry in Russia, where he wrote significant works like his "Essai sur le principe generateur des constitutions politiques ("General principles of human institutions," 1810), and "Du pape" ("On the Pope," 1819). Of interest also is his "Les soirées de St. Petersbourg" ("Nights in St. Petersburg," 1821).

Makarii (Macarius), Metropolitan (1482–1563)

Church writer and Russian metropolitan from 1542, who presided at the councils of 1547 and 1549, representing the views of Iosif Volotskii. On 16 January 1547 he crowned Ivan IV (the Terrible) using Byzantine ceremonies, and in 1551 presided over the council of Russian bishops, the *Stoglav* (Council of 100 Chapters); he is quoted as saying of Tsar Ivan, "God has chosen you, o Sovereign, to rule this land in His place." Makarii considered tsarist autocracy indispensable for Orthodoxy.

Maximus the Greek (Mikhail Trivolis) (1475–1556)

Greek Orthodox monk, humanist scholar, and linguist, who received an outstanding education in Europe. He came to Russia in 1518, chosen by the patriarchate of Constantinople to correct church texts used in Russia. He translated many original Greek canonical, liturgical, and theological texts into Russian, which involved him in the dispute between Possessors (who were led by Iosif of Volokolamsk [Volotskii] and favored autocratic monarchy) and Nonpossessors (led by Nil Sorskii, 1433–1508); he supported the latter group, which lost. Condemned by the Church councils of 1525, he was arrested and spent 20 years imprisoned in the monastery of Volokolamsk, near Moscow, where Iosif was abbot, from 1531 until his release in 1551.

Maximus the Confessor (580–662)

Outstanding Byzantine theologian of the 7th century. His commentaries on the Christian Neoplatonist Pseudo-Dionysius the Areopagite and other Greek Church Fathers influenced medieval Christian mystical theology deeply. He is remembered for his opposition to the Monothelites, who affirmed that Christ had two distinct natures, divine and human, in one Person, but with only one will. After involvement in a regional church council under Pope Martin I (649), he was arrested by the emperor Constans II, imprisoned two years (653–55), exiled, and died near the Black Sea. His major works developed a

Christocentric theology; important are his *Opuscula theologica et polemica* (*Short Theological and Polemical Treatises*), *Ambigua* (*Ambiguities* [in the works of Gregory of Nazianzus]), *Scholia* (on Pseudo-Dionysius the Areopagite), and 400 *Capita de caritate* (*Four Hundred Chapters on Charity*). In the latter he advised a humane asceticism integrated with ordinary life and active charity.

Maiakovskii, Vladimir Vladimirovich (1893–1930)

Russian and Soviet poet; spokesman for the Russian Futurist group (1912) and leading poet of the 1917 Revolution, producing utilitarian, topical poetry. Of interest are popular poems like *Oda revolutsi* (*Ode to the Revolution*, 1918), the 3,000-line elegy on the death of Vladimir Il'ich Lenin (1924), and satirical sketches, *Moe otkrytie Ameriki* (*My Discovery of America*, 1926). His reforms of poetic language, using street language and daring technical innovations, made a deep impact on subsequent 20th-century Soviet poetry.

Mekhmet II the Conqueror (1432–81)

Turkish sultan of 1444 and 1451–81, who pursued an aggressive policy in the Balkans and Asia. In 1453 he conquered Constantinople and turned it into the capital of Ottoman Empire.

Merezhkovskii, Dmitrii Sergeevich (1866–1941)

Russian writer and religious philosopher who emigrated in 1920. Noteworthy publications include *Khristos i Antikhrist* (*Christ and Antichrist*, 1895–1905), *Aleksandr I* (1911–12), and *L. Tolstoi i Dostoevskii* (L. Tolstoi and Dostoevskii, 1901–02).

Meyendorff, John (1926–92)

Theologian, prolific writer, dean of St. Vladimir's Seminary (1984–92), and professor of Church History and Patristics (1959–92). His work follows up on that of Georges Florovsky. Among his important works are: *Christian Spirituality: Origins to the Twelfth Century*, ed. with B. McGinn (1985); *Christian Spirituality: High Middle Ages and Reformation*, ed. with J. Raitt and B. McGinn (1987); *Vision of Unity* (1987); *Imperial Unity and Christian Divisions. The Church 450–680 AD* (1989); *Christian Spirituality: Post-Reformation and Modern*, ed. with L. Dupe and D. E. Saliers (1989); *Imperial Unity and Christian Divisions: The Church 450–680 AD* (1989); *The Legacy of St Vladimir*, ed. with Fr. J. Breck and E. Silk, (1990); *Vizantiia i Moskovskaia Rus': Ocherk po istorii tserkovnykh i kul'turnykh sviazei v XIV veke* (translation of *Byzantium and the Rise of Russia: A Study of Byzantine-Russian Relations in the Fourteenth Century*, 1990); *The Primacy of Peter: Essays in Ecclesiology and the Early Church* (rev. ed., 1992).

Mongolian-Tatar Yoke (1243–1480)

Traditional name for the system by which Russia was exploited under the Mongolian Tatars. This "Yoke" existed nominally after the battle of Kulikovo (1380), and was altogether overthrown in 1480, during the reign of Ivan III. Although the occupation halted Russia's development, it also fostered centralization of political power in Moscow.

Monomakh, Vladimir Vsevolodovich (1053–1125)

Grand prince of Kiev from 1113 to 1125, son of Grand Prince Vsevolod I Iaroslavich (ruling 1078–93) and Irina, daughter of Byzantine emperor Constantine IX Monomachus. With his father he defeated cousins Oleg Sviatoslavich and Boris Viacheslavich at Chernigov (1078) and opposed endless internal warfare among princes of Rus. As grand prince of Kiev he fought the Polovtsy, who had been raiding from the southeast steppe region since 1061. The *Testament*, or *Precept*, written for his sons, constitutes the earliest known example of Old Russian literature written by a layman, and recounts participation in 83 military campaigns. An excellent administrator and builder, he also founded the city of Vladimir on the Kliazma River (northeastern Russia), to replace Kiev as seat of the grand prince (end of the 12th century).

Monophysite

Term for an early Christian controversy of the 5th century. Monophysites argued for Christ having a single nature (*monos, physis*) in which the human and divine would be fused, or the divine nature appear in human flesh. The council of Chalcedon (451) declared this position heretical, defending Christ's double nature, both human and divine, in one person.

Muromets (see **Il'i a**)

Muscovia

A name for Russia in foreign literary and historical sources of the 16th and 17th centuries. This was the period in which Moscow took a leading role in Russian affairs, replacing former centers like Kiev and Vladimir.

Narodnichestvo

Russian term for a political movement focused on the peasants, or the Russian people (*narod*). As an ideological movement of Russian *raznochintsi*, projecting a type of socialistic utopia, it characterized the period 1861–95. Founders of *narodnichestvo* were A. I. Hertzen and N. G. Chernyshevskii. The movement opposed both serfdom and capitalism in Russia.

"Neo-Patristic Synthesis"

Term used by Georges Florovsky to encourage renewed study of early Eastern church fathers, as part of a revival of contemporary religious philosophy.

Neoplatonism

A 3rd-century A.D. reformulation of Platonism and synthesis of Aristotelian and Stoic positions, attributed to Plotinus (205–70). He accented the transcendence of the divine One; it can only be described by negatives, apophatically. The Nous, or intellectual principle, proceeds from the One, by emanation. The world as we know it also emanates from the One via intermediaries, the Ideas or Forms of Nous, which are introduced in the world through the World Soul animating it. Neoplatonism is mystical, and regards contemplation as the highest state; union is experienced as a result of ascetic effort of will and understanding.

Nesmelov, Viktor Ivanovich (1863–1920)

Russian writer, professor of logic and philosophy at the Academy in Kazan. Nesmelov is remembered for his development of an Orthodox Christian anthropology.

Nestor (late 11th and early 12th century)

Early Russian writer and monk of the Kievan-Pechersk monastery; he is considered one of the greatest historians of the Middle Ages and author of the earliest version of *Povest' o Vremennykh Let* (*The Tale of Bygone Years*). Nestor is also regarded as the author of *Skazanie o Borise i Glebe* (*The Tale of Boris and Gleb*).

Nicholas I (Nikolai Pavlovich) (1796–1855)

Russian emperor (1825–55), the personification of classic autocracy, known for his reactionary policies. The ideological expression of his approach was given by the minister of education, Count Sergei Uvarov in his doctrine of "Official Nationality" (1833): Orthodoxy, Autocracy, and Nationality.

Nicholas of Cusa (Nikolaus Cusanus) (1401–64)

German model Renaissance scholar, mathematician, experimental scientist, Catholic cardinal, and influential philosopher who stressed the incompleteness of human knowledge of God and the universe. He supported the supremacy of general councils over the papacy in 1433, with his *De concordantia catholica* (*On Catholic Concordance*), but by 1437 changed his view in support of Pope Eugenius IV. His scientific work anticipated that of Copernicus by discerning a movement in the universe not centered in the earth. As philosopher he preferred Neoplatonists to Aristotelians who deny the compatibility of contradictories. Nicholas described God as the "coincidence of opposites" who in his infinity embraces all things in perfect unity. Since absolute truth escapes man, the proper attitude is "learned ignorance."

Nietzsche, Friedrich (1844–1900)

German classical scholar, philosopher, and critic of culture. He attempted to overturn the scholarly results of the Enlightenment. Well known are his statement "God is dead" and his works *Die Geburt der Tragödie* (*The Birth of Tragedy*, 1872), *Also sprach Zarathustra* (*Thus Spoke Zarathustra*, 1883–85) and *Jenseits von Gut und Böse* (*Beyond Good and Evil*, 1886).

Nihilism

In Russia in the 1860s the term was symbolized by the hero of I. S. Turgenev's *Fathers and Sons*, with his slogan: "First, it is necessary to break everything down." All revolutionaries of the 1870s and 1880s are regarded as nihilists. S. L. Frank, affirming that the "intelligentsia does not acknowledge absolute values," regarded nihilistic morals as the basic characteristic of the Russian intelligentsia.

Nikon the Great (d. 1088)

Early Russian writer, and father superior of the Kievan-Pechersk monastery from 1074. According to some Russian historians, Nikon authored one of the sources for *Povest' o vremennykh let* (*The Tale of Bygone Years*).

Nirvana

An Indian and Buddhist term referring to complete extinction of individuality, without losing consciousness, in beatific union with the metaphysical world-ground or highest reality, which completely lacks the multiplicity and manifold character of phenomena.

Nonviolence/Active Nonviolence

A political philosophical term introduced in the 20th century by Mahatma Gandhi of India. The Hindi equivalent *satiagraha* means "truth force" or "devotion to truth." Introduced by Gandhi first in 1906 in response to a South African law discriminating against Asians, it became the leading principle for Indian resistance to British imperialism and has been adopted by many protest groups. Active nonviolence seeks the truth in a spirit of peace and love, confronting evil with a determined but nonviolent response (using fasting or economic boycott) in a search not for victory but renewed harmony. Gandhi was influenced by Lev Tolstoi, Henry David Thoreau, the Christian Bible, the Bhagavadgita, and other Hindu writings.

Noösphere

Biological term connected with evolutionary theories, based on the Greek *nous*, mind; also given as "anthroposphere." It was introduced by the Russian scientist Vladimir Ivanovich Vernadskii (1863–1945), the founder of biogeochemistry, who developed theories about the Earth's envelope changing from being determined by biological processes to determination by conscious human intellectual effort. He referred to the layer of consciousness as the noösphere, as such opposed to the geosphere (nonliving world) and biosphere (living world). The French paleontologist and theologian Pierre Teilhard de Chardin developed this idea as a bridge between biology and religion.

Novalis (Friedrich von Hardenberg) (1772–1801)

German poet and philosopher, early representative of Romanticism in Germany.

October Revolution – see "Great October"

Obkom

Shortened expression for *oblastnoi komitet* (regional committee).

Oblomov

Main character in Goncharov's novel of that title, and personification of idleness and weakness of will.

Old Believers – see Schism

Origen (184–254)

The most important theologian and biblical scholar of the early Greek church. His great work the *Hexapla* gives a synopsis of six versions of the Old Testament.

St. Paissii (Velichkovskii) (1722–94)

Monastic spiritual leader or *starets* (elder) and abbot of the monastery of Neamts in Romania, responsible for the Slavonic edition of the *Philokalia*. This publication stimulated a revival of Hesychast traditions in the monasteries, with Optina Pustyn' as the outstanding example.

Palamas, Gregory (1296–1359)

Orthodox monk at Mount Athos from 1316, and theologian, well acquainted with ancient philosophy and the Church fathers. Palamas is noted for defence of Hesychast (from Greek *hesychia*, quiet) ascetic mystical prayer using formulas, a designated posture, and controlled breathing; it was attacked by Western scholastic theologians and rationalistic humanists, including Barlaam. Important in this battle is his *Triad* or *Apology for the Holy Hesychasts* (1338), arguing that the mystical experience involves the entire human person, body and soul, in a process of *theosis* or deification through an inner union of man with God in the depths of his spirit. Such prayer communion with God through vision of "divine light" or "uncreated energy" is explained on the example of Christ's transfiguration on Mount Tabor (Matt. 16.17; Mark 8.9). Palamas was appointed bishop of Thessalonica in 1347 and became the acknowledged leader for the monastic mystical school known as Hesychasm. Through the intervention of Philotheus, Patriarch of Constantinople, who supported Hesychasm, Gregory Palamas was acclaimed doctor of the Greek Orthodox Church at the synod of 1368.

Panentheism

Religious philosophical position which is distinguished from theism and pantheism in that it regards the divine as both beyond and within our world. This position, associated with the 20th-century American Charles Hartshorne, is based on the principle that the perfect knower includes within himself that which he knows; it also implies that God is moved and changed by that knowledge, while retaining his integrity.

Pantheism

Religious philosophical position which identifies God with the world: "God is everything, and everything is God." The term is based on the Greek *pan* (everything) and *theos* (god). Thus it denies the biblical transcendence of God over his creation. It is usually connected with a monistic ontology and fatalism regarding the human role in the world, without true freedom.

Peter I (the Great) (1672–1725)

Russian emperor from 1694, son of Tsar Alexis, reigning from 1682–1725; Peter's social, technological, military, and academic reforms remained important for the next two centuries of Russian history. Peter built a navy and in 1703 laid the foundations of his new capital, St. Petersburg, at the mouth of the Neva River, to secure direct sea access to Western Europe. His triumph over Sweden (1711) secured diplomatic concessions for Russia, and the élites of conquered European territories helped introduce German education, science, and culture. Peter's "Spiritual Regulation" (*Dukhovnyi Reglament*) reformed the Orthodox church on the German model, abolishing the patriarchate and introducing a "Holy Governing Synod" under a high commissioner, or *Oberprokuror*, who had cabinet rank and was responsible for Church administration. No patriarch was elected from the death of Patriarch Adrian in 1700 until 1917.

Philokalia

Based on the Greek, meaning literally "Love of the Good, the Beautiful," it is the title of a prose anthology of Greek Christian monastic texts going back to Origen. In modern times writings of major Hesychasts (or hermits) of the Christian East, from Evagrius Ponticus to Gregory Palamas, were gathered and published by the Greek monk Nikodimos and Makarios (bishop of Corinth), in 1782. These texts promote "inner asceticism," daily recollection of death and judgment, remembrance of God as omnipresent, and ceaseless prayer. It was translated into Church Slavonic by Paissii Velichkovskii in 1793 as *Dobrotoliubie*, and was instrumental in the spiritual renewal of 19th-century monasticism as well as Orthodox laity led by monastic spiritual leaders (*startsy*).

Philotheus – see **Filofei**

Pisareva, Elena Fedorovna (d. 1940s)

Founding member of the Russian Theosophical Association (1908), and first major supporter of Rudolf Steiner in Russia. She established a theosophical center on the family estate outside Kaluga, close to the Optina Pustyn' monastery. She lectured widely, translated and published numerous popular works, including *O skrytom smysle zhizni* (*On the Hidden Meaning of Life*) and *Elena Petrovna Blavatskaia, A Biographical Sketch* (pub. 1966); in 1922 she emigrated to Italy.

Platonov, Sergei Fedorovich (1860–1933)

Outstanding Russian historian, member of the Russian Academy of Science from 1920. His special interest was the "Time of Troubles" (1598–1613), the chaotic period between the end of the Riurik dynasty and the first Romanov tsar, to which he devoted the *Ocherki po istorii smuty v Moscovscom gosudarstve XVI-XVII vv.* (*Studies in the History of the Time of Troubles in the Muscovite State During the 16th and 17th Centuries*, 1899). Also important are his *Istoriia Rossii* (*History of Russia*, 1909) and *Lektsii po russkoi istorii* (*Lectures on Russian History*, 1899). In the late 1920s he was attacked by Marxist critics, was arrested (1930), and exiled to Samara where he died.

Pomerants, Grigorii Solomonovich (b. 1918)

Religious writer and pantheist reductionist. Important among his numerous books published are: *Krishnamurti i problema religioznogo nigilizma* (*Krishnamurti and the Problem of Religious Nihilism*) and *Dzen i ego nasledie* (*Zen and its Heritage*).

Pomor'e

Russian term for a coastal area, and historical name for the White Sea coast in the 15–17th centuries.

Pseudo-Dionysius – see Dionysius the Areopagite

Purana

Old Indian Buddhist treatises, of cosmological, mythological and legendary character, including ethical, philosophical, and scientific observations.

Pushkin, Alexandr Sergeevich (1799–1837)

The most famous Russian poet, writer, playwright, and founder of the modern Russian language; his poetry exemplifies harmonious art in Russian literature. He was the first to accent problems of society in Russian literature. Important works are *Boris Godunov* (1825), *Evgenii Onegin* (1823–31), *Povesti Belkina* (*Belkin's Stories*, 1830), and *Pikovaia dama* (*The Queen of Spades*, 1833).

Radishchev, Aleksandr Nikolaevich (1749–1802)

Russian philosopher and publicist, well-known for his treatise *Puteshestvie iz Peterburga v Moskvu* (*Travels from Petersburg to Moscow*). Realistic social details in this work led to his exile to Siberia under Catherine the Great (1729–1796). Amnestied in 1796, he participated actively with the Imperial Committee on the new civil code.

Rahner, Karl (1904–84)

Jesuit priest and outstanding Roman Catholic theologian of the 20th century, known for his Christology and integration of a personalist existential philosophy with Thomistic realism. He studied with Martin Heidegger, taught at various universities, and served as editor of the *Lexikon für Theologie und Kirche* (*Lexicon for Theology and the Church*, 10 vols., 1957–68). Important works include *Geist in Welt* (*The Spirit in the World*, 1939), *Hörer des Wortes* (*Hearers of the Word*, 1941), *Sendung und Gnade* (*Mission and Grace*, 1966), and *Grundkurs des Glaubens* (*Foundations of Christian Faith*, 1976).

Raskol'niki – see Schism

Raznochintsy

Term used for a social grouping of Russian society of the late 18th and 19th century. *Raznochintsy* represented the nobility, gentry, clergy, merchants, or peasantry; they were well educated, but estranged from their social background, considering themselves "superfluous people." They greatly influenced Russian cultural, educational, and social developments; the term took on political meaning by the 1860s, becoming synonymous with "democrats."

Renan, (Joseph-)Ernest (1823–92)

French philosopher, historian, scholar of religion, and leader of the French school of critical philosophy. While preparing for the priesthood he experienced a crisis of faith which led him to leave the Roman Catholic church (1845). His outstanding work, the *Vie de Jésus* (*Life of Jesus*) appeared in 1863, and was immediately denounced by the church for its "mythical" account of the source of Christianity. He followed this with *Les Apôtres* (*The Apostles*, 1866) and *Saint Paul* (1869), as parts of a series, *Histoire des origines du christianisme* (*The History of the Origins of Christianity*).

Roerich, (Rerikh, Roerikh), Elena (1879–1955)

Religious philosopher, wife of N. K. Roerich, who took part in both his expeditions and worked in India from 1924. She developed *agni-yoga*, the teaching of "living ethics," on the foundation of Indian spiritual tradition.

Roerich, (Rerikh, Roerikh), Nikolai Konstantinovich (1874–1947)

Russian designer of scenes for Sergei Pavlovich Diaghilev's "Ballets Russes," archaeologist, landscape painter and popular mystic. His outstanding work was done for the Polovtsian Dances (1909) from Aleksandr Borodin's *Prince Igor'*, depicting 12th-century Russia. He emigrated to the United States in 1920, where he soon gained a reputation as a painter and seer.

Riurik (ca. 862)

Founder of the dynasty of *Riurikovichi* whose rule of Kievan Rus ended with Fedor Ioannovich (1557–98). According to legend Riurik commanded the Varangian detachment and was invited by Slavs to rule in Novgorod. His successor Oleg (d. 912) conquered Kiev and established his control over trade along the Dnepr from Novgorod to the Black Sea. Among his descendants Vladimir (ruling ca. 980–1015) organized his subject territory into a confederation, introduced Christianity, and provided the first law code.

Rublev, Andrei (ca. 1360–1439)

Famous medieval icon painter, whose masterpiece, the icon of "The Trinity" is now kept in the Tretiakov Gallery in Moscow. He worked as assistant of Theophanes the Greek, and late in life became a monk at the Trinity-St. Sergius monastery (Sergiev Posad) and Andronikov monastery of Moscow. Other icons attributed to him include panels of St. John the Baptist, St. Paul, St. Peter, and the Ascension for the Cathedral of the Dormition of the Virgin (Vladimir, 1408), as well as the Archangel Michael and the Savior from Zvenigorod. No later Russian painter equaled Rublev in handling or interpretation of the subject.

Russian idea

This term appeared in the 19th century with Slavophiles, especially Dostoevskii, and has at least three meanings: 1) the whole complex of specific features, typical of Russian culture and mentality in historical perspective; 2) the level of the national self-consciousness at any given period of Russia's history; and 3) the co-existence (or clash) of older and new (East and Western) elements in the social, cultural and political development of Russia.

Sakharov, Andrei Dmitrievich (1921–89)

Physicist, theoretician, and public figure; he was one of the Soviet creators of the H-bomb (1953). From the late 1950s he spoke out against the testing of nuclear weapons, for which he received the Nobel Peace prize in 1975, but suffered political repression at home. Sakharov left his *Vospominaniia* (*Memoirs*, pub. 1990) and other works.

Saltykov-Shchedrin, Mikhail Evgrafovich (1826–89)

Russian writer, author of satyrical works, and publicist.

Samarin, Iurii Fedorovich (1819–76)

Russian philosopher, historian, and publicist; one of the early ideologists of Slavophilism.

Samizdat

Russian abbreviation for *samostoiatel'noe izdatel'stvo* (independent publication). This term was used during the Soviet period for writings either published secretly in the USSR (*samizdat*) or abroad (*tamizdat*) to get around ideological censorship.

Samsara

Indian Buddhist term for transmigration of the soul in a cycle or "wheel" of incarnations, through birth and death, justified through karma.

Schlegel, Friedrich (1772–1829)

German critic, philosopher, philologist, writer, and theorist of romanticism.

Schelling, Friedrich Wilhelm Joseph (1775–1854)

German philosopher, representative of German classical idealism.

Schism (*Raskol*)

In Russia the Orthodox Church experienced a serious schism in the 17th century; this happened as a result of Patriarch Nikon's correction of ecclesiastical books, and strict application of what he believed to be more authentic forms of worship based on old Greek liturgical texts. Maximus the Greek had done a preliminary correction, but inadequate knowledge of Slavonic led to inaccuracies; he was exiled to a distant monastery. Corrections stimulated by the church council of 1550 and several visits of foreign patriarchs did not erase problems with the Greek text, and from 1653 Nikon undertook the necessary reforms. Many Russians, under the leadership of Avakkum, considered the subsequent innovations in Orthodox liturgical rites a betrayal of their faith and the Orthodoxy of the Russian church, and refused to accept them; they interpreted contemporary events apocalyptically, as a sign of the reign of the Antichrist. The council of 1666–67 forced a separation of "Old Believers" (*staroobriadtsi*, i.e., those holding to old rites), who rejected the Church Reform of 1653–56; until 1906 they were persecuted, and the church was greatly weakened.

Scholasticism

The term used primarily for a medieval Christian system of education, based on the Greek *scholadzein* (to have leisure, or devote oneself to a master, as a student) and Latin *doctores scholastici*. By the 9th century it was used for instruction in the seven liberal arts and philosophy, as well as theology, regarding revelation as an aid to human reason, and subordinating philosophy to theology. The method was characterized by disputation (defense of a position against adversaries), logic, and syllogistic argument. The golden period of scholasticism is marked by the 12th-century translations of Aristotle and Aquinas's integration of Aristotelianism in Christian theology.

St. Sergii of Radonezh (ca. 1321–91)

Founder and father superior of Holy Trinity Monastery, now the Troitse-Sergiev Monastery in Sergiev Posad, ca. 100 km. from Moscow.

Sermon on the Mount – see Beatitudes

Shakhmatov, Mstislav Viacheslavovich (1888–1943)

A historian who identified with Eurasian positions. He was a member of the Russian Historical Society in Prague in the 1920s and wrote numerous articles about constitutional government, many of which have been published in journals and collections by Eurasianists, like the *Evraziiskii vremennik (The Eurasian Contemporary)*.

Shatov

Character in Dostoevskii's *The Devils*, usually regarded as the person expressing Dostoevskii's own ideas about the "godbearing" nature of the Russian people.

Shelom'an

This older Russian term represents a watershed ridge and is used figuratively to indicate the breaking up of Rus' as a single "island" into a multiplicity of regions.

Sil'vestr (16th century)

Early Russian Orthodox writer and thinker, known for codification of rules for practical life in the *Domostroi*, the daily wisdom through which the pious Christian could "save his soul" and "serve his lord, and please God."

St. Simeon the New Theologian (ca. 949–1032)

Byzantine monk, mystic, poet, and abbot of St. Mamas monastery near Constantinople from 980–1009. His mystical theology and spiritual experience prepared the way for Hesychastic mysticism.

Skoptsi (Eunuchs)

Those who practiced voluntary emasculation among Christians in order to avoid sexual temptation; the tradition goes back to the Christian theologian Origen (184–254). It is based on the text of Matthew 19.12 and Matthew 5.28–30.

Slavophilism/*Slavianofilstvo*

A Russian movement beginning in the 19th century, emphasizing independent development of Russia with respect to Europe. Slavophiles from Khomiakov to Katkov affirmed the uniqueness of Russia, with special reference to its own historical, religious, and cultural traditions: the Slavic world should stimulate renewal and enlightenment in Europe, rather than be subjected to European ways. *Slavianofilstvo* was deeply religious; it regarded the church and its faith as the foundations of history and society. Its philosophical position can be summarized as follows: 1) emphasis on spiritual integrity, affirming the accessibility of true knowledge for the people in its entirety (*sobornost'*); 2) the priority of inner freedom as opposed to outward necessity; 3) faith as the determining factor in history, culture, ethics and thought in general.

Smutnoe vremia/Smuta (Time of Troubles)

A Russian term for the chaotic social and political conditions of the late 16th and early 17th century, before the Romanovs came to power.

Sobornost'

Special term of Russian religious philosophy, variously translated as "conciliar," "communal," "catholic/universal," or "collective"; given by Khomiakov, it is etymologically associated with "*sobor*" (cathedral, and council), and came to represent the central idea of *Slavianofilstvo*. *Sobor* has two important meanings: 1) a meeting of authorities to solve problems or answer questions; and 2) the actual church building being used by the clergy (of several parishes) to conduct the liturgy. For Khomiakov, *sobor* expresses the idea of "unity in multiplicity"; for him the Russian Orthodox Church combines principles of freedom with unity, unlike the Catholic Church, whose unity is without freedom, and the Protestant Church, which has freedom without unity. The principle of *sobornost'* indicates the divine foundation of church life, and can only exist in the Orthodox Church. For Khomiakov and the Slavophiles a communal (*sobornyi*) sense characterizes Russian consciousness, and guarantees the spiritual unity of the Russians as a people. They traced such a mystical "collectivity" to early Muscovite history. Marxists politicized the Slavophile idea of *sobornost'* as a socio-collectivistic principle and used state means to enforce its conception of collectivism.

Snorri Sturluson (1178–1241)

Icelandic epic poet. His saga *Heimskringla* describes the history of Norway to 1177.

Solonevich, Ivan Luk'ianovich (1891–1953)

Political thinker. During the Civil War he took part in the White Movement; he lived in Soviet Russia in the 1920s, but was imprisoned in a concentration camp by 1930. He managed to flee, and published Russian newspapers in Sophia, Berlin, and Argentina. His main work, *Narodnaia monarkhiia* (*Popular Monarchy*), prescribes a combination of autocracy and self-government for Russia.

Solov'ev, Sergei Mikhailovich (1820–79)

Famous Russian historian and professor of Russian history at Moscow University from 1850, well known for studies of Peter the Great and Alexander I. His most important work is the *Istoriia Rossii s drevneishikh vremen* (*History of Russia From Ancient Times*, 29 vols., 1851–79); here Solov'ev gives a masterful survey of Russia's political development as an organic process toward a centralized, autocratic state.

Solov'ev, Vladimir Sergeevich (1853–1900)

Russian religious philosopher, poet, publicist, and critic; son of the well-known historian. Reacting to rational Enlightenment philosophy, Solov'ev provided a synthesis of religious philosophy, science, and ethics. Already noted for his dissertation *Krizis zapadnoi filosofii (protiv pozitivistov)* (*The Crisis of Western Philosophy: Against the Positivists*, 1874), he also attracted considerable attention with the St. Petersburg *Chteniia o Bogochelovechestve* (*Lectures on Godmanhood*, 1880). His proposal for the union of Eastern Orthodoxy with the Roman Catholic church was less favorably received. Influenced by Spinoza and Hegel, Solov'ev emphasized an evolutionary dialectical process of the contradictory multiplicity of cosmic elements finally becoming reintegrated with its original single source, Absolute Being. Among important later publications are *Istoriia budushchei teokratii* (*The History and Future of Theocracy*, 1887), *Smysl liubvi* (*The Meaning of Love*, 1894), *Zhiznennaia drama Platona* (*Plato's Life Drama*, 1898), and *Tri besedy* (*Three Conversations*, 1900). He greatly influenced a succeeding generation of religious philosophers in what is called Russia's Silver Age, including N. A. Berdiaev, S. N. Bulgakov, P. A. Florenskii, and S. L. Frank.

Solzhenitsyn, Aleksandr Isaevich (b. 1918)

Russian novelist and historian, of Cossack descent, awarded the Nobel Prize for Literature for 1970. First arrested in 1945 for criticizing Stalin, he spent many years in prison, camps, and exile. Rehabilitated in 1956, his short novel *Odin den' Ivana Denisovicha* (*One Day in the Life of Ivan Denisovich*, 1962) gave him immediate popularity. After the fall of Khrushchev (1964) he was increasingly harassed over attempts at publication; he turned to *samizdat* (self-published) literature, circulated secretly, and often published abroad, as was his *V kruge pervom* (*The First Circle*, 1968), *Rakovy korpus* (*Cancer Ward*, 1968), *Avgust 1914* (*August 1914*, 1971), and *Arkhipelag Gulag* (*The Gulag Archipelago*, 1973), the latter followed by arrest and forced exile. He settled in the USA; his works circulated more freely in the Soviet Union with the *"glasnost'"* of the 1980s. His citizenship was restored in 1990 and he returned in 1994. Solzhenitsyn rejects Western democracy and individual freedom, favoring a benevolent authoritarian regime that relies on Russia's traditional Christian values.

Sophiology (*sofiologiia*)

A position of Russian religious philosophy on Sophia, as God's Wisdom, particularly associated with Vladimir Solov'ev and his followers in the early 20th century, especially Sergei Bulgakov. Sophiology is based on passages from Proverbs 8.1–36 and 9.1–12: "The Lord brought me forth as the first of his works, before his deeds of old; I was appointed from eternity, from the beginning, before the world began." As an ontological, philosophical, and theological teaching, sophiology is focused on issues of the relationship of God and the world, and the origin of evil. Of special interest for sophiology is the role of Mary as "mother of God" and the many churches which have been dedicated to Sophia in Kiev, Novgorod, and Arkhangelsk.

Sorokin, Pitirim Aleksandrovich (1889–1968)

Russian and American sociologist, known for his research on social and cultural mobility. He was exiled from Russia in 1922; in the USA he became president of the American Sociological Association in 1964.

Stankevich, Sergei Borisovich

Russian political figure prominent during the *perestroika* years. A graduate of Moscow State University in history, he worked with the mayor of Moscow, G. Popov, and the city government, and later also with the federal government. After accusations of corruption he moved to Poland, where he continues to live; requests for deportation back to Russia have not been successful.

Stoglav (100 Chapters)

A church deliberative body so called because the resolutions from its meeting consisted of 100 chapters. Tsar Ivan IV presented the council of 1551 with urgent questions regarding church liturgy and rites, judicial power over clergy, and improvement of public morals; the answers of the clergy were compiled as the *Stoglav* (*100 Chapters*), a collection of laws and rules.

Stolpniki (Stylites)

Christian ascetics who lived on top of a column or pillar (Greek: *stylos*). The first was St. Simeon Stylites (the Elder) who took up residence atop a column in Syria in A.D. 423. The practice never spread in the West, but in the East such ascetics became famous holy men and attracted crowds who asked them for advice on matters of Christian life and thought.

Struve, Petr Berngardovich (1870–1944)

Russian economist and political scientist, historian, publicist. He was known for an early work, a Marxist analysis of Russian capitalism, *Kriticheskie zametki k voprosu ob ekonomicheskom razvitii Rossii* (*Critical Remarks on Russia's Economic Development*, 1894), and composed the Russian Social Democratic Workers' Party manifesto (1898). In exile he turned to constitutional liberalism, critical of tsarist autocracy. Back in Russia after the Revolution of 1905, he joined the Constitutional Democratic Party (*Kadets*) and was elected to the second Duma (1907). Opposing the 1917 Revolution, he participated in White Guard resistance before settling in Paris, and, after 1928, in Belgrade.

Sviatoslav (reigning 945–72)

Early prince of Kievan Rus', descendant of the Varangian Riurik, son of Igor' (ruling 912–45) and Ol'ga, and responsible for broadening the territories ruled.

The Tale of Bygone Years (Povest' o vremennykh let)

The text of this old Russian epic was compiled by Nestor early in the 12th century; it contains a chronicle from the 11th and earlier centuries. In *The Tale of Bygone Years* Russia's history is connected with world history and that of the Slavs.

Tamizdat

Russian abbreviation for *izdatel'stvo tam*, publication "there," i.e., abroad. See also *samizdat*.

Teilhard de Chardin – see **Chardin**

Theocracy

Term referring to a political form recognizing the direct rule of God in the nation's affairs; etymologically, from the Greek *theos* (god) and *kratos* (power, rule). The idea is based on Old Testament rule of the king on God's behalf; the term is also used more broadly for recognition of divine control of the public life of a people, whether through its prophets or some other form of revelation.

Theodosius of Pechora – see **Feodosii**

Theosis

Greek theological term for "deification," in Russian, *obozhenie*. It refers to reconciliation with God and sanctification, as aspects of the process of salvation which depend on divine grace. Salvation as a process of "becoming divine" is based on 2 Peter 1.4, referring to "participation in the divine nature." It is based on original human creation in the image of God; salvation thus implies a re-creation. Whether or not it was interpreted synergistically and depending on human response, *theosis* was a central teaching of the Hesychast movement.

Theosophy

A religious and philosophical term based on the Greek *theos* (God) and *sophia* (wisdom); it represents esoteric and intuitive knowledge of (occult) divine mysteries. It is applied to the system of Jakob Boehme (1575–1624), and more specifically to the teachings promulgated by Elena Blavatskaia, a synthesis of Christian Gnostic with Hindu and Buddhist pantheist mystical elements. She regarded God as a transcendent impersonal consciousness, and supported teachings about karma, reincarnation, the ultimate unity of all, and use of occult powers.

Thomism, Thomist scholasticism – see **Scholasticism, Aquinas**

Tolstoi, Count Lev Nikolaevich (1828–1910)

Russian author, master of realistic fiction and one of the world's greatest novelists. He is best known for his two long works, *War and Peace* (1863–69) and *Anna Karenina* (1873–77); a shorter novella, *The Death of Ivan Il'ich* is also regarded as exemplary. In the last years he was known as a moral and religious teacher for his teaching of nonresistance to evil, which influenced Gandhi.

Toporov, Vladimir Nikolaevich (b. 1928)

Specialist in History of World Culture and member of the Russian Academy of Sciences, Department of Literature and Language.

Total-unity – see **All-unity**

Tracy, A. Destutte de (1754–1836)

French nobleman who survived imprisonment during the Reign of Terror and founded the philosophical school of *"idéologie."* His most important work is *Éléments d'idéologie* (*The Elements of Ideology*, 4 vols., 1801–15); he also wrote the *Traité de la volonté et de ses effects* (*Treatise on the Will and its Effects*, 1805) and *Logique* (*Logic*, 1805). His emphasis on the role of sense-perception for knowledge demonstrates the influence of John Locke and Francis Bacon. Napoleon supported the intent of *"idéologie"* from 1795–99, but later attributed all the ills of the Revolution to it and suppressed the movement after 1803.

Troy

The Trojan city of the legendary wealthy king Priam, on the Dardanelles, was surrounded by Danaean Greeks for ten years; it became famous through the epic poetry of Homer, the *Iliad*, describing the Trojan war. The Greeks finally broke the stalemate by using the "Trojan horse" to capture the city.

Trubetskoi, Evgenii Nikolaevich (1863–1920)

Russian religious philosopher, lawyer, prince, brother of S. N. Trubetskoi. Important works are his *Mirosozertsanie Solovëva* (*Worldview of Solov'ev*, 1912), *Smysl zhizni* (*The Meaning of Life*, 1918), and *Entsiklopediia zakona* (*Encyclopedia of Law*, 1901; reprint, 1982).

Tselkovskii, Konstantin Eduardovich (1857–1935)

Russian thinker and scientist, responsible for a new scientific trend in rocket dynamics and astronautics; his essays developed a cosmist philosophy.

Turovskii, Kirill (ca. 1130–1182)

Early Russian church writer, preacher, Bishop of Turov, canonized by the Russian Orthodox Church. Author of *Slova* (*Words*) and various prayers and sayings.

Tiutchev, Fedor Ivanovich (1803–73)

Famous Russian poet, known for his statements about the impossibility of "understanding Russia with the mind," and the necessity of a "special standard" to measure its "particular condition."

***Unia* of Florence (1439)**

Early in the 15th century the Byzantine empire, under great pressure from the Ottoman empire, sought the support of Western Christians, especially the Pope. The Byzantine emperor John IV (1425–48) expected to receive help from the West under pretense of the Greek Church submitting to Pope Eugene IV. At the ecumenical Council of Florence (1437–39) representatives of both East and West signed the "Unia"; only Mark, Metropolitan of Ephesus and representative of the Patriarch of Jerusalem abstained. The Patriarchs of Alexandria, Antioch, as well as Jerusalem opposed the "Unia"; at the Council of Jerusalem (1443) all supporters of the "Unia" were excommunicated. The Greek Isidor, Metropolitan of Moscow, who represented the Russian church, was expelled and replaced.

Uvarov, Count Sergei (1786–1855)

Minister for education under Tsar Nicholas I from 1833–49, responsible for a report declaring that education be guided by "principles of Orthodoxy, Autocracy, and Nationality." These principles represented loyalty to dynastic tsarism, traditional Orthodox faith, and romantic glorification of the Russian people. Implementation led to reactionary policies restricting opportunities for students of the lower classes and tightened control over the university curriculum, but education in technical and vocational fields was expanded.

Vasilii Buslaev – see Buslaev

***Vekhi* (*Landmarks*)**

Title of a collection of articles by leading Russians of the Silver Age movement of religious philosophy, including Frank, Berdiaev, and Bulgakov. It was published just before the 1917 Revolution and was sharply critical of Marxism; it roused a considerable stir in Russia.

Vernadskii, Vladimir Ivanovich (1863–1945)

Russian thinker and naturalist. Vernadskii is known for his theory of the biosphere, and was one of the creators of "anthropocosmism," a system synthesizing historical, natural, social, and cultural aspects of science.

St. Vladimir (Vladimir I) (?–1015)

Prince of Kiev from 980, a descendant of Riurik, the youngest son of Sviatoslav I (d. 972), known for his wars against Bulgaria, Byzantium, and Poland. Under his reign Russia was Christianized (ca. 988). He provided its first law code.

Vladimir II Monomakh – see Monomakh

Volokolamskii (Volotskii), Iosif (Ivan Sanin) (1439–1515)

Famous Russian polemist, canonized in 1579; founder and father superior of the Iosifo-Volokolamskii monastery. His basic work is *Prosvetitel'* (*The Enlightener*). He represented the Possessors, and was close to the tsar, conferring a halo of divinity on the ruler's authority.

Voloshin (Kirienko-Voloshin), Maksimilian Aleksandrovich (1877–1932)

Russian poet and water-color painter.

Weber, Max (1864–1920)

German jurist in Heidelberg who later taught political economy and founded the German Society for Sociology; he focused on sociology of religion. He also worked on the constitution for Germany as a republic, arguing for popular election of the president.

World-Soul

The immaterial life principle of the universe, particularly connected with the philosophical systems of Neoplatonism. As a single animating principle universal soul is to guarantee world unity, and reintegration of multiplicity into unity.

Xenophanes of Kolofon (ca. 570–478 B.C.)

Ancient Greek poet and philosopher, associated with the Milesian school of thought and contemporary of Pythagoras. His critique of anthropomorphic gods was well-known: "The gods of the Ethiopian are dark-skinned and snub-nosed; the gods of the Thracians are fair and blue-eyed. If oxen could paint, their gods would be oxen."

Zek

A Soviet term for prisoner, *zakliuchennyi chelovek* (lit. a person confined).

Zenkovskii, Vasilii Vasil'evich (1881–1962)

Russian philosopher, theologian, literary critic, and historian of Russian philosophical thought. He emigrated in 1919, and from 1926 lectured at the Theological Institute in Paris. Important publications are *Russkie mysliteli i Evropa* (*Russian Thinkers and Europe*, 1926), *Dar svobody* (*The Gift of Freedom*, 1926), *O chudesakh* (*On Miracles*, 1928), *Das Bild des Menschen in Oestlichen Kirche* (*The Image of Man in the Eastern Church*, 1953), *Grundlagen der orthodoxen Anthropologie* (*Foundations of Orthodoxy Anthropology*, 1953), *Istoriia russkoi filosofii* (*A History of Russian Philosophy*, 1953).

Zinov'ev, Aleksandr (b. 1922)

Russian émigré writer and philosopher, living in Germany and highly critical of post-Soviet Russia. Known for works like *Katastroika* (1990) and *Russkii eksperiment* (*The Russian Experiment*, 1995).

Bibliography

1. Collections and Reference Works

Billington, James. *The Icon and the Axe: An Interpretive History of Russian Culture*. New York: Vintage Books, Random House, 1970.

Dvornik, Francis. *The Slavs in European History and Civilization*. New Brunswick, NJ: Rutgers University Press, 1962.

Kuvakin, Valery A., ed. *A History of Russian Philosophy, from the Tenth through the Twentieth Centuries*. 2 vols. Buffalo, NY: Prometheus Books, 1994.

Lossky, N. O. *History of Russian Philosophy*. New York: International Universities Press, 1951.

Maslin, M. A., ed. *Russkaia ideia* [The Russian idea]. Moscow: Respublika, 1992.

———, ed. *Russkaia filosofiia: Slovar'* [Russian philosophy: A dictionary]. Moscow: Respublika, 1995.

Raeff, Marc. *Russian Intellectual History: An Anthology*. New York: Harcourt, Brace & World, 1966.

Riasanovsky, Nicholas V. *A History of Russia*. 5th ed. New York and Oxford: Oxford University Press, 1993.

Shatz, M. S. and J. E. Zimmerman, eds. and trans. *Vekhi – Landmarks*. Armonk, NY: M. E. Sharpe, 1994.

Shein, Louis J., comp., ed., and trans. *Readings in Russian Philosophical Thought*. The Hague and Paris: Mouton, 1968.

Walicki, Andrzej. *A History of Russian Thought from the Enlightenment to Marxism*. Stanford: Stanford University Press, 1979.

Zenkovsky, Vasilii Vasil'evich. *A History of Russian Philosophy*. Translated by George L. Kline. 2 vols. New York: Columbia University Press; London: Routledge & Kegan Paul, 1953.

Zweerde, Evert van der, ed. *Russische filosofie na de perestrojka*. Amsterdam: Krisis/Parrèsia, 1995.

2. Russian Sources

Belinskii, V. G.
    "Letter to Gogol" (1847). In *Russian Intellectual History: An Anthology*, edited by Marc Raeff, 252–61. New York: Harcourt, Brace & World, 1966.
    Selected Philosophical Works. Moscow: Foreign Languages Publishing House, 1956.

Berdiaev, N. A.
    The Russian Idea. New York: The MacMillan Co., 1947.

Chaadaev, P. Ia.
    "First Letter." In *Russian Intellectual History: An Anthology*, edited by Marc Raeff, 160–73. New York: Harcourt, Brace & World, 1966.

Dostoevskii, F. M.
    "Pushkin: A Sketch." In *Russian Intellectual History: An Anthology*, edited by Marc Raeff, 288–300. New York: Harcourt, Brace & World, 1966.

Fedotov, G. P.
    The Russian Religious Mind. 2 vols: Vol. 1, *Kievan Christianity: The Tenth to the Thirteenth Centuries*; Vol. 2, *The Middle Ages: The Thirteenth to the Fifteenth Centuries*. Cambridge: Harvard University Press, 1946.
    Sud'ba i grekhi Rossii: Izbrannye stat'i po filosofii russkoi istorii i kul'tury [The fate and sins of Russia: Selected articles on the philosophy of Russian history and culture]. St. Petersburg: Sofiia, 1991–92.

Florenskii, P. A.
    Stolp i utverzhdenie istiny: Opyt pravoslavnoi feoditsii v dvenadtsati pis'makh [The pillar and ground of truth: An essay in Orthodox theodicy in twelve letters]. Moscow, 1914; reprint, Westmeade, Farnborough, England: Gregg International, 1970. Reproduced in P. A. Florenskii, *Sobranie sochinenii*. Vol. 4. Paris: YMCA Press, 1989.
    The Pillar and Ground of Truth: An Essay in Orthodox Theodicy in Twelve Letters. Translated by Boris Jakim. Princeton: Princeton University Press, 1997.

Florovsky, G.
    "Tvar' i tvarnost'" [Creature and creatureliness]. Translated as "Creation and Creaturehood" in *The Collected Works of Georges Florovsky*, vol. 3, *Creation and Redemption*, 43–78. Belmont, MA: Nordland Publishing Company, 1976.
    Puti russkogo bogosloviia [Ways of Russian theology]. Paris: YMCA-Press, 1983.
    Ways of Russian Theology. Translated by Robert L. Nichols. Belmont, MA: Nordland Publishing Company, 1987.

Kireevskii, I. V.
  "On the Nature of European Culture and Its Relation to the Culture of Russia." In *Russian Intellectual History: An Anthology,* edited by Marc Raeff, 174–207. New York: Harcourt, Brace & World, 1966.
  "Sur la necessité et la possibilité de principes nouveaux en philosophie." In Ivan Kiréievski, *Essais philosophiques,* translated by François Rouleau, 141–80. Paris: Editions Lethielleux, 1988.

Solov'ev, V. S.
  L'Idée russe, as *Russkaia Ideia.* In *Rossiia glazami russkogo: Chaadaev, Leont'ev, Solov'ev* [Russia through Russian eyes: Chaadaev, Leont'ev, Solov'ev]. Edited by A. F. Zamaleev. St. Petersburg: "Nauka," 1991.
  Lectures on Godmanhood [Chtenie o Bogochelovechestve] (1877–81). Translated by Peter P. Zouboff. London: Dennis Dobson, 1948. The Russian text is found in the third volume of *Sobranie sochinenii Vladimira Solov'eva.* 2nd ed. Edited by S. M. Solov'ev and E. L. Radlov. 10 vols. St. Petersburg: Prosveshchenie, 1911–14; reprinted with two vols. added, Brussels: Zhizn' s Bogom, 1966–70). Important sections of the *Lectures* are also found in S. L. Frank. *A Solovyov Anthology.* Translated by N. Duddington. London: SCM, 1950.
  Rossiia i vselenskaia tserkov' (1911). Translated by G. A. Rachinskii. In *Sobranie sochinenii Vladimira Solov'eva,* 11: 139–348. Brussels: Zhizn' s Bogom, 1969. Originally published as *La Russie et l'église universelle.* Paris, 1889. Reprint, Paris: Librairie Stock, 1922.
  Russia and the Universal Church. Translated by Herbert Rees. London: G. Bles, 1948.
  Sochineniia v dvukh tomakh [Collected work in two volumes]. Edited by A. F. Losev and A. V. Gulyga. Filosofkoe nasledie, vols. 110–11. Moscow: Akademiia nauk SSSR, Institut filosofii, Mysl', 1990, first pub. 1988).
  Sochineniia v dvukh tomakh [Works in two volumes]. Edited by N. V. Kotrelev. Introductory essay by V. F. Asmus. Notes by N. V. Kotrelev and E. B. Rashkovskii. Moscow: Pravda, 1989.
  A Solovyov Anthology. Edited by S. L. Frank. Translated by N. Duddington. London: SCM Press, 1950.

3. Contemporary Sources

Abramov, A. I. "Reflections on Russia's Destiny in the Philosophical Work of Russian Romanticism." *Russian Studies in Philosophy* 35: 3 (1996–97): 6–18.

Agursky, M. *The Third Rome.* Boulder, CO and London: Westview Press, 1987.

Aizlewood, Robin. "The Return of the 'Russian Idea' in Publications, 1988–91." *Slavonic and East European Review* 71: 3 (1993): 490–99.

———. "Revisiting Russian Identity in Russian Thought: From Chaadaev to the Early Twentieth Century." *Slavonic and East European Review* 78: 1 (2000): 20–43.

Alfeev, Hilarion. "Reviving the Russian Orthodox Church, A Task both Theological and Secular." In *Russia's Fate through Russian Eyes: Voices of the New Generation*, edited by Heyward Isham, 235–49. Boulder, CO: Westview Press, 2001.

Andreyev, Nikolay. "Filofey and his Epistle to Ivan Vasil'yevich." *Slavonic and East European Review* 38: 90 (1959): 1–31.

Bercken, William Van den. *Christian Thinking and the End of Communism*. Utrecht-Leiden: Interuniversity Institute for Missiological and Ecumenical Research, 1993.

Billington, James and Kathleen Parthé. *Second Colloquium on Russian National Identity: Final Report*. Washington, DC: The Library of Congress, 1999.

———. *Third Colloquium on Russian National Identity: Final Report*. Washington, DC: The Library of Congress, 2000.

Blane, Andrew, ed. *Georges Florovsky: Russian Intellectual and Orthodox Churchman*. Crestwood, NY: St.Vladimir's Seminary Press, 1993.

Brougher, V. G. "The Occult in Russian Literature of the 1990s." *Russian Review* 56: 1 (1997): 110–24.

Boyle, Kevin and Juliet Sheen, eds. *Freedom of Religion and Belief: A World Report*. London: Routledge, 1997.

Carlson, Maria. *"No Religion Higher than Truth": A History of the Theosophical Movement in Russia, 1875–1922*. Princeton: Princeton University Press, 1993.

———. "Gnostic Elements in the Cosmogony of Vladimir Soloviev." In *Russian Religious Thought*, edited by Judith Deutsch Kornblatt and Richard F. Gustafson, 49–67. Madison, WI: University of Wisconsin Press, 1994.

Chafetz, G. "The Struggle for a National Identity in Post-Soviet Russia." *Political Science Quarterly* 111: 4 (1996–97): 661–88.

Cioran, Samuel D. *Vladimir Solov'ev and the Knighthood of the Divine Sophia*. Waterloo, Ontario: Wilfrid Laurier Press, 1977.

Devlin, Judith. *Enemies of Democracy in Modern Russia*. London: Macmillan Press, 1999. See, in particular, chap. 3, "Russian Orthodoxy and Nationalism," 61–89.

Duncan, P. J. S. *Russian Messianism: Third Rome, Holy Revolution, Communism and After*. London and New York: Routledge, 2000.

Dunlop, John B. *The Faces of Contemporary Russian Nationalism*. Princeton: Princeton University Press, 1983.

———. "Russia: In Search of an Identity?" In *New States, New Politicis: Building the Post-Soviet Nations*, edited by Ian Bremmer and Ray Taras, 29–74. Cambridge: Cambridge University Press, 1997.

Feifer, G. "Utopian Nostalgia: Russia's 'New Idea.'" *World Policy Journal* 16 (1999): 111–18.

Findlay, John N. "Hegelianism and Platonism." In *Hegel and the History of Philosophy. Proceedings of the 1972 Conference of the Hegel Society of America*, edited by Joseph J. O'Malley, Keith W. Algozin, and Frederick G. Weiss, 62–82. The Hague: Nijhoff, 1973.

Fink, Hilary L. *Bergson and Russian Modernism, 1900–1930*. Evanston, IL: Northwestern University Press, 1998.

Gaidenko, P. P. "Chelovek i chelovechestvo v uchenii V. S. Solov'eva" [The human being and humanity in the teaching of V. S. Solov'ev]. *Voprosy filosofii*, no. 6 (1994): 47–54.

Giddens, Anthony. *Beyond Left and Right: The Future of Radical Politics*. Cambridge: Polity Press, 1994.

———. *A Contemporary Critique of Historical Materialism*. 2nd ed. London: MacMillan, 1995.

Groys, Boris. "Russia and the West: The Quest for Russian National Identity." *Studies in Soviet Thought* 43 (1992): 185–98.

Gulyga, A. *Russkaia ideia i ee tvortsy* [The Russian idea and its creators]. Moscow: Soratnik, 1995.

Gvosdev, Nikolas K. "The Orthodox Church and Russian Politics." *Orthodox Christian News Service*, 20 December 1999, http://www.orthodoxnews.com.

Hartshorne, Charles. "Total Unity in Russian Metaphysics: Some Reactions to Zenkovsky's and Lossky's Theories." In *The Logic of Perfection, and Other Essays in Neoclassical Metaphysics*, 263–79. LaSalle, IL: Open Court Publishing Co., 1973). First published in *Review of Metaphysics* 7 (1954).

Helleman, Wendy E. *Hellenization Revisited*. Lanham, MD: University Press of America, 1994.

———. "Orthodoxie en platonisme." *Beweging* 61: 2 (1997): 63–67.

———. "Reading Plato for the 21st Century." *Philosophia Reformata* 64 (1999): 148–64.

———. "The 'Russian Idea.'" *Oil and Gas Eurasia* 4 (June 2001): 12–14.

———. "Solovyov and Sophia." In *Vladimir Solov'ëv, Reconciler and Polemicist*, edited by W. van de Bercken, M. de Courten, and E. van de Zweerde, 163–84. Leuven: Peeters Publishers, 2000.

———. "Solovyov's Plato." In *Solov'evskii sbornik: Materialy mezhdunarodnoi konferentsii "V. S. Solov'ev i ego filosofskoe nasledie." Avgust 2000* [A Solov'ev anthology: Materials from the international conference "V. S. Solovyov and his philosophical heritage." August 2000], edited by I. V. Borisova and A. P.

Kozyrev, 197–219. Moscow: Institut filosofiii RAN, Fenomenologiia-Germenevtika, 2001.

Hesli, V. L., E. Erdem, Wm. Reisinger, and A. Miller. "The Patriarch and the President: Religion and Political Choice in Russia." *Demokratizatsiia* 7: 1 (1999): 42–69.

Hosking, Geoffrey A. "The Institutionalization of Soviet Literature." In *Perspectives on Literature and Society in Eastern and Western Europe*, edited by G. Hosking and G. V. Cushing, 55–75. Houndmills, London: Macmillan, 1989.

Hosking, Geoffrey A. and Robert Service, eds. *Russian Nationalism, Past and Present*. Houndmills, London: Macmillan, 1998.

Hough, Jerry F. *Democratization and Revolution in the USSR, 1985–1991*. Washington, DC: Brookings Institution Press, 1997.

Isham, Heyward, ed. *Remaking Russia: Voices from Within*. New York: M. E. Sharpe, 1995.

Isham, Heyward et al., eds. *Russia's Fate through Russian Eyes: Voices of the New Generation*. Boulder, CO: Westview Press, 2001.

Ivanov, Vyacheslav. "In My Beginning is My End: Traditional Values in Russian Social Life and Thought." In *Remaking Russia: Voices from Within*, edited by Heyward Isham, 23–36. New York: M. E. Sharpe, 1995.

Kämpfer, F. "The Image of Russian Christianity in the West and the concept of 'Holy Russia.'" In *The Christianization of Ancient Russia: A Millennium, 988–1988*, edited by Yves Hamant, 193–204. New York: UNESCO, 1998.

Kharkhordin, Oleg. "Civil Society and Orthodox Christianity." *Europe-Asia Studies* 50: 6 (1998): 949–68.

Khoruzhii, S. S. "Filosofskii parokhod" [The ship of philosophers]. In *Posle pereryva: Puti russkoi filosofii. Uchebnoe posobie* [After the interval: The ways of Russian philosophy. Study materials], 189–208. St. Petersburg: Aleteiia, 1994.

———. "Filosofskii protsess v Rossii kak vstrecha filosofii i pravoslaviia" [The philosophical process in Russia as a meeting of philosophy and Orthodoxy]. *Voprosy filosofii*, no. 5 (1991): 26–57.

———. "Khomiakov i printsip sobornosti" [Khomiakov and the principle of *sobornost'*]. *Zdes' i teper'*, no. 2 (1992): 80–81.

Klibanov, A. I. *History of Religious Sectarianism in Russia, 1860s–1917*. Translated by E. Dunn. Oxford and New York: Pergamon Press, 1982.

Klibansky, Raymond. *The Continuity of the Platonic Tradition during the Middle Ages, Outlines of a Corpus Platonicum Medii Aevi*. London: The Warburg Institute, 1939.

Kline, George L. "Hegel and Solovyov." In *Hegel and the History of Philosophy: Proceedings of the 1972 Conference of the Hegel Society of America*, edited by

Joseph J. O'Malley, Keith W. Algozin, and Frederick G. Weiss, 159–70. The Hague: Nijhoff, 1973.

Kornblatt, Judith Deutsch. "Vladimir Solov'ev on Spiritual Nationhood, Russia and the Jews." *The Russian Review* 56: 2 (1997): 157–77.

Kornblatt, Judith Deutsch and Richard F. Gustafson, eds. *Russian Religious Thought*. Madison, WI: University of Wisconsin Press, 1994.

Linzey, Sharon, and Ken Kaisch, eds. *God in Russia: The Challenge of Freedom*. Lanham, MD: University Press of America, 1999.

Lossky, Vladimir. *The Mystical Theology of the Eastern Church*. London: James Clarke, 1957. Originally published as *Essai sur la théologie mystique de l'Eglise d'Orient* (Paris: Aubier, 1944).

Maksimov, V. "Svoboda dukhovnaia dolzhna predshestvovat' svobode politicheskoi" [Spiritual freedom must precede political freedom]. *Novoe russkoe slovo*, 18 June 1978.

McDaniel, Tim. *The Agony of the Russian Idea*. Princeton: Princeton University Press, 1996.

McGann, L. L. "The Russian Orthodox Church under Patriarch Aleksii II and the Russian State: An Unholy Alliance?" *Demokratizatsiia* 7: 1 (1999): 12–27.

Meerson, Michael A. "Put' Against Logos: The Critique of Kant and NeoKantianism by Russian Religious Philosophers." *Studies in East European Thought* 47 (1995): 225–43.

Mihajlov, M. "The Great Catalyzer: Nietzsche and Russian Neo-Idealism." In *Nietzsche in Russia*, edited by Bernice Glatzer Rosenthal, 127–45. Princeton: Princeton University Press, 1986.

Mil'don, V. I. "The Russian Idea at the End of the Twentieth Century." *Russian Studies in Philosophy* 35 (1997): 24–38.

Miller, A. H., V. L. Hesli, and Wm. M. Reisinger. "Conceptions of Democracy among Mass and Elite in Post-Soviet Societies." *British Journal of Political Science* 27 (1997): 157–90.

Miller, J. "Alternative Visions of the Russian Future." In *Russia in Search of Its Future*, edited by Amin Saikal and William Maley, 190–205. Cambridge: Cambridge University Press, 1995.

Nethercott, Frances. *Russia's Plato: Plato and the Platonic Tradition in Russian Education, Science and Ideology (1840–1930)*. Aldershot, UK: Ashgate Publishing, 2000.

Neumann, Iver B. *Russia and the Idea of Europe*. London: Routledge, 1996.

Novik, Fr. Veniamin. "Russia – Between Past and Future." *Religion, State and Society* 22: 2 (1994): 183–89.

———. "Social Doctrine: Will the Russian Orthodox Church Take a Daring Step?" *Religion, State and Society* 26: 2 (1998): 197–203.

Pammett, J. H. "Elections and Democracy in Russia." *Communist and Post-Communist Studies* 32 (1999): 45–60,
Paradowsky, R. "The Eurasian Idea and Leo Gumilev's Scientific Ideology." *Canadian Slavonic Papers* 41: 1 (1999): 19–32.
Parthé, Kathleen F. *Russian Village Prose: The Radiant Past.* Princeton: Princeton University Press, 1992.
———, "Russia's 'Unreal Estate': Cognitive Mapping and National Identity." Kennan Institute For Advanced Russian Studies, Occasional Paper #265. Washington, DC: The Woodrow Wilson Center, 1997.
Pavlov, A. T. "The Question of the Uniqueness of Russian Philosophy." *Russian Studies in Philosophy* 33 (1994): 37–49.
Pelikan, Jaroslav. *Christianity and Classical Culture: The Metamorphosis of Natural Theology in the Christian Encounter with Hellenism.* New Haven: Yale University Press, 1993.
Petro, Nicolai N. *The Rebirth of Russian Democracy: An Interpretation of Political Culture.* Cambridge, MA: Harvard University Press, 1995.
Piskunov, V. M. *Russkaia Ideia* [The Russian Idea]. Moscow: Iskusstvo, 1994.
Pospielovsky, D. "Russian Nationalism: An Update." *Report on the USSR* 2: 6 (9 February 1990): 8–17.
Raeff, Marc. "Enticements and Rifts: Georges Florovsky as Russian Intellectual Historian." In *Georges Florovsky: Russian Intellectual, Orthodox Churchman,* edited by Andrew Blane, 219–86. Crestwood, NY: St. Vladimir's Seminary Press, 1993.
———. *Political Ideas and Institutions in Imperial Russia.* Boulder, CO: Westview Press, 1994.
Scanlan, James P. "Interpretations and Uses of Slavophilism in Recent Russian Thought." In *Russian Thought after Communism: The Recovery of a Philosophical Heritage,* edited by James P. Scanlan, 31–61. Armonk, NY: M. E. Sharpe, 1994.
———. "Is Russia Really in Need of Russian Philosophy?" [Nuzhna li Rossii russkaia filosofiia?]. *Voprosy filosofii,* no. 1 (1994): 61–65.
———. "The Russian Idea from Dostoevskii to Ziuganov." *Problems of Post-Communism* 43 (August 1996): 35–42.
Scanlan, James P., ed. *Russian Thought after Communism: The Recovery of a Philosophical Heritage.* Armonk, NY: M. E. Sharpe, 1994.
Schlapentokh, D. "The End of the Russian Idea." *Studies in Soviet Thought* 43 (1992): 199–217.
Serebriany, Sergei. "Culture in Russia and Russian Culture." In *Russia in Search of Its Future,* edited by Amin Saikal and William Maley, 158–77. Cambridge: Cambridge University Press, 1995.

Shapovalov, Viktor F. "The Categories of the Cultural Historical Process in Russia." *Russian Studies in Philosophy* 33 (1994): 7–22.

———. "Liberalism and the Idea of Russia." *Russian Politics and Law* 35 (1997): 31–47.

Slater, Wendy. "Russia's Imagined History: Visions of the Soviet Past and the New 'Russian Idea.'" *Journal of Communist Studies and Transition Politics* 14 (1998): 69–86.

Slesinski, Robert. *Pavel Florensky: A Metaphysics of Love.* New York: St. Vladimir's Seminary Press, 1984.

Smirnova, Z. V. "The Debates about Slavophilism: Some Methodological Aspects of the Study of Early Slavophilism." *Soviet Studies in Philosophy* 27 (1988–89): 35–62.

Solzhenitsyn, Aleksandr, Mikhail Agurskii, A. B., Evgenii Barabanov, Vadim Borisov, F. Korsakov, Igor' Shafarevich, *From Under the Rubble.* Boston and Toronto: Little, Brown and Company, 1975. Originally published as *Iz-Pod glub* (Paris: YMCA Press, 1974).

———. *Pis'mo vozhdiam Sovetskogo Soiuza* [Letter to the leaders of the Soviet Union]. Paris: YMCA Press, 1974.

———. *The Russian Question: At the End of the 20th Century.* Translated by Yermolai Solzhenitsyn. New York: Farrar, Strauss and Giroux, 1995.

Starobin, Paul. "Vladimir Putin: More Questions Than Answers So Far." *Business Week Online*, 2 January 2000. http://www.businessweek.com.

Strémooukhoff, Dimitri N. *Vladimir Soloviev et son ouevre messianique.* Strasbourg: University of Strasbourg, 1935; Paris: L'Age d'Homme, 1935; Paris: Société d'édition Les Belles Lettres, 1935; reprint, Paris: L'Age d'Homme, 1976.

———. *Vladimir Soloviev and His Messianic Work.* Translated by Elizabeth Meyendorff. Edited by Phillip Guilbeau and Heather Elise MacGregor. Belmont, MA: Nordland Publishing Co., 1980.

Suny, R. G. "Provisional Stabilities, the Politics of Identities in Post-Soviet Eurasia." *International Security* 24: 3 (1999–2000): 139–78.

Taivans, Leons G. "Russia on the Threshold: Orthodox Tradition and Protestant Ethics." *Religion in Eastern Europe* 21: 1 (2000): 1–15.

Tigerstedt, Eugène Napoleon. *The Decline and Fall of the Neoplatonic Interpretation of Plato: An Outline and Some Observations.* Helsinki: Societas Scientarum Fennica, 1974.

———. *Interpreting Plato.* Stockholm: Almqvist and Wiksell International, 1977.

Timberlake, Charles E., ed. *Religious and Secular Forces in Late Tsarist Russia: Essays in Honor of Donald W. Treadgold.* Seattle: University of Washington Press, 1992. See the Introduction by Timberlake, "Religious Pluralism, the

Spread of Revolutionary Ideas, and the Church-State Relationship in Tsarist Russia," 3–29.

Torbakov, Igor. "The Statists and Ideology of Russian Imperial Nationalism." *RFE/RL Research Report* 1: 49 (1992): 10–16.

Tolz, Vera. "Forging the Nation: National Identity and Nation Building in Post-Communist Russia." *Europe-Asia Studies* 50: 6 (1998): 993–1022.

Troitskii, Evgenii Sergeevich. *Vozrozhdenie russkoi idei: Sotsial'no-filosofskie ocherki* [The renaissance of the Russian idea: Social-philosophical essays]. Moscow: Filosofskoe obshchestvo SSSR, 1991.

Tulaev, Pavel Vladimirovich. "*Sobor* and *Sobornost'*." *Russian Studies in Philosophy* 31 (1993): 31–46.

Urban, Michael. "Remythologising the Russian State." *Europe-Asia Studies* 50: 6 (1998): 969–92.

Valliere, Paul. *Modern Russian Theology: Bukharev, Soloviev, Bulgakov. Orthodox Theology in a New Key*. Grand Rapids, MI: Wm. B. Eerdmans, 2000.

Vainshtein, G. "The Authoritarian Idea in the Public Conscious and Political Life of Contemporary Russia." *Journal of Communist Studies and Transition Politics* 11: 3 (1995): 272–85.

Volkogonova, Olga D. "Est' li budushchee u russkoi idei?" [Is there a future for the Russian idea?]. *Mir Rossii/ Universe of Russia* 9: 2 (2000): 28–52.

Walicki, Andrzej. "Po povodu 'russkoi idei' v russkoi filosofii" [Concerning the 'Russian idea' in Russian philosophy]. *Voprosy filosofii*, no. 1 (1994): 68–72.

White, S. and A. Pravda, eds. *Ideology and Soviet Politics*. London: Macmillan and the School of Slavonic and East European Studies, University of London, 1998.

Yanov, Alexander. *The Russian Challenge and the Year 2000*. Translated by I. J. Rosenthal. Oxford: Basil Blackwell, 1987.

———. *The Russian New Right: Right-Wing Ideologies in the Contemporary USSR*. Berkeley, CA: Institute of International Studies, University of California, 1978.

Zernov, Nicolas. *The Russian Religious Renaissance of the Twentieth Century* London: Darton, Longman and Todd, 1963.

Ziuganov, G. *My Russia*. Armonk, NY: M. E. Sharpe, 1997.

About the Authors

Part I. The Russian Idea: Cultural, Historical, and Ideological Aspects

VLADIMIR KARLOVICH KANTOR (b. 1945) finished a basic education in the Philological Faculty of Moscow State University in 1969, continued his studies with the Institute of the History of Fine Arts of the Ministry of Culture (USSR), and received his doctorate from the Institute of Philosophy (RAN) in 1988. Since 1974 he has participated on the editorial staff of the journal *Voprosy filosofii* (*Issues in Philosophy*), and since 1981 has taught at the Moscow State Linguistic University. He has published numerous monographs dealing with Russian and European cultural factors, contributed to several collections on the history of Russian philosophy, culture, and aesthetics, and written many articles on the problems of Russian mentality.

MIKHAIL VASIL'EVICH IL'IN (b. 1947), Candidate in Philological Sciences, general director of the journal *Polis*, professor at MGIMO, MID, RF completed basic studies in literature with his master's degree (1976) focused on William Shakespeare. From 1977–82 he worked at a student center in Prague. Back in Moscow in the 1980s he began comparative study of civil society and political forms, from 1988 at the Russian Academy of Sciences. Serving as vice director of the Institute of Comparative Politics from 1991–94, he taught comparative politics at MGIMO after 1994 . Further study of political organization led to a monograph on political typology in 1995. The article in this collection is part of a larger publication, *Slova i smysly* (*Words and Meanings*, 1997), on basic political concepts. Il'in has worked as editor and general director of *Polis* since the early 1990s; in 1997 he was chosen President of the Russian Association of Political Science.

VLADIMIR SOLOMONOVICH BIBLER (1918–2000), a specialist in philosophical logic and philosophy of culture, graduated from the faculty of history of Moscow State University in 1941, defended a dissertation on dialectical logic in 1951, and until 1959 taught philosophy at the State University of Tajikistan. Back in Moscow he taught and led a seminar on philosophy of culture and dialogics, and served on the editorial boards of journals like *Arbor mundia* and *Odyssei*. In 1962 he began to work at the Institute of the History of Natural Sciences and Technology of the Academy of Sciences, transferring in 1968 to the Institute of General History, and from 1980

Helleman, Wendy, ed. *The Russian Idea: In Search of a New Identity*. Bloomington, IN: Slavica, 2004, 263–66.

worked at the Institute of Psychology. From 1989 he served as scientific director of the group "The Dialogue of Culture" at the Russian State University for the Humanities. The 20th-century crisis of reason does not, for Bibler, entail irrationalism, but a new kind of dialogical reason of culture evidenced in the arts as well as daily human life. He influenced new educational directions at "schools of the dialogue of culture" in leading cities of the USSR. Among Bibler's major publications are *Myshlenie kak tvorchestvo: Vvedenie v logiku myslennogo dialoga* (*Reflection as a Creative Activity: Introduction to Logic as Reflective Dialogue*, 1975); *Ot naukoucheniia k logike kul'tury* (*From the Teaching of Science to a Logic of Culture*, 1991); *M. M. Bakhtin ili poetika kul'tury* (*M. M. Bakhtin or a Poetics of Culture*, 1991); and *Kul'tura, nravstvennost', sovremennost'* (*Culture, Morality, Modernity*, 1991).

LEONID ALEKSANDROVICH SEDOV (b. 1934), graduated from the Moscow Institute of Foreign Languages in 1957. He continued studies with the Oriental Institute of the USSR Academy of Sciences, specializing in SouthEast Asian medieval history. In 1964 he defended his candidate's thesis and became actively involved in theoretical discussions on the nature of human society, looking for an explanation of social reality alternative to Marxism. While working with the Institute of Concrete Social Studies of the USSR Academy of Sciences, his signature on a letter protesting political persecution led to considerable pressure, and removal from the institute in 1972. He found work as an editor with the Soviet Encyclopedia Publishing House and co-authored a famous two-volume encyclopedia, *Myths of the Peoples of the World*. In 1988 he was invited to work with the National Center for Public Opinion Research (WCIOM) as senior researcher for political and culturological issues. At present he serves as deputy director for WCIOM.

ANDREI PAVLOVICH ZABIAKO (b. 1960) was born in Blagoveshchensk, where he received his education in history at the Pedagogical Institute. In 1989 he completed post-graduate studies at the Faculty of Philosophy of Moscow State University with the degree of candidate in philosophy. From 1991–95 he chaired the department of history of culture at the Pedagogical Institute of Blagoveshchensk. He is the author of more than 30 scientific research essays in the study of religion and history of culture, and the textbook *The History of Old Russian Culture* (1995). In 1999 he completed the doctoral degree in the Department of the Study of Religion, in the Faculty of Philosophy, Moscow State University.

EVGENII BORISOVICH RASHKOVSKII (b. 1940) completed a basic education at the Moscow Historical Archival Institute in 1964, and pursued doctoral work in history with the Institute of Oriental Studies (Academy of

Sciences USSR, 1974), and Institute of World Economy and Internal Relations (Russian Academy of Sciences, 1997). From 1964–67 Rashkovskii worked as bibliographer with the Fundamental Library of Social Siences, Moscow, from 1971–90 as research fellow with the Institute of Oriental Studies, and since 1990 as leading research fellow with the Institute of World Economy and Internal Relations. From 1994–97 he also served as research fellow with the Bible Society of Russia (UBS). Among important publications are *The Genesis of the Studies of Science in Asia and Africa, 1960s–1970s* (1985); *Scientific Knowledge, Institutions of Science and Intellectuals in Asia: XIX-XX Centuries* (1990); and *The Axis of Time: Essays in Philosophy of History* (1999). Rashkovskii has also translated numerous works, including poetry, from Hebrew, and prepared informational and children's books based on the Bible.

Part II. The Russian Idea and Russian Religious Philosophy

KONSTANTIN KONSTANTINOVICH IVANOV was born in 1942 during the battle of Stalingrad; after 1945 the family transferred to St. Petersburg, where Ivanov attended St. Petersburg State University, studying philosophy. He completed his dissertation on "Philosophical Questions of Modal Logics" in the late 1960s, but was soon advised to leave his university teaching post because he was visiting a church by this time. Baptized in 1971, he had to take employment in a variety of nonacademic jobs, while leading religious philosophical discussions, writing and educational work "underground" together with well-known leaders like Fathers Sergei Zheludkov, Anatolii Vaneev, and Aleksandr Men'. With the onset of *perestroika* he organized the St. Petersburg school "Open Christianity" for religious and philosophical studies, and was president and chief lecturer for ten years. At present Ivanov serves as dean of the theological faculty of the Dietrich Bonhoeffer University (sponsored by Korean Presbyterians) of St. Petersburg.

ALEKSEI VASIL'EVICH ZHURAVSKII (b. 1953), completed basic studies at MGIMO and received the degree of candidate of historical sciences in 1980. He has specialized in the history of Islam and Christianity, with special attention to Russian religious philosophy of the 19th and 20th centuries, and continues to work on questions of the mutual relationship and possibility for dialogue between Muslims and Christians. At present he serves as pro-rector of the Biblical-Theological Institute of St. Andrew's (Moscow), and also lectures at the Institute of Eastern Culture (Russian State University for the Humanities). He recently published *Khristianstvo i islam* (*Christianity and Islam*, 1990) and *Khristiane i musul'mane* (*Christians and Muslims*, 2000).

LEONID IVANOVICH VASILENKO (b. 1946), a specialist in philosophy of religion and Russian religious philosophy, completed studies at the Moscow

Physical-Technical Institute (1970), continuing with graduate studies at the Institute of Philosophy (RAN), defending a dissertation on philosophical problems of ecology in 1976. Until 1990 he worked at the Institute of Philosophy, then taught philosophy at the Moscow Theological Seminary, and since 1995 has been teaching the history of Russian religious philosophy at the Orthodox Theological Institute of St. Tikhon. His publications include the *Vvedenie v istoriiu russkoi religioznoi filosofii* (*Introduction to the History of Russian Religious Philosophy*, 1999), *Kratkii religiozno-filosofskii slovar'* (*Short Religious-Philosophical Dictionary*, 1998), and many articles on the theme of philosophy of religion, Russian cosmism, ecology, and culture.

SERGEI SERGEEVICH KHORUZHII (b. 1941), doctor of mathematical physics, has long occupied himself with the study of Russian religious philosophy. He completed basic education in physics at Moscow State University in 1964, and worked at the Mathematical Institute of V. A. Steklov from 1967. He has contributed numerous articles on Russian religious philosophy and the theory of literature to the *Filosofskaia entsiklopediia* (1960–70). Khoruzhii is the author of *Lev Karsavin: Religiozno-filosofkie sochineniia* (*The Religious-Philosophical Writings of Lev Karsavin*, 1992), and co-author of the complete translation of James Joyce's *Ulysses* in Russian. He has also written numerous articles and books on Florenskii, on asceticism, and hesychasm, and continues work on Palamas and an Orthodox anthropology based on an understanding of energism and synenergism.

ANDREI VIACHESLAVOVICH KURAEV (b. 1963), a specialist in Christian philosophy, studied at the Faculty of Philosophy of Moscow State University, finishing his basic degree in 1984, and also completed a course of studies at the Moscow Theological Academy in 1992. From 1990–93 he worked for the Moscow Patriarchate, and from 1993 served as dean of the Philosophical-Theological Faculty of the Russian Orthodox University of St. John the Divine. According to Kuraev, philosophy is both Christian and Orthodox when studied from the perspective of Christian Orthodox spirituality. Even if philosophy is a-dogmatic, and has a degree of autonomy in the answers it provides, it cannot avoid issues like the meaning of Easter as the victory over man's fallen nature. Kuraev is professor at the St. Tikhon Orthodox Theological Institute and teaches philosophy of religion at Moscow State University. He has written many articles and monographs, often polemical and apologetic, dealing with issues of faith.

Index

Abraham 17, 143, 146, 147
Absolute 76, 78, 101, 155, 181, 185–187, 191, 193–95, 198–201
absolutes 3, 12, 18, 46
alienation 17, 115, 117, 179
All-Unity 18, 43, 167, 169–73, 176–77, 192
Arianism 139, 145
atheism 16, 77, 132
autocracy 7, 23, 44, 48, 59, 61–63, 69

Belarus 10, 69
Belinskii 13–14, 33–35, 46, 80
Berdiaev 9–10, 16–18, 24, 74, 116, 124, 129–34, 159–61, 178
Blavatsky 18, 179, 181, 182, 186, 189, 196, 198–99
Bolshevik 16, 24, 25, 172
Bolshevism 3, 31, 130
Boris and Gleb, Ss. 14, 42, 45
Buddha, the 78, 81
Buddhism 19, 195, 201, 203
Bulgakov 12, 17–18, 106, 157–61, 170, 172, 178, 200

Caesar 15, 116–19, 143
Catholicism 10, 12, 15, 70, 87, 114, 148
Chaadaev 1, 4, 16, 23, 26, 40, 51–52, 60, 80, 137–40, 173
chance (avos') 15, 33, 38, 53, 90–91
chauvinism 4, 68
Christianity 12, 14, 16, 19, 28, 39–40, 43, 61, 79, 81, 82–83, 86–88, 92, 104, 112, 118, 131, 134–36, 139–41, 143–44, 153, 158–59, 168, 175, 177–79, 182–83, 186, 187, 188–89, 192–94, 196, 199, 202–03

civil society 12, 14–15, 30, 54, 62, 113, 116–26
collective 23–24, 31, 75
Communism 2, 4, 6, 9, 10, 13, 16, 43, 54, 132, 136
cosmism 16–17, 151–52, 154–57, 161, 163
creation 3, 11–12, 18, 161, 180–84, 186, 193, 200

Danilevskii 9, 139
democracy 7, 8, 10, 14, 51, 58, 62–63, 69, 73, 114
Descartes 3, 167, 178–79, 194
destiny 9, 10, 13, 33–39, 41–45
dissidents 6, 8, 29
Dostoevskii 4, 9, 13, 14, 24, 25, 27, 29, 35–36, 44, 58, 65, 83–84, 91, 96, 97, 101, 103, 133, 143–44, 148
dualism 17, 153

economy 13, 15, 29–30, 116, 119, 140, 151
Empire, Russian 2, 34, 58
enlightenment (religious/philosophical) 14, 28, 34, 47, 48, 50, 51, 142
Enlightenment, the 3, 138
eschatology 49, 159
ethics 76, 105, 124, 152, 212
evil 16, 18, 19, 23, 35, 37, 45, 68, 82, 89, 104, 108, 132, 147, 152, 168, 194, 196, 197–202
evolutionism 151–65, 171

fairy-tale 38, 109–10
Fall of Man 17, 155, 181
fascism 14

fatalism 14, 91, 145
fate 15, 33, 37, 46, 47, 50, 52–53, 80, 98, 106, 116, 137, 145
Fathers, Church 179, 191
Fedotov 1, 24, 75
Filofei 14, 48–49
Florenskii 12, 17, 96, 152–54, 159–61, 170, 172
Florovsky 12, 18, 50, 129, 130–31, 165–66, 171, 174–76, 181, 193
freedom 7, 8, 12, 15, 17–19, 24, 28, 30, 40, 45, 55, 82–83, 89, 100–01, 114, 116–19, 124, 143, 145, 152–53, 156, 160–61, 168, 180, 182–83, 187–88, 192, 195–96, 201, 202
France 64, 67

Genesis 3, 146
Germany 3, 6, 33, 64, 101
Gorbachev 5, 52, 59

heresy 7, 48, 82, 144, 145
hesychasm 18, 172–73, 176–77, 183
Hilarion, Metropolitan 13, 41–43, 46, 48
Hinduism 19, 203
historiosophy 141, 143
holiness 14, 37, 45, 48–49, 78, 82, 83, 105, 133

idealism 3, 167, 177–78
idleness 15, 106–10, 112, 133
imiaslavie 172
imperialism 9, 10, 69
individualism 13, 79
instability 1, 38, 123
integrality (tselnost') 18
intelligentsia 22, 25, 28–29, 79, 120, 129, 132–34, 136
Islam 11, 16–17, 40, 73, 81, 83, 86, 88, 89, 137–49, 187
isolationism 4, 9, 25, 30, 163
Italy 3, 6, 67

Judaism 39, 87, 138, 139, 143, 146, 148

Kant 3, 4, 114, 171, 195–96
Kiva 14, 58–61, 69–70

landscape 15, 101
law 9, 15, 30, 42, 60, 64, 73, 75, 114, 117, 119, 122–23, 139, 140, 145, 146, 147, 149–55, 179, 182, 187, 188, 192, 196
laziness 15, 96, 97, 106, 107, 108, 110
legends 40, 142
Lenin 5, 14, 51
Logos 17, 34, 154, 155, 156
love, divine 18, 186, 187, 189

mafia 15, 24, 122, 123, 124
Marxism 9, 14, 51, 74, 76, 81, 92, 93, 132, 178
Massignon 17, 144, 147
materialism 87–88, 158, 178
messianism 9, 10, 13, 14, 25–26, 31, 51, 58, 134
metaphysics 17, 18, 116, 167, 169–73, 176–77, 180, 190, 202
Mohammed 138, 144, 146, 147
monotheism 140, 178–204
morality 17, 118, 122, 148, 195, 200
myth 4, 13, 14, 27, 31, 37, 38, 39–40, 41, 45, 50–53, 97, 109, 110, 143, 159, 162–63, 180, 177, 203

narodniki 15, 123
nationalism 2, 4, 6, 8–9, 10, 14, 19, 29, 68–69, 121, 132
naturalism 147
nature 18, 19, 85, 91, 97, 98, 142, 152, 155, 158–60, 180–81, 193, 197, 202
Nestor 13–14, 41, 45
nihilism 16, 123, 125–26, 193
Nikon, Patriarch 13–14, 41, 42, 43

occultism 16, 18, 156, 177, 179, 180, 196, 198–99, 204
ontology 18, 167–68, 177, 179–82
Orthodoxy 3, 4, 7, 9–12, 14, 16, 23, 25, 34–35, 43, 48, 50, 59, 61–63, 69, 79–84, 92, 105, 131, 134, 149, 170–79, 202

Palamist 18, 172–73, 176–77
pantheism 18–19, 135, 185–204
Paradise 1, 16, 30, 79, 85, 90, 92, 159, 160
Party, Communist 2, 5, 27
patriotism 7, 31, 49
patristic 16, 18, 165–83
perestroika 4, 13–14, 52
Peter I the Great 50, 75
Plato 3, 11–12, 17–18, 57, 70, 85, 139, 153, 168–70, 175, 177, 180, 183, 188
pochvennichestvo 81
Pomerants 18, 203
Pospielovsky 8–9
pragmatism 158
principle, national 2, 13, 35, 36

Rahner 16, 140, 141
rationalism 256
Reformation, Protestant 15, 114
re-integration 17
revelation 11, 34, 85, 140, 142–43, 147, 161, 175, 183, 190
Revolution (Bolshevik) 1, 5, 7, 10, 18, 24, 29, 41, 51, 74, 79–80, 106, 129, 132, 136, 156, 171, 182
ritual 54, 111, 130, 177
Roerichs 18, 193, 201
Rome, Third 10, 16, 47–50, 75, 83, 130–31, 134
rossiiskaia 2, 23
Sakharov 8, 122
samizdat 7, 9, 29
schism 10, 16, 50, 83, 129–37
ecularization 7, 49, 167, 179
Slavophilism 7, 31, 162

Solov'ev 9, 12, 16, 17–18, 25, 37, 82–83, 86, 91–93, 115, 122, 124, 138–49, 154–61, 167–71, 173, 178, 196–97, 201
Solzhenitsyn 6–10, 106
Sophia 17, 34, 154–55, 159
soul 3, 7, 17, 46, 89, 91, 93, 101, 105, 106, 111, 114, 126, 133, 135, 136, 138, 151, 154–57, 161, 163, 169–71, 183, 178–79, 182–83, 188, 198, 200, 202, 203
Soviet Union 2, 5, 7, 59
space exploration 10, 12
statism 8, 9, 31
suffering 16, 27, 75, 77–78, 91, 106, 124, 132–33, 189, 203
summer 15, 98, 104
supra-national 5, 66
syncretism 16, 18, 19, 178, 203

theocracy 16, 17, 41, 50, 122, 141–42, 146
theosophy 179, 182–83, 188, 198–99
this-worldliness 14, 83, 89
totalitarianism 7, 10, 14, 116, 122
total-unity 17, 154–57, 200
Tracy, Destutte de 3, 53
Truth 14, 25, 29, 34, 42–43, 46, 85–86, 89, 95, 120, 134, 139, 148, 161, 162, 171, 175, 192, 201, 203
tsars 3, 7, 14, 25, 27, 34, 43, 46, 48, 52, 86, 90, 109, 130–31, 134–35
tyranny 17, 24, 28, 125, 157

Ukraine 5, 10, 69
unification 17, 58, 179, 182
USSR 1, 5–6, 8–9, 37, 40, 51, 77
utopia 4, 10, 12, 16, 26–27, 109–10, 118, 131–36, 141, 162, 203
Uvarov 7, 14, 58–63, 67, 69–70

Vladimir, St. 42, 106

winter 15, 98, 104, 112

Yanov 6–9
Yeltsin 2, 5, 13, 19

Zhirinovskii 2, 8, 13
Ziuganov 2, 4, 13